FIJI ISLANDS
HANDBOOK
THIRD EDITION

FIJI ISLANDS HANDBOOK

THIRD EDITION

DAVID STANLEY

MOON
PUBLICATIONS, INC.

FIJI ISLANDS HANDBOOK, 3RD EDITION
(Formerly *Finding Fiji*)

Published by
Moon Publications, Inc.
P.O. Box 3040
Chico, California 95927-3040, USA

Printed by
Colorcraft Ltd., Hong Kong

© Text, maps, illustrations, and photos copyright 1993
David Stanley. All rights reserved.

Some photos and illustrations are used by permission
and are the property of the original copyright owners.

Library of Congress Cataloging in Publication Data
Stanley, David
Fiji Islands handbook / David Stanley— 3rd ed.
    p.   cm.
Includes bibliographical references and index.
ISBN 0-918373-92-1
1. Fiji—Handbooks, manuals, etc.   2. Fiji—Guidebooks
I. Title.
DU600.S73   1993.   92-42320
9119.61104—dc20   CIP

Editors: Mark Arends, Taran March
Copy Editors: Gina Wilson, Asha Johnson
Layout: Carey Wilson
Cartographers: Bob Race, Brian Bardwell
Index: Mark Arends

Front cover photo: Douglas Peebles
Frontispiece: Diana Lasich-Harper

Printed in Hong Kong

Please send all comments,
corrections, additions,
amendments, and critiques to:

**DAVID STANLEY
c/o MOON PUBLICATIONS, INC.
P.O. BOX 3040
CHICO, CA 95927-3040, USA**

Printing History
1st edition—May 1985
    Reprinted—July 1986
2nd edition—March 1990
    Reprinted—January 1992
3rd Edition—April 1993

CONTENTS

MAPS

MAP SYMBOLS

HIGHWAYS, ROADS, STREETS
FOOT TRAILS
BRIDGE

MOUNTAIN
WATERFALL
WATER
REEF

o ■ SIGHTS, POINTS OF INTEREST
O TOWNS, CITIES
o VILLAGES

CHARTS

ABBREVIATIONS

A$—Australian dollar
a/c—air-conditioned
C—centigrade
C$—Canadian dollar
d—double
DM—deutsche mark
EC—European Community
EEZ—Exclusive Economic Zone
G.P.O.—General Post Office
F$—Fiji dollar
Fr—franc
HK$—Hong Kong dollar
km—kilometer
kmph—kilometers per hour
LMS—London Missionary Society
MV—motor vessel
no.—number
N.Z.—New Zealand
NZ$—New Zealand dollar
OW—one-way

P.A.—Postal Agency
PNG—Papua New Guinea
pp—per person
P.W.D.—Public Works Department
RR—railroad
RT—roundtrip
s—single
S$—Singapore dollar
SDA—Seventh-Day-Adventist
SPF—South Pacific Forum
t—triple
tel.—telephone
US$—U.S. dollar
WW II—World War Two
YHA—Youth Hostel Association
YWCA—Young Women's Christian
    Association

SPELLING AND PRONUNCIATION

When 19th-century English missionaries created a written form of Fijian they rendered "mb" as "b," "nd" as "d," "ng" as "g," "ngg" as "q," and "th" as "c." For the convenience of travelers we use the phonetic form, spelling "Ba" as Mba, "Nadi" as Nandi, "Sigatoka" as Singatoka, "Qamea" as Nggamea, and "Cicia" as Thithia. Most official Fiji government maps also use phonetic spelling. We feel that in a practical travel guide it's better to risk upsetting purists than have visitors going around mispronouncing place names and words. (The surnames of individuals are written in the Fijian manner, however.) Always keep this factor in mind as most local signs use the indigenous spelling. Turn to "Alternative Place Names" just before the index for a list of the most common such names.

ACKNOWLEDGEMENTS

Special thanks to the Fiji Visitors Bureau for help in updating resort and recreational information, to Eileen Chambers for valuable help and advice, to Andrew Hempstead and Nadina Purdon for 22 pages of notes on the second edition (!), to Dianne Bain for information on yacht charters around Fiji, to Peter McQuarrie for checking facilities around Suva, to Debra Minto and Eric Harper for a complete report on Kandavu, to Trudi Unger for collecting all the latest brochures, to Hans J. Camerer for returning his handbook full of useful notes, to Jim Matheson for the map of Savusavu, to Tjalling Terpstra of Amber Travel Agency, Amsterdam, for help in updating Pacific air routes, to Margaret Argue of the South Pacific Peoples Foundation of Canada for a big box of resources, to Bill Weir for getting my computer operational, and to Ria de Vos for providing the support I needed to continue updating this book.

Thanks, too, to the following readers who took the trouble to write us letters about their trips: Lisa Arman, Andrea and Thomas Bachmann, Katrin and Carsten Bartels, Robert Bisordi, Peter Bossew, Albert Büchi, Robert Buckley, Louisa Bungey, Rick Carson, Ronald L. Challis, Pundy Christopher, Miguel DaSilva, Alexandra Ganter, Thom Garfat, Siegfried Gebel, Thomas Gerber, Brian Grant, Neil and Nora Hagen, Emil Kappus, Kurt and Trudi Keller, Sanford Kent, Marko Knepper, Eric Kobbe, Christoph Kokolt, Real Leboeuf, Hans-Peter Liecht, John Maident, Petra Maierhofer, Bernd Marks, Nick Miller, Jonathan Mitchell, Dr. Wolfram Müller, David Nash, Margit Oppitz, Ingrid Pickel, William de Prado, Hanne Rasmussen, Marian Riach, Isei Rokonaceva, Gerald Ryder, Horst A. Sach, Mark John Schlagböhmer, Peter Schüfer, Manfred Seitz, S. Wanda Sippl, Peter Sprenger, Hans-Jörg Stahmeier, Gerhard Stief, Robert Leger Teitelbaum, Helgor Trachet-Vandevoorde, Gernot Vogels, Jochen Wadsack, Gisela Walther, Mag. Martin Zausner, Dr. Waltraud Zausner, and Johanna Ziegler. You can have your name included here next edition for the price of a postage stamp.

**Attention Hotel Keepers,
Tour Operators, Divemasters:**

The best way to keep your listing in *Fiji Islands Handbook* up to date is to send us current information about your business. If you don't agree with what we've written, tell us why—there's never any charge or obligation for a listing. Thanks to the following island tourism workers and government officials who *did* write in: Ofa and Haroon Ali, Elain Barrett-Power, Denis Beckmann, Agnes Bibi, Nolyn Blanchette, Wendy Brooks, Luisa Bulavakarua, John Bullock, Do Cammick, Colleen E. Condon, Henry Crawford, Linda S. Crowl, Mary Crowley, Michael Dennis, Gordon Edris, Richard V. Elms, Lorraine Evans, Sicely Eyre, Anne Fairlie, Capt. Fritz Falkner, John D. Flatt, Bob Forster, Valerie Gadway, Val Gavriloff, Burnie Grayson, Betty and Brian Greenwood, Eric Harper, Mark Hinton, Brad Hoopes, Roger Hoskins, Gabrielle Hunt, Rozita Ibrahim, Thomas W. Jacobus, Walter Kamm, Helene Kelly, Folke von Knobloch, H.D. Kruse, Champak Lal, Leslie G. Lewis, Peter D. Marks, Brenda L. McCroskey, Mrs. B.F. McElrath, Roger Miles, Debra Minto, Andrew W. Mitchell, Douglas Mitchell, Joan B. Moody, Mrs. Edward A. Morris, Kathryn Lyman Nickel, Nicholas Panza, Graham Pettitt, C. Gregory Posey, Keith Potter, Niranjan Prasad, Gianni Proios, Saimoni Ratu, A. Raywadee, Humphrey Reece, Theresa Rietberg, Taeko I. Ruggiero, Brian Rutherford, Lauraine Sharan, Mrs. Suruj Singh, Ved P. Singh, Joanne Slater, E. Sovea, Max Storck, Gillian Summers, Saras L. Swamy, Geoff Taylor, George Taylor, Mary Tuisago, Kim D. Waters, John Weir, Johno Wells, Brigid Whitton, Roy F. Whitton, and Marge D. Williams.

While out researching my books I find it cheaper to pay my own way, and nothing in this book is designed to repay freebies from hotels, tour operators, or airlines. I prefer to arrive unexpected and uninvited and to experience things as they really are. On the road I seldom identify myself to anyone. The companies and organizations included in this book are there for information purposes only, and a mention in no way implies an endorsement.

IS THIS BOOK OUT OF DATE?

Travel writing is like trying to take a picture out the window of a bus: time frustrates the best of intentions. Some things are bound to have changed, so if our information is out of date, please let us hear about it. Did anything lead you astray or inconvenience you? In retrospect, is there anything that would have made your trip easier? If you're an island entrepreneur with a service or product to offer travelers, do bring it to our attention. When writing, please be as precise and accurate as you can. Make notes in your copy of *Fiji Islands Handbook* as you go along, then send us a summary when you get home. Recycle used travel brochures by forwarding them to us when you're done with them. If this book helped you out, please help us make it even better. Address your letters to:

David Stanley,
c/o Moon Publications Inc.,
P.O. Box 3040
Chico, CA 95927-3040, U.S.A.

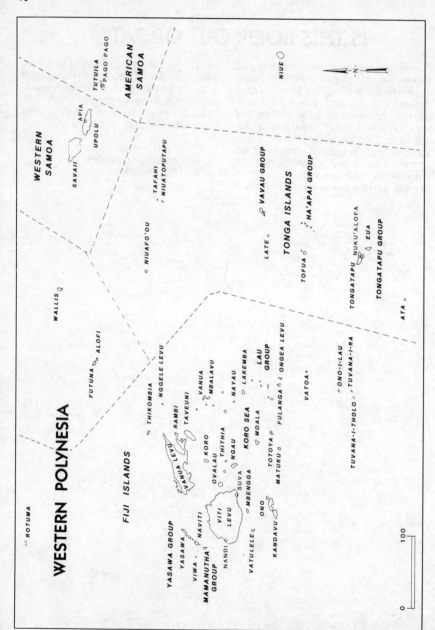

SALVATORE CASA

INTRODUCTION

Once notorious as the "Cannibal Isles," Fiji is now the colorful crossroads of the Pacific. Of the 322 islands that make up the Fiji Group, over 100 are inhabited by a rich mixture of vibrant, exuberant Melanesians, East Indians, Polynesians, Micronesians, Chinese, and Europeans, each with a cuisine and culture of their own. Here Melanesia mixes with Polynesia, ancient India with the Pacific, tradition with the modern world, in a unique blend. There's a diversity of landforms and seascapes, and a fascinating human history. Prices are affordable, with a wide range of accommodation and travel options. Whatever your budget, Fiji gives you good value for your money and plenty of ways to spend it.

Fiji preserves an amazing variety of traditional customs and crafts such as kava drinking, the presentation of whales' teeth, firewalking, fish driving, turtle calling, tapa beating, and pottery making. Fiji offers posh resorts, good food and accommodations, nightlife, historic sights, outer-island living, hiking, camping, surfing, snorkeling, scuba diving, and river-running, plus travel by small plane, interisland ferry, copra boat, outboard canoe, open-sided bus, or air-conditioned coach. Fiji's sun-drenched beaches, blue lagoons, panoramic open hillsides, lush rainforests, and dazzling reefs are truly magnificent. You'll barely scratch the surface of all there is to see and do.

THE PHYSICAL SETTING

THE LAND

Fiji sits in the middle of the main air route between North America and Australia, 4,450 km southwest of Hawaii and 2,730 km northeast of Sydney. Nandi is the hub of Pacific air routes, while Suva is a regional shipping center. The 180th meridian cuts through Fiji, but the international date line swings east so the entire group can share the same day. Together the Fiji Islands are scattered over 1,290,000 square km of the South Pacific Ocean.

The name Fiji is a Tongan corruption of the

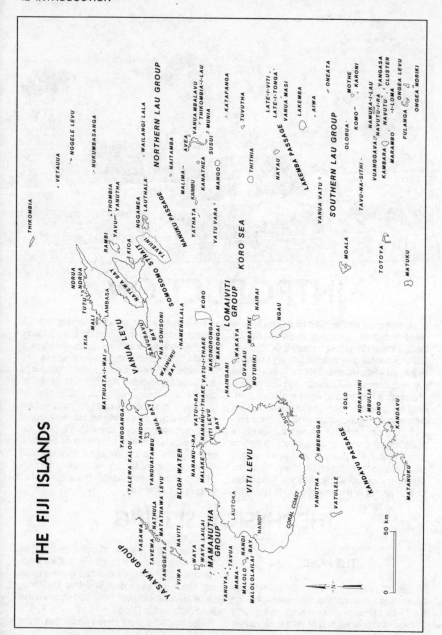

THE FIJI ISLANDS

indigenous name "Viti." The Fiji Islands are arrayed in a horseshoe configuration, with Viti Levu ("Great Fiji") and adjacent islands to the west, Vanua Levu ("Great Land") and Taveuni to the north, and the Lau Group to the east. This upside-down-U-shaped archipelago encloses the Koro Sea, which is relatively shallow and sprinkled with the Lomaiviti, or central Fiji group of islands.

If every single island were counted, the isles of the Fiji archipelago would number in the thousands. A mere 322 are judged large enough for human habitation, however, and of these only 106 are inhabited. That leaves 216 uninhabited islands, most of them prohibitively isolated or lacking fresh water.

Most of the Fiji Islands are volcanic, remnants of a sunken continent that stretched through Australia. This origin accounts for the mineral deposits on the main islands. None of Fiji's volcanoes are presently active, though there are a few small hot springs. The two largest islands, Viti Levu and Vanua Levu, together account for 87% of Fiji's 18,376 square km of land. Viti Levu has 57% of the land area and 75% of the people, while Vanua Levu, with 30% of the land, has 18% of the population. Viti Levu alone is bigger than all five archipela-

gos of Tahiti-Polynesia together; in fact, Fiji has more land and people than all of Polynesia combined.

The 1,000-meter-high Nandrau Plateau in central Viti Levu is cradled between Tomanivi (1,323 meters) on the north and Monavatu (1,131 meters) on the south. On different sides of this elevated divide are the Tholo-East Plateau drained by the Rewa River, the Navosa Plateau drained by the Mba, the Tholo-West Plateau drained by the Singatoka, and the Navua Plateau drained by the Navua. Some 29 well-defined peaks rise above Viti Levu's interior; most of the people live in the river valleys or along the coast.

The Nandi River slices across the Nausori Highlands, with the Mt. Evans Range (1,195 meters) towering above Lautoka. Other highland areas are cut by great rivers like the Singatoka, Navua, Rewa, and Mba, navigable far inland by outboard canoe or kayak. Whitewater rafters shoot down the Navua and Mba, while the lower Singatoka flows gently through Fiji's "market garden salad bowl." Fiji's largest river, the Rewa, pours into the Pacific through a wide delta just below Nausori. After a hurricane the Rewa becomes a dark torrent worth a visit to Nausori just to see. Sharks have been known to

FIJI AT A GLANCE

ISLAND	AREA (sq. km)	HIGHEST POINT (meters)	POPULATION (mid-1988 est.)	PERCENT FIJIAN*
Viti Levu	10,429	1,323	508,777	40.5
Vanua Levu	5,556	1,032	117,790	43.3
Taveuni	470	1,241	8,799	72.7
Kandavu	411	838	9,936	98.1
Ngau	140	747	3,054	99.4
Koro	104	522	3,654	98.5
Ovalau	101	626	6,660	88.3
Rambi	69	463	2,771	5.0
Rotuma	47	256	3,204	1.9
Mbengga	36	439	1,488	98.6

* Viti Levu, Vanua Levu, and Taveuni have sizable Fijian Indian populations, while Rambi is Micronesian and Rotuma is Polynesian.

enter both the Rewa and the Singatoka and swim far upstream.

Vanua Levu has a peculiar shape, with two long peninsulas pointing northeast. A mountain range between Lambasa and Savusavu reaches 1,032 meters at Nasorolevu. Navotuvotu (842 meters), east of Mbua Bay, is Fiji's best example of a broad-shield volcano, with lava flows built up in layers. The mountains are closer to the southeast coast, and a broad lowland belt runs along the northwest. Of the rivers only the Ndreketi, flowing west across northern Vanua Levu, is large; navigation on the Lambasa is restricted to small boats. The interior of Vanua Levu is lower and drier than Viti Levu, yet scenically superb: the road from Lambasa to Savusavu is a visual delight.

Vanua Levu's bullet-shaped neighbor Taveuni soars to 1,241 meters, its rugged east coast battered by the southeast trades. Taveuni and Kandavu are known as the finest islands in Fiji for their scenic beauty and agricultural potential. Geologically, the uplifted limestone islands of the Lau Group have more in common with Tonga than with the rest of Fiji. Northwest of Viti Levu is the rugged limestone Yasawa Group.

Fringing reefs are common along most of the coastlines, and Fiji is outstanding for its many barrier reefs. The Great Sea Reef off the north coast of Vanua Levu is the fourth longest in the world, and the Astrolabe Reef north of Kandavu is one of the most colorful. Countless other unexplored barrier reefs are found off northern Viti Levu and elsewhere. The many cracks, crevices, walls, and caves along Fiji's reefs are guaranteed to delight the scuba diver.

CORAL REEFS

Coral reefs cover some 200,000 square km worldwide, between 35 degrees north and 32 degrees south latitude. A reef is created by the accumulation of millions of tiny calcareous skeletons left by myriad generations of tiny coral polyps. Though the skeleton is usually white, the living polyps are many different colors. They thrive in clear, salty water where the temperature never drops below 18°C. They must also have a base not over 50 meters below the surface on which to form.

The coral colony grows slowly upward on the consolidated skeletons of its ancestors until it reaches the low-tide mark, after which development extends outward on the edges of the reef. Sunlight is critical for coral growth. Colonies grow quickly on the ocean side due to clearer water and a greater abundance of food. A strong, healthy reef can grow four to five cm a year. Fresh or cloudy water inhibits coral growth, which is why villages and ports all across the Pacific are located at the reef-free mouths of rivers.

Polyps extract calcium carbonate from the water and deposit it in their skeletons. All reef-building corals also contain limy encrustations of microscopic algae within their cells. The algae, like all green plants, obtain their energy from the sun and contribute this energy to the growth of the reef's skeleton. As a result, corals behave (and look) more like plants than animals, competing for sunlight just as terrestrial plants do. Many polyps are also carnivorous; with minute, stinging tentacles they supplement their energy by capturing tiny planktonic animals and organic particles at night. A small piece of coral is a colony composed of large numbers of polyps.

Coral Types

Corals belong to a broad group of stinging creatures, which includes polyps, soft corals, stony corals, sea anemones, sea fans, and jellyfish. Only those types with hard skeletons and a single hollow cavity within the body are considered true corals. Stony corals such as brain, table, staghorn, and mushroom have external skeletons and are important reef builders. Soft corals, black corals, and sea fans have internal skeletons. The fire corals are recognized by their smooth, velvety surface and yellowish brown color. The stinging toxins of this last group can easily penetrate human skin and cause swelling and painful burning that can last up to an hour. The many varieties of soft, colorful anemones gently waving in the current might seem inviting to touch, but beware! Many are also poisonous.

The corals, like most other forms of life in the Pacific, colonized the ocean from the fertile seas of Southeast Asia. Thus the number of species declines as you move east. Over 600 species of coral make their home in the Pacific, compared

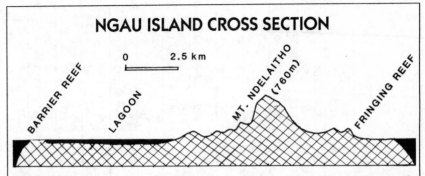

NGAU ISLAND CROSS SECTION

The difference between barrier and fringing reefs is illustrated in this southwest-northeast cross section of Ngau Island (see map on page 166). The vertical scale has been exaggerated. The barrier reef of Ngao's southwestern shore is separated from the main island's coast by a deep lagoon, while only a tidal flat lies between Ngau's northeastern coast and the edge of the fringing reef.

to only 48 in the Caribbean. The diversity of coral colors and forms is endlessly amazing. This is our most unspoiled environment, a world of almost indescribable beauty.

Exploring A Reef

Until you've explored a good coral reef, you haven't experienced one of the greatest joys of nature. Dive shops throughout Fiji rent scuba and snorkeling gear, so do get into the clear, warm waters around you. Be careful, however, and know the dangers. Practice snorkeling in the shallow water; don't head into deep water until you're sure you've got the hang of it. Breathe easily; don't hyperventilate.

When snorkeling on a fringing reef, beware of deadly currents and undertows in channels that drain tidal flows. Observe the direction the water is flowing before you swim into it. If you feel yourself being dragged out to sea through a reef passage, try swimming across the current, rather than against it. If you can't resist the pull at all, it may be better to let yourself be carried out. Wait till the current diminishes, then swim along the outer reef face until you find somewhere to come back in. Or use your energy to attract the attention of someone onshore. Most beach drownings occur in such situations, so try not to panic.

Snorkeling on the outer edge or drop-off of a reef is thrilling for the variety of fish and corals, but attempt it only on a very calm day. Even then it's best to have someone stand onshore or on the edge of the reef (at low tide) to watch for occasional big waves, which can take you by surprise and smash you into the rocks. Also, beware of unperceived currents outside the reef—you may not get a second chance.

A far better idea is to limit your snorkeling to the protected inner reef and leave the open waters to the scuba diver. The local divemasters know their waters and will be able to show you the most amazing things in perfect safety. Many of the scuba operators listed in this book offer scuba certification courses at reasonable rates, with a level of personal attention you won't find elsewhere. It's a great way to acquire a new skill while having a holiday, and in Fiji you'll probably have a diving instructor all to yourself. All prospective scuba divers must have a medical report from their doctors indicating that they are in good physical condition. Experienced divers should bring their certification card, buoyancy compensator, and regulator.

Diving is possible year-round, with marinelife most profuse July to November. Facilities for scuba diving exist in the Mamanutha Group, along Viti Levu's Coral Coast, on Mbengga, Ono, and Kandavu, at Suva and Savusavu, and on Taveuni and adjacent islands. Low-budget divers should turn to the Kandavu or Taveuni chapters in this book. Many fantastic

FIJI CLIMATE CHART

LOCATION		JAN.	FEB.	MAR.	APRIL	MAY	JUNE	JULY	AUG.	SEPT.	OCT.	NOV.	DEC.	ALL YEAR
Nandi airport, Viti Levu	C	27.0	26.9	26.7	26.2	25.0	24.0	23.3	23.8	24.5	25.2	25.9	26.6	25.4
	mm	294	291	373	195	99	78	51	62	88	73	137	181	1922
Yasawa Island	C	27.0	26.9	26.6	26.4	26.0	25.3	24.6	24.8	25.1	25.7	26.1	26.7	25.9
	mm	281	287	344	168	110	106	45	68	90	78	187	165	1929
Mba, Viti Levu	C	27.2	27.1	26.9	26.5	25.3	24.1	23.3	23.8	24.7	25.5	26.1	26.1	25.6
	mm	322	409	387	203	101	67	46	65	72	91	126	228	2117
Nandarivatu, Viti Levu	C	21.6	22.0	21.5	21.0	20.0	18.9	18.3	18.8	19.0	20.1	20.6	21.1	20.2
	mm	599	668	689	362	181	99	89	125	126	136	220	400	3694
Rakiraki, Viti Levu	C	27.6	27.6	27.3	26.8	25.9	24.9	24.2	24.6	25.1	25.9	26.6	27.1	26.2
	mm	307	371	372	236	122	66	47	68	74	83	140	221	2107
Suva, Viti Levu	C	26.8	26.9	26.8	26.1	24.8	23.9	23.1	23.2	23.7	24.4	25.3	26.2	25.1
	mm	314	299	386	343	280	177	148	200	212	218	268	313	3158
Vunisea, Kandavu I.	C	26.4	26.8	26.1	25.4	24.2	23.2	22.4	22.6	23.1	23.9	24.7	26.1	24.6
	mm	239	225	313	256	208	102	112	121	122	126	151	177	2152
Nambouwalu, Vanua Levu	C	26.9	27.1	26.7	26.3	25.5	24.7	23.9	24.0	24.4	25.2	25.4	26.3	25.6
	mm	328	354	352	275	198	130	96	114	139	164	208	279	2637
Lambasa, Vanua Levu	C	26.8	26.8	26.6	26.2	25.3	24.4	23.8	24.2	24.7	25.4	25.9	26.4	25.6
	mm	449	457	465	236	97	86	38	60	77	96	210	263	2534
Vunikondi, Vanua Levu	C	26.6	26.7	26.6	26.3	26.0	25.3	24.6	24.7	25.0	25.6	25.9	26.6	25.8
	mm	302	377	409	225	143	131	92	90	114	132	264	220	2499
Rotuma Island	C	27.4	27.3	27.2	27.4	27.2	26.8	26.4	26.5	26.7	26.8	27.0	27.2	27.0
	mm	358	390	430	278	262	244	207	230	277	283	327	331	3617
Matuku, Lau Group	C	26.8	27.0	26.8	26.3	25.1	24.1	23.1	23.6	24.2	25.0	25.7	26.4	25.3
	mm	231	230	265	192	151	116	114	78	110	97	139	152	1875
Ono-i-Lau, Lau Group	C	26.3	26.5	26.4	25.7	24.3	23.4	22.4	22.4	22.7	23.6	24.5	25.3	24.4
	mm	201	199	266	196	144	109	90	94	106	114	128	145	1792

dives are just 10 or 15 minutes away from the resorts by boat, while at Australia's Great Barrier Reef the speedboats often have to travel over 60 km to get to the dive sites. The worst underwater visibility conditions in Fiji are the equivalent of the very best off the Florida coast. In the Gulf of Mexico, you've about reached the limit if you can see for 15 meters; in Fiji visibility begins at 15 meters and increases to 45 meters in some places. The main constraint is financial: snorkeling is free, while scuba diving does get expensive.

CLIMATE

Along the coast the weather is warm and pleasant, without great variations in temperature. The southeastern trades prevail from June to Oct., the best months to visit. In Feb. and March the wind often comes directly out of the east. These winds dump 3,000 mm of annual rainfall on the humid southeastern coasts of the big islands, increasing to 5,000 mm inland. The drier northwestern coasts, in the lee, get only 1,500-2,000 mm. Yet even during the rainy months (Dec. to April), bright sun often follows the rains.

The official dry season (June to Oct.) is not always dry at Suva, although much of the rain falls at night. In addition, Fiji's winter (May to Nov.) is cooler and less humid, the best months for mountain trekking. During the drier season, the reef waters are clearest for the scuba diver. Summer (Dec. to April) is hurricane season, with Fiji, Samoa, and Tonga receiving up to five

Notes on the climate chart: The top figure indicates the average monthly temperatures in degrees and tenths centigrade, while the monthly rainfall average in millimeters (mm) is given below. The last column gives the annual temperature and the total precipitation during the year. These figures have been averaged over a minimum of 10 years, in most cases much longer. Altitude is a factor at Nandarivatu (835 meters); all of the others are very near sea level. It will be seen that temperatures don't vary too much year-round, but that there is a pronounced dry season midyear. Note too that some areas of Fiji are far drier than others.

SUVA'S CLIMATE

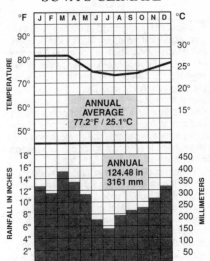

ANNUAL AVERAGE 77.2°F / 25.1°C

ANNUAL 124.48 in 3161 mm

storms annually. But even in summer the refreshing tradewinds relieve the high humidity.

In Fiji you can obtain weather information by dialing 301-642.

NANDI'S CLIMATE

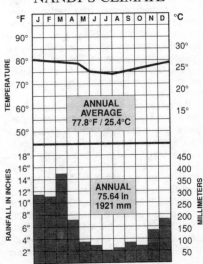

ANNUAL AVERAGE 77.8°F / 25.4°C

ANNUAL 75.64 in 1921 mm

FLORA

The flora of Fiji originated in the Malaysian region; ecological niches are filled by similar plants in the two regions. There are over 3,000 species of plants in Fiji, a third of them endemic. Of the large islands, Taveuni is known for its rare climbing *tangimauthia* flower. The absence of leaf-eating animals in Fiji allowed the vegetation to develop largely without the protective spines and thorns found elsewhere, and one of the only poisonous plants is the *salato,* a tree with large, hairy leaves that inflict painful wounds when touched.

Patterns of rainfall are in large part responsible for the variety of scenery here. The wetter sides of the high islands are heavily forested, with occasional thickets of bamboo and scrub. Natural forests cover 40% of Fiji's total land area and about a quarter of this is classified as production forest suitable for logging. The towering *ndakua* tree, once carved into massive Fijian war canoes, has already disappeared from Viti Levu, and the last stands are now being logged on Vanua Levu for export to New Zealand.

Coconut groves fill the coastal plains. On the drier sides, open savanna or *talasinga* of coarse grasses predominates where the original vegetation has been destroyed by slash-and-burn agriculture. Sugarcane is now cultivated in the lowlands here, and Caribbean pine has been planted in many dry hilly areas, giving them a Scandinavian appearance. The low islands of the Lau Group are restricted to a few hardy, drought-resistant species such as coconuts and pandanus.

Mangroves can occasionally be found in river deltas and along some high-island coastal lagoons. The cable roots of the saltwater-tolerant mangroves anchor in the shallow upper layer of oxygenated mud, avoiding the layers of hydrogen sulfide below. The tree provides shade for tiny organisms dwelling in the tidal mudflats—a place for birds to nest and fish, or for shellfish to feed and spawn. The mangroves also perform the same task as land-building coral colonies along the reefs. As sediments are trapped between the roots, the trees extend farther into the lagoon, creating a unique natural environment. The past decade has seen widespread destruction of the mangroves as land is reclaimed for agricultural use in northwest Viti Levu and around Lambasa.

Though only introduced to Fiji in the late 1860s, sugarcane probably originated in the South Pacific. On New Guinea the islanders have cultivated the plant for thousands of years, selecting vigorous varieties with the most colorful stems. The story goes that two Melanesian fishermen, To-Kabwana and To-Karavuvu, found a piece of sugarcane in their net one day. They threw it away, but after catching it again on the next two days decided to keep it and painted the stalk a bright color. Eventually the cane burst and a woman came forth. She cooked food for the men but hid herself at night. Finally she was captured and became the wife of one of the men. From their union sprang the whole human race.

FAUNA

Of the 70 species of land birds, 22 are endemic, including broadbills, cuckoos, doves, fantails, finches, flycatchers, fruitdoves, hawks, honey eaters, kingfishers, lorikeets, parrots, pigeons, rails, silktails, and warblers. The Fijian names of some of these birds, such as the *kaka* (parrot) and *kikau* (giant honey eater), imitate their calls. Of the seabirds, boobies, frigate birds, petrels, and tropic birds are present. More in evidence is the introduced Indian mynah (with its yellow beak and legs), the bulbul, and the Malay turtledove. The best time to observe forest birds is in the very early morning—they move around a lot less in the heat of the day.

pink-billed parrot finch

DIANA LASICH-HARPER / 3

tree frog

The only native mammals are the monkey-faced fruit bat or flying fox, the insect-eating bat, and the Polynesian gray rat. Two species of snakes inhabit Fiji: the very rare, poisonous *bolo loa* and the harmless Pacific boa, which can grow up to two meters long. Venomous sea snakes are common on some coasts, but docile and easily handled. The land- and tree-dwelling native frogs are noteworthy for the long suction discs on their fingers and toes. Because they live deep in the rainforests and feed at night, they are seldom seen. Some Fijian clans have totemic relationships with eels, prawns, turtles, and sharks and are able to summon these creatures with special chants.

One of the more unusual creatures found in Fiji and Tonga is the banded iguana, a lizard which lives in trees and can grow up to 70 cm long (two-thirds of which is tail). The iguanas are emerald green, and the male is easily distinguished from the female by his bluish gray cross stripes. Banded iguanas change color to control their internal temperature, becoming darker when in the direct sun. Their nearest relatives are found in South America and Madagascar, and no lizards live farther east in the Pacific than these. In 1979 a new species, the crested iguana, was discovered on Yanduatambu, a small island off the west coast of Vanua Levu.

The Indian mongoose was introduced by planters in the 1880s to combat rats, which were damaging the plantations. Unfortunately, no one realized at the time that the mongoose hunts by day, whereas the rats are nocturnal; thus, the two seldom meet. Today, the mongoose is the scourge of chickens, native ground birds, and other animals, though Kandavu, Ngau, Ovalau, and Taveuni are mongoose-free (and thus the best islands for birdwatching). In 1936 the giant toad was introduced from Hawaii to control beetles, slugs, and millipedes. When this food source is exhausted, they tend to eat each other. At night gardens and lawns may be full of them.

banded iguana

Four of the world's seven species of sea turtles nest in Fiji: the green, hawksbill, loggerhead, and leatherback. Nesting occurs from Nov. to Feb., at night when there is a full moon and a high tide. The female struggles up the beach and lays as many as 100 eggs in a hole, which she digs and then covers with her hind flippers. The eggs are protected by law in Fiji, as are leatherback turtles, turtles with shells under 46 cm long, and all turtles during the nesting season. Persons who take eggs or turtles at this time are violating the Fisheries Act and face heavy fines.

HISTORY

The Pre-European Period

The first people to arrive in Fiji were of a broad-nosed, light-skinned Austronesian-speaking race, probably the Polynesians. They originated in insular Southeast Asia and gradually migrated east past the already occupied islands of Melanesia. Distinctive *lapita* pottery, decorated in horizontal geometric bands and dated from 1290 B.C., has been found in the sand dunes near Singatoka, indicating they had reached here by 1500 B.C. or earlier. Much later, about 500 B.C., Melanesian people arrived, bringing with them their distinct pottery traditions. From the fusion of these primordial peoples the Fijian race was born.

The hierarchical social structure of the early Fijians originated with the Polynesians. Status and descent passed through the male line and power was embodied in the *turanga* (chief). The hereditary chiefs possessed the *mana* of an ancestral spirit or *vu*. This feudal aristocracy combined in confederations or *vanua* and extended its influence through war. Treachery and cannibalism were an intrinsic part of these struggles; women were taken as prizes or traded to form alliances.

Villages were fortified with ditches or built along ridges or terraced hillsides for defense.

The native aristocracy practiced customs that today seem barbarous and particularly cruel. The skull cap of a defeated enemy might be polished and used as a *yanggona* (kava) cup to humiliate the foe. Some chiefs even took delight in cooking and consuming bodily parts as their agonizing victims looked on. Men were buried alive to hold up the posts of new houses, war canoes were launched over the living bodies of young girls, and the widows of chiefs were strangled to keep their husbands company in the spirit world. The farewells of some of these women are remembered today in dances and songs known as *meke*.

These feudal islanders were, on the other hand, guardians of one of the highest material cultures of the Pacific. They built great ocean-going double canoes *(ndrua)* up to 30 meters long, constructed and adorned large solid, thatched houses *(mbures)*, performed marvelous song-dances called *meke*, made tapa, pottery, and sennit (coconut cordage), and skillfully plaited mats. For centuries the Tongans came to Fiji to obtain sandalwood for carving and great logs from which to make canoes.

Fijian ndrua: These heavy, double-hulled canoes were sometimes more than 30 meters in length. William Lockerby, an early Pacific traveler, described one in which he was held prisoner in 1808: "The canoe I was held in was one of the largest size of double canoe; it consisted of two single ones joined together by a platform, in the middle of which the mast was fixed. Round the sides of the platform there was a strong breast work of bamboo, behind which they [the Fijians] stand in engaging the enemy. There was also a house on the platform which is erected and taken down as circumstances require. The number of men on board amounted to 200. Captain Cook's account of the sailing of these vessels is quite correct, however incredible it may appear to those who have not seen them. With a moderate wind they will sail 20 miles an hour." Nineteenth-century Fijians showed great skill in handling these large catamaran canoes.

European Exploration

In 1643 Abel Tasman became the European discoverer of Fiji when he sighted Taveuni, though he didn't land. Tasman was searching for *terra australis incognita,* a great southern continent believed to balance the continents of the north. He also hoped to find new markets and trade routes. Unlike earlier Spanish explorers, Tasman entered the Pacific from the west rather than the east. Apart from Fiji, he was the first European to see Tasmania, New Zealand, and Tonga. By sailing right around Australia from the Dutch East Indies he proved New Holland (Australia) was not attached to the elusive southern continent.

In 1774, Capt. Cook anchored off Vatoa (which he named Turtle Island) in southern Lau. Like Tasman he failed to proceed farther or land, and it was left to Capt. William Bligh to give Europeans an accurate picture of Fiji for the first time. After the *Bounty* mutiny in May 1789, Bligh and his companions were chased by canoe-loads of Fijian warriors just north of the Yasawa Islands as they rowed through on their escape route to Timor. Some serious paddling, a timely squall, and a lucky gap in the Great Sea Reef saved the Englishmen from ending up as the main course at a cannibal feast. The section of sea where this happened is today known as Bligh Water. Bligh cut directly across the center of Fiji between the two main islands, and his careful observations made him the first real European explorer of Fiji, albeit an unwilling one. Bligh returned to Fiji in 1792, but once again stayed aboard ship.

Beachcombers And Chiefs

All of these early explorers stressed the perilous nature of Fiji's reefs. This, combined with tales told by the Tongans of cannibalism and warlike Fijian natives, caused most travelers to shun the area. Then in 1804 a survivor from the shipwrecked U.S. schooner *Argo* brought word that sandalwood grew abundantly along the Mbua coast of Vanua Levu. This precipitated a rush of traders and beachcombers to the islands. A cargo of sandalwood bought from the islanders for $50 worth of trinkets could be sold to the Chinese at Canton for $20,000. By 1814 the forests had been stripped to provide joss sticks and incense, and the trade collapsed.

During this period Fiji was divided among warring chieftains. The first Europeans to actually mix with the Fijians were escaped convicts from Australia, who instructed the natives in the use of European muskets and were thus well received. White beachcombers such as the Swedish adventurer Charles Savage and the German Martin Bushart acted as middlemen between traders and Fijians and took sides in local conflicts. In one skirmish Savage was separated from his fellows, captured, and eaten. With help from the likes of Savage, Naulivou, the cannibal chief of tiny Mbau Island just off eastern Viti Levu, and his brother Tanoa extended their influence over much of western Fiji.

In his book *Following the Equator,* Mark Twain had this to say about the beachcombers:

> *They lived worthless lives of sin and luxury, and died without honor—in most cases by violence. Only one of them had any ambition; he was an Irishman named Connor. He tried to raise a family of fifty children and scored forty-eight. He died lamenting his failure. It was a foolish sort of avarice. Many a father would have been rich enough with forty.*

From 1827 to 1850 European traders collected bêche-de-mer, a sea slug that, when smoked and dried, also brought a good price in China. While the sandalwood traders only stayed long enough to take on a load, the bêche-de-mer collectors set up shore facilities where the slugs were processed. Many traders, such as David Whippy, followed the example of the beachcombers and took local wives, establishing the part-Fijian community of today. By monopolizing the bêche-de-mer trade and constantly warring, Chief Tanoa's son and successor, Ratu Seru Cakobau (pronounced Thakombau), became extremely powerful in the 1840s, proclaiming himself Tui Viti, or King of Fiji.

The beginnings of organized trade brought a second wave of official explorers to Fiji. In 1838 the Frenchman Dumont d'Urville and his crew landed on Mbau Island and met Tanoa. The Frenchmen caused consternation and confusion by refusing to drink *yanggona* (kava), preferring their own wine. The American Exploring Expedition of 1840, led by Commodore

Charles Wilkes, produced the first recognizable map of Fiji. When two Americans, including a nephew of Wilkes, were speared on a beach at Malolo Island in a misunderstanding, Wilkes ordered the offending fortified village stormed, and 87 Fijians were killed. The survivors were made to water and provision Wilkes' ships as tribute. Captain H.M. Denham of the HMS *Herald* prepared accurate navigational charts of the group in 1855-56, making regular commerce possible.

European And Tongan Penetration

As early as the 1830s an assortment of European and U.S. beachcombers had formed a small settlement at Levuka on the east coast of Ovalau Island just northeast of Mbau, which whalers and traders used as a supply base. In 1846 John Brown Williams was appointed U.S. commercial agent. On 4 July 1849 William's home on Nukulau Island, near present Suva, burned down. Though the conflagration was caused by the explosion of a cannon during William's own fervent celebration of his national holiday, he objected to the way Fijian onlookers carried off items they rescued from the flames. A shameless swindler, Williams had purchased Nukulau for only $30, yet he blamed the Tui Viti for his losses and sent Cakobau a $5001.38 bill. Claims by the U.S. for damages eventually rose to $44,000, and in 1851 and 1855 American gunboats called and ordered Cakobau to pay up. This threat hung over Cakobau's head for many years, the 19th-century equivalent of 20th-century third-world debt.

The early 1830s also saw the arrival from Tonga of the first missionaries. Though Tahitian pastors were sent by the London Missionary Society to Oneata in southern Lau as early as 1830, it was the Methodists based at Lakemba after 1835 who made the most lasting impression by rendering the Fijian language into writing. At first Christianity made little headway among these fierce, idolatrous people. Only after converting the powerful chiefs were the missionaries successful. Methodist missionaries Cargill and Cross were appalled by what they saw during a visit to Mbau in 1838. A white missionary, Rev. Thomas Baker, was clubbed and eaten in central Viti Levu by the *kai tholo* (hill people) as late as 1867.

In 1847 Enele Ma'afu, a member of the Tongan royal family, arrived in Lau and began building a personal empire under the pretense of defending Christianity. In 1853 King George of Tonga made Ma'afu governor of all Tongans resident in Lau. Meanwhile there was continuing resistance from the warlords of the Rewa River area to Cakobau's dominance. In addition the Europeans at Levuka suspected Cakobau of twice ordering their town set afire and were directing trade away from Mbau. With his power in decline Cakobau accepted Christianity in 1854 in exchange for an alliance with King George. In 1855, with the help of 2,000 Tongans led by King George himself, Cakobau was able to put down the Rewa revolt. In the process, however, Ma'afu became the dominant force in Lau, Taveuni, and Vanua Levu.

During the early 1860s, as Americans fought their Civil War, the world price of cotton soared, and large numbers of Europeans arrived in Fiji hoping to establish cotton plantations. In 1867 the USS *Tuscaroga* called at Levuka and threatened to bombard the town unless the still-outstanding U.S. debt was paid. The next year an enterprising Australian firm, the Polynesia Company, paid off the Americans in exchange for a grant from Cakobau of 80,000 hectares of choice land, including the site of modern Suva. The British government later refused to recognize this grant, though they refunded the money paid to the Americans and accepted the claims of settlers who had purchased land from the company. Settlers soon numbered around 2,000, and Levuka boomed.

It was a lawless era and a need was felt for a central government. An attempt at national rule by a council of chiefs failed in 1867; three regional governments were then set up in Mbau (western), Lau (eastern), and Mbua (northern), but these were only partly successful. With cotton prices collapsing as the U.S. South resumed production, a national administration under Cakobau and planter John Thurston was established at Levuka in 1871.

However, Cakobau was never strong enough to impose his authority over the whole country, so with growing disorder in western Fiji, infighting between Europeans and Fijian chiefs, and a lack of cooperation from Ma'afu's rival confederation of chiefs in eastern Fiji, Cakobau decided he should cede his kingdom to Great Britain. The British had refused an invitation to annex Fiji in 1862, but this time they accepted rather than risk seeing the group fall into the hands of another power. On 10 Oct. 1874 Fiji became a British colony. In 1877 the Western Pacific High Commission was set up to protect British interests in the surrounding unclaimed island groups as well. At first Levuka was the colony's capital, but in 1881 the government moved to a more spacious site at Suva.

The Making Of A Nation
The first British governor, Sir Arthur Gordon, and his colonial secretary and successor, Sir John Thurston, created modern Fiji almost single-handedly. They realized that the easiest way to rule was indirectly, through the existing Fijian chiefs. To protect the communal lands on

Blackbirded Solomon Islanders, brought to work on European-owned plantations in Fiji, wait aboard ship off Levuka around the turn of the century. In 1910 the Melanesian labor trade was finally terminated by the British, but a few of the Solomon Islanders stayed on and small communities of their descendants exist on Ovalau and near Suva.

CAINES JANIF LTD., SUVA

which the chieftain system was based, they ordered that native land could not be sold, only leased. Not wishing to disturb native society, Gordon and Thurston ruled that Fijians could not be required to work on European plantations. The blackbirding of Melanesian laborers from the Solomons and New Hebrides had been restricted by the Polynesian Islanders Protection Act in 1872.

By this time sugar had taken the place of cotton and there was a tremendous labor shortage on the plantations. Gordon, who had previously served in Trinidad and Mauritius, saw indentured Indian workers as a solution. The first arrived in 1879, and by 1916, when Indian immigration ended, there were 63,000 present. To come to Fiji the Indians had to sign a labor contract *(girmit)* in which they agreed to cut sugarcane for their masters for five years. During the next five years they were allowed to lease small plots of their own from the Fijians and plant cane or raise livestock. Over half the Indians decided to remain in Fiji as free settlers after their 10-year contracts expired, and today their descendants form about half the population, many of them still working small, leased plots.

Though this combination of European capital, Fijian land, and Indian labor did help preserve traditional Fijian culture, it also kept the Fijians backward—they remained envious onlookers passed over by European and (later) Indian prosperity. The separate administration and special rights for indigenous Fijians installed by the British over a century ago continue in force today. In early 1875 Cakobau and two of his sons returned from a visit to Australia infected with measles. Though they themselves survived, the resulting epidemic wiped out a third of the Fijian population. As a response to this and other public health problems, the Fiji School of Medicine was founded in 1885. At the beginning of European colonization there were about 200,000 Fijians, approximately 114,748 in 1881, and just 84,000 by 1921.

The Colonial Period
In 1912 a Gujerati lawyer, D.M. Manilal, arrived in Fiji from Mauritius to fight for Indian rights, just as his contemporary Mahatma Gandhi was doing in South Africa. Indentured Indians continued to arrive in Fiji until 1916, but the protests

led to the termination of the indenture system throughout the empire in 1920 (Manilal was deported from Fiji after a strike that year).

Although Fiji was a political colony of Britain, it was always an economic colony of Australia; the big Australian trading companies Burns Philp and W.R. Carpenters dominated business. The ubiquitous Morris Hedstrom is a subsidiary of Carpenters. Most of the Indians were brought to Fiji to work for the Australian-owned Colonial Sugar Refining Company, which controlled the sugar industry from 1881 right up until 1973, when it was purchased by the Fiji government for $14 million.

No representative government existed in Fiji until 1904, when a Legislative Council was formed with six elected Europeans and two Fijians nominated by the Great Council of Chiefs, itself an instrument of colonial rule. In 1916 the governor appointed an Indian member to the council. A 1929 reform granted five seats to each community: three elected and two appointed Europeans and Indians, and five nominated Fijians. The council was only an advisory body and the governor remained in complete control. The Europeans generally sided with the Fijians against any further demands for equality from the Indians—divide and rule.

During WW I an indigenous resistance movement to this colonial exploitation emerged in the form of the Viti Kabani, or Fiji Company, led by Apolosi Ranawai, a commoner from western Viti Levu. The company began as a reaction to profiteering by Fijian chiefs and white traders who bought and sold village products, but it soon moved beyond economic matters to question the whole eastern-dominated chiefly system, which allowed the British to rule so easily. The chiefs reacted by having the movement branded seditious and Apolosi exiled.

Fijians were outstanding combat troops on the Allied side in the Solomon Islands campaign during WW II, and again in 1952-56, suppressing Malaya's national liberation struggle. So skilled were the Fijians at jungle warfare against the Japanese that it was never appropriate to list a Fijian as "missing in action"—the phrase used was "not yet arrived." Until 1952, Suva, the present Fijian capital, was headquarters for the entire British Imperial Administration in the South Pacific.

In 1963 the Legislative Council was expanded but still divided along racial lines; women and Fijians got the vote for the first time. Wishing to be rid of the British, whom they blamed for their second-class position, the Indians pushed for independence, but the Fijians had come to view the British as protectors and were somewhat reluctant. After much discussion, a constitution was finally adopted in 1970. Some legislature members were to be elected from a common roll (voting by all races), as the Indians desired, while other seats remained ethnic (voting in racial constituencies) to protect the Fijians. On 10 Oct. 1970 Fiji became a fully independent nation. The first Fijian governor-general was appointed in 1973—none other than Ratu Sir George Cakobau, great-grandson of the chief who had ceded Fiji to Queen Victoria 99 years previously.

Political Development

During the 1940s Ratu Sir Lala Sukuna, paramount chief of Lau, played a key role in the creation of a separate administration for indigenous Fijians, with native land (83% of Fiji) under its jurisdiction. In 1954 he formed the Fijian Association to support the British governor against Indian demands for equal representation. In 1960 the National Federation Party (NFP) was formed to represent Indian cane farmers.

In 1966 the Alliance Party, a coalition of the Fijian Association, the General Electors' Association (representing Europeans, part-Fijians, and Chinese), and the Fiji Indian Alliance (a minority Indian group), won the legislative assembly elections. In 1970 Alliance Party leader Ratu Sir Kamisese Mara led Fiji into independence, and in 1972 his party won Fiji's first postindependence elections. He served as prime minister almost continuously until the 1987 elections.

In 1975 Mr. Sakeasi Butadroka, a member of parliament previously expelled from the Alliance Party, introduced a motion calling for all Indians to be repatriated to India at British expense. This was rejected, but during the April 1977 elections Butadroka's Fijian Nationalist Party took enough votes away from the Alliance to allow the predominantly Indian NFP to obtain a majority in parliament. After a few days' hesitation, the governor-general reappointed

Ratu Mara as prime minister, but his minority Alliance government was soon defeated. Meanwhile, Butadroka had been arrested for making racially inflammatory statements in violation of the Public Order Act, and in new elections in September 1977 the Alliance recovered its majority, due in part to a split of the NFP into Hindu and Muslim factions.

The formation of the Fiji Labor Party (FLP) in July 1985, headed by Dr. Timoci Bavadra, dramatically altered the political landscape. Fiji's previously nonpolitical trade unions had finally come behind a party that campaigned on bread-and-butter issues rather than race. Late in 1986 Labor and the NFP formed a coalition with the aim of defeating the Alliance in the next election. Dr. Bavadra, a former director of Primary and Preventive Health Services and president of the Fiji Public Service Association, was chosen as Coalition leader. In the 12 April 1987 elections, the Coalition won 28 of 52 House of Representatives seats; 19 of the 28 elected Coalition members were Indians. What swung the election away from Alliance was not a change in Indian voting patterns but support for Labor from urban Fijians and part-Fijians, which cost Alliance four previously "safe" seats around Suva.

The Coalition had a broad base of public support, and all cabinet positions of vital Fijian interest (Lands, Fijian Affairs, Labor and Immigration, Education, Agriculture and Rural Development) went to indigenous Fijian legislators, though none of them was a chief. Coalition's progressive policies marked quite a switch from the conservatism of the Alliance—a new generation of political leadership dedicated to tackling the day-to-day problems of members of all races rather than perpetuating the privileges of the old chiefly oligarchy. Medical care was expanded, an Institute for Fijian Language and Culture was created, and Fijians were given greater access to loans by the Fiji Development Bank, which had previously been going mostly to foreign corporations.

The new government also announced that nuclear warships would be banned from a nonaligned Fiji. Foreign Minister Krishna Datt said he would join Vanuatu and New Zealand in pressing for a nuclear-free Pacific at the 24 May 1987 meeting of the South Pacific Forum. Alleged corruption in the previous administration was also to be investigated. Ratu Mara himself had allegedly accumulated a personal fortune of $4-6 million on his annual salary of $100,000. Given time the Coalition might have required the high chiefs to share the rental monies, which they received from leasing lands to Indians, more fairly with ordinary Fijians. Most significant of all, the Coalition would have transformed Fiji from a plural society where only indigenous Melanesian Fijians were called Fijians to a truly multiracial society where all citizens would be Fijians.

The First Coup

After the election the extremist Fiji-for-Fijians Taukei (landowners) movement launched a destabilization campaign by throwing barricades across highways, organizing protest rallies and marches, and carrying out firebombings. On 24 April 1987 Senator Inoke Tabua and former Alliance cabinet minister Apisai Tora organized a march of 5,000 Fijians through Suva to protest "Indian domination" of the new government. Mr. Tora told a preparatory meeting for the demonstration that Fijians must "act now" to avoid ending up as "deprived as Australia's aborigines." (In fact, under the 1970 constitution the Coalition government would have had no way of changing Fiji's land laws without indigenous Fijian consent.) During the following weeks five gasoline bombs were thrown against government offices, though no one was injured. On 13 May 1987 Alliance Senator Jona Qio was arrested for arson.

At 1000 on Thurs. 14 May 1987 Lieutenant Colonel Sitiveni Rabuka (pronounced Rambuka), an ambitious officer whose career was stalled at the third-ranking position in the Fijian Army, and 10 heavily armed soldiers dressed in fatigues, their faces covered by gas masks, entered the House of Representatives in Suva. Rabuka ordered Dr. Bavadra and the Coalition members to follow a soldier out of the building, and when Dr. Bavadra hesitated the soldiers raised their guns. The legislators were loaded into army trucks and taken to Royal Fiji Military Forces headquarters. There was no bloodshed, though Rabuka later confirmed that his troops would have opened fire had there been any resistance. At a press conference five hours after the coup, Rabuka claimed he had acted to prevent violence and had no political ambitions of his own.

Most Pacific governments denounced the region's first military coup. Governor-General Ratu Sir Penaia Ganilau attempted to reverse the situation by declaring a state of emergency and ordering the mutineers to return to their barracks. They refused to obey. The next day the *Fiji Sun* ran a black-bordered editorial that declared, "Democracy died in Fiji yesterday. What right has a third-ranking officer to attack the sacred institutions of Parliament? What right has he to presume he knows best how this country shall be governed? The answer is none." Soon after, Rabuka's troops descended on both daily papers and ordered publication suspended. Journalists were evicted from the buildings.

Later that day Rabuka named a 15-member Council of Ministers, chaired by himself, to govern Fiji, with former Alliance prime minister Ratu Mara as foreign minister. Significantly, Rabuka was the only military officer on the council; most of the others were members of Ratu Mara's defeated administration. Rabuka claimed he had acted to "safeguard the Fijian land issue and the Fijian way of life."

On 19 May Dr. Bavadra and the other kidnapped members of his government were released after the governor-general announced a deal negotiated with Rabuka to avoid the possibility of foreign intervention. Rabuka's Council of Ministers was replaced by a 19-member, caretaker Advisory Council, appointed by the Great Council of Chiefs, which would govern until new elections could take place. The council would be headed by Ratu Ganilau, with Rabuka in charge of Home Affairs and the security forces. Only two seats were offered to Dr. Bavadra's government, and they were refused.

The Sunday before the coup, Ratu Mara was seen playing golf with Rabuka at Pacific Harbor. At the time of the coup he was at the Fijian Hotel chairing a meeting of the Pacific Democratic Union, a U.S.-sponsored grouping of ultraright politicians from Australia, New Zealand, and elsewhere. Though Ratu Mara expressed "shock" at the coup, he accepted a position on Rabuka's Council of Ministers the next day, prompting New Zealand Prime Minister David Lange to accuse him of treachery under Fiji's constitution by acquiescing to military rule. Lange said Ratu Mara had pledged allegiance to the Queen but had brought about a rebellion in one of her countries. Ratu Ganilau was also strongly criticized for legitimizing a traitor by accepting Rabuka on his Advisory Council.

Behind The Coup

U.S. interest in the South Pacific picked up in 1982 after the U.S. ambassador to Fiji, William Bodde, Jr., told a luncheon audience at the Kahala Hilton in Hawaii that the creation of a South Pacific nuclear-free zone would be "the most potentially disruptive development to U.S. relations with the region . . . I am convinced that the United States must do everything possible to counter this movement. It will not be an easy task, but it is one that we cannot afford to neglect." In 1983 Bodde's diplomacy resulted in the lifting of a ban on visits to Fiji by U.S. nuclear warships, and Fiji was soon rewarded by becoming the first South Pacific country to receive direct U.S. aid. Substantial grants to the Fiji army for "weapons standardization" soon followed, and from 1984 to 1986 U.S. aid to Fiji tripled.

Immediately after the coup, rumors circulated throughout the South Pacific that the U.S. government was involved. On 16 June 1987 at a press conference at the National Press Club in Washington, D.C., Dr. Bavadra publicly accused William Paupe, director of the South Pacific regional office of U.S. AID, of channeling US $200,000 to right-winger Apisai Tora of the Taukei movement for destabilization purposes. Later Dr. Bavadra dropped the charge, which Paupe and Tora emphatically denied.

From 29 April to 1 May 1987 General Vernon A. Walters, U.S. ambassador to the U.N. and a former CIA deputy director, visited Fiji. At a long meeting with Foreign Minister Datt, Walters tried to persuade the new government to give up its antinuclear stance. Walters told the Fiji press that the U.S. "has a duty to protect its South Pacific interests." Walters is believed to have been involved in previous coups in Iran

(1953) and Brazil (1964), and during his stay in Fiji he also met with Rabuka and William Paupe. During his 10-country Pacific trip, Walters spread a bogus Libya scare, diverting attention from what was about to happen in Fiji.

On 22 Oct. 1987 the U.S. Information Service in New Zealand revealed that the amphibious assault ship USS *Belleau Wood* was just west of Fiji immediately after the coup, supported by three C-130 Hercules transport planes, which staged through Nandi Airport 20-22 June. The same release mentioned four other C-130s at Nandi that month to support the gigantic hospital ship USNS *Mercy*, which was at Suva 23-27 June—an unprecedented level of military activity. By chance or design the U.S. would have been ready to intervene militarily within hours had anything gone wrong.

Yet the evidence of U.S. involvement in the coup is circumstantial and inconclusive. In an article published in the *Sydney Morning Herald* on 16 Nov. 1987 the U.S. ambassador to Australia, William Lane, categorically denied the U.S. was behind the coup. In *No Other Way*, an official biography of Rabuka by Eddie Dean, Rabuka is quoted as saying: "Everyone involved in my coup of 14 May were people I personally picked and trained . . . no foreigners came into the country to help." The coup caught the Australian and New Zealand intelligence services totally by surprise, indicating that few knew of Rabuka's plans in advance.

Until the coup the most important mission of the Royal Fiji Defense Force was service in South Lebanon and the Sinai with peacekeeping operations. Half of the 2,600-member Fijian army was on rotating duty there, with the Sinai force financed by the U.S., and the troops in Lebanon by the United Nations. During WW II Fiji Indians refused to join the army unless they received the same pay as European recruits; indigenous Fijians had no such reservations, and the force has been 95% Fijian ever since. Service in the strife-torn Middle East gave the Fiji military a unique preparation for its present role in Fiji itself.

The mass media presented the coup in simplistic terms as a racial conflict between Indians and Fijians, though commentators with a deeper knowledge of the nature of power in Fiji saw it differently. Anthony D. van Fossen of Griffith University, Queensland, Australia, summed it up this way in the *Bulletin of Concerned Asian Scholars* (Vol. 19, No. 4, 1987):

Although the first coup has been most often seen in terms of ethnic tensions between indigenous Fijians and Fijian Indians, it may be more accurately seen as the result of tensions between aristocratic indigenous Fijians and their commoner allies defending feudalism, on the one hand, and the cause of social democracy, small-scale capitalism, and multi-ethnic nationalism represented by middle-class indigenous Fijian commoners and Hindus on the other.

In their Oct. 1987 issue *Pacific Islands Monthly* published this comment by noted author Brij V. Lal of the University of Hawaii:

More than anything else, the coup was about power. The emergence in an incipient form of a class-minded multi-racial politics, symbolized by the Labor Party and made possible by the support of many urban Fijians, posed a grave threat to the politics of race and racial compartmentalization preached by the Alliance and thus had to be nipped in the bud. The ascent of Dr. Bavadra, a chief from the long-neglected western Viti Levu, to the highest office in the land posed an unprecedented challenge to the traditional dominance of eastern chiefs, especially from Lau and Thakaundrove.

Constitutional Reform

Prior to 14 May 1987 the Fijian Parliament was composed of two houses. The House of Representatives had 52 members, 12 elected by the indigenous Fijian community, 12 by the Indian community, and three by "general electors" (Europeans, part-Fijians, Chinese, etc.). Another 10 Fijians, 10 Indians, and five general electors were chosen by a "common roll" of all voters. The 22-member Senate included eight members appointed by the Great Council of Chiefs, seven by the prime minister, six by the leader of the opposition, and one by the Council of Rotuma. Although the House of Representatives was by far the more important body,

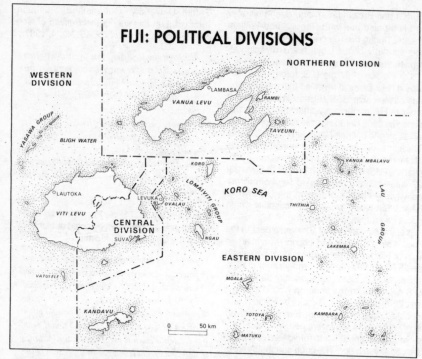

FIJI: POLITICAL DIVISIONS

NORTHERN DIVISION

WESTERN DIVISION

LAMBASA

RAMBI

VANUA LEVU

YASAWA GROUP

BLIGH WATER

TAVEUNI

VANUA MBALAVU

KORO

LOMAIVITI GROUP

KORO SEA

LAU GROUP

LAUTOKA

LEVUKA

OVALAU

THITHIA

VITI LEVU

CENTRAL DIVISION

SUVA

NGAU

LAKEMBA

EASTERN DIVISION

VATUIELE

MOALA

KANDAVU

0   50 km

TOTOYA

KAMBARA

MATUKU

changes to the constitution and many laws of special concern to indigenous Fijians (such as land laws) required a 75% majority vote in both houses. A governor-general represented the British Crown. He had the right to dissolve Parliament and order new elections.

The Great Council of Chiefs *(Mbose Levu Vakaturanga)* included the high chiefs of Fiji, the members of Parliament, and others appointed by the Minister for Fijian Affairs. After the coup parliamentarians were excluded from the council. Government at the village *(koro)* level was and still be led by a village herald *(turangani-koro)* chosen by consensus. The villages are grouped into districts *(tikina),* the districts into 14 provinces *(yasana),* and the provinces into four administrative divisions: central, eastern, northern, and western. The Micronesians of Rambi govern themselves through a council of their own. City and town councils also function. After the coups Fijians in western Fiji formed a fourth

confederacy, the Yasayasa Vakara, to balance the power of the eastern elite in the three previous confederacies, the Kumbuna, Mburembasanga, and Tovata.

In July and August 1987 a committee set up by Governor-General Ganilau studied proposals for constitutional reform. The Great Council of Chiefs asked that in a new, 71-member, unicameral Parliament indigenous Fijians be given 40 seats, all of them appointed by the Provincial Councils, the Great Council of Chiefs, and the prime minister. Indigenous Fijians would not vote directly again. The prime minister would be a Fijian elected by these Fijian members. The Labor-NFP Coalition called for a return to the 1970 constitution, while the Taukei extremists demanded a parliament comprised exclusively of indigenous Fijian members. On 4 Sept. talks between Alliance and Coalition leaders under the chairmanship of Ratu Ganilau began at Government House in Suva. With no hope of a consensus on a revised constitution, the talks were aimed at preparing for new elections.

The Second Coup

On Fri., 26 Sept. 1987, Rabuka struck again, just hours before the governor-general was to announce a Government of National Unity to rule Fiji until new elections could be held. The plan, arduously developed over four months and finally approved by veteran political leaders on all sides, would probably have resulted in Rabuka being sacked. Rabuka quickly threw out the 1970 constitution and pronounced himself "head of state." Some 300 prominent community leaders were arrested and Ratu Ganilau was confined to Government House. Newspapers were shut down, trade unions repressed, the judiciary suspended, the public service purged, the activities of political opponents restricted, a curfew imposed, and the first cases of torture reported.

At midnight on 7 Oct. 1987 Rabuka declared Fiji a republic. Rabuka's new Council of Ministers included Taukei extremists Apisai Tora and Filipe Bole, Fijian Nationalist Party leader Sakeasi Butadroka, and other marginal figures. Rabuka appeared to have backing in the Great Council of Chiefs, which wanted a return to the style of customary rule threatened by the Indian presence and Western democracy. Regime ideologists trumpeted traditional culture and religious fundamentalism. Rabuka said he wanted Christianity adopted as Fiji's official religion, and henceforth all trading (except at tourist hotels), sports, and public transport would be banned on Sunday. Rabuka even called for the conversion of Hindu and Muslim Indians to Christianity.

On 16 Oct. Ratu Ganilau resigned as governor-general and two days later Fiji was expelled from the British Commonwealth (perhaps for good, as Commonwealth rules require a unanimous vote from other members for readmission). On 6 Nov. Rabuka allowed the *Fiji Times* to resume publication after it pledged self-censorship, but the more independent *Fiji Sun* has never appeared again. Nobody accused the U.S. of having anything to do with Rabuka's second coming and even Ratu Mara seemed annoyed that Rabuka had destroyed an opportunity to reestablish the prestige of himself and Ratu Ganilau. Clearly Rabuka had become his own man.

The Republic Of Fiji

Realizing that Taukei military rule was a recipe for disaster, on 5 Dec. 1987 Rabuka appointed Ratu Ganilau president and Ratu Mara prime minister of his new republic. The 21-member cabinet included 10 members of Rabuka's military regime, four of them army officers. Rabuka himself (now a self-styled brigadier) was once again Minister of Home Affairs. This interim government set itself a deadline of two years to frame a new constitution and return Fiji to freely elected representative government. By mid-1988 the army had been expanded into a highly disciplined, 6,000-member force loyal to Brigadier Rabuka, who left no doubt he would intervene a third time if his agenda were not followed. The Great Council of Chiefs was to decide on Fiji's republican constitution.

The coups devastated the Fijian economy. In 1987 Fiji experienced 11% negative growth in the gross domestic product. To prevent a massive flight of capital the Fiji dollar was devalued 17.75% on 30 June 1987 and 15.25% on 7 October. Inflation, which had been under 2% before the coups, was up to 11.9% by the end of 1988. At the same time the public service (half the work force) had to accept a 25% wage cut as government spending was slashed. Food prices skyrocketed, causing serious problems for many families. At the end of 1987 the per capita average income was 11% *below* what it had been in 1980. Thousands of Indian professionals—accountants, administrators, dentists, doctors, lawyers, nurses, teachers—left for Australia, Canada, New Zealand, and the United States. In 1987 there were 18,359 emigrants, in 1988 another 10,360, crippling losses for a country with a total population of under 750,000.

The coups also undermined the independence struggles of the Kanaks in New Caledonia, gave comfort and support to French colonialism in the South Pacific, weakened the influence of the South Pacific Forum on the international stage, revealed the impotence of constitutional monarchy as a defender of democracy, set a dangerous precedent for other Pacific countries, such as Tonga, which are now trying to establish representative government, institutionalized racism in what had been a model of multiracialism, reduced the human rights of all Fijians, and stifled the social and political development of the country. In effect Rabuka and the old oligarchs had pushed Fiji squarely back into the third world.

Internal Security

On 31 May 1988 Australian customs officials at Sydney discovered a mysterious 12-tonne arms shipment bound for Lautoka, Fiji. In a container that had arrived from North Yemen were Czech-made weapons including AK-47 rifles, rocket launchers, antitank mines, and explosives. Evidently a second container had slipped into Fiji in April 1988, and by 8 June raids by security forces in western Fiji had netted over 100 rifles and other weapons, with 20 arrests.

For whom the arms were actually intended has never been precisely established, and the Fiji police were unable to establish any link to the Coalition. Right from the start Dr. Bavadra had consistently advocated nonviolence. Australian officials implicated Mohammed Rafiq Kahan, an ex-resident of Fiji with a long criminal background, as the one responsible for the shipment. Kahan, who fled Australia when the arms were uncovered, was apprehended in London, England. In March 1989 a London court considering his extradition to Fiji was told that the defendant had mentioned Alliance supporter Motibhai Patel, owner of the duty-free emporium at Nandi Airport, and Ratu Mara himself in connection with the arms shipment. Kahan was released on grounds that the case was political.

Kahan had been photographed wearing a military uniform in the Queen Elizabeth Barracks, Suva, just two months before the arms were discovered, and on the same visit to Fiji Kahan developed contacts with key Alliance ministers Apisai Tora, Taniela Veitata, and Ahmed Ali. The shipments appeared to have been either in preparation for a countercoup against Rabuka by disgruntled Alliance elements or the pretense for a crackdown on the political opposition within Fiji by the security forces.

On 17 June 1988 the regime issued an 86-section Internal Security Decree giving the police and military unlimited powers to arrest and hold anyone up to two years without charge, to impose curfews, to shoot to kill within declared security areas, to search vehicles or premises without a warrant, to seize land and buildings,

and to cancel passports. No inquests would be held into any killings under decree powers, and the penalty for possession of firearms or explosives was life imprisonment. The decree also made it illegal to publish anything "prejudicial to the national interest and security of Fiji." The decree was modeled on similar laws in Malaysia and Singapore, which have led to widespread human-rights violations. On 17 Nov. 1988 the decree was suspended but not repealed.

On 22 June 1988, 10 people were arrested in Suva, including the secretary of the Fiji Law Society, who had merely called a meeting to discuss the new security decree, and two lawyers who had defended persons charged with arms offenses. Several prominent Muslim businessmen suspected of financing the arms shipment were also held. Despite a one-month amnesty to surrender arms, declared by Rabuka on 23 June, the arrests continued, with families fearing their relatives had "disappeared." Most were held incommunicado about a week, then released. Many reported being beaten in confinement.

The most notorious of the 22 June arrests was that of Som Prakash, a lecturer in English at the University of the South Pacific who wrote a critical review of Rabuka's biography. The review castigated the brigadier's "Messiah syndrome" and his intolerance of races and religions other than his own and questioned Rabuka's claim that he had acted to prevent "bloodshed," suggesting that political considerations were paramount. Mr. Prakash was held in solitary confinement without legal advice or access to his family until 6 July, when he was released on the condition that he not speak to the news media. It was reported he had been beaten during his detention. Amnesty International called Mr. Prakash a "prisoner of conscience."

Meanwhile France stepped in with $8 million in military aid to Fiji, including 53 Renault vehicles for the army and a helicopter for Rabuka. France hoped that by backing the military regime in Fiji it could divide the opponents of French nuclear testing in the South Pacific. As the U.S., Australia, New Zealand, and Britain maintained their freeze on military aid to Fiji, the country turned to undemocratic regimes in South Korea, Taiwan, and mainland China for military training and supplies.

Interim Government

In May 1989 the interim government eased Sunday restrictions on work, trading, and sports. This drew loud protests from Rev. Manasa Lasaro, fundamentalist general secretary of the Methodist Church of Fiji and a leader of the Fijian Christian Nationalist Party, who organized Sunday roadblocks in Lambasa, leading to the arrest and conviction of himself and 56 others for unlawful obstruction. On 9 Aug. Rabuka flew to Lambasa by helicopter and arranged the release of Rev. Lasaro and the others on his own authority. On Sun. 15 Oct. 1989 members of a Methodist youth group carried out firebombings against Hindu and Sikh temples and a Muslim mosque at Lautoka.

In Nov. 1989 Dr. Bavadra died from spinal cancer at age 55 and 60,000 people attended his funeral at Viseisei, the largest in Fijian history. Right up until his death Dr. Bavadra maintained a courageous critical posture against the militarization of Fijian society and politics.

Though the political situation remained unstable, Fiji's economy began to recover, with 2% positive growth in 1988 and 12.1% growth in 1989. Inflation was reduced to 6.1% in 1989 and 8.1% in 1990. Ratu Mara, who considered Rabuka an unpredictable upstart, insisted that he choose between politics or military service, so in late 1989 the general and two other army colonels were dropped from the cabinet. Rabuka kept his post as army commander.

In May 1990 Fiji expelled the entire staff of the Indian Embassy in Suva after India's Minister for External Affairs called for an international campaign against the institutionalization of racism in Fiji. The expulsion was in preparation for the launching of a new Fijian constitution approved by the Great Council of Chiefs in June and promulgated by President Ganilau on 25 July 1990. This constitution gives the chiefs the right to appoint the president and 24 of the 34 members of the senate. In addition, one senator is appointed by the Rotuman Council and nine senators are appointed by the president to represent the other communities. The president has executive authority and appoints the prime minister from among the ethnic Fijian members of the House of Representatives. Cabinet ministers may be from either house.

The 70-member House of Representatives is elected directly, with voting racially segregated. Ethnic Fijians are granted 37 seats, 32 from 14 provincial constituencies and only five from five urban constituencies, despite the fact that 33% of indigenous Fijians live in towns and cities. The provincial Fijian constituencies are gerrymandered to ensure eastern dominance. For example, Mba, with an ethnic Fijian population of 55,000, gets three Fijian seats, the same number as Lau with only 14,000 inhabitants. Fiji Indians (nearly half the population) get 27 seats based on 27 constituencies, while there is one Rotuman seat and five for other races (Chinese, part-Fijians, Europeans, etc.).

The new constitution not only guarantees ethnic Fijians a majority in both houses, but the posts of president, prime minister, and army chief are explicitly reserved for Fijians. Christianity is the official religion and Rabuka's troops are granted amnesty for any offenses committed during the 1987 coups. Fijian customary laws have become the law of the land, and all decisions of the Native Lands Commission are final with no further recourse to the courts. Continued military interference in civilian government is allowed for by the vague identification of the army as the final arbiter in determining "the security, defense, and well-being of Fiji and its peoples."

The Coalition quickly rejected this constitution as undemocratic and racist and threatened to boycott elections held under it unless a referendum took place. They claimed the rigged voting system used race as a device to divide Fijians and perpetuate the power of the eastern elite. Urban and western Fijians, the very groups that challenged the status quo by voting Labor in 1987, are discriminated against, and Indians are relegated to the fringes of political life. Complicated registration requirements also deprive many rural Fijian commoners of the vote.

On 18 Oct. 1990 a copy of the new constitution was burned during a nonviolent protest by a small group of academics and students. Six days later one of those involved, Dr. Anirudh Singh, a lecturer in physics at the University of the South Pacific, was abducted by five soldiers and taken to Tholo-i-Suva where he was tortured with lit cigarettes and had his hands broken by an iron bar during "interrogation." Later he was released. On 29 Oct. three journalists of the *Daily Post* were arrested for publishing a story suggesting that there might be a second constitution burning, and on 31 Oct. Dr. Singh and six other alleged constitution burners were arrested and charged with sedition. After a public outcry the soldiers who had tortured Dr. Singh were turned over to police by the army, given a brief trial, fined F$340 each, and set free. Incredibly, just a few months later the Fiji Army picked one of the convicted torturers, Capt. Sotia Ponijiase, to head Fiji's contingent in a U.N. observer team sent to Kuwait. When the story came to light, Capt. Ponijiase was sent packing back to Fiji by the United Nations

Not satisfied with control of the senate, in early 1991 the Great Council of Chiefs formed the Fijian Political Party, or Soqosoqo ni Vakavulewa ni Taukei (SVT), to project their power into the lower house. This provoked strong criticism from many who saw it as another move by the eastern oligarchs to monopolize power. To avoid the embarrassment of a defeat for the chiefs and allow more time for voter registration, the interim government postponed the elections several times. Meanwhile Fiji's multiethnic unions continued to rebuild their strength by organizing garment workers and leading strikes in the mining and sugar industries.

In June 1991 Major-General Rabuka rejected an offer from Ratu Mara to join the cabinet as Minister of Home Affairs and co-deputy prime minister, since it would have meant giving up his military power base. Instead Rabuka attempted to widen his political appeal by making public statements in support of striking gold miners and cane farmers, and even threatening a third coup. Rabuka's ambition to become prime minister had become obvious, and his new role as a populist rabble-rouser seemed designed to outflank both the Labor Party and the chiefs (Rabuka himself is a commoner). President Ganilau (Rabuka's paramount chief) quickly applied pressure, and in July the volatile general reversed himself and accepted the cabinet posts he had so recently refused. As a condition for reentering the government, Rabuka was forced to resign as army commander, and the president's son, Major-General Epeli Ganilau, was appointed his successor. With Rabuka out of the army everyone breathed a little easier, and the chiefs decided to co-opt a potential trouble-

maker by electing Rabuka president of their Fijian Political Party (SVT).

The 1992 Elections

In July 1991 the NFP decided at its annual meeting that it would field candidates for the 27 Indian seats after all, to avoid their being won by "irresponsible persons." By late 1991 some 17 political parties had formed to contest the 1992 elections. The old Alliance Party had split into three main factions: the SVT, the Indian Liberal Party, and the General Voters Party—all of them accepting the power of the traditional chiefs. Several indigenous parties, including the Fijian Conservative Party, the Christian Fijian Nationalist Party, and the All National Congress, used racial issues to appeal to Fijian commoners. After a bitter internal debate, the Fiji Labor Party (FLP), now led by Mahendra Chaudhry, decided not to boycott the elections.

The long-awaited parliamentary elections took place in late May 1992 under the new constitution. The SVT captured 30 of the 37 indigenous Fijian seats, with another five going to Sakeasi Butadroka's Fijian Nationalist United Front (FNUF) and two to independents. The 27 Indian seats were split between the NFP with 14 and the FLP with 13. The five other races' seats went to the General Voters Party (GVP).

Just prior to the election Ratu Mara (who had retired from party politics) was named vice-president of Fiji by the Great Council of Chiefs. An intense power struggle developed in the SVT between Ratu Mara's chosen successor, former Finance Minister Josevata Kamikamica, and ex-general Rabuka. Since the party lacked a clear majority in the 70-seat house, coalition partners had to be sought, and after much repositioning the pro-big business camp lined up behind Kamikamica, with NFP and GVP support. Rabuka had the backing of the FNUF, but most SVT members opposed a coalition with Butadroka's racial extremists, and in a remarkable turn of events populist Rabuka gained the support of the FLP by offering concessions to the trade unions and a promise to review the constitution and land leases. Thus Sitiveni Rabuka became prime minister thanks to the very party he had ousted from power at gunpoint exactly five years before. The SVP has formed a coalition with the GVP and a lively opposition seems assured.

preparing a *lovo* or underground oven at Korovou, central Viti Levu (D. Stanley)

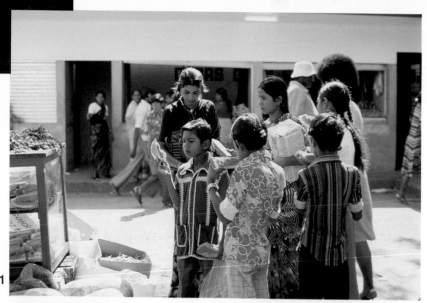

1. a Fiji Indian family enjoying watermelon at Nandi (John Penisten);
2. pineapple vendor, Nandi Market (John Penisten)

Taro, which grows marvelously well in the rich soils of Fiji's bush gardens, is one of the staples of the Pacific and ensures a steady supply of nourishing food for the villagers.

MINISTRY OF INFORMATION, GOVERNMENT OF FIJI

ECONOMY

Economic Development

Fiji has a diversified economy based on sugar production, tourism, garment manufacturing, timber, commercial fishing, gold mining, and coconut products. From WW II until 1987 a series of five-year plans guided public investment and resulted in the excellent modern infrastructure and advanced social services Fiji enjoys today. Aside from this cash economy, subsistence agriculture makes an important contribution to the life of indigenous Fijians in rural areas. About 40% of the work force has paid employment; the remainder is involved in subsistence agriculture, with manioc, taro, yams, sweet potato, and corn the principal subsistence crops.

While eastern Viti Levu and the Lau Group dominate the country politically, western Viti Levu is Fiji's economic powerhouse, with sugar, tourism, timber, and gold mining all centered there. Almost all of Fiji's sugar is produced by small independent Indian farmers on contract to the government-owned Fiji Sugar Corporation,

which took over from the Australian-owned Colonial Sugar Refining Company in 1973. Some 23,000 farmers cultivate cane on holdings averaging 4.5 hectares leased from indigenous Fijians. The corporation owns 644 km of 0.610-meter narrow-gauge railway, which it uses to carry the cane to the mills at Lautoka, Mba, Rakiraki, and Lambasa. About half a million tonnes of sugar are produced annually.

Timber is increasingly important as thousands of hectares planted in western Viti Levu and Vanua Levu by the Fiji Pine Commission and private landowners in the late 1970s reach maturity. Each year Fiji exports about F$12 million in sawed lumber and F$14 million in wood chips (the export of raw logs was banned in 1987). Yet Fiji's native forests are poorly protected from the greed of foreign logging companies and shortsighted local landowners, and each year large tracts of pristine rainforest are lost. Now that all of the lowland forests have been cleared, attention is turning to the highlands. The pine

HOW A SUGAR MILL WORKS

The sugarcane is fed through a shredder towards a row of huge rollers, which squeeze out the juice. The crushed fiber (bagasse) is burned to fuel the mill or is processed into paper. Lime is then added to the juice and the mixture is heated. Impurities settle in the clarifier and mill mud is filtered out to be used as fertilizer. The clear juice goes through a series of evaporators, in which it is boiled into steam under partial vacuum to remove water and create a syrup. The syrup is boiled again under greater pressure in a vacuum pan, and raw sugar crystals form. The mix then enters a centrifuge, which spins off the remaining syrup (molasses—used for distilling or cattle feed). The moist crystals are sent on to a rotating drum where they are tumble-dried using hot air. Raw sugar comes out in the end.

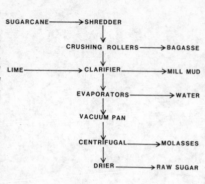

project has had the added benefit of reducing pressure on the natural forests to supply Fiji's timber needs.

Commercial fishing is booming, with a major tuna cannery at Levuka supplied in part by Fiji's own fleet of 17 longline vessels. The 15,000 metric tonnes of canned tuna produced each year comprise Fiji's third-largest export, shipped mostly to Britain and Canada.

Mining activity centers on gold at Vatukoula on Viti Levu, and extensive low-grade copper deposits at Namosi àre now being considered for development. Fiji now grows almost half its own rice needs and is trying to become self-sufficient. Much of the rice is grown around Nausori and Navua. Most of Fiji's copra is produced in Lau, Lomaiviti, Taveuni, and Vanua Levu, half by European or part-Fijian planters and the rest by indigenous Fijian villagers.

Yet, in spite of all this potential, unemployment is turning into a major social problem as four times more young people leave school than there are jobs to take them. To stimulate industry, firms that export 95% of their production are granted 13-year tax holidays, the duty-free import of materials, and the freedom to repatriate capital and profit. The garment industry is growing fast, with female employees earning an average of F$30 a week. Women working in the industry have complained of being subjected to body searches and sexual harassment, with those who protest or organize collective action being fired and blacklisted. The clothing is exported mostly to Australia and New Zealand, where partial duty- and quota-free entry is allowed under the South Pacific Regional Trade and Economic Cooperation Agreement (SPARTECA) for products with at least 50% local content, and many manufacturers in those countries have moved their factories to Fiji to take advantage of the lower labor costs. Food processors and furniture and toy makers are also prominent in the tax-free exporting sector, and it's believed that within a decade manufacturing may overtake both sugar and tourism as the main source of income for the country.

Trade And Aid

Fiji is an important regional trading center. Although Fiji imports 50% more than it exports, some of the imbalance is later sold to tourists who pay in foreign exchange. In the Pacific islands Fiji's trade deficit is exceeded only by that of Tahiti-Polynesia and has grown much larger in recent years due to sharply increased imports of machinery and supplies by tax-free zone industry. Raw sugar accounts for over half of the nation's visible export earnings, followed by garments, unrefined gold, canned fish, wood chips, sawed timber, and coconut oil, in that order. Huge trade imbalances exist with Australia, Japan, and New Zealand.

Fiji has long-term contracts to sell sugar to New Zealand, Singapore, Malaysia, Britain, and the European Community at fixed rates. These contracts cover over 300,000 tonnes annually, with the surplus sold on the world market. A distillery at Lautoka produces alcohol, including rum and other liquors.

Mineral fuels used to be Fiji's most expensive import item, but this declined as the Monasavu Hydroelectric Project and other self-sufficiency measures came on-line. Machinery, vehicles, manufactured goods, food, fuels, and chemicals account for most of the import bill.

Fiji is the least dependent Pacific nation (excluding Nauru). In 1989 overseas aid totaled only A$75 per capita (as compared to A$1838 per capita in Tahiti-Polynesia); it accounts for just 7% of government expenditures. Development aid is well diversified among over a dozen donors; the largest amounts come from Australia, Japan, New Zealand, France, Germany, and the United Kingdom, in that order, with Australia alone contributing nearly half. U.S. and Canadian aid to Fiji is meager. Increasingly Fiji is looking to Asian countries such as Japan, China, Taiwan, South Korea, and Singapore for aid.

Tourism
Tourism is the leading moneymaker, earning around F$350 million a year—more than sugar and gold combined. In 1991 some 259,350 tourists visited Fiji—twice as many as visited Tahiti and twelve times as many as visited Tonga. Things appear in better perspective, however, when Fiji is compared to Hawaii, which is about the same size in surface area. Hawaii gets six million tourists, 20 times as many as Fiji. Gross receipts figures from tourism are often misleading, as 58 cents on every dollar is repatriated overseas by foreign investors or used to pay for tourism-related imports. In real terms sugar is far more profitable for Fiji.

The main tourist resorts are centered along the southern coast of Viti Levu and in the Mamanutha Islands off Nandi/Lautoka, with major new developments planned for Saweni Beach near Lautoka, Ndenarau Beach at Nandi, and Natandola Beach south of Nandi. For years the Fiji government swore there would be no hotel development in the Yasawas, but several resort projects are presently underway there, and only the Lau Group is now without regular hotels. The huge Japanese group Electrical and Industrial Enterprises (EIE) has investments in Fiji worth a half billion dollars, including the Sheraton and Regent of Fiji hotels at Nandi and a stake in Air Pacific.

BALANCE OF TRADE

TOTAL IMPORTS A$889 MILLION (1989)

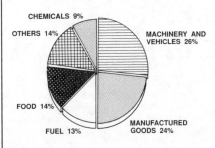

CHEMICALS 9%

OTHERS 14%

MACHINERY AND VEHICLES 26%

FOOD 14%

FUEL 13%

MANUFACTURED GOODS 24%

TOTAL EXPORTS A$455 MILLION (1989)

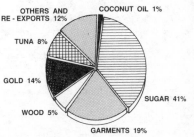

OTHERS AND RE - EXPORTS 12%

COCONUT OIL 1%

TUNA 8%

GOLD 14%

WOOD 5%

GARMENTS 19%

SUGAR 41%

The 1987 military coups ended a decade of steady increases in tourism to Fiji. Fiji's image as a trouble-free Pacific paradise has been shattered and the Fiji Visitors Bureau had to scrap their former marketing slogan, "The Way the World Should Be." From Jan. to April 1987 arrivals increased 10%; from May to Dec. they dropped 42%. Visitor arrivals peaked at 257,824 in 1986, dropped to 189,866 in 1987, and then rose to 208,155 in 1988, 250,565 in 1989, and 278,996 in 1990. Continental Airlines severed service to Fiji after the 1987 coup and never returned.

About 40% of Fiji's tourists come from Australia, 15% from the U.S., 10% each from New Zealand and continental Europe, and 8% from Canada. The vast majority of visitors arrive in Fiji en route to and from Auckland, Sydney, and Honolulu. North Americans tend to view Fiji as a mere stopover on the way down under and spend far less time in the country than Australians or New Zealanders: over half of Australians stay longer than a week, while a majority of Americans stay three days or less.

Most of the large resort hotels in Fiji are foreign-owned, and 80% of their purchases for food, beverages, linen, glassware, etc., are imported at concessional rates. The Fiji government has diverted large sums from its capital-improvements budget to provide infrastructure such as roads, airports, and other services to the resorts, yet the hotels can write off 55% of their capital expenditure against taxes over a period of six years. Management of the foreign-owned hotels is usually European, with Fiji Indians filling technical positions, such as maintenance, cooking, accounting, etc., and indigenous Fijians working the high-profile positions, such as receptionists, waiters, guides, and housekeepers. Now Fiji is beginning to get a reputation as an expensive destination as prices at the luxury hotels go up and up. Fortunately there are still lots of low-budget alternatives.

THE PEOPLE

The Fijians

Fiji is a transitional zone between Polynesia and Melanesia. The Fijians bear a physical resemblance to the Melanesians, but like the Polynesians the Fijians have hereditary chiefs, patrilineal descent, a love of elaborate ceremonies, and a fairly homogeneous language and culture. Fijians have interbred with Polynesians to the extent that their skin color is lighter than that of other Melanesians. In the interior and west of Viti Levu, where there was less contact, the people tend to be somewhat darker than the easterners. Yet Fijians still have Melanesian frizzy hair, while most—but not all—Polynesians have straight hair.

The Fijians live in villages along the rivers or coast, with anywhere from 50 to 400 people led by a hereditary chief. *Matanggali* (clans) are grouped into *yavusa* of varying rank and function. Several *yavusa* form a *vanua*, a number of which make up a *matanitu*. Chiefs of the most important *vanua* are known as high chiefs. In western Viti Levu the units are smaller, and outstanding commoners could always achieve the prestige reserved for high chiefs in the east. Away from the three largest islands the population is almost totally Fijian. The traditional thatched *mbure* is fast disappearing from Fiji

as villagers rebuild (usually following destructive cyclones) in tin and panel. Grass is not as accessible as cement, takes more time to repair, and is less permanent. About 78% of Fijians are Methodist, 8.5% Catholic.

Fijians work communal land individually, not as a group. Each Fijian is assigned his piece of native land. They grow most of their own food in village gardens, and only a few staples, such as tea, sugar, flour, etc., are imported from Suva and sold in local co-op stores. A visit to one of these stores will demonstrate just how little they import and how self-sufficient they are. Fishing, village maintenance work, and ceremonial presentations are done together. While village life provides a form of collective security, individuals are discouraged from rising above the group. Fijians who attempt to set up a business are often stifled by the demands of relatives and friends. This pattern makes it difficult for Fijians to compete with Indians, for whom life has always been a struggle.

The Indians

Most of the Indians now in Fiji are descended from indentured laborers recruited in Bengal and Bihar a century ago. In 1879, the first year of the system, some 450 Indians arrived in Fiji to

CAINES JANNIF LTD., SUVA

The descendants of late 19th-century arrivals, such as this characterful young woman, make up the majority of Fiji's population today. These indentured laborers faced many hardships and indignities, one of which stemmed from a British policy of allowing only 40 Indian women to be brought to the islands for every 100 men.

work in the cane fields. By 1883 the total had risen to 2,300, and in 1916, when the last indentured laborers arrived, 63,000 Indians were present in the colony. In 1920 the indenture system was finally terminated, the cane fields were divided into four-hectare plots, and the Indian workers became tenant farmers on land owned by Fijians. Indians continued to arrive until 1931, though many of these later arrivals were Gujerati or Sikh businesspeople.

In 1940 the Indian population stood at 98,000, still below the Fijian total of 105,000. But by the 1946 census Indians had outstripped Fijians 120,000 to 117,000—making Fijians a minority in their own home. In the wake of the coups the relative proportions changed when some 30,000 Indians emigrated to North America and Australia, and by early 1989 indigenous Fijians once again outnumbered Fiji Indians. At the end of 1991, Fiji's estimated total population was 746,326, of which approximately 49.4% were Fijian, while 45.6% were Indian (compared to 46% Fijian and 48.7% Indian at the 1986 census).

Unlike the village-oriented Fijians, a majority of Indians are concentrated in the cane-growing areas and live in isolated farmhouses, small settlements, or towns. Many Indians also live in Suva, as do an increasing number of Fijians. Within the Fiji Indian community are divisions such as between Hindu (80%) versus Muslim (20%), northern Indian versus southern Indian, and Gujerati versus the rest. The Sikhs and Gujeratis have always been somewhat of an elite as they immigrated freely to Fiji outside the indenture system.

The different groups have kept alive their ancient religious beliefs and rituals. Hindus tend to marry within their caste, although the restrictions on behavior that characterize the caste system in India have disappeared. Indian marriages are often arranged by the parents, while Fijians generally choose their own partners. Rural Indians still associate most closely with other members of their extended patrilineal family group, and Hindu and Muslim religious beliefs still restrict Indian women to a position subservient to men.

It's often said that Indians concentrate on accumulation, while Fijians emphasize distribution. Fiji's laws, which prevent Indians or anyone else from purchasing native communal land, have encouraged the Indians to invest their savings in business, which they now almost monopolize at the middle levels. (Big business is the domain of Europeans.) This has created envy on the part of the less business-oriented Fijians. If some Indians seem money-minded, keep in mind it's because they have been forced into that role. When one considers their position in a land where most have lived three generations and where they form about half the population, their industriousness and patience are admirable.

Land Rights

When Fiji became a British colony in 1874, the land was divided between white settlers who had bought plantations and the *taukei ni ngele*, the Fijian "owners of the soil." The government assumed title to the balance. Today the alienated (privately owned) plantation lands are known as "freehold" land—about 10% of the total. Another 7% is Crown land and the remaining 83% is inalienable Fijian communal land, which can be leased (about 30% is) but may never be sold. Compare this 83% (much of it not arable) with only 3% Maori land in New Zealand and almost zero native Hawaiian land. Land ownership has provided the Fijian with a security that allows him to preserve his traditional culture, unlike most indigenous peoples in other countries.

Communal land is administered on behalf of some 6,600 clan groups *(matanggali)* by the Native Land Trust Board, a government agency established in 1940. In 1966 the Agricultural Landlords and Tenants Act increased the period for which native land can be leased from 10 to 30 years. The 30-year leases will begin coming up for renewal in 1996, and Fiji's 23,000 Indian sugarcane farmers are apprehensive about the new terms they'll receive. If rents are greatly increased or the leases terminated (as Rabuka and others have suggested), Fiji's sugar industry could be badly damaged and an explosive social situation created. The difficulty in obtaining land has led to a serious squatter problem: people simply occupy unused areas without concerning themselves about who holds the title.

At the First Constitutional Conference in 1965, Indian rights were promulgated, and the 1970 independence constitution asserted that everyone born in Fiji would be a citizen with equal rights. But land laws, right up to the present, have very much favored "Fiji for the Fijians." Fiji Indians have always accepted Fijian ownership of the land, provided they are granted satisfactory leases. Now the leases seem endangered and many Indians fear they will be driven from the only land they've ever known. The stifling of land development may keep Fiji quaint for tourists, but it also condemns a large portion of Fijians of both races to backwardness and poverty.

Other Groups

The 5,000 Fiji-born Europeans or *Kai Viti* are descendants of Australians and New Zealanders who came to create cotton, sugar, or copra plantations in the 19th century. Many married Fijian women and the 13,000 part-Europeans or *Kai Loma* of Fiji today often call themselves part-Fijians. Many other Europeans are present in Fiji on temporary contracts or as tourists. The 5,000 Chinese in Fiji are descended from free settlers who came to set up small businesses a century ago. Fiji Chinese tend to intermarry freely with the other racial groups. There is almost no intermarriage between Fijians and Fiji Indians.

The people of Rotuma, a majority of whom now live in Suva, are Polynesians. On neighboring islands off Vanua Levu are the Micronesians of Rambi (from Kiribati) and the Polynesians of Kioa (from Tuvalu). The descendants of Solomon Islanders who were blackbirded during the 19th century still live in communities near Suva, Levuka, and Lambasa. The Tongans in Lau and other Pacific islanders who have immigrated to Fiji make this an ethnic crossroads of the Pacific.

DAVID STANLEY

The three largest ethnic groups in Fiji are Indians, Fijians, and Polynesians.

Social Conditions

Some 98% of the country's population was born in Fiji. The partial breakdown in race relations after the Rabuka coups was a tragedy for Fiji, though racial antagonism has been exaggerated. Despite the rhetoric and recent provocations, the different ethnic groups have always gotten along well together, with remarkably little animosity. As important as race are the variations between rich and poor, urban (39%) and rural (61%). About 9% of the population lives in absolute poverty. Avenues for future economic growth are limited, and there's chronic unemployment. The population is growing at an annual rate of 3% (compared to 0.9% in the U.S.), and the subsistence economy simply can't absorb these numbers. The lack of work is reflected in the increasing crime rate.

Though literacy is high at 80%, most schools are operated by religious groups and local communities. Tuition fees must be paid at all levels. The Fiji Institute of Technology was founded at Suva in 1963, followed by the University of the South Pacific in 1968. The university serves the 12 Pacific countries that contribute to its costs. Medical services in Fiji are heavily subsidized. The main hospitals are at Lambasa, Lautoka, and Suva, though smaller hospitals, health centers, and nursing stations are scattered throughout the country. The most common infectious diseases are influenza, gonorrhea, and syphilis.

Language

Fijian is a member of the Austronesian family of languages spoken from Easter Island to Madagascar. In 1835 two Wesleyan missionaries, David Cargill and William Cross, devised the form of written Fijian used in Fiji today. Since all consonants in Fijian are separated by vowels, they spelled *mb* as *b, nd* as *d, ng* as *g, ngg* as *q,* and *th* as *c.* (For convenience this book employs phonetic spelling for place names and words, but Fijian spelling for the names of individuals.) Fijian vowels are pronounced as in Latin or Spanish, while the consonants sound similar to English. Syllables end in a vowel and the next-to-last syllable is usually the one emphasized. Where two vowels appear together, they are sounded separately.

Though Cargill and Cross worked at Lakemba in the Lau Group, the political importance of tiny Mbau Island just off Viti Levu caused the Mbauan dialect of Fijian to be selected as the "official" version of the language, and in 1850 a dictionary and grammar were published. When the Bible was translated into Mbauan, that dialect's dominance was assured, and it is today's spoken and written Fijian.

Hindustani or Hindi is the household tongue of most Fiji Indians. Fiji Hindi has diverged from that spoken in India with the adoption of many words from English and other Indian languages, such as Urdu. Though a quarter of Fiji Indians are descended from immigrants from southern India where Tamil and Telegu are spoken, few use these languages today, even in the home. Fiji Muslims speak Hindi out of practical considerations, though they might consider Urdu their mother tongue. In their spoken form Hindi and Urdu are very similar. English is the second official language in Fiji and is understood by almost everyone. All schools teach exclusively in English after the fourth grade.

CUSTOMS

Fijians and Fiji Indians are very tradition-oriented people who have retained a surprising number of their own ancestral customs, despite the flood of conflicting influences that have swept the Pacific over the past century. Rather than becoming a melting pot where one group assimilated another, Fiji is a patchwork of varied traditions.

The obligations and responsibilities of Fijian village life include not only the erection and upkeep of certain buildings, but also personal participation in the many ceremonies that give their lives meaning. Hindu Indians, on the other hand, practice firewalking and observe festivals, such as Holi and Diwali, just as their forebears in India did for thousands of years.

Fijian Firewalking

In Fiji, both Fijians and Indians practice firewalking, although the Fijians walk on heated stones instead of hot embers. Legends tell how the ability to walk on fire was first given to a warrior named Tui-na-vinggalita from Mbengga Island, just off the southern coast of Viti Levu, who had spared the life of a spirit god he caught while fishing for eels. The freed spirit gave to Tui-na-vinggalita the gift of immunity to fire. Today his descendants act as *mbete* (high priests) of the rite of *vilavilairevo* (jumping into the oven). Only members of his tribe, the Sawau, perform the ceremony. The Tui Sawau tribe lives at Ndakuimbengga village on Mbengga, but firewalking is now performed only at the resort hotels on Viti Levu.

Fijian firewalkers (men only) are not permitted to have contact with women or to eat any coconut for two weeks prior to a performance. In a circular pit about four meters across, hundreds of large stones are first heated by a wood fire until they're white-hot. If you throw a handkerchief on the stones, it will burst into flames. Much ceremony and chanting accompanies certain phases of the ritual, such as the moment when the wood is removed to leave just the red-hot embers. The men psych themselves up in a nearby hut, then emerge, enter the pit, and walk briskly once around it. Bundles

of leaves and grass are then thrown on the stones and the men stand inside the steaming pit again to chant a final song. They seem to have complete immunity to pain and there's no trace of injury. The men appear to fortify themselves with the heat, to gain some psychic power from the ritual.

Indian Firewalking

By extraordinary coincidence Fiji Indians brought with them the ancient practice of religious firewalking. In southern India, firewalking occurs in the pre-monsoon season as a call to the goddess Kali (Durga) for rain. Fiji Indian firewalking is an act of purification, or fulfillment of a vow to thank the god for help in a difficult situation.

In Fiji firewalking is performed in most Hindu temples once a year, at full moon sometime between May and Sept., according to the Hindu calendar. The actual event takes place on a

Spikes piercing their cheeks, Fiji Indians walk over hot coals at a religious festival, to purify themselves or give thanks to Durga for assistance rendered.

THE FIJI TIMES

Sun. at 1600 on the Suva side of Viti Levu, and at 0400 on the Nandi/Lautoka side. In Aug. there is firewalking at the Sangam Temple on Howell Rd., Suva. During the 10 festival days preceding the walk, participants remain in isolation, eat only unspiced vegetarian food, and spiritually prepare themselves. There are prayers at the temple in the early morning and a group singing of religious stories at about 1900 from Mon. through Thursday. The yellow-clad devotees, their faces painted bright yellow and red, often pierce their cheeks or other bodily parts with spikes as part of the purification rites. Their faith is so strong they feel no pain.

The event is extremely colorful; drumming and chanting accompany the visual spectacle. Visitors are welcome to observe the firewalking, but since the exact date varies from temple to temple according to the phases of the moon (among other factors), you have to keep asking to find out where and when it will take place. To enter the temple you must remove your shoes and any leather clothing.

The Yanggona Ceremony

Yanggona (kava), a tranquilizing, nonalcoholic drink that numbs the tongue and lips, comes from the waka (dried root) of the pepper plant (Macropiper methysticum). This ceremonial preparation is the most honored feature of the formal life of Fijians, Tongans, and Samoans. It is performed with the utmost gravity according to a sacramental ritual to mark births, marriages, deaths, official visits, the installation of a new chief, etc.

New mats are first spread on the floor. Next, a handcarved tanoa (wooden bowl) nearly a meter wide is placed on a mat. A long fiber cord decorated with cowrie shells and fastened to the bowl leads to the guests of honor. To step over this cord during the ceremony is forbidden. As many as 70 men take their places before the bowl. The officiants are adorned with tapa, fiber, and croton leaves, their torsos smeared with glistening coconut oil, their faces usually blackened.

The guests present a bundle of waka to the hosts, along with a short speech explaining their visit, a custom known as sevu sevu. The sevu sevu is received by the hosts and acknowledged with a short speech of acceptance. The waka are then scraped clean and pounded in a tambili (mortar). Formerly they were chewed. Nowadays the pulp is put in a cloth sack and mixed with water in the tanoa. In the chiefly ceremony the yanggona is kneaded and strained through vau (hibiscus) fibers.

The mixer displays the strength of the grog (kava) to the mata ni vanua (master of ceremonies) by pouring out a cupful into the tanoa. If the mata ni vanua considers the mix too strong, he calls for "wai" ("water"), then says "lose" ("mix"), and the mixer proceeds. Again he shows the consistency to the mata ni vanua by pouring out a cupful. If it appears right the mata ni vanua says "lomba" ("squeeze"). The mixer squeezes

Draped in croton leaves, the cupbearer offers a bowl of yanggona to a visiting chief at a formal kava ceremony.

the remaining juice out of the pulp, puts it aside, and announces *"sa lose oti saka na yanggona, vaka turanga"* ("the kava is ready, my chief"). He runs both hands around the rim of the *tanoa* and claps three times.

The *mata ni vanua* then says *"talo"* ("serve"). The cupbearer squats in front of the *tanoa* with a *mbilo* (half coconut shell), which the mixer fills. The cupbearer then presents the first cup to the guest of honor, who claps once and drains it, and everyone claps three times. The second cup goes to the guests' *mata ni vanua*, who claps once and drinks. The man sitting next to the mixer says *"aa,"* and everyone answers *"matha"* ("empty"). The third cup is for the first local chief, who claps once before drinking, and everyone claps three times after. Then the *mata ni vanua* of the first local chief claps once and drinks, and everyone says *"matha".* The same occurs for the second local chief and his *mata ni vanua.*

After these six men have finished their cups, the mixer announces *"Sa matha saka tu na yanggona, vaka turanga"* ("the bowl is empty, my chief"), and the *mata ni vanua* says *"Thombo"* ("Clap"). The mixer then runs both hands around the rim of the *tanoa* and claps three times. This terminates the full ceremony, but then a second bowl is prepared and everyone drinks. During the drinking of the first bowl complete silence must be maintained.

Social Kava Drinking

While the above describes one of several forms of the full *yanggona* ceremony, which is performed only for high chiefs, abbreviated versions are put on for tourists at the hotels. However, the village people have simplified grog sessions almost daily. Kava drinking is an important form of Fijian entertainment and a way of structuring friendships and community relations. Even in government offices a bowl of grog is kept for the staff to take as a refreshment at *yanggona* breaks. Some say the Fijians have *yanggona* rather than blood in their veins.

Visitors to villages are invariably invited to participate in informal kava ceremonies, in which case it's customary to present 200 grams or more of kava roots to the group. Do this at the beginning, before anybody starts drinking, and make a short speech explaining the purpose of your visit (be it a desire to meet the people and learn about their way of life, an interest in seeing or doing something in particular on their island, or just a holiday from work). Don't hand the roots to anyone, just place them on the mat in the center of the circle. The bigger the bundle of roots, the bigger the smiles. (The roots are easily purchased at any town market for about F$10 a half kilo. Kava doesn't grow well in dry, cane-growing areas or in the Yasawas, so carry a good supply with you when traveling there, as it can be hard to buy more. Kava is prohibited entry into the U.S., so don't consider bringing home any leftovers.)

Clap once when the cupbearer offers you the *mbilo*, then take it in both hands and say *"mbula"* just before the cup meets your lips. Clap three times after you drink. Remember, you're a participant, not an onlooking tourist, so don't take photos if the ceremony is rather formal. Even though you may not like the appearance or taste of the drink, do try to finish at least the first cup. Tip the cup to show you're done.

It's considered extremely bad manners to turn your back on a chief during a kava ceremony, to walk in front of the circle of people when entering or leaving, or to step over the long cord attached to the *tanoa*. At the other end of the cord is a white cowry, which symbolizes a link to ancestral spirits.

Presentation Of The *Tambua*

The *tambua* is a tooth of the sperm whale. It was once presented when chiefs exchanged delegates at confederacy meetings and before conferences on peace or war. In recent times, the *tambua* is presented during chiefly *yanggona* ceremonies as a symbolic welcome for a respected visitor or guest or as a prelude to public business or modern-day official functions. On the village level, *tambuas* are still commonly presented to arrange marriages, to show sympathy at funerals, to request favors, to settle disputes, or simply to show respect.

Old *tambuas* are highly polished from continuous handling. The larger the tooth, the greater its ceremonial value. *Tambuas* are prized cultural property and may not be exported from Fiji. Endangered Species laws prohibit their entry into the U.S., Australia, and many other countries.

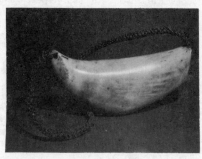

tambua: Yanggona (or kava) the Fijians share with the Polynesians, but the tambua, or whale's tooth, is significant only in Fiji. The tambuas obtained from the sperm whale have always played an important part in Fijian ceremonies. During great festivals they were hung around the necks of warriors and chiefs in the 19th century, and even today they are presented to distinguished guests and are exchanged at weddings, births, deaths, reconciliations, and also when personal or communal contracts or agreements are entered into. Tambuas, contrary to popular belief, have never been used as currency and cannot purchase goods or services. To be presented with a tambua is a great honor.

Fijian Dancing (Meke)

The term *meke* describes the combination of dance, song, and theater performed at feasts and on special occasions. Brandishing spears, their faces painted with charcoal, the men wear frangipani leis and skirts of shredded leaves. The war club dance reenacts heroic events of the past. Both men and women perform the *vakamalolo,* a sitting dance, while the *seasea* is danced by women flourishing fans. The *taralala,* in which visitors may be asked to join, is a simple two-step shuffle danced side-by-side (early missionaries forbade the Fijians from dancing face-to-face). As elsewhere in the Pacific the dances tell a story, though the music now is strongly influenced by Christian hymns and contemporary pop. Less sensual than Polynesian dancing, the rousing Fijian dancing evokes the country's violent past. Fijian *meke* are often part of a *mangiti* or feast performed at hotels. The Dance Theater of Fiji at Pacific Harbor is well regarded.

Stingray Spearing And Fish Drives

Stingrays are lethal-looking creatures with caudal spines up to 18 cm long. To catch them, eight or nine punts are drawn up in a line about a kilometer long beside the reef. As soon as a

closing the ring during a Mbengga fish drive

stingray is sighted, a punt is paddled forward with great speed until close enough to hurl a spear.

Another time-honored sport and source of food is the fish drive. An entire village participates. Around the flat surface of a reef at rising tide, sometimes as many as 70 men and women group themselves in a circle measuring a kilometer or more in circumference. All grip a ring of connected liana vines with leaves attached. While shouting, singing, and beating long poles on the seabed, the group slowly contracts the ring as the tide comes in. The shadow of the ring alone is enough to keep the fish within the circle. The fish are finally directed landward into a net or stone fish trap.

The Rising Of The *Mbalolo*

Among all the Pacific Island groups, this event takes place only in Samoa and Fiji. The *mbalolo (Eunice viridis)* is a segmented worm of the Coelomate order, considered a culinary delicacy throughout these islands. It's about 45 cm long and lives deep in the fissures of coral reefs, rising to the surface only twice a year to propagate and then die. This natural almanac keeps both lunar and solar times, and has a fixed day of appearance—even if a hurricane is raging—one night in the third quarter of the moon in Oct., and the corresponding night in November. It has never failed to appear on time for over 100 years now—you can even check your calendar by it.

Because this thin, jointed worm appears with such mathematical certainty, Fijians are waiting in their boats to scoop the millions of writhing, reddish brown (male) and moss green (female) spawn from the water when they rise to the surface just before dawn. Within an hour after the rising the sacs burst, and the fertile milt spawns the next generation of *mbalolo*. This is one of the most bizarre curiosities in the natural history of the South Pacific, and the southeast coast of Ovalau is a good place to observe it.

CRAFTS

The traditional art of Fiji is closely related to that of Tonga. Fijian canoes, too, were patterned after the more-advanced Polynesian type, although the Fijians were timid sailors. War clubs, food bowls, *tanoas* (kava bowls), eating utensils, clay pots, and tapa cloth *(masi)* are considered Fiji's finest artifacts. The Government Handicraft Center behind Ratu Sukuna House in Suva has the most authentic designs.

There are two kinds of woodcarvings: the ones made from *nawanawa (Cordia subcordata)* wood are superior to those of the lighter, highly breakable *vau (Hibiscus tiliaceus)*. In times past it often took years to make a Fijian war club, as the carving was done in the living tree and left to grow into the desired shape. The best *tanoas* are carved in the Lau Group.

Though many crafts are alive and well some Fijians have taken to carving mock New Guinea masks painted with black shoe polish to look like ebony for sale to tourists. Also avoid crafts made from endangered species such as sea turtles (tortoiseshell) and marine mammals (whales' teeth, etc.). Prohibited entry into most countries, they will be confiscated by Customs if found.

Pottery Making

Fijian pottery making is unique in that it is a Melanesian art form. The Polynesians forgot how to make pottery thousands of years ago. Today the main center for pottery making in Fiji is the Singatoka Valley on Viti Levu. Here, the women shape clay using a wooden paddle outside against a rounded stone held inside the future pot. The potter's wheel was unknown in the Pacific.

A saucerlike section forms the bottom; the sides are built up using slabs of clay, or coils and strips. These are welded and battered to shape. When the form is ready the pot is dried inside the house for a few days, then heated over an open fire for about an hour. Resin from the gum of the *dakua* (kauri) tree is rubbed on the outside while the pot is still hot. This adds a varnish that brings out the color of the clay and improves the pot's water-holding ability.

This pottery is extremely fragile, which accounts for the quantity of potsherds found on ancient village sites. Smaller, less-breakable pottery products, such as ashtrays, are now made for sale to visitors.

Fijian pottery making has changed very little since this 1845 Sherman and Smith engraving.

MERIAM LIBRARY, CSU CHICO

Fijian masi *(tapa)*

Tapa Cloth

This is Fiji's most characteristic traditional product. Tapa is light, portable, and inexpensive, and a piece makes an excellent souvenir to brighten up a room back home. It's made by women on Vatulele Island off Viti Levu and on certain islands of the Lau Group.

To make tapa, the inner, water-soaked bark of the paper mulberry *(Broussonetia papyrifera)* is stripped from the tree and steeped in water. Then it's scraped with shells and pounded into a thin sheet with wooden mallets. Four of these sheets are applied one over another and pounded together, then left to dry in the sun.

While Tongan tapa is decorated by holding a relief pattern under the tapa and overpainting the lines, Fijian tapa *(masi kesa)* is distinctive for its rhythmic geometric designs applied with stencils made from green pandanus and banana leaves. The stain is rubbed on in the same manner by which one makes temple rubbings from a stone inscription.

The only colors used are red, from red clay, and a black pigment obtained by burning candlenuts. Both powders are mixed with boiled gums made from scraped roots. Sunlight deepens and sets the colors. Each island group has its characteristic colors and patterns, ranging from plantlike paintings to geometric designs. Sheets of tapa feel like felt when finished.

HOLIDAYS AND EVENTS

Public holidays in Fiji include New Year's Day (1 Jan.), Good Friday and Easter Monday (March/ April), Queen Elizabeth's Birthday (a Mon. around 14 June), Constitution Day (a Mon. around 27 July), Fiji Day (a Mon. around 10 Oct.), Diwali (Oct. or Nov.), Prince Charles's Birthday (a Mon. around 14 Nov.), Prophet Mohammed's Birthday (anytime from Sept. to Dec.), and Christmas Days (25 and 26 Dec.). Some dates vary from year to year.

Check with the Fiji Visitors Bureau to see if any festivals are scheduled during your visit. The best known are the Mbula Festival in Nandi (July), the Hibiscus Festival in Suva (Aug.), and the Sugar Festival in Lautoka (Sept. or October). Before Diwali, the Hindu festival of lights, Hindus clean their homes, then light lamps or candles to mark the arrival of spring. Fruit and sweets are offered to Lakshmi, goddess of wealth. Holi is an Indian spring festival in Feb. or March.

The soccer season in Fiji is Feb. to Nov., while rugby is played from April to September. Rugby is played only by Fijians, while soccer teams are predominantly Indian. Cricket is played from Nov. to March, mostly in rural areas. Lawn bowling is also popular. Sports of any kind are forbidden on Sunday.

CONDUCT

It's a Fijian custom to smile when you meet a stranger and say something like "good morning," or at least "hello." Of course you needn't do this in the large towns, but you should almost everywhere else. If you meet someone you know, stop for a moment to exchange a few words. Fijian villages are private property and it's important to get permission before entering one. Of course it's okay to continue along a road that passes through a village, but do ask before leaving the road. It's good manners to take off your hat while walking through a village, where only the chief is permitted to wear a hat. Some villagers also object to sunglasses. Don't point at people in villages. If you wish to surf off the coast of a village or picnic on their beach, you should also ask permission. If you approach the Fijians with respect you're sure to be so treated in return.

Shorts are not proper dress for women in villages, so carry a *sulu* to cover up. Topless sunbathing by women is not allowed in Fiji. Men should always wear a shirt in town and women should forgo halter tops, see-through dresses, and short shorts. Scanty dress in public shows a lack of respect. Notice how the locals are dressed.

Take off your shoes before entering a *mbure,* and stoop as you walk around inside. Clap three times when you join people already seated on mats on the floor. Men should sit cross-legged, women with their legs to the side. Sitting with your legs stretched out in front is insulting. Fijian villagers consider it offensive to walk in front of a person seated on the floor (pass behind instead) or to fail to say *"tilou"* (excuse me) as you go by. Never place your hand on another's head and don't sit in doorways. Do you notice how Fijians rarely shout? Keep your voice down. Don't stand up during a *sevu sevu* to village elders. When you give a gift, hold it out with both hands, not one hand.

Fijian children are very well behaved. There's no running or shouting when you arrive in a village, and they'll leave you alone if you wish. Also, Fijians love children, so don't hesitate to bring your own. You'll never have to worry about finding a babysitter.

Take care if a local invites you to visit his home in a main tourist center such as Nandi or Suva, as you may be seen mainly as a source of beer and other goods. Women should have few problems traveling around Fiji on their own, so long as they're prepared to cope with frequent offers of marriage. Littering is punished by a minimum F$40 fine, and breaking bottles in public can earn six months in jail.

DAVID STANLEY

Clad in a *sulu, the all-purpose garment of the Pacific, a Fijian poses before a traditional* mbure.

ACCOMMODATIONS

A 10% government turnover tax is added to all accommodation prices, and the prices herein do not include this tax. Fiji offers a wide variety of places to stay, from low budget to world-class, and in this book we list them all. Standard big-city international hotels are found in Nandi and Suva, while most of the huge upmarket beach resorts are on small islands in the Mamanutha Group off Nandi and along the Coral Coast on Viti Levu's south side.

In recent years smaller luxury resorts have multiplied on the outer islands, from the guest-accepting plantations near Savusavu and on Taveuni to isolated beach resorts on remote islands such as Turtle, Yasawa, Vatulele, Mbengga, Kandavu, Tomberua, Wakaya, Nukumbati, Namenalala, Nggamea, Matangi, Lauthala, and Kaimbu. Prices at these begin at several hundred dollars a day. A few such as Mbengga, Matana and Matangi are marketed almost exclusively to scuba divers. If heading for any of these pick up a bottle of duty-free liquor on the way.

The Mamanutha resorts are secluded, with fan-cooled *mbure* accommodations, while at the Coral Coast hotels you often get an a/c room in a main building. The Coral Coast has more to offer in the way of land tours, shopping, and entertainment/eating options, while the offshore resorts are preferable if you want a rest or are

into water sports. The Coral Coast beaches are only good at high tide. Most guests at the deluxe hotels in both areas are on package tours. For economy and flexibility, avoid prepaying hotel accommodations from home.

Many hotels, both in cities and at the beach, offer dormitory beds as well as individual rooms. Most of the dorms are mixed. Women can sometimes request a women-only dorm when things are slow, but it's usually not guaranteed. At some budget hotels you can get a small discount on dormitory accommodation by showing a youth hostel card.

Budget accommodations are spread out, with concentrations in Nandi, Korolevu, Suva, Lautoka, Levuka, Savusavu, and on Taveuni. Low-cost outer-island beach resorts exist on Kandavu, Ono, Leleuvia, Naingani, Nananu-i-ra, and Tavewa. Some Suva hotels lock their front doors at 2300, so ask first if you're planning a night on the town. A few of the cheapies double as whorehouses, making them cheap in both senses of the word. Government resthouses exist in out-of-the-way places like Nandarivatu, Nambouwalu, and Lakemba, and advance bookings are often required. Some islands with air service from Nausori, including Koro, Moala, Ngau, Rambi, Rotuma, and Thithia, have no facilities whatsoever for visitors, so it really helps

Campers, Kandavu Island. Where hotels don't exist, your tent is your home away from home.

DAVID STANLEY

to know someone before heading that way.

Camping facilities (own tent) are found near Momi Bay south of Nandi, on Nukulau Island off Suva, and on Kandavu, Ono, Ovalau, and Taveuni islands. Elsewhere, get permission before pitching your tent as all land is owned by someone and land rights are a sensitive issue in Fiji. Some freelance campers on beaches such as Natandola near Nandi have been robbed, so take care. Don't ask a Fijian friend for permission to camp beside his house in the village itself. Although he may feel obligated to grant the request of a guest, you'll be proclaiming to everyone that his home isn't completely to your liking. Of course in places like Tavewa Island, that receive visitors regularly, this isn't a problem; elsewhere if all you really want is to camp, make this clear from the start and get permission to do so on a beach or by a river, but *not* in the village. A *sevu sevu* should always be presented in this case. Never camp directly under a coconut tree: falling coconuts are lethal.

Staying In Villages

A great way to meet the people and learn a little about their culture is to stay in a village for a few nights. Since the Fiji Visitors Bureau hasn't set up a regular homestay program yet, you'll have to arrange this for yourself. If you befriend someone from a remote island, ask them to write you a letter of introduction to their relatives back in the village. Mail a copy of it ahead with a polite letter introducing yourself, then start heading slowly that way.

In places off the beaten tourist track, you could just show up in a village and ask permission of the *turanga-ni-koro* to spend the night. Rarely will you be refused. Similarly, both Fiji Indians and native Fijians will spontaneously invite you in. The Fijians' innate dignity and kindness should not be taken for granted, however.

All across the Pacific it's customary to reciprocate when someone gives you a gift—if not now, then sometime in the future. Visitors who accept gifts (such as meals and accommodations) from islanders and do not reciprocate are undermining traditional culture and causing resentment, often without realizing it. It's sometimes hard to know how to repay hospitality, but Fijian culture has a solution: the *sevu sevu*. This can be money, but it's usually a 500-gram bundle of kava roots *(waka)*, which can be easily purchased at any Fijian market for about F$10. *Sevu sevus* are more often performed between families or couples about to be married, or at births or christenings, but the custom is certainly a perfect way for visitors to show their appreciation.

The Fiji Rucksack Club recommends that its members donate a minimum of F$10 pp per night to village hosts. The *waka* is additional, and anyone traveling in remote areas of Fiji should pack some (take whole roots, not powdered kava). If you give the money up front with the *waka* as a *sevu sevu,* they'll know you're not a freeloader and you'll get much better treatment, though in all cases it's absolutely essential to contribute something.

The *sevu sevu* should be placed before (not handed to) the *turanga-ni-koro* or village chief so he can accept or refuse. If he accepts (by touching the package), your welcome is confirmed and you may spend the night in the village. It's also possible to give some money to the lady of the house upon departure, with your thanks. Just say it's your goodbye *sevu sevu* and watch the smile. A Fijian may refuse the money, but will not be offended by the offer if done properly. You could also take some gifts along, such as lengths of material, T-shirts, badges, pins, knitting needles, hats, acoustic guitar strings, schoolbooks, colored pens, toys, playing cards, fishhooks, line, or lures, or a big jar of instant coffee. Keep in mind, however, that Seventh Day Adventists are forbidden to have coffee, cigarettes, or kava, so you might ask if there are any SDAs around in order to avoid embarrassment. One thing *not* to take is alcohol, which is always sure to offend somebody.

When choosing your traveling companions for a trip that involves staying in Fijian villages, make sure you agree on this before you set out. Otherwise you could end up subsidizing somebody else's trip, or worse, have to stand by and watch the Fijian villagers subsidize it. Never arrive in a village on a Sunday and don't overstay your welcome.

A final note from Josje Hebbes of the Netherlands:

If people only meet Indians on the street or in tourist centers they will get a totally wrong idea of Indian culture. To appreciate their hospitality and friendliness one should also try to spend some time in rural Indian settlements. If you go on a day hike you might be invited for lunch. First they will serve you something sweet like juice or tea. That's their way. Make sure you don't leave Fiji with a mistaken impression of Fiji Indians!

Village Life

Staying in a village is definitely not for everyone. Most houses have no electricity, running water, toilet, furniture, etc., and only native food will be offered. Water and your left hand serve as toilet paper. You should also expect to sacrifice most of your privacy, to stay up late drinking grog, and to sit in the house and socialize when you could be out exploring. On Sunday you'll have to stay put the whole day. The constant attention and lack of sanitary conditions may become tiresome, but it would be considered rude to attempt to be alone or refuse the food or grog. Remember that villagers are not paid performers here to entertain tourists but humans like yourself living real lives, so put your heart in it or stay away.

When you enter a Fijian village, people will want to be helpful and will direct or accompany you to the person or place you seek. If you show genuine interest in something and ask to see how it is done, you will usually be treated with respect and asked if there is anything else you would like to know. Initially Fijians may hesitate to welcome you into their homes because they fear you will not wish to sit on a mat and eat native foods with your fingers. Once you show them that this isn't true, you'll receive the full hospitality treatment.

Consider participating in the daily activities of the family, such as weaving, cooking, gardening, and fishing. Your hosts will probably try to dissuade you from "working," but if you persist you'll become accepted. Staying in the villages of Fiji offers one of the most rewarding travel experiences in the South Pacific, and if everyone plays fair it will always be so.

FOOD AND ENTERTAINMENT

Unlike some other South Pacific nations, Fiji has many good, cheap eateries. Chinese restaurants are everywhere. On the western side of Viti Levu, Indian restaurants sometimes use the name "lodge." Indian dishes are spicy, often curries with rice and *dhal* (lentil) soup. Goat curry is a unique Indian dish, but orthodox Hindus don't eat beef and Muslims forgo pork. Instead of bread Indians eat *roti*, a flat tortilla-like pancake. The Hot Bread Kitchen chain of bakeries around Fiji serves delicious fresh-fruit loaves, cheese-and-onion loaves, muffins, and other assorted breads. The Morris Hedstrom supermarket chain is about the cheapest, and many have milk bars with ice cream and sweets.

Many restaurants are closed on Sun., and a 10% tax is added to the bill. Fijians have their own pace and trying to make them do things more quickly is often counterproductive. Their charm and the friendly personal attention you'll receive more than make up for the occasionally slow service at restaurants.

Real Fijian dishes, such as baked fish *(ika)* in coconut cream *(lolo)* with cassava *(tavioka),* taro *(ndalo),* breadfruit, and sweet potato *(kumala),* take a long time to prepare and must be served fresh, which makes it difficult to offer them in a restaurant. Try *nduruka,* a native vegetable tasting something like a cross between artichoke and asparagus. Taro leaves are used to make *palusami* (with coconut cream) and *rourou* (the local spinach).

Raw fish *(kokonda)* is an appetizing dish. To prepare it, clean and skin the fish, then dice the fillet. Squeeze lemon or lime juice over it, and store in a cool place about 10 hours. When it's ready to serve, add chopped onions, garlic, green peppers, tomatoes, and coconut cream to taste. Local fishmongers know which species makes the best raw fish, but know what you're doing before you join them—island stomachs are probably stronger than yours. It's sometimes safer to eat well-cooked food and to peel your own fruit.

The sweet potato is something of an anomaly—it's the only Pacific food plant with a South American origin. How it got to the islands is not known, but it and tobacco seem to have been introduced into New Guinea about 1600, suggesting the possibility of a Hispanic connection. Taro is an elephant-eared plant cultivated in freshwater swamps. Although yams are considered a prestige food, they're not as nutritious as breadfruit and taro. Yams can grow up to three meters long and weigh hundreds of kilos. Papaya *(pawpaw)* is nourishing: a third of a cup contains as much vitamin C as 18 apples. To ripen a green papaya overnight, puncture it a few times with a knife. Don't overeat papaya—unless you *need* an effective laxative.

The ancient Pacific islanders, who stopped making pottery over a millennium ago, developed an ingenious way of cooking in an underground earth oven *(lovo)*. First a stack of dry coconut husks is burned in a pit. Once the fire is going well, stones are heaped on top. When most of the husks have burnt away, the food is wrapped in banana leaves and placed on the hot stones, fish and meat below, vegetables above. A whole pig may be cleaned, then stuffed with banana leaves and hot stones. This cooks the beast from inside out, as well as outside in, and the leaves create steam. The food is then covered with more leaves and stones, and in about 2½ hours everything will be cooked.

The famous Fiji Bitter beer is brewed by Australian-owned Carlton Brewery Ltd., with breweries in Suva and Lautoka. South Pacific Distilleries Ltd. in Lautoka produces brandy, gin, rum, vodka, and whiskey under a variety of brand names. Drinking alcoholic beverages on the street is prohibited.

Breadfruit

The breadfruit is the plant most often associated with the South Pacific. The theme of a man turning himself into such a tree to save his family during famine often recurs in South Pacific legends. Ancient voyagers brought breadfruit shoots or seeds from Southeast Asia. When baked in an underground oven or roasted over flames, the now-seedless Polynesian variety resembles bread. Joseph Banks, botanist on Capt. Cook's first voyage, wrote: "If a man should in the course of his lifetime plant 10 trees, which if well done might take the labor of an hour or thereabouts, he would completely fulfill his duty to his own as well as future generations."

The breadfruit *(Artocarpus altilis),* a tall tree with broad, green leaves, provides shade as well as food. A well-watered tree can produce as many as 1,000 pale green breadfruits a year. Robert Lee Eskridge described a breadfruit thus: "Its outer rind or skin, very hard, is covered with a golf-ball-like surface of small irregular pits or tiny hollows. An inner rind about a half-inch thick surrounds the fruit itself, which when baked tastes not unlike a doughy potato. Perhaps fresh bread, rolled up until it becomes a semifirm mass, best describes the breadfruit when cooked." The starchy, easily digested fruit is rich in vitamin B. When consumed with a protein,

slicing breadfruit

DAVID STANLEY

such as fish or meat, it serves as an energy food. Like the coconut, the breadfruit tree itself had many uses, including the provision of wood for outrigger canoes.

The Coconut Palm

Human life would not be possible on most of the Pacific's far-flung atolls without this all-purpose tree. It reaches maturity in eight years, then produces about 50 nuts a year for 60 years. Aside from its aesthetic value and usefulness in providing shade, the water of the green coconut provides a refreshing drink, and the white meat of the young nut is a delicious food. The harder meat of more mature nuts is grated and squeezed, giving rise to a coconut cream used alone or in cooking. The oldest nuts are cracked open, the hard meat removed, then dried to be sold as copra. Copra is pressed to extract the oil, which in turn is made into candles, cosmetics, and soap. Millionaire's salad is made by shredding the growth cut from the heart of the tree. For each salad, a fully mature tree must be sacrificed.

The nut's hard inner shell can be used as a cup and makes excellent firewood. Rope, cordage, brushes, and heavy matting are pro-

DIANA LASICH-HARPER

Every part of the coconut tree (Cocos nucifera) can be used. The husk provides cord, mats, brushes, and fuel; the leaves thatch, baskets, and fans; and the trunk building material. Food and oil from the nuts are the greatest prize. A healthy tree will produce 50 nuts a year for over 60 years.

duced from the coir fiber of the husk. The smoke from burning husks is a most effective mosquito repellent. The leaves of the coconut tree are used to thatch the roofs of the islanders' cottages or are woven into baskets, mats, and fans. The trunk provides timber for building and furniture. Actually, these are only the common uses: there are many others besides.

Entertainment

Considering the strong Aussie presence and the temperature, it's not surprising that Fiji has its share of colorful bars where bottled Fiji Bitter beer is consumed cold in amazing quantities. Some bars become discos after 2100. Respectable visitors are welcome at the ex-colonial "clubs," where the beer prices are generally lower and the clientele more sedate. Barefoot beachcombers in T-shirts and shorts may be refused entry. Don't overlook the resort bars, where the swank surroundings cost only slightly more. Unlike in Australia and New Zealand, it's not customary to bring your own booze into restaurants.

The large hotels around Nandi or on the Coral Coast often stage a weekly *lovo,* usually accompanied by a Fijian *meke,* or song and dance performance in which legends, love stories, and historical events are told in song and gesture. Alternatively, firewalking may be presented. This is a good opportunity to taste the local food and see traditional dancing for about F$40 pp. If you don't want to splurge on the meal it's often possible to witness the spectacle from the bar for the price of a drink. These events are held weekly on certain days, so ask. For the locals Fri. night is the time to let it all hang out; on Sat. many people are preparing for a family get-together or church; everything grinds to a halt Sat. at midnight, and Sun. is *very quiet*—a good day to go hiking or to the beach.

In Fiji it's cheap to go to the movies, usually romance, horror, or adventure. Good psychological films are the exception. Video fever is the latest craze, and you'll often see throngs of locals crowded into someone's living room watching an inane tape rented from one of the ubiquitous video rental shops. Many guesthouses have video too, so make sure your room is well away from it.

SHOPPING

Shops in Fiji close at 1300 on Sat., except in Nausori town, where they stay open all day Sat. but only half a day on Wednesday. The 1987 military coups placed Fiji firmly in the South Pacific Bible Belt, which also encompasses Tonga, Western Samoa, and Cook Islands, so no commercial business may be conducted on Sunday (hotels excepted). Fiji Indians dominate the duty-free trade. If you're buying from an Indian merchant always bargain hard and consider all sales final. Indigenous Fijians usually begin by asking a much lower price, in which case bargaining isn't so important.

Fiji's duty-free shops such as Prouds or Tappoo are not really duty-free, as all goods are subject to a 10% fiscal tax plus the 10% value-added tax. Bargaining is the order of the day, but only in Suva is the selection really good. You'll sometimes get an additional last-minute discount by offering to pay in U.S. dollars cash. To be frank, Americans can usually buy the sort of Japanese electrical merchandise sold "duty-free" in Fiji cheaper in the States, where they get more recent models. If you do buy something, get an itemized receipt and guarantee and watch that they don't switch packages and unload a demo on you. Once purchased, items cannot be returned, so don't let yourself be talked into something. Camera film is cheap, however, and the selection good—stock up.

If you'd like to do some shopping in Fiji, locally made handicrafts such as tapa cloth, mats, kava bowls, war clubs, woodcarvings, etc., are a better investment (see "Crafts" above). The four-pronged cannibal forks available everywhere make unique souvenirs. The Government Handicraft Center in Suva is a good place to learn what's available and familiarize yourself with prices. If you're willing to spend serious money for top-quality work, visit the Fiji Museum beforehand. Try to purchase your souvenirs directly from the Fijian producers at street markets, etc.

Videos

It's becoming the thing to buy commercial travel videotapes of the places you visit. Keep in mind that there are three incompatible video systems loose in the world: NTSC (used in North America), PAL (used in Britain, Germany, Japan, and Australia), and SECAM (used in France and Russia). Don't buy prerecorded tapes abroad unless they're of the system used in your country.

---

cannibal fork: It has been said that the Fijians were extremely hospitable to any strangers they did not wish to eat. Native voyagers who wrecked on their shores, who arrived "with salt water in their eyes," were liable to be killed and eaten, since all shipwrecked persons were believed to have been cursed and abandoned by the gods. Many European sailors from wrecked vessels shared the same fate. Cannibalism was a universal practice, and prisoners taken in war, or even women seized while fishing, were invariably eaten. Most of the early European accounts of Fiji emphasized this trait to the exclusion of almost everything else; at one time, the island group was even referred to as the "Cannibal Isles." By eating the flesh of the conquered enemy, one incorporated their mana, or psychic power. One chief on Viti Levu is said to have consumed 872 people and to have made a pile of stones to record his achievement. The leaves of a certain vegetable (Solanum uporo) were wrapped around the human meat, and it was cooked in an earthen oven. Wooden forks such as the one pictured were employed at cannibal feasts by men who relied on their fingers for other food, but used these because it was considered improper to touch human flesh with fingers or lips. Present-day Fijians do not appreciate tourists who make jokes about cannibalism.

VISAS

Everyone needs a passport valid at least three months beyond the date of entry. No visa is required of visitors from Europe, North America, or most Commonwealth countries for stays of 30 days or less, although everyone needs a ticket to leave. All journalists and TV crews do require entry permits approved by the Minister of Information, however. Tourists are forbidden to become involved in any sort of political activity, to engage in political studies, or to conduct research. The required vaccination against yellow fever or cholera only applies if you're arriving directly from an infected area, such as the Amazon jungles or the banks of the Ganges River.

Extensions of stay are given out two months at a time (up to a maximum of six months) free of charge by the immigration offices in Suva and at Nandi Airport. If you extend your stay somewhere else the police have to send your passport to Suva, and this process will take a week at least. You must apply before your current permit expires. Bring your passport, onward or return ticket, and proof of sufficient funds. After six months you must leave and aren't supposed to return until another six months have passed.

Fiji has four ports of entry for yachts: Suva, Lautoka, Levuka, and Savusavu. Calling at an outer island before clearing customs is prohibited. Levuka is by far the easiest place to check in or out, as all of the officials have offices right on the main wharf. To visit the outer islands, yachts require a letter of authorization from the Secretary of Fijian Affairs in Suva or the commissioner (at Nausori, Lambasa, Lautoka, or Levuka) of the division they wish to visit. The army searches all arriving yachts for guns and charges a F$20 fee for the service.

Here's a list of Fiji's diplomatic offices around the world where you can inquire about the possibility of working in Fiji (special skills required) or just get information.

DIPLOMATIC OFFICES

Permanent Mission of Fiji to the United Nations,
One U.N. Plaza, 26th Floor,
New York, NY 10017, U.S.A.

Embassy of Fiji,
Suite 240, 2233 Wisconsin Ave. NW,
Washington, DC 20007, U.S.A.

Honorary Consulate of Fiji,
Suite 750, 130 Slatter St.,
Ottawa K1P 6E2, Canada

Honorary Consulate of Fiji,
1437 West 64th Ave.,
Vancouver V68 2N5, Canada

Embassy of Fiji,
9 Beagle St.,
Canberra, ACT 2600, Australia

Consulate General of Fiji,
10th floor, 225 Clarence St.,
Sydney, NSW 2000, Australia

Embassy of Fiji,
13th Floor, Plimmer Towers,
Boulcott St. and Glimmer Terrace,
Wellington, New Zealand

Consulate General of Fiji,
3rd Floor, Tower Block, 47 High St.,
Auckland, New Zealand

Embassy of Fiji,
34 Hyde Park Gate,
London SW7 5BN, England

Embassy of Fiji,
66 Ave. De Cortenberg,
1040 Brussels, Belgium

Embassy of Fiji,
Noa Building (10th Floor),
3-5, Chome Azabudai, Minato-Ku,
Tokyo 106, Japan

Honorary Consulate of Fiji,
Jalan Jend. Sudiman, Kar 21,
Jakarta 12910, Indonesia

Embassy of Fiji,
Suite 203, Wisma Equity,
150 Jalan Ampang,
Kuala Lumpur 54050, Malaysia

MONEY AND COMMUNICATIONS

Money

The currency is the Fiji dollar, which is lower than the U.S. dollar in value (about US$1 = F$1.50). It's based on a basket of currencies which means it doesn't fluctuate much. There are bills of F$1, F$2, F$5, F$10, and F$20, and despite Fiji's expulsion from the Commonwealth in 1987 the portrait of Queen Elizabeth appears on them (and the Union Jack still forms part of the country's flag). Always try to have lots of small bills handy, and don't expect to change foreign currency outside the main towns. Tipping isn't customary in Fiji, although some luxury resorts have a staff Christmas fund, to which contributions are welcome.

Banking hours are Mon.-Thurs. 1000-1500, Fri. 1000-1600. Commercial banks operating in Fiji include the ANZ Bank, the Indian-owned Bank of Baroda, the Pakistani-owned Habib Bank, the National Bank of Fiji, and the Westpac Banking Corporation. There are banks in all the towns, but it's usually not possible to change traveler's checks on the outer islands; credit cards are strictly for the cities and resorts (the best cards to bring are American Express, Diners Club, MasterCard, and Visa), though most banks give cash advances. Many banks will

hold a sealed envelope for you in their vault for a nominal fee—a good way to avoid carrying unneeded valuables with you all around Fiji.

The import of foreign currency is unrestricted, but only F$100 in Fiji banknotes and F$500 in foreign banknotes may be exported. Larger quantities of cash are subject to confiscation, though there's no restriction on the amount one carries in traveler's checks. Avoid taking any Fijian banknotes out of the country at all, as Fijian dollars are difficult to change and heavily discounted outside Fiji. Change whatever you have left over into the currency of the next country on your itinerary.

Currency controls have spawned a small black market offering about 10% better than the official rate for cash dollars, though foreigners caught wheeling and dealing have been roughed up by the authorities and cheated by the marketeers. Pawnshop proprietors are often knowledgeable about such matters. Also take care changing at hotels, which often give a much lower rate than the banks. If you need money sent, have your banker make a telegraphic transfer to any Westpac Bank branch in Fiji. If you're having money wired, have an odd amount (such as $501.35) sent. If there's an error, a figure like this would be easier to trace in bank ledgers or computer printouts than a round figure like $500, which might be one of dozens of similar transactions.

The bulk of your travel funds should be in traveler's checks. American Express is probably the best kind to have, as they have offices in Suva (4th Floor, ANZ House, 25 Victoria Parade; tel. 302-333) and Nandi (Nandi Airport Concourse; tel. 722-100). If your American Express checks are lost or stolen, contact either of these or call 61-2-886-0689 in Sydney, Australia, collect.

On 1 July 1992 Fiji introduced a 10% value-added tax (VAT).

Post And Telephone

Post offices are generally open weekdays 0800-1600. Always use airmail when posting letters from Fiji. Airmail takes two weeks to reach North America and Europe, surface mail takes up to five months. The weight limit for overseas parcels is 10 kilograms. When writing to Fiji, use the words "Fiji Islands" in the address (otherwise the letter might go to Fuji, Japan) and underline Fiji (so it doesn't end up in Iceland). Try to include the post-office-box number of the individual or business, since mail delivery is rare. If it's a remote island or small village you're writing to, the person's name will be sufficient. To send a picture postcard to an islander is a very nice way to say thank you.

When collecting mail at poste restante (general delivery), be sure to check for the initials of your first and second names, plus any initial that is similar. Have your correspondents print and underline your last name. Such mail is held two months. Be aware that there are two post offices at Nandi which hold such mail, one in town, the other at the airport.

Most post offices have public telephones, which are often bright red. Lift the receiver, wait for a dial tone, then deposit a coin and dial. Over half the pay phones may be out of order, with long lines of people waiting to use the rest. Alternatively, ask a shopkeeper if you may use his/her phone for a small additional fee. To make a long-distance call you'll have to call the operator, tel. 012. A better way to place a long-distance call is to go to the Fiji International Telecommunications (FINTEL) office on Victoria Parade, Suva, or any post office. The basic charge for three minutes is F$4.80 to Australia or New Zealand, F$8.10 to North America or Europe. If the line is inaudible, hang up and tell the operator to try again. International calls placed from hotel rooms are always much more expensive.

Fiji has direct dialing via satellite and undersea cables. If you want to place a call to Fiji from outside the region, first dial the international access code (check your phone book), then the country code (679), then the number. Calling from the U.S. to Fiji is *much* cheaper than going in the other direction, so if you want to receive calls during your trip leave a list of dates and numbers where your friends or relatives can reach you.

Electric Currents

If you're taking along a plug-in razor, radio, or other electrical appliance, be aware that Fiji uses 240 AC voltage, 50 cycles. Most appliances require a converter to change from one voltage to another. You'll also need an adapter to cope with three-prong sockets with the two on top at angles. Pick up both items before you leave home, as they're hard to find in Fiji. Keep voltages in mind if you buy duty-free appliances: dual voltage (110-220 V) items are best.

Time

The international date line generally follows 180 degrees longitude and creates a difference of 24 hours in time between the two sides. It swings east at Tuvalu to avoid slicing Fiji in two. Everything in the Eastern Hemisphere west of the date line is a day ahead; everything in the Western Hemisphere east of the line is a day behind. Air travelers lose a day when they fly west across the date line and gain it back when they return. Keep track of things by repeating to yourself, *If it's Sunday in Samoa, it's Monday in Melbourne.*

The islanders operate on "coconut time"—the coconut will fall when it's ripe. In the languid air of the South Seas, punctuality takes on a new meaning. Appointments are approximate and the service relaxed. Even the seasons are fuzzy: sometimes wetter, sometimes drier, but almost always hot. Slow down to the island pace and get in step with where you are. You may not get as much done, but you'll enjoy life a lot more.

HEALTH

Fiji's climate is a healthy one and malaria is unknown. The sea and air are clear and usually pollution-free. The humidity nourishes the skin, and the local fruit is brimming with vitamins. If you take a few precautions, you'll never have a sick day. The information provided below is intended to make you knowledgeable, not fearful. Health care in Fiji is good, with an abundance of hospitals, health centers, and nursing stations scattered around the country. Attention at these is free or quite cheap, but in the towns it's less time-consuming to visit a private doctor. Their fees are also very reasonable. U.S.-made medications may by unobtainable in Fiji, so bring a supply of whatever you think you'll need. Antibiotics should only be used to treat serious wounds, and only after medical advice.

Don't go from winter weather into the steaming tropics without a rest before and after. Scuba diving on departure day can give you a severe case of the bends. Avoid jet lag by setting your watch to Fiji time as soon as you board the flight. Airplane cabins have low humidity, so drink lots of juice or water instead of carbonated drinks, and don't overeat in-flight. It's also best to forgo coffee, as it will only keep you awake. Alcohol helps dehydrate you. If you start feeling seasick on board ship, stare at the horizon, which is always steady, and stop thinking about it. Anti-motion-sickness pills are available.

Frequently the feeling of thirst is false and only due to mucous-membrane dryness. Gargling or taking two or three gulps of warm water should be enough. Other means to keep moisture in the body are to have a hot drink like tea or black coffee, or any kind of slightly salted or sour drink in small quantities. Salt in fresh lime juice is remarkably refreshing.

The tap water in Fiji is usually drinkable except just after a cyclone or during droughts, when care should be taken. If in doubt, boil it or use purification pills. Tap water that is uncomfortably hot to touch is usually safe. Allow it to cool in a clean container. If the tap water is contaminated, local ice will be too. Avoid brushing your teeth with water unfit to drink. If you're preparing your own meals, wash your fruit and vegetables very carefully. Cooked food is less subject to contamination than raw.

Sunburn

Though you may think a tan will make you *look* healthier and more attractive, it's very damaging to the skin, which becomes dry, rigid, and prematurely old and wrinkled, especially on the face. And a burn from the sun greatly increases your risk of getting skin cancer. Begin with short exposures to the sun, perhaps half an hour, followed by an equal time in the shade. Drink plenty of liquids to keep your pores open. Avoid the sun from 1000 to 1400. Clouds and beach umbrellas will not protect you fully. Wear a T-shirt while snorkeling to protect your back. Beware of reflected sunlight. Sunbathing is the main cause of cataracts to the eyes, so wear sunglasses and a wide-brimmed hat.

Use a sunscreen lotion containing PABA rather than oil (don't forget your nose, lips, forehead, neck, hands, and feet). Sunscreens protect you from ultraviolet rays (a leading cause of cancer), while oils magnify the sun's effect. A 29- or 30-factor sunscreen, such as Presun 29 or Sundown 30, will provide adequate protection. Apply the lotion *before* going to the beach to avoid being burned on the way, and reapply periodically to replace sunscreen washed away by perspiration. After sunbathing take a tepid shower rather than a hot one, which would wash away your natural skin oils. Stay moist and use a vitamin E evening cream to preserve the youth of your skin. Calamine ointment soothes skin already burned, as does coconut oil. Pharmacists recommend Solarcaine to soothe burned skin. Rinsing off with a vinegar solution reduces peeling. Aspirin relieves some of the pain and irritation. Vitamin A and calcium counteract overdoses of vitamin D received from the sun. The fairer your skin, the more essential it is to take care.

Ailments

Cuts and scratches infect easily in the tropics and take a long time to heal. Prevent infection from coral cuts by washing with soap and fresh water, then rubbing vinegar or alcohol (whisky will do) into the wounds—painful but effective. The locals usually dab coral cuts with lime juice. All cuts turn septic quickly in the tropics, so try to keep them clean and covered. For bites, burns, and cuts, an antiseptic such as Solarcaine speeds healing and helps prevent infection. Bites by nono flies itch for days and can become infected.

Prickly heat, an intensely irritating rash, is caused by wearing heavy, inappropriate clothing. When the glands are blocked and the sweat is unable to evaporate, the skin becomes soggy and small red blisters appear. Synthetic fabrics like nylon are especially bad in this regard. Take a cold shower, apply calamine lotion, dust with talcum powder, and take off those clothes! Until things improve, avoid alcohol, tea, coffee, and any physical activity that makes you sweat. If you're sweating profusely, increase your intake of salt slightly to avoid fatigue, but not without concurrently drinking more water.

Use antidiarrheal medications sparingly. Rather than take drugs to plug yourself up, drink plenty of unsweetened liquids like green coconut milk or fresh fruit juice to help flush yourself out. Egg yolk mixed with nutmeg helps diarrhea, or have a rice-and-tea day. Avoid dairy products. Most cases of diarrhea are self-limiting and require only simple replacement of fluids and salts lost in diarrheal stools. If the diarrhea is persistent or you experience high fever, drowsiness, jaundice, or blood in the stool, stop traveling, rest, and consider attending a clinic. For constipation eat pineapple or any peeled fruit.

If you're sleeping in villages or with the locals you may pick up head or body lice. Pharmacists and general stores usually have an emulsion that will eliminate the problem in minutes (pack a bottle with you if you're uptight). You'll know you're lousy when you start to scratch: pick out the little varmints and snap them between your thumbnails for fun. Intestinal parasites (worms) are also widespread. The hookworm bores its way through the soles of your feet, and if you go barefoot through gardens and plantations you're sure to pick up something.

AIDS is now present in Fiji (four cases by Feb. 1992) and sexually transmitted diseases (syphilis, gonorrhea, herpes) have reached almost epidemic proportions in urban areas. By 1991, 67 full-blown cases of AIDS and another 229 HIV infections had been diagnosed in the Pacific islands, though the South Pacific Commission estimated that the real number of victims was probably 50 times higher.

Toxic Fish

Over 400 species of tropical reef fish, including wrasses, snappers, groupers, barracudas, jacks, moray eels, surgeonfish, and shellfish, are known to cause seafood poisoning (ciguatera). There's no way to tell if a fish will cause ciguatera: a species can be poisonous on one side of the island but not on the other.

Several years ago scientists on Tahiti determined that micro-algae called dinoflagellates were the cause. Normally these algae are found only in the ocean depths, but when a reef is disturbed by natural or human causes they can multiply dramatically in a lagoon. The toxins have no effect on the fish that feed on them but become concentrated in large, predatory fish and enter the food chain.

There's no treatment except to relieve the symptoms (tingling, prickling, itching, nausea, vomiting, joint and muscle pains), which usually subside in a few days. Induce vomiting and take castor oil. Symptoms can recur for up to a year, and victims can become allergic to all seafoods. Avoid biointoxication by cleaning fish as soon as they're caught, discarding the head and organs, and taking special care with oversized fish. Whether the fish is consumed cooked or raw has no bearing on this problem. Local residents often know from experience which species may be eaten.

Other Diseases

Infectious hepatitis A is a liver ailment transmitted from person to person or through unboiled water, uncooked vegetables, or other foods contaminated during handling. The risk of infection is highest for those who eat village food. If you'll be spending much time in rural areas an immune globulin shot is recommended. You'll know you've got the hep when your eyeballs and urine turn yellow. Time and rest are the only cure. Serum hepatitis B is spread through sexual or blood contact.

There have been sporadic outbreaks of cholera in the Gilbert and Caroline islands (in Micronesia). Cholera is acquired via contaminated food or water, so avoid uncooked foods, peel your own fruit, and drink bottled drinks if you happen to arrive in an infected area. Horrible disfiguring diseases such as leprosy and elephantiasis are hard to catch, so it's unlikely you'll be visited by one of these nightmares of the flesh.

There's no malaria, but a mosquito-transmitted disease known as dengue fever is rampant in Fiji. Signs are headaches, sore throat, pain in the joints, fever, nausea, and rash. It can last anywhere from five to 15 days; although you can relieve the symptoms somewhat, the only real cure is to stay in bed and wait it out. It's painful, but dengue fever usually only kills infants. No vaccine exists, so try to avoid getting bitten.

Vaccinations

Officially, most visitors are not required to get any vaccinations at all before coming to Fiji. Since 1977 no naturally transmitted cases of smallpox have been recorded anywhere in the world, so forget that one. Tetanus, typhoid fever, polio, and diphtheria shots are not required, but they're a good idea if you're going off the beaten track. Tetanus and diphtheria shots are given together, and a booster is required every 10 years. Typhoid fever is every three years, polio every five years.

The cholera vaccine is only 50% effective, valid just six months, and bad reactions are common, so forget it unless you're headed for an infected area (such as Micronesia). Immune globulin (IG) isn't 100% effective against hepatitis A, but it does increase your general resistance to infection. IG prophylaxis must be repeated every five months. Hepatitis B vaccination involves three doses over a six-month period (duration of protection unknown). While yellow fever is confined to the jungles of South America and Africa, this vaccination is listed as a requirement if you're coming from those areas. Since the vaccination is valid 10 years, get one if you're an inveterate globetrotter.

THE
Fiji Times

INFORMATION

The **Fiji Visitors Bureau** (G.P.O. Box 92, Suva) sends out, free upon request, general brochures and a list of hotels with current prices. In Fiji they have walk-in offices in Suva and at Nandi Airport. For a list of their overseas offices, see "Tourist Offices" below.

The **Fiji Hotel Association** (Private Mail Bag, G.P.O. Suva) will mail you a brochure listing all upmarket hotels, with specific prices, though budget accommodations are not included.

The **Ministry of Information** (Box 2225, Government Buildings, Suva) publishes a few general brochures on the political and economic situation in the country.

The free *Fiji Magic* magazine (Box 12511, Suva; tel. 313-944) is useful to get an idea of what's on during your visit. Also browse the local bookstores, **Desai Bookshops, Zenon Book Shops**, and the **Singatoka Book Depot**, with branches all over Fiji.

The *Fiji Times* (G.P.O. Box 1167, Suva; tel. 304-111), "the first newspaper published in the world today," was founded at Levuka in 1869 but is now owned by publishing mogul Rupert Murdoch's estate. The *Daily Post* (Box 7010, Valelevu, Nasinu; tel. 395-855) is an independent morning newspaper with a local focus. Both regional newsmagazines, *Islands Business* and *Pacific Islands Monthly,* are published in Suva.

Fiji Voice, published by the Fiji Independent News Service (Box 78, Balmain, Sydney, NSW 2041, Australia; US$40 a year to North America), is a bimonthly newsletter on political devel-

TOURIST OFFICES

Fiji Visitors Bureau,
GPO Box 92,
Suva, Fiji Islands

Fiji Visitors Bureau,
Box 9217,
Nandi Airport, Fiji Islands

Fiji Visitors Bureau,
5777 West Century Blvd.,
Suite 220,
Los Angeles, CA 90045, U.S.A.

Fiji Visitors Bureau,
127 West 6th Ave.,
Vancouver, BC V6H 1A6,
Canada

Fiji Visitors Bureau,
9th floor, 225 Clarence St.,
Sydney, NSW 2000, Australia

Fiji Visitors Bureau,
Suite 204, 620 St. Kilda Rd.,
Melbourne 3000, Australia

Fiji Visitors Bureau,
Box 1179,
Auckland, New Zealand

Fiji Embassy,
10th Floor, Noa Building,
3-5, 2-Chome, Azabudai,
Minatu-Ku,
Tokyo 106, Japan

Marketing Services,
Suite 433, High Holborn House,
52-54 High Holborn,
London WC1V 6RB, England

D&S Touristie Represantanz,
Klugstrasse 114,
8000 München 19, Germany

opments in Fiji. The same organization puts out a monthly *Fiji Situation Report.*

The Fiji Broadcasting Commission (Box 334, Suva; tel. 314-333) operates two public AM radio stations heard throughout the islands: Radio Fiji 1 in English and Fijian (BBC world news at 0800), and Radio Fiji 2 in English and Hindi (local news in English at 0700 and 1900). Radio Fiji 3-FM in English and FM 98 in Hindi cannot be heard everywhere. Radio West is based in Lautoka. Communications Fiji Ltd. (Private Mail Bag, Suva; tel. 314-766) operates two commercial FM stations that broadcast around the clock: FM 96 in English and Fijian; and FM 96, broadcast in Hindi to Navtarang. Radio Australia on 11.86 shortwave gives a weather forecast for the whole Pacific area at 0830. There have been numerous announcements of the introduction of television to Fiji, but nothing permanent has yet materialized. VCRs are quite common in Fiji.

Freedom of the Press

Until 1987 Fiji had a free media, and although there's no official censorship and a certain degree of press criticism is tolerated, newspapers are now "self-censored" by editors who face intimidation and arrest if the wrong stories find their way into print, especially those which might arouse racial or political tensions. After the *Fiji Sun* was shut down for the second time in 1987 it refused to reopen under these conditions and no longer exists.

A government plan to directly control the media through one-year licenses was dropped after strong objections from publishers, but libel has been upgraded from a civil to a criminal offense. Fiji's Public Order Act allows the government to arrest journalists for "malicious publication," and on 29 Oct. 1990 these wide, sweeping powers were used when the publisher, the chief subeditor, and a reporter from the *Daily Post* were arrested in connection with a story about a planned antigovernment protest. The three were promptly freed after Amnesty International took an interest in the case.

Journalists are harassed by defamation suits,

such as the $1.5-million suit brought against the *Fiji Times* by Prime Minister Ratu Mara in 1989, when an article in the paper included one line criticizing him for keeping a scheduled meeting with President Bush in Washington D.C. instead of attending Dr. Bavadra's funeral. Back in Fiji, foreign journalists were refused permission to cover the funeral.

The government's Ministry of Information has issued persistent and vociferous criticisms of "irresponsible" and "inaccurate" reporting by foreign journalists, yet when the SPF organized a "media workshop" at Rarotonga in 1990 to discuss such complaints, ministry officials declined to attend. The state radio is a propaganda arm of the government, and the Ministry of Information has made it clear that television will be strictly censored when it is installed in Fiji.

Since Feb. 1988 foreign journalists and television crews are required to have work permits to enter Fiji, are given time limits, and are restricted as to whom they may interview (government ministers are usually unavailable). Such permits are routinely denied, and coverage of the many regional organizations based in Fiji is severely restricted. About the only foreign journalists officially welcome in the country are travel writers sponsored by the Fiji Visitors Bureau, and such writers never include anything in their articles which might displease those who gave them their free rooms, flights, and meals. International human-rights organizations are not welcome in Fiji.

In May 1990 the Fiji government expelled from Fiji the Pacific islands' only regional news service, the German-funded PacNews, after a leading broadcaster refused to apologize to the Minister of Information for previous criticism (PacNews is now based in Honiara in the Solomon Islands). In Sept. 1990 the Fiji Intelligence Service (FIS) was set up, with the power to intercept all mail, faxes, and telephone calls entering or leaving Fiji. FIS spies have the right to enter private residences, to seize documents, to plant listening devices, and to arrest anyone who interferes with their activities or publicly identifies their agents.

WHAT TO TAKE

Packing

Assemble everything you simply must take and cannot live without—then cut the pile in half. If you're still left with more than will fit into a medium-size suitcase or backpack, continue eliminating. Now put it all into your bag. If the total (bag and contents) weighs over 16 kilograms, you'll sacrifice much of your mobility. If you can keep it down to 10 kilograms, you're traveling *light*. Categorize, separate, and pack all your things into plastic bags or stuff sacks for convenience and protection from moisture. In addition, you'll want a day pack or flight bag. When checking in for flights, carry anything that can't be replaced in your hand luggage.

Your Pack

A medium-size backpack with a lightweight internal frame is best. Big, external-frame packs are fine for mountain climbing but are very inconvenient on public transport. Make sure your pack carries the weight on your hips, has a cushion for spinal support, and doesn't pull backward. The pack should strap snugly to your body but also allow ventilation to your back. It should be made of a water-resistant material, such as nylon, and have a Fastex buckle. The best packs have a zippered compartment in back where you can tuck in the straps and hip belt before turning your pack over to an airline.

Look for a pack with double, two-way-zipper compartments and pockets you can lock with miniature padlocks. These might not *stop* a thief but could be deterrent enough to make him look for another mark. A 60-cm length of lightweight chain and another padlock will allow you to fasten your pack to something. Keep valuables locked in your bag, out of sight.

Camping Equipment And Clothing

A small nylon tent guarantees you a place to sleep every night. It *must* be mosquito- and waterproof. Get one with a tent fly. You'll seldom need a sleeping bag in the tropics. A youth-hostel sleeping sheet is ideal—all youth hostel association handbooks give instructions on how to make your own. You don't really need to carry a bulky foam pad, as the ground is seldom cold.

For clothes take loose-fitting cotton washables, light in color and weight. Synthetic fabrics are hot and sticky in the tropics. The dress is casual, with slacks and a sports shirt okay for men, even at dinner parties. Local women wear long, colorful dresses in the evening, but shorts are okay in daytime. If you're in doubt, pack clothes that can be discarded and buy tropical garb here. Stick to clothes you can rinse in your room sink. In midwinter (July, Aug.) it can be cool at night, so a light sweater may come in handy.

The lavalava or *sulu* is a bright, two-meter piece of cloth that both men and women wrap around themselves as an all-purpose garment. Any islander can show you how to wear it. Missionaries taught the South Sea island women to drape their attributes in long, flowing gowns, called muumuus in Hawaii. In the South Pacific, for the muumuu-attired nursery-rhyme character who "went to the cupboard to fetch her poor dog a bone," the dress is better known as a Mother Hubbard.

Take comfortable shoes that have been broken in. Running shoes and rubber thongs (zories) are very handy for day use but will bar you from night spots with dress codes. Scuba divers' rubber booties are lightweight and perfect for both crossing rivers and reefwalking, though an old pair of sneakers may be just as good. Below we've provided a few checklists to help you assemble your gear. The listed items combined weigh well over 16 kilograms, so eliminate what doesn't suit you.

> pack with internal frame
> day pack or airline bag
> nylon tent and fly
> tent-patching tape
> mosquito net
> synthetic sleeping bag
> youth-hostel sleeping sheet
> sun hat
> essential clothing only
> swimsuit

hiking boots
rubber thongs
rubber booties
mask and snorkel

Photography

Look at the ads in photographic magazines for the best mail-order deals on cameras and film, or buy at a discount shop in any large city. Run a roll of film through your camera to be sure it's in good working order. Register valuable cameras or electronic equipment with Customs before you leave home so there won't be any argument about where you bought the items when you return, or at least carry the original bill of sale.

The type of camera you choose could depend on the way you travel. If you'll be staying mostly in one place, a heavy single-lens reflex with spare lenses and other equipment won't trouble you. If you'll be moving around a lot for a considerable length of time a 35-mm compact camera may be better. The compacts are useful mostly for close-up shots; landscapes will seem spread out and far away. A wide-angle lens gives excellent depth of field, but hold the camera upright to avoid converging verticals. A polarizing filter prevents reflections from glass windows. Avoid overexposure at midday by reducing the exposure half a stop; *do* overexpose when photographing dark-skinned islanders, however. High-speed film is required for shooting in dark rainforests. Ask permission before photographing people. If you're asked for money (extremely rare) you can always walk away—give your subjects the same choice. There is probably no country in the world where the photographer will have as interesting and willing subjects as in Fiji.

Keep your camera in a plastic bag during rain and while traveling in motorized canoes, etc. In the tropics the humidity can cause film to stick to itself; silica-gel crystals in the bag will protect film from humidity and mold growth. Protect camera and film from direct sunlight and load film in the shade. Whenever loading, check that the takeup spool revolves when winding on. Never leave camera or film in a hot place like a car floor or glove compartment. When packing protect your camera against vibration. Remove the batteries from your camera when in storage at home for long periods.

Checked baggage is scanned by powerful airport X-ray monitors, so carry both camera and film aboard the plane in a clear plastic bag and ask security for a visual inspection. Some airports will refuse to do this. Otherwise use a lead-laminated pouch. The old high-dose X-ray units are the worst, but even low-dose inspection units can ruin fast film (400 ASA and above). Beware of the cumulative effect of X-ray machines. Whenever purchasing film in Fiji take care to check the expiration date.

Accessories

A clip-on book light with extra batteries allows campers to read at night, and a small, folding umbrella will protect you from the rain. If you're a serious scuba diver, write to the operators you'll be diving with and ask about their equipment requirements. Serious scuba divers will bring their own regulator, buoyancy-control device, and perhaps a wetsuit for protection against coral. A mask and snorkel are essential equipment—you'll be missing half of Fiji's beauty without them.

Also take along postcards of your hometown, snapshots of your house, family, workplace, etc; islanders love to see these. Always keep a promise to mail the islanders photos you take of them. Think of some small souvenirs of your country (such as lapel pins bearing kangaroos or maple leafs, or Kennedy half dollars) that you can take along as gifts. Miniature compasses sold in camping stores also make good gifts.

Neutral gray eyeglasses protect your eyes from the sun and give the least color distortion. Take an extra pair (if you have them). Keep the laundry soap inside a couple of layers of plastic bags. To cook at campsites you'll often need a small stove: trying to keep rainforest wood burning will drive you to tears from smoke and frustration. Camping fuel cannot be carried on commercial airlines, however, so choose a stove that uses a common fuel like kerosene or gasoline.

camera and five rolls of film
compass
pocket flashlight
extra batteries
candle
pocket/alarm calculator

1. guard at Government House, Suva (David Bowden); **2.** handicraft seller, Nandi (Doug Hankin);
3. market scene (Karl Partridge); **4.** along Numbukalou Creek, Suva (D. Stanley);
5. Suva market (D. Stanley)

1. Matuku I., Moala Group (Robert Kennington); **2.** Mount Victoria, Viti Levu (D. Stanley);
3. road near Mbukuya, Viti Levu (Don Pitcher); **4.** vegetation on the hike to Lovoni,
Ovalau (Don Pitcher); **5.** Rewa River near Vunindawa, Viti Levu (D. Stanley)

pocket watch
inflatable neck pillow
soft-wax earplugs
sunglasses
padlock and lightweight chain
collapsible umbrella
twine for a clothesline
powdered laundry soap
sink plug (one that fits all)
minitowel
sewing kit
miniscissors
nail clippers
fishing line for sewing gear
plastic cup
can and bottle opener
corkscrew
penknife
spoon
water bottle
matches
tea bags
dried fruits
nuts
crackers
plastic bags
gifts

stick deodorant
shampoo
comb and brush
skin creams
makeup
tampons or napkins
white toilet paper
multiple vitamins and minerals
Cutter's insect repellent
PABA sunscreen
lip balm
motion-sickness remedy
contraceptives
iodine
water-purification pills
delousing powder
diarrhea medication
Tiger Balm
cold medication
Alka-Seltzer
aspirin
antihistamine
antifungal
calamine lotion
antibiotic ointment
painkiller
antiseptic cream
disinfectant
simple dressings
sterile bandages, various sizes

Toiletries And Medical Kit

Since everyone has his/her own medical requirements and since brand names vary from country to country, there's no point going into detail here. Note, however, that even the basics (such as aspirin) are unavailable on some outer islands, so be prepared. Bring medicated powder for prickly heat rash. Charcoal tablets are useful for diarrhea and poisoning (they absorb the irritants). Bring an adequate supply of any personal medications, plus your prescriptions (in generic terminology).

High humidity causes curly hair to swell and bush, straight hair to droop. If it's curly have it cut short or keep it long in a ponytail or bun. A good cut is essential with straight hair. Water-based makeup is best, as the heat and humidity cause oil glands to work overtime. See "Health" above for more ideas.

soap in a plastic container
soft toothbrush
toothpaste

Money And Documents

All post offices have passport applications. If you lose your passport you should report the matter to the local police at once, obtain a certificate or receipt, then proceed to your consulate for a replacement. If you have your birth certificate with you, it facilitates things considerably.

Traveler's checks are widely accepted, and in Fiji American Express is by far the most efficient company when it comes to providing refunds for lost checks. Credit cards can be used at travel agencies and deluxe hotels. Bring along a small supply of US$1 and US$5 bills to use if you don't manage to change money immediately upon arrival or if you run out of local currency and can't get to a bank. Quantities of foreign banknotes over F$500 should not be shown to officials (see "Money and Communcations" above).

Become a life member of the Youth Hostel

Association if you feel the wanderlust in your veins. If you have a car at home, bring along the insurance receipt so you don't have to pay insurance every time you rent a car. Ask your agent about this.

Carry your valuables in a money belt worn around your waist or neck under your clothing; most camping stores have these. Make several photocopies of the information page of your passport, personal identification, driver's license, scuba-certification card, credit cards, airline tickets, receipts for purchase of traveler's checks, etc.—you should be able to get them all on one page. A brief medical history with your blood type, allergies, chronic or special health problems, eyeglass and medical prescriptions, etc., might also come in handy. Put these inside plastic bags to protect them from moisture. Carry the lists in different places, and leave one at home.

- passport
- vaccination certificates
- airline tickets
- scuba-certification card
- driver's license
- traveler's checks
- credit card(s)
- some U.S. cash
- photocopies of documents
- money belt
- address book
- notebook
- envelopes
- extra ballpoint pens

GETTING THERE

Fiji's geographic position makes it the hub of transport for the whole South Pacific. Nandi Airport is the region's most important international airport, with long-haul services to points all around the Pacific Rim. Eight international airlines fly into Nandi: Air Caledonie International, Air Marshall Islands, Air Nauru, Air New Zealand, Air Pacific, Air Vanuatu, Qantas Airways, and Solomon Airlines. Air Marshall Islands, Air Nauru, and Air Pacific also use Suva's Nausori Airport, a regional distribution center with flights to many of the nearby Polynesian countries to the east.

Only Air New Zealand flies direct from Los Angeles to Fiji via Honolulu. Qantas passengers originating in Los Angeles or San Francisco must change planes in Honolulu, where Canadian Airlines International also connects from Toronto and Vancouver. It's a five-hour flight from California to Hawaii, then another six hours from Hawaii to Fiji.

From Australia you can fly to Nandi on Air Pacific or Qantas, both of which arrive from Brisbane, Melbourne, and Sydney. From Auckland, New Zealand, to Nandi, it's a choice of Air New Zealand or Air Pacific. From Tokyo you'll fly Air New Zealand or Air Pacific.

Fiji's national airline, **Air Pacific**, was founded as Fiji Airways by Australian aviator Harold Gatty in 1951. Gatty flew around the world in eight days with American Willy Post to set a record in 1931. In 1972 the airline was reorganized as a regional carrier and the name changed to Air Pacific. Aside from the flights mentioned above they also arrive at Nandi from Apia, Honiara, Port Vila, and Tongatapu. Plans call for direct Air Pacific flights from Fiji to Los Angeles by 1995, though a similar Air Pacific "Project America" in 1985 resulted in heavy losses. Air Pacific has a U.S. office at 6151 W. Century Blvd., Suite 524, Los Angeles, CA 90045, U.S.A. (tel. 213-417-2236). Flying with Air Pacific means you'll enjoy the friendly flavor of Fiji from the moment you leave the ground.

Other regional carriers landing in Nandi include Air Caledonie International (from Nouméa and Wallis), Air Marshall Islands (from Majuro, Tarawa, and Funafuti), Air Nauru (from Nauru), Air New Zealand (from Rarotonga), Air Vanuatu (from Port Vila), and Solomon Airlines (from Honiara).

Airlines offering direct flights to Suva include Air Marshall Islands (from Funafuti), Air Nauru (from Nauru), and Air Pacific (from Apia and Tongatapu). Some Air Pacific flights to Nandi from Port Vila carry on to Suva.

AIR SERVICES

From North America

Air New Zealand and Qantas are the carriers

LOUISE FOOTE

serving Fiji from North America. Their South Pacific fares vary according to seasons: basic (April to July), shoulder (March, Aug. to Nov.), and peak (Dec. to Feb.). The month of outbound travel from the U.S. determines which seasonal airfare you pay. The airlines have made March to Nov., the best months in Fiji, their "low" season because it's winter in Australia and New Zealand. If you're only going to the islands and come at this time it certainly works to your advantage! The main problems with both these carriers are their schedules, which are built around Auckland, Sydney, and Los Angeles: they'll drop you off at Nandi in the middle of the night.

Roundtrip excursion fares to Nandi from Los Angeles or San Francisco are US$1237/-1335/1497 basic/shoulder/peak. You can buy your ticket anytime and have a year to complete the trip. The Advance Purchase Excursion (APEX) fare for this same roundtrip is slightly cheaper at US$1104/1202/1364 basic/shoulder/peak, but there are a few strict rules. You must book and pay at least 14 days in advance, and there's a 35% cancellation fee within 14 days of departure. You can change your return date without penalty but must do so at least 14 days in advance. If you decide to change the return on shorter notice, you'll pay a heavy penalty. You may only stay three months. Both fares allow a free stopover at Honolulu, but to extend either ticket beyond Fiji to Australia and New Zealand will cost US$300-700 extra.

Cheaper still are Independent Tour Excursion (ITX) fares, available to passengers who prepay a land package. Normal economy tickets carry no restrictions at all but cost almost double the excursion fares.

Circle-Pacific Fares
Thanks to agreements between the carriers mentioned above and Asian or U.S. companies, such as Cathay Pacific, Japan Airlines, Malaysian Airlines, Northwest Airlines, Singapore Airlines, and United Airlines, you can get a "Circle-Pacific" fare that combines the South Pacific with Singapore, Bangkok, Hong Kong, Taipei, Tokyo, etc. These tickets must be purchased 21 days in advance, but they're valid up to six months and only the initial flight has to be booked 21 days ahead. The rest of the ticket can be left open-dated.

Prices run US$1970 RT from Los Angeles/San Francisco/Seattle, C$2599 from Vancouver, A$2131 from Brisbane/Sydney, or HK$12,200 from Hong Kong. You're allowed four free stopovers; additional stopovers are US$50 apiece, to a total of six stops maximum. Different carriers offer different routes in Asia, so ask your travel agent to explain the alternatives to you. The Circle-Pacific fares are excellent values if you have enough time for such a wide-ranging trip.

From Australia
To help subsidize Qantas, the state-owned carrier, the Australian government keeps airfares out of Australia as high as it can; it also requires foreign carriers to set high fares. The APEX and Circle-Pacific fares described above are available, however, so see a travel agent. The carriers often offer specials during the off months. Ask Qantas about their South Pacific Pass, which allows three flights (for example, Sydney-Nandi-Auckland-Sydney) for A$790 (not available to residents of Australia, New Zealand, or Fiji). For information on special fares available from Student Travel Australia, see "Student Fares" below.

Air Pacific offers a special "triangle fare," Sydney-Fiji-Port Vila-Sydney, of A$1034 RT (A$1227 from Melbourne, A$820 from Brisbane). The maximum stay is 60 days—an excellent way to combine Fiji with Vanuatu.

From New Zealand
Low unrestricted airfares to Fiji are surprisingly hard to come by in New Zealand. Some of the best tickets have advance-purchase requirements, so you have to start shopping well ahead. Government regulations limit what Student Travel Services in Auckland and Wellington can offer, but they do have an Auckland-Fiji-Honolulu-Los Angeles student fare and Air New Zealand has 21-day, advance-purchase EPIC fares to Fiji. Again, see your travel agent.

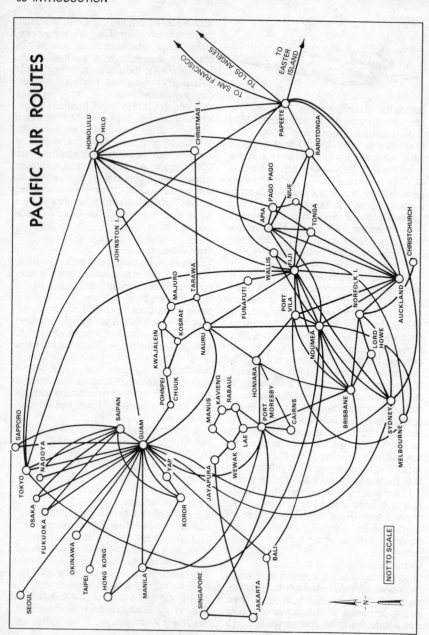

PACIFIC AIR ROUTES

NOT TO SCALE

AIRFARES

Tickets

Your plane ticket will be your biggest single expense, so spend some time considering the possibilities. Start by calling the airlines directly over their toll-free 800 numbers to get current information on fares. In North America, these numbers are available by calling toll-free information at (800) 555-1212 (all 800 numbers are free). Call both Air New Zealand and Qantas and say you want the *lowest possible fare.* Ask about restrictions. If you're not happy with the answers you get, call back later and try again. Many different agents take calls on these lines and some are more knowledgeable than others. The numbers are busy during business hours, so call at night or on the weekend. *Be persistent.*

Travel Agents

Any travel agent worth his/her commission will probably want to sell you a package tour, and some vacation packages actually cost less than regular roundtrip airfare! If they'll let you extend your stay to allow you some time to yourself this could be a good deal, especially with the hotel thrown in for "free." But check the restrictions.

Pick your agent carefully, as many are pitifully ignorant about Fiji and may know little about discounts, cheap flights, or alternative routes. With alarming frequency, travel agents give wrong or misleading information in an offhand manner. Ask an airline to suggest a travel agent. They won't *recommend* any, but they will give you the names of a few in your area that specialize in Pacific travel. Agencies belonging to the American Society of Travel Agents (ASTA) or Alliance of Canadian Travel Associations (ACTA) must conform to a strict code of ethics. A travel agent's commission is paid by the airline, so you've got nothing to lose.

Even if you decide to take advantage of the convenience of an agent, do call the airlines yourself beforehand so you'll know if you're getting a good deal. Airline tickets are often refundable only in the place of purchase, so ask about this before you invest in a ticket you may not use. There can be tremendous variations in what different passengers on the same flight have paid for their tickets, so allow yourself time

to shop around. An hour on the phone, asking questions, could save you hundreds of dollars.

One of the most knowledgeable Canadian travel agencies for Fiji tickets is the **Adventure Centre** (17 Hayden St., Toronto, ON M4Y 2P2, Canada; tel. 800-661-7265), with offices in Calgary, Edmonton, Toronto, and Vancouver. They sell most tickets listed above and below. Their U.S. branch, the **Adventure Center** (1311 63rd St., Ste. 200, Emeryville, CA 94608-2103, U.S.A.; tel. 510-654-1879), has the best tickets on the market. They also have six-day tours for scuba divers to Fiji's Matangi Island (US$1120, double occupancy, including diving and meals, airfare extra).

Cheap Flights

Check the travel section in a Sunday newspaper, like the *San Francisco Examiner,* or a major entertainment weekly. They often carry ads for "bucket shops," agencies that deal in bulk and sell seats for less than airline offices will. Most airlines have more seats than they can market through normal channels, so they sell their unused long-haul capacity on this gray market at discounts of 40-50% off the official IATA tariffs.

There are well-known centers around the world where globe-trotters regularly pick up onward tickets (Amsterdam, Athens, Bangkok, Hong Kong, London, Penang, San Francisco, and Singapore are only a few—unfortunately Fiji isn't one). Rates are competitive, so check a few agencies before deciding. Despite their shady appearance, most of the bucket shops are perfectly legitimate, and your ticket will probably be issued by the airline itself. Most discounted tickets look and are exactly the same as regular full-fare tickets. They're usually nonrefundable.

From Singapore And Bangkok

The bucket shops of Southeast Asia are famous for selling air tickets at enormous discounts. For example, discount Air New Zealand tickets (Singapore-Auckland-Fiji-Rarotonga-Tahiti-Los Angeles) are available in Singapore and Penang for about US$1000 OW. These are open tickets valid up to a year on any flight.

One recommended agency is **German Asian Travels Ltd.** (126 Telok Ayer St. #02-01, Singapore 0106; tel. 221-5539; fax 221-4220). Among the many variations available at Ger-

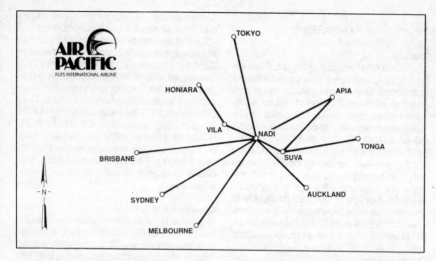

man Asian is Singapore-Auckland-Nandi-Raro-tonga-Papeete-Los Angeles (S$1705).

Similar tickets are available from **MAS Travel Center Ltd.** (19 Tanglin Rd., #06-01 Tanglin Shopping Center, Singapore 1024; tel. 737-8877) and **K. Travel Service** (21/33 Soi Ngam Dupli, near Malaysia Hotel, Bangkok 10120, Thailand; tel. 286-1468). All of these companies have been operating for many years.

Some of the cheap tickets sold in Southeast Asia are for UTA French Airlines services through Nouméa. Fiji is easily accessible from there on a Pacific Triangle fare (Nouméa-Fiji-Port Vila-Nouméa) costing Fr63,200 (about US$650), valid one year. Agence de Voyages Jean Brock in Nouméa will have details.

From Europe

Flights from London to Australia via the U.S. and the Pacific used to be more expensive than Eastern Hemisphere flights. Things have changed. Now **Trailfinders** (42-50 Earls Court Rd., Kensington, London W8 6EJ; tel. 071-938-3366) includes Honolulu and Fiji in their discount flights to Sydney (£862 RT). Around the world from London is £995 via Fiji. Check the ads in *Time Out* for others.

In Amsterdam **Reisbureau Amber** (Da Costastraat 77, 1053 ZG Amsterdam; tel. 20-

685-1155) and **Malibu Travel** (Damrak 30, 1012 LJ Amsterdam) have low round-the-world fares that include Fiji.

In Switzerland try **Globetrotter Travel Service** (Rennweg 35, 8001 Zürich; tel. 01-211-7780) with offices in Zürich, Bern, Basel, Luzern, St. Gallen, Winterthur, and Baden. For example, Globetrotter offers Frankfurt-New York-San Francisco-Papeete-Nandi-Auckland-Singapore-Colombo-Frankfurt for US$2260, valid one year. A return flight from Frankfurt to Fiji, with stops in Los Angeles and Papeete, is US$1860, valid 180 days. From Munich they have return tickets to Fiji via Canada for only US$1790.

In Germany ask about the Pacific-Airpass that allows travel from Frankfurt to Fiji and four other South Pacific countries for DM2500 RT (valid six months).

STUDENT FARES

If you're a student or recent graduate you can benefit from lower student fares by booking through a student travel office. There are two rival organizations of this kind: **Council Travel Services**, with offices in college towns across North America, and **Student Travel Australia** (called the **Student Travel Network** in the U.S.). A similar company in Canada is **Travel CUTS**. These organizations require you to pay a nominal fee for an official student card, and to get the cheapest fares you'll have to prove you're really a student. Slightly higher fares on the same routes are available to nonstudents, however, so check them out.

Student Travel Australia and their North American affiliate, the **Student Travel Network** (tel. 800-777-0112), have been flying students across the Pacific for years. Basically, they'll sell you the same APEX and Circle-Pacific tickets described above but at a lower price and without any restrictions whatsoever. For example, their round-trip student fare from Los Angeles to Fiji is US$909/989/1119 basic/shoulder/peak (see "From North America" above, for the seasons). The tickets are refundable with only a US$25 penalty. One-way tickets are about half the roundtrip price. Reservations may be changed at will, and the ticket is refundable.

Here's a partial list of the 120 STA/STN offices and affiliates around the world:

North America
STN, 1208 Massachusetts Ave., Cambridge, MA 02138, U.S.A.; tel. (617) 576-4623
STN, 273 Newbury St., Boston, MA 02116, U.S.A.; tel. (617) 226-6014
STN, 82 Shattuck Square, Berkeley, CA 94704, U.S.A.; tel. (510) 841-1037
STN, 914 Westwood Blvd., Los Angeles, CA 90024, U.S.A.; tel. (310) 824-1574
STN, 7202 Melrose Ave., Los Angeles, CA 90046, U.S.A.; tel. (213) 934-8722
STN, 17 E. 45th St., New York, NY 10017, U.S.A.; tel. (212) 986-9470
STN, 48 E. 11th St., New York, NY 10003, U.S.A.; tel. (212) 477-7166
STN, 5131 College Ave., Ste. B, San Diego, CA 92115, U.S.A.; tel. (619) 286-1322
STN, 166 Geary St., Ste. 702, San Francisco, CA 94108, U.S.A.; tel. (415) 391-8407
CUTS, 187 College St., Toronto, ON M5T 1P7, Canada; tel. (416) 979-2406
CUTS has other offices in Calgary, Edmonton, Fredericton, Guelph, Halifax, Montreal, Ottawa, Quebec City, Saskatoon, St. John's, Sudbury, Vancouver, Victoria, Waterloo, and Winnipeg.

Australia/New Zealand
STA, 220 Faraday St., Carlton, Melbourne 3053, Australia; tel. 03-347-6911
STA, 1a Lee St., Railway Square, Sydney, NSW 2000, Australia; tel. 02-212-1255
STA has many other offices in Adelaide, Brisbane, Canberra, Perth, etc.
Student Travel, 64 High St., Auckland, New Zealand; tel. 09-39-9723
Student Travel, 207 Cuba St., Wellington, New Zealand; tel. 04-850560
Student Travel has other offices in Christchurch, Dunedin, and Hamilton

Student fares are also available from **Council Travel Services,** a division of the Council on International Educational Exchange. They're much stricter about making sure you're a "real" student: you must first obtain the widely recognized International Student Identity Card (US$14) to get a ticket at the student rate. Some fares are limited to students and youths under 26 years of age, but part-time students and teachers also qualify. Circle-Pacific and Around the World routings are available, though Council Travel is oriented toward student travel to Europe.

Here are a few Council Travel offices:

2511 Channing Way, Berkeley, CA 94704, U.S.A.; tel. (510) 848-8604
729 Boylston St., Boston, MA 02116, U.S.A.; tel. (617) 266-1926
1153 N. Dearborn St., 2nd Floor, Chicago, IL 60610, U.S.A.; tel. (312) 951-0585
1093 Broxton Ave., Ste. 220, Los Angeles, CA 90024, U.S.A.; tel. (310) 208-3551
205 E. 42nd St., New York, NY 10017, U.S.A.; tel. (212) 661-1450
715 S.W. Morrison, Ste. 600, Portland, OR 97205, U.S.A.; tel. (503) 228-1900
953 Garnet Ave., San Diego, CA 92109, U.S.A.; tel. (619) 270-6401
312 Sutter St., Ste. 407, San Francisco, CA 94108, U.S.A.; tel. (415) 421-3473
1314 N.E. 43rd St., Ste. 210, Seattle, WA 98105, U.S.A.; tel. (206) 632-2448

REGIONAL CARRIERS

Air Nauru

Air Nauru (80 Collins St., Melbourne, Victoria 3000, Australia) links the South Pacific to Micronesia through Nauru, a tiny phosphate-rich island in the central Pacific. They offer Boeing 737 flights to Nauru from Auckland, Sydney, Melbourne, Guam, and Manila, and their fares are reasonable. Most are based on a journey via Nauru, so fit two of these one-way economy fares to Nauru together: Auckland (NZ$563), Chuuk (US$245), Guam (US$227), Honiara (A$140), Kosrae (US$130), Manila (US$319), Melbourne (A$389), Nandi (F$198), Nouméa (A$211), Pohnpei (US$176), Suva (F$198), Sydney (A$335), Tarawa (A$103). For north-south passengers traveling between Micronesia and Fiji, Air Nauru is much cheaper than competing services on Air Marshall Islands.

Over the years Air Nauru has earned a reputation for canceling flights on a moment's notice and bumping confirmed passengers to make room for local VIPs, but things are said to have improved recently. Add to all Air Nauru fares the compulsory A$10 airport departure tax everyone (even through passengers continuing on the same aircraft) is charged at Nauru.

Sidetrips From Fiji

Air Pacific has two different triangle fares from Fiji, a good way to get around and experience the South Pacific's variety of cultures: Fiji-Apia-Tonga-Fiji (F$667) and Fiji-Port Vila-Nouméa-Fiji (F$747), plus F$15 tax if purchased in Fiji. Both are valid for one year and can be purchased at any travel agency in Fiji or direct from the airlines. The coupons are accepted by all carriers flying the routes, and the dates can be changed at will. When using such a fare to travel to Samoa and Tonga, be aware that it's much better to go Fiji-Apia-Tonga-Fiji than vice versa, because the flights between Apia and Fiji are often full, while it's easy to get on between Tonga and Fiji. More important, the flight from Apia to Tonga operates in the late morning, while Tonga to Apia is late at night.

A Pacific Air Pass allows 30 days travel from Fiji to Apia, Tonga, and Port Vila (US$499) or Apia, Tonga, Port Vila, and Honiara (US$549).

These tickets may be purchased only from Qantas Airways offices in North America and are only valid on Air Pacific services. They're good value if you want to see a lot in a short period.

Air Pacific also has 28-day RT excursion fares from Fiji to Apia (F$545), Tonga (F$428), Port Vila (F$560), and Honiara (F$1015), about 25% off the regular fare. These can also be bought in Fiji.

Polynesian Airlines's Polypass, which allows 30 days of unlimited travel between Samoa, Tonga, Cook Islands, New Zealand, and Australia for US$999, is not valid for travel to Fiji.

Solomon Airlines and **Air Caledonie** combine to offer a 30-day Discover Pacific Pass that includes two flights on either airline for US$399, three flights for US$499, four flights for US$599. Possible four-coupon routings are Nandi-Wallis-Nouméa-Port Vila-Nandi or Nandi-Honiara-Port Vila-Nouméa-Nandi. Extensions to Australia or New Zealand are US$100 extra. These tickets can only be purchased in North America (through APR, Inc., 5777 West Century Blvd., Ste. 875, Los Angeles, CA 90045, U.S.A.; tel. 310-670-7302; fax 310-338-0708) and Europe (through Mr. Karl Philipp, Guillettsrasse 30, 6000 Frankfurt, Germany; tel. 69-172260; fax 69-729314). It's an excellent value.

BAGGAGE

All international airlines allow 20 kilograms of baggage, and on flights to/from North America you can take two pieces of up to 32 kilos each, within certain size limits. Small commuter aircraft restrict you to as few as 10 kilos, so pack according to the lowest common denominator. Bicycles, folding kayaks, and surfboards can usually be checked as baggage (sometimes for an additional US$50 charge), but sailboards may have to be shipped airfreight. If you do travel with a sailboard, be sure to call it a surfboard at checkin.

Tag your bag with name, address, and phone number inside and out. Stow anything that could conceivably be considered a weapon (scissors, penknife, toy gun, Mace, etc.) in your checked luggage. Incidentally, it can be considered a criminal offense to make jokes about bombings or hijackings in airports or aboard aircraft.

One reason for lost baggage is that people fail to remove used baggage tags after they claim their luggage. Get into the habit of tearing off old baggage tags, unless you want your luggage to travel in the opposite direction! As you're checking in, look to see if the three-letter city codes on your baggage tag and boarding pass are the same. If you're headed to Nandi the tag should read NAN (Suva is SUV).

If your baggage is damaged or doesn't arrive at your destination, then unless you inform the airline officials *immediately* and have them fill out a written report future claims for compensation will be compromised. Airlines will usually reimburse out-of-pocket expenses if your baggage is lost or delayed over 24 hours. The amount varies from US$25 to US$50, and your chances of getting it are better if you're polite but firm. Keep receipts for any money you're forced to spend to replace missing articles.

Claims for lost luggage can take weeks to process. Keep in touch with the airline to show your concern and hang on to your baggage tag until the matter is resolved. If you feel you did not receive the attention you deserved, write the airline an objective letter outlining the case. Get the names of the employees you're dealing with so you can mention them in the letter. Of course, don't expect pocket money or compensation on a remote outer island. Report the loss, then wait till you get back to their main office. Whatever happens, try to avoid getting angry. The people you're dealing with don't want the problem any more than you do.

BY BOAT

Even while Pacific shipping was being sunk during WW II, airstrips were springing up on all the main islands. This hastened the inevitable replacement of the old steamships with modern aircraft, and it's now extremely rare to arrive in Fiji by boat (private yachts excepted). Those bitten by nostalgia for the slower prewar days may like to know, however, that a couple of passenger-carrying freighters still call at Fiji, though fares are much higher than those charged by the airlines.

A specialized agency booking such passages is **TravLtips** (Box 188, Flushing, NY 11358, U.S.A.; tel. 800-872-8584 in the U.S. and 800-548-7823 in Canada). They can place you aboard a British-registered **Banks Line** container ship on its way around the world from England via the Panama Canal and both Suva and Lautoka in Fiji. A round-the-world ticket for the four-month journey is US$11,750, but segments are sold if space is available 30 days before sailing. Similarly, TravLtips books German-registered **Columbus Line** vessels, which make 45-day roundtrips between Los Angeles and Australia via Suva (US$5400 RT, double occupancy). One-way segments (when available) are half price. These ships only accommodate about a dozen passengers, so inquire well in advance.

If a voyage to/from Fiji aboard a luxury cruise ship is more what you had in mind, ships of the **Royal Cruise Line** (One Maritime Plaza, San Francisco, CA 94111, U.S.A.; tel. 415-956-7200) ply between Australia and Ensenada, Mexico, once a year, stopping for about eight hours in Fiji. With careful advance planning you might be able to fly to Fiji, have a holiday, then pick up one of their *Odyssey*-class vessels for a leisurely one-month cruise back to the States via Tonga, Samoa, Cook Islands, Tahiti, and Hawaii. If you need to ask the price, this trip isn't for you, though by booking four months in advance you can get 25% off.

ORGANIZED TOURS

Packaged Holidays

While this book is written for independent travelers rather than packaged tourists, greatly reduced group airfares and hotel rates make some tours worth considering. If there are two of you with limited time and a desire to stay at a first-class beach hotel, this is the cheapest way to go. Special-interest tours are very popular among sportspeople who want to be sure they'll get to participate in the various activities they enjoy. The main drawback to the tours is that you're on a fixed itinerary among other tourists, out of touch with local life. Singles pay a healthy supplement.

Ted Cook's Islands in the Sun (Box 1398, Newport Beach, CA 92663, U.S.A.; tel. 714-645-8300), founded in 1965, was the first American travel company to specialize exclusively in the South Pacific (no connection with James or Thomas). Ted Cook offers packaged holidays at Coral Coast hotels and the resorts off Nandi, and books three-day Blue Lagoon cruises. He doesn't accept consumer inquiries, however, so you must work through a travel agent.

In Australia **Swingaway Holidays** (22 York St., Sydney, NSW 2000; tel. 237-0300) offers the same sort of beach holidays at 28 resorts around Fiji. By booking a seven-night hotel package through them you're eligible for specially reduced airfares, yet you can extend your stay up to 120 days. Ask your travel agent about this.

Jetabout Holidays (141 Walker St., North Sydney, NSW 2060, Australia; tel. 02-957-0768) offers much the same, and again, only travel agent inquiries are accepted. European travel agents can easily book all this through Jetabout's U.K. office (Jetabout Holidays, Sovereign House, 359-367 King St., Hammersmith, London W6 9NJ, England; tel. 0345-010900). **Hideaway Holidays** (994 Victoria Rd., West Ryde, NSW 2114, Australia; tel. 02-807-4222) specializes in off-the-beaten-track packages and can organize complicated itineraries.

In New Zealand try **ASPAC Vacations Ltd.** (Box 4330, Auckland; tel. 09-623-0259), which is similar to all of the above. They also have a "special interest" division, which deals with specific requests.

Scuba Tours

Facilities for divers are good in Fiji, but unless you've got unlimited time and are philosophical about disappointments, you'll probably want to go on an organized scuba tour. Prices aren't cheap, but the convenience of having all your arrangements made for you by a company able to pull weight with island suppliers is sometimes worth it. When booking, ask if meals, regulator, pressure and depth gauges, mask, snorkel, fins, etc., are provided. In addition to the regular phone numbers given below, many companies have toll-free numbers, which you can obtain by calling toll-free information at (800) 555-1212. Of course, diver certification is mandatory.

Poseidon Venture Tours (359 San Miguel Dr., Newport Beach, CA 92660, U.S.A.; tel. 714-644-5344; or 505 N. Belt, Ste. 675, Houston, TX

feeding fish

BOB HALSTEAD

77060, U.S.A.; tel. 713-820-3483) offers seven-night diving tours to Fiji's Mbengga Reef or Taveuni from US$1495 without meals, US$1980 with meals. The price includes five days of two-tank diving, airfare from the U.S. West Coast, hotels, taxes, and transfers. Poseidon also books two live-aboard dive boats, the *Matangi Princess,* an 18-meter cabin cruiser operating around Taveuni, and the *Pacific Nomad,* a 35-meter ex-freighter that takes divers to the Astrolabe Reef south of Suva. A seven-night stay on either of these vessels is more expensive at US$1880 (airfare extra), but the boat anchors right above the dive sites so no time is wasted commuting back and forth, all meals are included, and the diving is unlimited. The *Nomad,* which sleeps 18 divers in nine king-size a/c cabins (hot showers!), departs Suva or Pacific Harbor every Saturday.

Tropical Adventures (111 Second Ave. N, Seattle, WA 98109, U.S.A.; tel. 206-441-3483) sends divers to Fiji for eight days for as little as US$1725, including airfare, accommodations, meals, diving, taxes, and more. Seven nights aboard the 22-meter live-aboard cruiser *Mollie Dean,* based at Suva, costs US$1750 (airfare extra). Over 6,000 divers a year book through this company, which has been in business since 1973.

Live-aboard diving can also be booked through **See & Sea Travel Service** (50 Francisco St., Ste. 205, San Francisco, CA 94133, U.S.A.; tel. 415-434-3400). See & Sea's president is noted underwater photographer and author Carl Roessler.

Aqua-Trek (110 Sutter St., Suite 811, San Francisco, CA 94104, U.S.A.; tel. 415-398-8990) is *the* Fiji specialist, with packages at 10 different resorts, beginning at US$750 a week double occupancy (airfare extra). Aqua-Trek is the place to call if you want to stay at Mana Island (US$1250 a week) or any of the resorts on or near Taveuni. They also work with the three live-aboard dive boats mentioned above (from US$1540 a week plus airfare).

Sea Safaris (3770 Highland Ave., Suite 102, Manhattan Beach, CA 90266, U.S.A.: tel. 310-546-2464) sells almost everything mentioned above, and their brochure is well worth obtaining, as it clearly outlines prices for a wide variety of scuba tours.

Innerspace Adventures (13393 Sorrento Dr., Largo, FL 34644, U.S.A.; tel. 813-595-5296) books diving at Matangi, Kandavu, and Mbengga islands.

Alternatively you can make your arrangements directly with island dive shops. Information about these operators is included in the respective chapters of this book.

Tours For Active People

Among the most exciting tours to Fiji are the 13-day ocean kayaking expeditions offered four times a year in June and July by **World Expeditions** (3rd Floor, 441 Kent St., Sydney, NSW 2000, Australia; tel. 02-264-3366; fax. 02-261-1974). Their groups (12 persons maximum) paddle stable two-person sea kayaks up through the Yasawa chain past the wild limestone caves of Sawa-I-Lau. Accommodations are tents on the beach, and participants must be in reasonable physical shape, as up to four hours a day is spent on the water. The groups meet at Lautoka, and since the US$1695 price doesn't include airfare, these trips are just as accessible to North Americans as to Aussies! In New Zealand book through **Venturetreks** (Box 37610, Auckland; tel. 09-799-855), in the U.S. through **Mountain Travel/Sobek,** 6420 Fairmount Ave., El Cerrito,

CA 94530 U.S.A.; tel. 510-527-8100). Highly recommended.

From May to Oct. **New Frontiers Trek Fiji,** a division of Rosie Travel Service (see below), runs adventurous five- to nine-night hiking trips across the central highlands from Tavua to Nalawa. Horses carry trekkers' backpacks, so the trips are feasible for almost anyone in good condition. The F$88 pp daily price includes transport to the trailhead, food and accommodations at a few of the 11 Fijian villages along the way, guides, and an outboard ride on the Wainimbuka River. Trekkers only hike about five hours a day, allowing lots of time to get to know the people. Outer-island treks are also arranged. Also recommended.

Earthwatch (Box 403, Watertown, MA 02272-9104 U.S.A.; tel. 617-926-8200) is a nonprofit foundation that accepts expenses-paying volunteers who are willing to assist scientists with field research. The actual projects vary from year to year, but in Aug. 1991 two Earthwatch teams were at Malololailai studying coral communities. The US$1395 contributed by each U.S. participant was tax-deductible in the States. Overseas offices include Earthwatch Europe, Belsyre Court (57 Woodstock Rd., Oxford OX2 6HU, England; tel. 0865-311600) and Earthwatch Australia (Box C360, Clarence St., Sydney, NSW 2000; tel. 02-290-1492).

Yacht Tours

If you were planning on spending a substantial sum to stay at a luxury resort, consider chartering a private yacht instead! You'll find a yacht cruise a much more rewarding experience for a similar price, with all meals included. All charterers visit remote islands accessible only by small boat and thus receive special insight into Fijian life, unspoiled by normal tourist trappings. Of course, activities such as sailing, snorkeling, and general exploring by sea and land are included in the price.

Emerald Yacht Charters Ltd. (Box 15, Savusavu; tel. 850-440) has three skippered yachts based at Savusavu, which operate in three main areas: the Lomaiviti Group, Taveuni and adjacent islands, and Vanua Mbalavu. The latter is recommended for people who want a long ocean-sailing leg to and from the cruising area. The price, including a Fijian skipper/guide, is US$390 a day for two persons, US$425 daily for three, or US$465 daily for four, about 10% less for a weekly charter, plus 10% tax. Emerald's prices are about the lowest in Fiji, but guests are expected to help with the cooking. In the U.S., call (408) 243-1677 for information.

The *Whale's Tale* (Oceanic Schooner Co., Box 9625, Nandi Airport; tel. 722-455) is a 30-meter schooner based at The Regent of Fiji, Nandi. Six guests are accommodated on three-day "Taste of the Blue Lagoon" cruises to the Yasawa Islands at US$3660, plus 10% tax. Yasawa cruises on the topsail schooner *La Violante* (Stardust Cruises Ltd., Private Mail Bag, Nandi Airport, Nandi; tel. 662-215) are cheaper at F$750 a day for up to four people. Between trips you'll find this boat anchored at Musket Cove on Malololailai Island.

Perhaps the finest charter yacht available at Fiji is the 14-meter ketch *Seax of Legra*, based at Taveuni (Box 89, Waiyevo, Taveuni; fax 679-880-141). The charge is US$595 daily for two persons, US$625 for three, US$660 for four, all-inclusive. Warwick and Dianne Bain will be your distinguished hosts on an unforgettable cruise. Larger groups could consider the 27-meter ketch *Tau* at the Tradewinds Marina, Suva, which charges US$8750 a week for up to six persons, meals included. For full information on these and other boats available in Fiji waters, write **Fiji Yacht Charter Association**, Box 3084, Lami, Fiji Islands (tel. 361-256).

Bare-boat chartering is not available in Fiji due to the risks involved in navigating the poorly marked reefs. However, **Rainbow Yacht Charters** arranges "flotilla" charters out of Nandi among the Mamanutha and Yasawa islands. You sail your own boat but follow a lead yacht that knows the way. Those wishing to go off on their own must take along a Fijian sailor/guide. If you don't know how to sail, they'll teach you at their sailing school based at Musket Cove Resort on Malololailai Island. The two-day course is F$195 pp (four persons maximum). A four-day flotilla charter is F$680 pp for four people, an individual guided charter is F$350 a day for the boat (food extra), plus 10% tax. For more information contact Rainbow Yacht Charters, Box 8327, Symonds St., Auckland, New Zealand (tel. 09-780-719; fax 09-780-931), or Postfach 920 113, 8500 Nurn-berg 92, Germany (tel. 0911-304090).

In the U.S. **Cruising Connection** (Box 31160, San Francisco, CA 94131, U.S.A.; tel. 415-337-8330) can book private charters of all the yachts mentioned above. **Ocean Voyages Inc.** (1709 Bridgeway, Sausalito, CA 94965, U.S.A.; tel. 415-332-4681) is one of the only companies organizing share-boat sailing tours, where individuals and couples join others for a cruise and pay on a per-person basis—perfect if you're alone or in a party of two and can't afford to charter an entire yacht.

Minicruise Ships

Blue Lagoon Cruises Ltd. (Box 54, Lautoka; tel. 665-280) has been offering minicruises of the Yasawa Islands from Lautoka since 1950. The three-night "popular" trips (from F$590) leave daily at 1900, while the six-night "club" cruise (from F$1150) is weekly. Prices are per person, double or triple occupancy, and include meals (excluding alcohol), entertainment, and shore excursions, but the 10% tax is additional. On the three-night cruises they use older three-deck, 45-passenger vessels, while larger four-deck, 66-passenger minicruise ships are used on the six-night (and some of the three-night) voyages. The meals are often beach barbecue affairs, with Fijian dancing. In 1991 this company opened a specially built facility on Nanayu Lailai Island for "island beach party" use. You'll have plenty of opportunities to snorkel in the calm, crystal-clear waters (bring your own gear). Though expensive, these trips have a good reputation. There are daily departures but reservations are essential, as they're usually booked solid months ahead—they're that popular.

Customized Itineraries

If you want the security of advance reservations but aren't interested in joining a regular packaged tour, there are several companies specializing in prebooking Blue Lagoon cruises, first-class hotel rooms, airport transfers, sightseeing tours, rental cars, etc. Their prices are competitive with what you'd pay on the spot, and they're sometimes cheaper.

One of the largest of such companies is **United Touring International**, with offices in the U.S. (400 Market St., Ste. 260, Philadelphia, PA 19106-2551, U.S.A.; tel. 215-923-8700),

Britain (71-75 Uxbridge Rd., Ealing Broadway, London, W5 5SL, England; tel. 081-566-1660), and Japan (Koyata Bldg., 3F, 2-5 Yotsuya 2-chome, Shinjuku-ku, Tokyo 160, Japan; tel. 03-355-2391). **Sprint Australia** offices in Australia (3rd Floor, 40 Miller St., North Sydney, NSW 2060, Australia; tel. 02-957-3811) and New Zealand (44-48 Emily Place, Auckland 1, New Zealand; tel. 09-797-105) are part of the same organization. United Touring also has an office in the arrival concourse at Nandi Airport open around-the-clock. They can put together any itinerary you may wish, but you must work through your regular travel agent as they don't deal directly with the public. Write or call for their *Travel Planner* brochure, which provides hundreds of specific prices.

Mitchell Odysseys (Box 61482, Denver, CO 80206, U.S.A.; tel. 303-399-3839) specializes in putting together custom-designed journeys for small special-interest groups wishing to escape the usual tourist track. If you've got six or more colleagues or friends interested in activities such as sailing, snorkeling, fishing, horseback riding, rafting, staying in villages, or trekking, give travel adviser Doug Mitchell a call. He can arrange everything beforehand for a standard "professional fee."

The Nandi Airport office of **Rosie Travel Service** (Box 9268, Nandi Airport; tel. 722-935) can arrange hotels, transfers, cruises, tours, etc., for you upon arrival in Fiji. They open at 0800. Rosie's bus tours from Nandi and all the Coral Coast hotels are much cheaper than those of other companies because lunch isn't included. Rosie's also has the **Thrifty Car Rental** franchise, with unlimited mileage rates beginning at F$105 a day, collision insurance, and tax included. There's a 300-km limit on one-day rentals. The fourth and seventh days are free and after a week the daily rate drops to F$75. As a bonus, Thrifty provides a book of discount coupons for reductions on hotel rooms and meals, and free admission to certain attractions. In Australia bookings can be made through Rosie Travel Service (East Towers, Ste. 505, 9 Bronte Rd., Bondi Junction, Sydney, NSW 2022, Australia; tel. 02-389-3666), in Canada through Goway Travel (2300 Yonge St., Toronto, ON M4P 1E4, Canada; tel. 416-322-1034). This locally owned business has provided efficient, personalized service since 1974.

GETTING AROUND

By Air

While international flights are focused on Nandi, Fiji's domestic air service radiates from Suva. **Fiji Air** (Box 1259, Suva; tel. 314-666) is the main domestic carrier, with flights a couple of times a week from Nausori Airport to such out-of-the-way islands as Kandavu (F$47), Koro (F$47), Lakemba (F$89), Moala (F$66), Ngau (F$40), Rambi (F$76), Rotuma (F$184), Thithia (F$86), and Vanua Mbalavu (F$89). More common destinations, such as Lambasa (F$61), Levuka (F$27), Nandi (F$52), Savusavu (F$56), and Taveuni (F$73), are served several times daily (all fares OW). Standby fares are F$27 to Kandavu, F$17 to Levuka, F$47 to Nandi, F$33 to Savusavu, and F$47 to Taveuni.

Fiji Air's **Fiji Islands Pass** allows you to fly from Suva to Kandavu, Levuka, Nandi,

Savusavu, and Taveuni and back anytime within 30 days for F$180. You can also use it to go Savusavu-Taveuni. Your initial flight is booked when you buy the ticket, but subsequent reservations can be made no earlier than 24 hours in advance, and as flights to Kandavu are only four times a week, it's best to begin with that leg. If the local agent on an outer island tells you all seats to Suva are booked solid days ahead, call up the Suva office and check. You must show your passport every time you use the pass.

Seven-day RT excursion tickets are about 20% less than full fare. If you're a full-time student aged 25 or under, inquire about the 25% student reductions, though you'll need a current International Student Identity Card (ISIC). Always reconfirm your return flight immediately

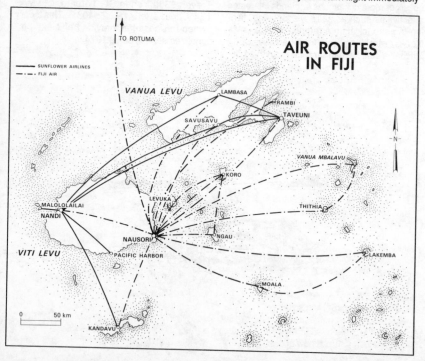

AIR ROUTES IN FIJI

SUNFLOWER AIRLINES
FIJI AIR

upon arrival at an outer island, as the reservation lists are sometimes not sent out from Suva. This is essential at Kandavu, where the local agent often gives Fijians priority over tourists. Fiji Air allows 15 kilograms of baggage only (overweight is about F$1 per kilogram). The service is reliable.

Sunflower Airlines (Box 9452, Nandi Airport; tel. 723-016) bases its domestic network in Nandi, with daily flights to Lambasa (F$82), Savusavu (F$82), and Taveuni (F$98). Kandavu (F$60) and Vatulele (F$48) are served from Nandi four times a week. Sunflower's seven-day RT excursion fare between Nandi and Lambasa is F$118. From Taveuni, Sunflower has flights to Savusavu (daily, F$38) and Lambasa (five a week, F$38). Unlike Fiji Air, Sunflower doesn't give standby fares to tourists. Flying in their 10-seat Britten Norman Islanders and Canadian-made Twin Otters is sort of fun. All flights are during daylight hours.

The busy little resort island of Malololailai gets eight flights a day by Sunflower Airlines (F$25), five by **Island Air** (Office Ste. 30, The Concourse, Nandi Airport, Nandi; tel. 722-371), and another four by Fiji Air. Sunflower's day excursion from Nandi to Malololailai is F$48 RT, lunch included. **Turtle Airways Ltd.** (Private Mail Bag, Nandi Airport, Nandi; tel. 722-988) flies their five Cessna floatplanes three times a day from Nandi to Castaway and Mana islands (F$70 OW, F$130 RT).

By Bus

Since most shipping operates out of Suva, passenger services by sea, both within Fiji and to neighboring countries, are listed in the "Suva" section, under "Transport."

Regular bus service is available all over Fiji, and fares are low. The most important routes are between Suva and Lautoka, the biggest cities. Fares from Suva are F$2 to Pacific Harbor, F$4.70 to Singatoka, F$6.80 to Nandi, F$7.10 to Nandi Airport, F$7.80 to Lautoka, and F$9 to Mba. To reserve a seat on a bus costs 50 cents extra. If you follow the southern route via Singatoka you'll be on Queen's Rd., the faster and smoother of the two. King's Rd. via Tavua is longer and can be rough and dusty, but you get to see a little of the interior. If you're from the States you'll be amazed how accessible, inex-

pensive, and convenient the service is. Local people are always happy to supply information about buses and to help you catch one. Right after the Rabuka coups buses were prohibited on Sun., but this is no longer the case and many services now operate daily.

Pacific Transport Ltd. (G.P.O. Box 1266, Suva; tel. 304-366) has nine buses a day along Queen's Rd., with expresses (five hours) leaving Suva for Lautoka at 0645, 0930, 1210, 1500, and 1730. These buses stop at Navua, Pacific Harbor, Singatoka (coffee break), Nandi, and Nandi Airport only. If you want off at a Coral Coast resort or some other smaller place, you must take one of the four local "stage" buses, which take 6½ hours to reach Lautoka via Queen's Road. The 1500 bus continues on to Mba.

Sunbeam Transport Ltd. (tel. 382-122) services the northern King's Rd. from Suva to Lautoka five times a day, with expresses (six hours) at 0645, 1330, and 1715. A Sunbeam express bus along King's Rd. is a comfortable way to see Viti Levu's picturesque backside. These expresses only stop at Nausori, Korovou, Vaikela, Tavua, and Mba. If you want off anywhere else you must take one of the two local buses, which take nine fun-filled hours to reach Lautoka via King's Road. Another local Sunbeam bus runs Suva-Vatukoula via Tavua daily (seven hours). **Reliance Transport** (tel. 382-296) also services King's Road.

There are many other local buses, especially closer to Suva or Lautoka. The a/c expresses cost twice as much and are not as much fun as the ordinary expresses, whose big open windows with roll-down canvas covers give you a panoramic view of Viti Levu. Bus service on Vanua Levu and Taveuni is also good. Local buses often show up late, but the long-distance buses are usually right on time. Bus stations are usually adjacent to local markets, though local buses will usually stop anywhere along their routes. Fares average about F$1.50 for each hour of travel.

Shared "running" taxis also shuttle back and forth between Suva, Nandi, and Lautoka, leaving when full and charging only a little more than the bus. Look for them in the markets around the bus stations. It's possible to hire a complete taxi from Nandi Airport to Suva for about F$50, with stops along the way for photos, resort visits, etc. Times are tough, and occasionally the drivers of private cars ask persons waiting at bus stops if they'd like a lift to Suva or Nandi for a bit more than bus fare. It's much faster than the bus, and they'll probably drop you off exactly where you want to go.

Passenger trucks serving as carriers charge set rates to and from interior villages. If you're hitching, be aware that truck drivers who give you a lift on the highway may expect the equivalent of bus fare; locals pay this without question.

Car Rentals

Car rental rates in Fiji are nearly double those charged in the U.S. (largely due to high import duties on vehicles) and a 10% tax is added. All of the large chains are represented, including Avis, Budget, Hertz, National, and Thrifty. Compare prices before you leave home by calling them up on their toll-free numbers. Local companies like Beta Rent-A-Car, Bula Rental Cars, Central Rent-A-Car, Dove and Cross Rentals, Dove Rent-A-Car, Khan's Rental Cars, Letz Rent-A-Car, Nandroga Car Hire, Roxy Rentals, Satellite Rentals, Sharmas Rental Cars, Sheik's Rent-A-Car, Skyline Rentals, and UTC Rent-A-Car are often cheaper, but check around as prices and service vary. The international companies rent only new cars, while the less expensive local companies may offer secondhand vehicles. If in doubt, check the vehicle carefully before driving off.

A dozen companies have offices in the concourse at Nandi Airport and three are also at Nausori Airport. Agencies with offices in Suva include Avis on Scott St. (tel. 313-833); Budget, 123 Forster Rd., Walu Bay (tel. 315-899); Central, 293 Victoria Parade (tel. 311-908); and Hertz, Ratu Mara Rd., Nambua (tel. 383-411). In Lautoka there's Budget, Marine Dr. (tel. 661-733); Central, 75 Vitongo Parade (tel. 664-511); and Dove and Cross, Queen's Rd. (tel. 664-959). Avis and Thrifty also have desks in many resort hotels on Viti Levu. On Vanua Levu, Avis is at Savusavu and Budget at Lambasa.

UTC Rent-A-Car and Avis allow you to drop the car off at any of their many offices on Viti Levu at no additional charge, while the others charge a F$30 delivery fee if you don't return the vehicle to the office where you rented it. By law third-party public liability insurance is compulsory for all vehicles and is included in the basic rate, with full collision/damage-waiver (CDW) insurance for about F$15 per day extra. Even with CDW, at Budget you're still responsible for the first F$500 in damage to the car, and at Central the first F$1500!

Both unlimited-kilometer and per-kilometer rates are available. On a per-kilometer basis, rates at Avis begin at F$43 a day plus 15 cents a km, F$15 CDW, and 10% tax. Thrifty asks F$27 a day, 27 cents a km, F$12 CDW, and 10% tax for the same. Budget has a weekend rate that gives you four days for the price of three, while UTC Rent-A-Car has the best unlimited-kilometer rates (from F$70 daily, F$420 weekly, plus F$10 a day CDW and 10% tax). Thrifty also offers good unlimited-kilometer prices (from F$105 daily, F$525 weekly) include CDW and tax. Ask about Thrifty's discount coupons that come with the car. Sharmas (tel. 701-055) advertises unlimited-kilometer rates of F$222 a week. Avis' unlimited-kilometer rates are only available for four days or more. Beware of companies like Central that list extremely low prices in their brochures, only mentioning in very small type at the bottom that these are the "off-season" rates (period not specified). Others, such as Budget, also advertise low prices with the qualification in tiny type below, that these apply only to four-day rentals. If you want the cheapest economy subcompact, reserve ahead.

Your home driver's license is recognized for your first six months in Fiji. Avis and Central won't rent to persons under age 25, while Budget and Thrifty will, so long as you're 21 or over. Most of the roads are atrocious (check the spare tire), with driving on the left-hand side (as in Britain and Japan), although Queen's Rd., which passes the Coral Coast resorts, is now completely paved from Lautoka to Suva, and there isn't a lot of traffic. If you plan to use a rental car to explore rough country roads in Viti Levu's mountainous interior, think twice before announcing your plans to the agency, as they may suddenly decline your business. The rental contracts all contain clauses stating that the insurance coverage is not valid under such conditions. Some companies offer four-wheel-drive Suzukis just made for mountain roads.

Speed limits are 50 kilometers an hour in

towns and 80 kilometers an hour on the highway. Pedestrians have the right of way at crosswalks. Unpaved roads can be very slippery, especially on inclines. Take care with local motorists, who sometimes stop in the middle of the road, pass on blind curves, and drive at high speeds. Driving at night can be a risky business. Seat belts must be worn in the front seat and the police are empowered to give roadside breath-analyzer tests. Tank up on Sat., as some gas stations are closed on Sunday. Small village stores sometimes sell fuel from drums, if you run out of gas in a rural area.

Taxis

Taxis are common within towns and relatively cheap, about F$3 for a short trip. If the cab doesn't have a meter, ask the fare first. Taxis returning to their stand after a trip will pick up passengers at bus stops and charge the regular bus fare (ask if it's the "returning fare"). Taxis are hard to find in Suva after dark or on Sun., though this is much less of a problem in Nandi/Lautoka.

Don't tip your driver; tips are neither expected nor necessary. Don't invite your driver for a drink or become overly familiar with him or he may abuse your trust. If you're a woman taking a cab alone in the Nandi area, don't let your driver think there is any "hope" for him, or you'll be in trouble.

OTHER TRAVEL OPTIONS

By Sailing Yacht

Hitch rides into the Pacific on yachts from California, New Zealand, and Australia, or around the yachting triangle Papeete-Suva-Honolulu. Check out the bulletin boards at yacht clubs and put up notices of your own. Meet people in the bars. Cruising yachts are recognizable by their foreign flags, wind-vane steering gear, sturdy appearance, and laundry hung out to dry. Rather than trying to find a yacht to the South Pacific, it's much easier to fly down and look for a boat already in the islands. After months of cruising, some of the original crew may have flown home or onward, opening a place for you.

The weather and seasons play a deciding role in any South Pacific trip by sailboat. You'll have to pull out of many beautiful places, or be unable to stop there, because of bad weather. Most important of all, be aware of the hurricane season: Nov. to March in the South Pacific. Few yachts will be cruising at this time. Also, know which way the winds are blowing; the prevailing tradewinds in the South Pacific are from the southeast, so you'll be able to travel westbound far more easily than eastbound. The South Pacific yachting "milk run" is from Tahiti to Vava'u or Suva in July, and from Fiji's Musket Cove Resort to Port Vila in September, then down to Australia or New Zealand in October.

Expense-sharing crew members pay US$50 a week or more per person. If you've never crewed before, it's better to try for a short passage the first time. Once at sea there's no way they'll turn around to take a seasick crew member back to port. Good captains evaluate crew on personality and attitude more than experience, so don't lie. Be honest and open when interviewing with a skipper—a deception will soon become apparent. It's also good to know what a captain's *really* like before you commit yourself to an isolated month with her/him. Once you're on a boat and part of the yachting enthusiast (yachtie) community, things are easy. If you've had a good trip, ask the captain to write you a letter of recommendation; it'll help you hitch another ride. The **Seven Seas Cruising Association** (521 South Andrews Ave., Ste. 10, Fort Lauderdale, FL 33301, U.S.A.; tel. 305-463-2431) is in touch with yachties all around the Pacific.

By Ocean Kayak

Ocean kayaking is experiencing a boom in Hawaii, but Fiji is still largely virgin territory. Virtually every island has a sheltered lagoon ready-made for the excitement of kayak touring, but this effortless new transportation mode hasn't yet arrived, so you can be a real independent 20th-century explorer! Many airlines accept folding kayaks as checked baggage at no charge.

Companies like **Long Beach Water Sports** (730 E. 4th St., Long Beach, CA 90802, U.S.A.; tel. 310-432-0187) sell inflatable one- or two-person sea kayaks for around US$1800, fully equipped. If you're new to the game, LBWS runs four-hour sea-kayaking classes (US$55) every Sat. morning and all-day advanced classes (US$80) every couple of months—a must for L.A. residents. They also rent kayaks by the day or week. Write for a free copy of their newsletter, *Paddle Strokes*.

Since 1977 **Baidarka Boats** (Box 6001, Sitka, AK 99835, U.S.A.; tel. 907-747-8996) has been a leading supplier of mail-order folding kayaks by Klepper and Nautiraid. **Aire** (Box 3412, Boise, ID 83703 U.S.A.; tel. 208-344-7506) makes the Sea Tiger self-bailing touring kayak, which weighs only 16 kilograms. Write these companies for their free catalogs.

For a better introduction to ocean kayaking than is possible here, check at your local public library for *Sea Kayaking, A Manual for Long-Distance Touring* by John Dowd (Seattle: University of Washington Press, 1981) or *Derek C. Hutchinson's Guide to Sea Kayaking* (Seattle: Basic Search Press, 1985). Noted author Paul Theroux toured the entire South Pacific by kayak, and his experiences are recounted in *The Happy Isles of Oceania: Paddling the Pacific* (London: Hamish Hamilton, 1992).

AIRPORTS

Nandi International Airport
Nandi International Airport (NAN) is between Lautoka and Nandi, 22 km south of the former and eight km north of the latter. There are frequent buses to these towns on the highway, just a short walk from the terminal. To catch a bus to Nandi (45 cents), cross the highway; those to Lautoka (90 cents) stop on the airport side. A taxi from the airport will be F$8 to downtown Nandi, F$20 to Lautoka. Most hotels around Nandi have their rates listed on a board inside the Customs area, so peruse the list while you're waiting for your baggage. The Fiji Visitors Bureau Office is to the left as you come out of Customs. They open for all international arrivals and can advise you on accommodations. Pick up some brochures, hotel lists, and the free tourist magazines.

There's a 24-hour ANZ Bank (50-cent commission) in the commercial arcade near the Visitors Bureau. Another bank is in the departure lounge. The airport restaurant serves good *kokonda*. Many travel agencies, car rental companies, and airline offices are also located in the arrivals arcade. The rent-a-car companies you'll find here are Avis, Budget, Bula, Central, Hertz, Khans, Letz, National, Roxy, Skyline, and Thrifty. The post office is across the road (ask). The luggage storage service in the departure terminal charges F$1 per bag per day. Most hotels around Nandi will store luggage. Check your change carefully if you buy anything at this airport, as the clerks might try to pass Australian and N.Z. coins off on you. Tourists probably do the same to them.

The airport never closes, so you can sleep on the benches on the departures side if you're leaving in the wee hours. Duty-free shops are found in both the departure lounge *and* the arrivals area near the baggage pickup. A departure tax of F$10 is payable on all international flights, but transit passengers connecting within 12 hours and children under the age of 16 are exempt.

Nausori Airport
Nausori Airport (SUV) is on the plain of the Rewa River delta, 23 km northeast of downtown Suva. The airport bus costs F$2 to the Air Pacific office in Suva (five times daily except Sun., 45 minutes). There's a local bus on the highway if you want to go to Nausori (35 cents). A taxi will run about F$4 to Nausori, F$15 to Suva, F$95 to Nandi Airport. Be very polite to the taxi drivers, but don't allow yourself to be hustled. Avis, Budget, and Hertz all have car rental offices in the terminal.

A lunch counter provides light snacks. The Bank of N.Z. counter opens Thurs. 1230-1400 only. There's the inevitable duty-free shop. You're not allowed to sleep overnight at this airport. The departure tax is F$10 on all international flights, but no tax is levied on domestic flights.

SALVATORE CASA

SOUTHWEST VITI LEVU
NANDI

Nandi (population 16,000), on the dry side of Fiji's largest island, offers a multitude of places to stay for incoming visitors landing at Nandi International Airport. A small airstrip existed at Nandi even before WW II, and after Pearl Harbor the Royal New Zealand Air Force began converting it into a fighter strip. Before long the U.S. military was there, building a major air base with paved runways for bombers and transport aircraft serving Australia and New Zealand. In the early 1960s Nandi Airport was expanded to take jet aircraft, and today the largest jumbo jets can land here. This activity has made Nandi what it is today.

All around Nandi are cane fields worked by the predominantly Indian population. In the nearby Mamanutha Group a string of sun-drenched Robinson Crusoe resorts soak up vacationers in search of a place to relax. Nandi town has a kilometer of concrete duty-free tourist shops with high-pressure sales staffs; mass-produced souvenirs are sold at the stalls behind the post office. Yet there's also a surprisingly colorful market (best on Sat. morning). It's a rather touristy town, so if you're not that exhausted after your transpacific flight you'd do better to head for Lautoka. Beware of the friendly handshake in Nandi, for you may find yourself buying something you neither care for nor desire.

Budget Accommodations In Town
Most of the hotels offer free transport from the airport. As you leave Customs you'll be besieged by a group of Indian men holding small wooden signs bearing the names of the hotels they represent. If you know which one you want, call out the name: if their driver is there, you'll get a free ride. If not, the **Fiji Visitors Bureau** (tel. 722-433) to the left will help you telephone them for a small fee. Don't be put off by the Indian hotel drivers at the airport, but question them about the rates and facilities before you let them drive you to their place. Add 10% tax to all prices quoted below.

There are several choices in the downtown area. The **Coconut Inn II** (Box 143, Nandi; tel.

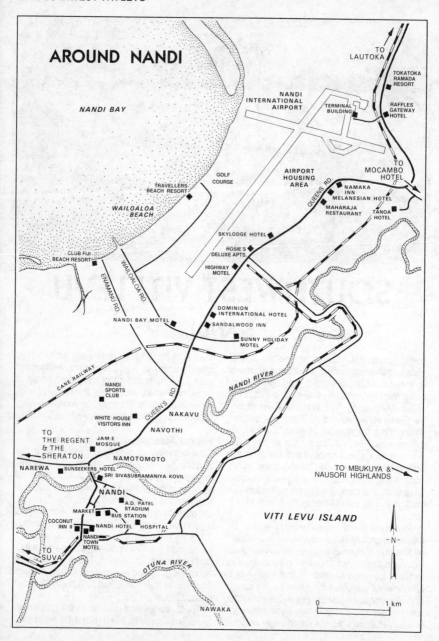

AROUND NANDI

NANDI BAY

TO LAUTOKA

TOKATOKA RAMADA RESORT

NANDI INTERNATIONAL AIRPORT

TERMINAL BUILDING

RAFFLES GATEWAY HOTEL

TO MOCAMBO HOTEL

GOLF COURSE

AIRPORT HOUSING AREA

QUEEN'S RD.

NAMAKA INN MELANESIAN HOTEL

MAHARAJA RESTAURANT

TANOA HOTEL

TRAVELLERS BEACH RESORT

WAILOALOA BEACH

SKYLODGE HOTEL

ROSIE'S DELUXE APTS.

CLUB FIJI BEACH RESORT

HIGHWAY MOTEL

ENAMANU RD.

WAILOALOA RD.

DOMINION INTERNATIONAL HOTEL

SANDALWOOD INN

NANDI BAY MOTEL

SUNNY HOLIDAY MOTEL

CANE RAILWAY

NANDI RIVER

NANDI SPORTS CLUB

QUEEN'S RD.

WHITE HOUSE VISITORS INN

NAKAVU

TO THE REGENT & THE SHERATON

NAVOTHI

JAM-E MOSQUE

NAMOTOMOTO

NAREWA

SUNSEEKERS HOTEL

SRI SIVASUBRAMANIYA KOVIL

TO MBUKUYA & NAUSORI HIGHLANDS

NANDI

A.D. PATEL STADIUM

MARKET

BUS STATION

COCONUT INN II

NANDI HOTEL

HOSPITAL

VITI LEVU ISLAND

TO SUVA

NANDI TOWN MOTEL

OTUNA RIVER

-N-

NAWAKA

0   1 km

701-011) is a two-story commercial hotel on Vunavou St. offering 17 a/c rooms upstairs with private bath beginning at F$35 s, d, or t, or F$7.50 for a dorm downstairs. Until recently this was the Fong Hing Hotel, but now the owners of Suva's famous Coconut Inn are making it a second Mecca for budget travelers, and prostitutes are no longer admitted. It's okay to go up and sit on the hotel roof.

Two other places have confusingly similar names and are located side-by-side but have separate managements. The **Nandi Town Motel** (Box 1326, Nandi; tel. 700-600) occupies the top floor of an office building opposite Khan's Service Station and looks rather basic at first glance, but the rooms are okay with fridge (broken?) and private bath. The price is F$18 s, F$22 d with fan, F$22 s, F$26 d with a/c, F$30 d with cooking facilities. The dormitory here is F$5 and basic rooms with shared bath are F$10 s, F$14 d. Their restaurant is not so cheap and the adjacent nightclub sends out a steady beat well into the morning. They arrange transport to Nananu-i-ra Island (F$21 pp).

Rates at the two-story **Nandi Hotel** (Box 91, Nandi; tel. 700-000), Koroivolu St., begin at F$25 s, F$30 d with fan, F$35 s, F$40 d with a/c, or F$9 pp in a dorm. The neat courtyard with a swimming pool out back and a variety of entertainment both at the hotel and nearby make this a pleasant, convenient place to stay. Nice people too, though some rooms are also subjected to nightclub noise.

The **Nandi Bridge Hotel** (Box 251, Nandi; tel. 700-019), on Main St. near the river on the north side of Nandi town, has 17 rooms with private bath at F$25 s, F$31 d with fan, F$28 s, F$40 d, F$49 t with a/c. There's also a F$6 dorm. Have a look at the room before accepting it. Their restaurant is open 24 hours a day, and on Tues. night there's Indian-style entertainment.

On Narewa Rd. at the north edge of Nandi is **Sunseekers Hotel** (Box 100, Nandi; tel. 700-400). The 20 rooms here are F$25 s, F$30 d without a/c, F$33 s, F$35 d with a/c, F$6 dorm (extra charge if you want a sheet, F$1 surcharge for one night, airport transfers F$3). There's a tiny pool out back and a cafe. It's a good place to meet other travelers, but it can be noisy.

The **White House Visitors Inn** (Box 174, Nandi; tel. 700-022), 40 Kennedy Ave. just off Queen's Rd., is a 10-minute walk north of central Nandi. The 12 rooms are F$20 d with shared bath, F$25 s, F$30 d with private bath, F$35 d with private cooking facilities, or F$8 pp in the dorm. Rooms with a/c are F$5 extra. This brand new hotel is a fairly peaceful place to stay, and there's a swimming pool, communal kitchen, video lounge, and free airport pickup. Baggage storage is F$1 per day.

Budget Airport Hotels
The budget hotel closest to the airport is **Kontiki Lodge** (Private Mail Bag, Nandi Airport; tel. 722-836), formerly Johal's Motel, set in cane fields a 15-minute walk in from the main highway, past the Mocambo Hotel. The 16 rooms go for F$15 s, F$20 s with private bath and fan, F$5 pp dormitory, or camp by the pleasant swimming pool. The motel lawns swarm with toads at night. Recommended, but avoid the noisy rooms near the active bar. Kontiki arranges daily transfers to Nananu-i-ra Island.

The **Namaka Inn** (Box 923, Nandi Airport; tel. 722-276), near the Maharaja Restaurant, has cheap rooms, but it's plain, noisy, and has little to recommend it except the low price. You might want to try a meal in the restaurant downstairs, however.

The **Melanesian Hotel** (Box 9242, Nandi Airport; tel. 722-438) has 16 rooms beginning at F$28 s, F$33 d, F$9 extra for a/c. A F$10 dorm is also available.

Also very basic is the **Highway Motel** (Box 9236, Nandi; tel. 723-761), formerly the Roadway Motel, F$20 s, F$25 d, all with private facilities. Rooms with a/c are F$5 more. The Highway partly makes up for the lack of a pool and bar by offering cooking facilities, a washing machine (F$1), and luggage storage.

The two-story **Sandalwood Inn** (John and Ana Birch, Box 9454, Nandi Airport; tel. 722-044), on Ragg St. just off Queen's Rd., is F$20 s, F$26 d, F$32 t for one of the five standard rooms with shared bath in the old wing, or F$26 s, F$32 d for the 20 rooms with fridge and private bath in the new wing (a/c rooms F$40 s, F$46 d). The cheaper rooms may be full. The layout is attractive with pool, bar, and a restaurant (authentic Fijian dishes!) where video movies are shown nightly after dinner. The Inn has a very good reputation—recommended.

Close by and less expensive is the nine-room **Sunny Holiday Motel** (Box 9335, Nandi Airport; tel. 722-844), 67 Northern Press Road. It's F$11 s, F$14 d, F$5 dorm (five beds), all with Continental breakfast included. Inveterate campers may like to know that this is about the only place around Nandi where you're able to unroll the tent. There's a pool table, games room, cooking facilities, and luggage storage. Show your YH card for a possible discount.

A few hundred meters down Wailoaloa Beach Rd., off the main highway and in the opposite direction from Sunny Holiday, is the 25-room **Nandi Bay Motel** (Box 1102, Nandi; tel. 723-599). Prices are F$25 s, F$35 d with fan, F$10 extra for private bath, F$20 extra for private bath and a/c, weight-watcher breakfast included. An apartment with cooking facilities is F$55 and there's also a F$10 dorm (20% discount on dormitory beds with a YH card). Coin-operated washing machines are available, plus a bar, restaurant, swimming pool, and luggage room. The roar of the jets on the adjacent runway can be jarring, yet the Nandi Bay is clean, comfortable, and good. Many "short-time" guests are seen discreetly coming and going weekends and evenings.

About the cheapest place to stay right on the beach is **Travellers Beach Resort** (Box 700, Nandi; tel. 723-322) on Wailoaloa Beach (also known as Newtown Beach) next to the seaplane base and golf club, three km from Nandi (take a taxi). The eight rooms with cooking facilities and private bath are F$25 s, F$30 d with fan, F$5 extra for a/c, or F$10 pp in a dorm. The restaurant/bar and pool make this a self-contained resort. Just 100 meters away is the **Newtown Beach Motel** (Box 787, Nandi; tel. 723-339), that charges F$25 s, F$30 d or t. A huge dinner is F$7. Similar is the new **Horizon Beach Resort** (Box 1401, Nandi; tel. 722-832) with 14 rooms at F$18 s, F$26 d with fan, F$27 s, F$30 d with a/c. Horizon's 10-bed dormitory is F$5 pp. One of these three aforementioned places is probably your best bet on the weekend.

Also on Wailoaloa Beach is **Club Fiji Beach Resort** (Box 9619, Nandi Airport; tel. 780-189). The 22 attractive thatched bungalows with veranda, private bath, solar hot water, and fridge are F$45 d (garden) or F$55 d (beach front). One bungalow has been converted into a four-bunk, eight-person dormitory at F$10 pp. The units have only tea- and coffee-making facilities (no cooking) but their restaurant serves a variety of dishes that are good when the cook resists the urge to put sugar in everything. The all-you-can-eat breakfast is F$5. Special evening events include the *lovo* on Wed., the *meke* on Fri., the Italian buffet on Sat., and the beach barbecue on Sunday. Club Fiji has a resident divemaster who charges F$70 for a two-tank dive or F$275 for a PADI scuba certification course. Horseback riding (F$10), sailing, water-skiing (F$15), and sailboarding are also available. Ask for their free bus at the airport. Recommended.

handicraft seller,
Nandi

DOUG HANKIN

Medium-priced Airport Hotels

The two-story **Raffles Gateway Hotel** (Box 9891, Nandi Airport; tel. 722-444) is just across the highway from the airport (easy walking distance). Its 93 a/c rooms begin at F$83 s, F$91 d, F$100 t. Happy hour in the Flight Deck Bar is 1800-1900 (half-price drinks) and there's disco dancing in the hotel restaurant Thurs., Fri., and Sat. after 2200—worth checking out if you're stuck in the terminal waiting for a flight.

The **Tokatoka Ramada Resort** (Box 9305, Nandi Airport; tel. 790-222), right next to the Raffles Gateway Hotel, caters to families by offering 70 villas with cooking facilities and videos for F$95 d and up. A supermarket and large swimming pool with water slide are on the premises.

Tanoa Hotel (Box 9211, Nandi Airport; tel. 722-300), one km from the airport, is on a hilltop overlooking the runway and surrounding countryside. In 1989 a kitchen fire gutted the 107-room hotel, and reconstruction work has been slow.

There are two good middle-priced choices between the airport and Nandi. The first is the **Skylodge Hotel** (Box 9222, Nandi Airport; tel. 722-200), four km from the airport. The Skylodge was constructed while Nandi Airport was being expanded to take jet aircraft in the early 1960s. The 56 a/c units begin at F$80 s, F$90 d. It's better to pay F$20 more and get a room with cooking facilities in one of the four-unit clusters, well-spaced among the greenery, rather than a smaller room in the main building or near the busy highway. If you're catching a flight in the middle of the night, you can get a room for "day use" until 2300 for half price. Pitch-and-putt golf, half-size tennis facilities, and a swimming pool are on the premises. Airport transfers are free.

Rosie's Deluxe Apartments (Box 9268, Nandi Airport; tel. 722-755) near the Skylodge offers new studio apartments that accommodate four at F$88, one-bedrooms for up to five at F$113, and two-bedrooms for up to eight at F$137.50. All eight units have cooking facilities and a private balcony. Rosie Travel Service at the airport arranges special car/apartment packages here (minimum stay four nights).

The **Dominion International Hotel** (Box 9178, Nandi Airport; tel. 722-255), a three-story building facing a pool, is near the Sandalwood Inn, halfway between the airport and town. The 85 a/c rooms with bright bedspreads and curtains are good values at F$77 s, F$82 d, F$87 t. Thrifty Car Rental has a desk in this hotel.

The two-story **New Westgate Hotel** (Box 10097, Nandi Airport; tel. 790-044), next to the Dominion International, has 62 rooms beginning at F$70 s, F$80 d with fan, or F$90 s, F$100 d with a/c. The F$40 d "budget rooms" are more like cement cells. A large swimming pool, restaurant, and Jessica's adult disco are on the premises. It's a good medium-priced choice for businesspeople.

Another new place to stay on Queen's Rd. is the **Rain Tree Resort** (Box 9043, Nandi Airport; tel. 790-088) between the New Westgate Hotel and Hamacho Japanese Restaurant. The 60 a/c rooms in this two-story complex go for F$65 s, F$75 d, F$85 t. Cooking facilities are not provided but there's a special curry dinner on Friday, a Fijian *lovo* on Saturday, and Chinese food on Sunday in the restaurant/bar on the premises. The Rain Tree also has a swimming pool in the courtyard.

Expensive Airport Hotels

A little inland from the Tanoa Hotel is the two-story **Nandi Travelodge Hotel** (Box 9203, Nandi Airport; tel. 790-277). The 114 a/c rooms are F$125 s or d, F$165 suite, and they also have a half-price day-use rate that gives you a room from noon until 2300 if you're leaving in the middle of the night (airport transfers free). Aside from the Indian curry buffet (F$20) offered some nights, the menu at Penny's Restaurant includes Fijian specialties. A swimming pool and lighted tennis courts are also on the grounds. Thrifty Car Rental has a desk here.

The **Fiji Mocambo Hotel** (Box 9195, Nandi Airport; tel. 722-000), a sprawling two-story hotel (near the Travelodge) two km inland from the airport, is the finest of the airport hotels. The 124 a/c rooms with patio or balcony begin at F$140 s, F$145 d. Secretarial services are arranged for businesspeople, and there's a par-27, nine-hole executive golf course (green fees F$10, clubs F$8) on the adjacent slope. Their much-touted French restaurant is reported to be overrated, so ask another guest about it before sitting down to a pricey meal. Alternatively, stick to the salads. Lots of in-house entertainment is laid on, including *mekes* four nights a week. The big event of the week is the Fijian firewalking Sat. at 1830, followed by a *lovo* feast and *meke* (F$32). A live band plays in the Vale Ni Marau Lounge every evening except Sunday.

Grande Luxe Beach Hotels

Nandi's two big international hotels, the **Regent** and the **Sheraton,** are on Ndenarau Beach opposite Yakuilau Island, seven km west of the bridge on the north side of Nandi town, a 15-minute drive from the airport. These are Nandi's only upmarket hotels right on the beach, though the gray sands can't compare with those on the Mamanutha Islands. Sidestepping the Waikiki syndrome, neither hotel is taller than the surrounding palms, though the manicured affluence has a Hawaiian, neighbor-island feel.

In mid-1988 the huge Japanese group Electronic and Industrial Enterprises (EIE) bought control of both the Regent and the Sheraton and plans eventually to build 618 villas, condominiums, a shopping center, a marina, and another four hotels here. In 1993 an 18-hole, par-72 championship golf course opened on the site of a former swamp adjacent to the Regent. Resort development here has deprived Fijians of free access to their traditional fishing grounds in this area.

The Regent of Fiji (Box 9081, Nandi Airport; tel. 780-000) is arguably Fiji's finest hotel. The 300 spacious a/c rooms in this sprawling se-

RICHARD GOODMAN

Grasping war clubs, Fijian men perform a meke.

ries of two-story clusters between golf course and beach begin at F$230 s or d. Facilities include an impressive lobby with shops to one side, a thatched pool bar you can swim right up to, and 10 lighted tennis courts. The Long Gallery at the Regent has some fine examples of contemporary Fijian art. A special event accompanies the buffet every night—notably firewalking and a *meke*. Yachties anchored offshore are not especially welcome at this hotel.

The Regent's neighbor, the **Sheraton-Fiji Resort** (Box 9761, Nandi Airport; tel. 701-777), has a more impersonal feel. Its 300 a/c rooms begin at F$295 s or d, including a buffet breakfast. This luxurious, $60 million, two-story hotel complex opened in 1987, complete with a 16-shop arcade and an 800-seat ballroom. Firewalking accompanies the barbecue and a *meke* goes with the *lovo* on certain nights (ask). Avis Rent-A-Car has a desk in each of the above hotels.

Food And Entertainment

Several places in Nandi town stand out. For Chinese and European food try **Poon's Restaurant** (tel. 700-896) upstairs, across from the Mobil service station on the main street on the north side of town. Poon's is recommended for its filling meals at reasonable prices, pleasant atmosphere, and friendly service. The **Jade Palace Restaurant** (tel. 701-011) on Vunavou St. serves a Chinese buffet smorgasbord (F$5.50) 1200-1400, while the **Curry Restaurant** (tel. 700-960) on Clay St. has a wide range of Indian dishes. The **Farmer's Cafe** (tel. 700-415) near the market is good and cheap.

Mama's Pizza Inn (tel. 700-221), 498 Queen's Rd., serves pizzas big enough for two or three people for F$8-11. The **Maharaja Restaurant** (tel. 722-962) out near the Skylodge Hotel is popular among flight crews who come for the good Indian curries. It's expensive but good.

For nightlife, ask about the barbecue and *meke* by the pool at the **Nandi Hotel** (tel. 700-000). The **Bamboo Palace Night Club** at the Nandi Hotel has a live band 2100-0100 on Thurs., Fri., and Sat. nights. Locals call it "the zoo." Near the airport the Tanoa and Mocambo hotels usually have live music after 2100 Tues.-Saturday.

During the sports season (Feb. to Nov.), see rugby or soccer on Sat. afternoon at the A.D. Patel Stadium, near the bus station. There are four movie houses in Nandi.

Activities

Many day cruises and bus tours that operate in the Nandi area are listed in the free tourist magazine *Fiji Magic*. Reservations can be made through hotel reception desks or at the travel agencies in the Nandi Airport arcade. Bus transfers to/from your hotel are included in the price, though some trips are arbitrarily canceled if not enough people sign up.

Rosie Travel Service (tel. 722-935) at Nandi Airport offers the cheapest "road tours" because lunch isn't included. Their day-trips to Pacific Harbor (F$40) and Suva (F$48) involve too much time on the bus, so instead go for the Singatoka Valley or Emperor Goldmines tours (each F$35). These trips only operate Mon.-Sat., but on Sun. Rosie offers a half-day drive to the Vunda Lookout and Lautoka for F$26 pp. Also ask about half-day bus tours to the Nausori Highlands, the easiest way to see this beautiful area.

A one-day cruise to the Mamanutha Group on the 30-meter schooner *Whale's Tale* (tel. 722-455) is F$125 pp, including Continental breakfast, lunch buffet, drinks, snorkeling, sailing, and sunset cocktails on the poop deck. This classic schooner, built at Suva in 1985 and now based at the Regent of Fiji, takes only 12 guests per trip, but they don't go every day, so check ahead.

The **Roaring Thunder Company** (Box 545, Nandi; tel. 780-029), Shop 2, 513 Queen's Rd., offers exciting whitewater rafting on the Mba River (F$70). The trips are restricted to those aged 15 to 45 (physically fit older persons can join by signing a liability disclaimer). Everybody gets wet.

For scuba diving call **South Sea Divers** (tel. 701-445) at Ndenarau Beach. **Tropical Divers** (Box 9063, Nandi; tel. 700-158) at the Sheraton offers scuba diving for F$81 one tank, F$106 two tanks, or F$478 for a PADI certification course.

Boat trips out to the surfing locales near Tavarua Island are organized by **Surf Fiji Pty. Ltd.** (tel. 780-322) in Nandi. After-hours call Stephen Turner at 722-744. Stephen also runs snorkeling trips.

The 18-hole, par-71 **Nandi Airport Golf Course** (tel. 722-148), between the airport runways and the sea, is said to be the toughest course in Fiji. Green fees are F$10 plus F$12 for clubs, though guests of the luxury hotels are admitted free. The course is reserved for competitions Thurs. afternoon and all day Sat., and it's closed on Sundays.

A Nandi company called **Peni's Waterfall Tours** charges F$140 for three nights of "real Fijian life" at Mbukuya, a mountain village in the Nausori Highlands. A Canadian reader wrote in complaining that instead of the promised *meke*, he was charged F$10 extra to see eight schoolchildren receive a dancing lesson; that scheduled visits to caves, a small waterfall, and a "promo chief" never occurred; that his group was charged F$20 pp extra for "river fishing," then left at the river with nothing to eat all day and given no chance to fish; that they were twice invited to sign guest books, then asked for donations to village or church "project funds"; that their meals deteriorated after Peni returned to Nandi, with the same food being served from one night to the next; and that sanitary conditions were low. In contrast, a German reader wrote that the food served on this trip was very good. Judge for yourself.

Transport

Turtle Airways (tel. 722-988) runs a quick seaplane shuttle to the offshore resorts for F$70 OW, F$130 RT (baggage limited to one 18-kilogram suitcase plus one carryon). Combined catamaran/seaplane trips to the resorts are F$90 RT. Scenic flights with Turtle are F$34 pp for 10 minutes, F$84 for 30 minutes (minimum of three persons).

If you're headed for the offshore resorts on Malololailai, Malolo, Castaway, or Mana islands, the 300-passenger catamaran *Island Express* of **South Seas Cruises** (Box 718, Nandi; tel. 722-988) departs Nandi's Regent Hotel twice daily at 0900 and 1330 (F$32 OW, F$56 RT). Interisland hops are F$20 each. A four-hour, four-island, nonstop roundtrip cruise on this 25-meter boat provides a fair glimpse of the lovely Mamanutha Group for F$29, or pay

F$54 for a day-trip to Mana Island (lunch included). Be prepared to wade on and off the boat. The same company operates day-trips to Plantation Resort on the two-masted schooner *Seaspray* (F$49 including lunch). The sunset cruise on the *Seaspray* is F$32 pp. Free bus pickups are made twice a day at most Nandi hotels.

Captain Cook Cruises (tel. 701-823) runs three-day cruises to the Yasawa Islands on the brigantine *Ra Marama* at F$299. You sleep in tents at night, the food is good with lots of fresh vegetables and salads, and the staff friendly and well organized. Your biggest disappointment will probably be that they have the diesel engine on all the time, and don't bother trying to use the sails (logical—they haven't got a clue how to sail).

Khan's Rental Cars (Box 299, Nandi; tel. 701-009), at the service station opposite the Nandi Town Motel and at the airport, has low, unlimited-mileage rates (from F$250 weekly), but ask about extra charges. With Khan's you *must* return the car to Nandi and cannot drop it off somewhere else. **Sheik's Rent-A-Car** (Box 9373, Nandi Airport; tel. 723-535), with an office just behind the Sandalwood Inn, is also very good on unlimited-mileage rentals, and they'll pick you up at the airport 24 hours a day if you call. **Thrifty Car Rental** (Box 9268, Nandi Airport; tel. 722-935) has competitive unlimited-mileage rates too, especially if you take the car for longer than three days. Look for the Rosie Travel Service office at Nandi Airport, which runs Thrifty.

You can bargain for fares with the collective taxis cruising the highway from the airport into Nandi. They'll usually take what you'd pay on a bus (45 cents), but ask first. Collective taxis take five passengers nonstop from Nandi to Suva in three hours for F$10 pp.

Pacific Transport (tel. 701-386) has express buses to Suva via Queen's Rd. at 0720, 0750, 0900, 1300, and 1820 daily (four-hour trip). The 0900 bus is the most convenient, as it begins its run at Nandi (the others all arrive from Lautoka). Four other "stage" buses also operate daily (five-hour trip). Nandi's bus station adjoining the market is an active place (except Sunday).

SOUTH OF NANDI

Momi Bay

On a hilltop overlooking Momi Bay, 28 km from Nandi, are two **British six-inch guns**, one named Queen Victoria (1900), the other Edward VIII (1901). Both were recycled from the Boer War and set up here in 1941 by the New Zealand army to defend the southern approach to Nandi Bay. Take a bus along the old highway to Momi, then walk three km west. The Nambilla village bus runs directly there from Nandi four times a day. The site is closed on Sunday.

Just a 10-minute stroll from the Momi Bay historical gun site is the **Surftrek Resort** (Box 9839, Nandi Airport; tel. 790-435), previously known as Trekkers, with dormitory accommodations for surfers at F$84 pp including all meals. Surftrek can arrange three-day camping tours to remote islands, but you'll need to bring your own tent. Day-trips for fishing, snorkeling, and surfing are also offered. It's spacious and located in an unspoiled rural setting, though the beach isn't that great.

Seashell Cove

Also on Momi Bay is **Seashell Cove Resort,** 37 km southwest of Nandi, (Box 9530, Nandi Airport; tel. 790-100). They have 28 duplex *mbures* with fans and cooking facilities at F$45 s, F$55 d, and clean rooms with shared bath in the lodge at F$35 s or d. There's no hot water. Larger units are available for families, and babysitters are provided. A big 25-bed dormitory is divided into five-bed compartments for F$15 pp, breakfast included (20% discount on the dorm rate with a YH card). Otherwise, pitch your own tent for F$6.50 per tent. Cooking facilities are not provided for campers or lodge or dormitory guests, and always eating at Seashell's restaurant can get expensive. Their coffee shop is open until midnight, with a pool table and table tennis. A small store is located at the entrance to the resort. Free baggage storage is available.

The beach here isn't exciting, but there's a swimming pool and day-trips to Natandola Beach (F$20 including lunch) and a deserted island (F$30), tennis (F$2 an hour), water-skiing, and volleyball (free). A *meke* (F$13) occurs Wed. and a Fijian feast (F$11) Sunday. If you're a **surfer** they'll take you to the Namotu Island breakers or Wilkes Passage for F$18.50 pp; otherwise consider the surfing possibilities around Momi Bay lighthouse. Scuba diving is F$60 (two tanks), and a PADI certification course is F$275. Airport transfers are F$6 pp. A public bus direct to Seashell Cove leaves Nandi bus station Mon.-Sat. at 0800, 1200, and 1545 (from Seashell to Nandi it leaves at 1215), and there's a good onward connection from the resort by public bus to Singatoka Mon.-Fri. at 0900. From the letters we get, opinions about Seashell are mixed.

Sonaisali Island Resort
This upmarket resort (Private Mail Bag, Nandi; tel. 790-411), which opened in June 1991, is located on a long, low island, just 300 meters off the coast of Viti Levu, in Momi Bay. The 32 a/c rooms in the main two-story building are F$190 s or d, and there are six thatched two-bedroom

mbures at F$245. The resort features a full-service marina, a swimming pool with a swim-up bar, and tennis courts.

Natandola Beach
The long, white, unspoiled sandy beach here has become popular for surfing and camping. You can camp on the beach, but campers and sunbathers should be aware that theft by locals is a daily occurrence and the police make no effort to stop it. It might be better to stay at Sanasana village by the river at the far south end of the beach. There's a store on the hill just before your final descent to Natandola. Development plans call for a 350-room hotel and golf course to be built on Natandola.

Get there on the bus to Sangasanga village, which leaves Nandi at 1630 (or catch one from Singatoka at 1130). You have to walk the last three km to the beach. Otherwise get off at the Maro School stop on the main highway and hitch 10 km to the beach. The sugar train passes close to Natandola, bringing day-trippers from the Coral Coast.

THE MAMANUTHA GROUP

The Mamanutha Group is a paradise of eye-popping reefs and sand-fringed isles shared by traditional Fijian villages and jet-age resorts. The white coral beaches and super snorkeling grounds attract visitors aplenty; boats and planes arrive constantly, bringing them in from nearby Nandi or Lautoka. These islands are in the lee of big Viti Levu, which means you'll get about as much sun here as anywhere in Fiji. Some of the South Pacific's best skin diving, surfing, game fishing, and yachting await you, and many nautical activities are included in the room prices. Dive spots include the Pinnacles, Sunflower Reef, Wilkes Passage, and Land of the Giants. As yet only a few have noticed the potential for ocean kayaking in this area. Unpack your folding kayak on the beach a short taxi ride from the airport, and you'll be in for some real adventure.

Malololailai Island

Malololailai or "Little Malolo," 22 km west of Nandi, is the first of the Mamanutha Group. It's a fair-sized island, eight km around (a nice walk). In 1860 an American sailor named Louis Armstrong bought Malololailai from the Fijians for one musket. In 1966 Dick Smith purchased it for many muskets. You can still be alone at the beaches on the far side of the island, but with two growing resorts, projects for a golf course and marina, and lots more time-share condominiums in the pipeline, it's in danger of becoming overdeveloped. An airstrip across the island's waist separates its two resorts; inland are rounded, grassy hills. At low tide you can wade to nearby **Malolo Island**, which is much bigger and has two Fijian villages. One of them, Solevu, is known to tourists as "shell village," for what the locals offer for sale.

Plantation Island Resort (Box 9176, Nandi Airport; tel. 722-333), on the southwest side of Malololailai, is one of the largest of the resorts off Nandi. The 110 rooms (beginning at F$135 s or d, meal plan F$50 pp extra) are divided between 67 individual *mbures*, big group or family *mbures*, and 43 a/c hotel rooms in a two-story building. In addition, three 12-bed dormitories are F$54 pp including meals. Unlike the better-known Beachcomber Island off Lautoka, this resort has **separate dormitories** for men, women, and couples (but no children). Plantation's excellent nightlife makes it a good place for the young or young-at-heart. Snorkeling gear, rowboats, and sailboarding are free, but boat trips cost extra. Coral viewing on Plantation's 30-passenger "yellow submarine" is F$26. **Captain Cook Cruises** (tel. 701-823) runs day cruises to Plantation from Nandi for F$49, including lunch.

Musket Cove Resort (Private Mail Bag, Nandi Airport; tel. 662-215), formerly known as Dick's Place and also on Malololailai Island, offers 24 fully-equipped *mbures* and six two-bedroom villas at F$180 s or d, F$250 for up to five. Unlike Plantation, at Musket Cove the units have small **kitchenettes,** which allow you to cook, and a well-stocked grocery store selling fresh fruit and vegetables is on the premises. There's also a bar and restaurant by the pool (meal package available). Entertainment is provided at the Thurs. night pig roast. Roundtrip airfare from Nandi Airport to Malololailai on Island Air is included for anyone who stays at least six nights.

Activities at Musket Cove—such as snorkeling, sailboarding, water-skiing, line fishing, and boat trips—are free for guests. Scuba diving with **Mamanutha Divers** is F$50 one tank, F$75 two tanks, or F$275 for the four-day PADI certification course, which begins every Wednesday. Certified divers can also rent tanks and other gear and organize their own beach diving for much less.

Malololailai is a favorite stopover for **cruising yachts.** Membership in the Musket Cove Yacht Club (F$1 for skippers, F$5 pp for crew) gets you water, clean showers, and half price at the weekly Fijian feast. The marked anchorage is protected and 15 meters deep, with good holding. Fuel and groceries are sold ashore. Several charter yachts, such as the schooner *La Violante*, are also based here. **Rainbow Yacht Charters** runs a sailing school at Musket Cove with two-day courses at F$195 pp (maximum of four persons). Shorter half-day (F$50) and one-day (F$75) "cruise 'n learn" sailing is also available.

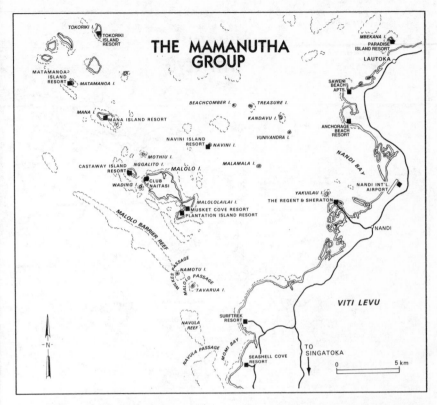

THE MAMANUTHA GROUP

In mid-Sept. there's a yacht regatta at Musket Cove, culminating in a yacht race from Fiji to Port Vila. Among the unique rules: the first yacht to arrive at Vila is disqualified unless it can be proven that blatant cheating occurred. The "race" is timed for the boats' annual departure east, prior to the onset of the hurricane season. It costs F$30 pp to enter the regatta, but for that you'll get feasts, parties, prizes, groceries, exemption from harbor fees at Port Vila, and more. If you're on a boat in Fiji at this time, Musket Cove is *the* place to be and if you're trying to hitch a ride as a crewmember you can't go wrong. Stories are even told of people being *paid* to serve as crew for the race! Most evenings at 1700 there's also a "cocktail-hour race" with four rum-punch-primed boats racing for prizes.

Malololailai's grass-and-gravel airstrip is the busiest one in the Mamanutha Group and serves as a distribution point for the other resorts. You can fly to Malololailai from Nandi (F$25 OW, F$32 same day return) eight times a day on Sunflower Airlines, five times a day on Island Air or Fiji Air. A same-day roundtrip by these airlines is F$32 without lunch, F$48 with lunch. Otherwise take the twice-daily 25-meter catamaran *Island Express* from Nandi's Regent Hotel for F$26 OW, F$46 RT (tel. 722-988 for free pickup).

Malolo Island

Club Naitasi (Box 10044, Nandi Airport; tel. 790-192) is at the western tip of Malolo Island, largest of the Mamanutha Group. The 28 one-bedroom bungalows with fan go for F$175 s or

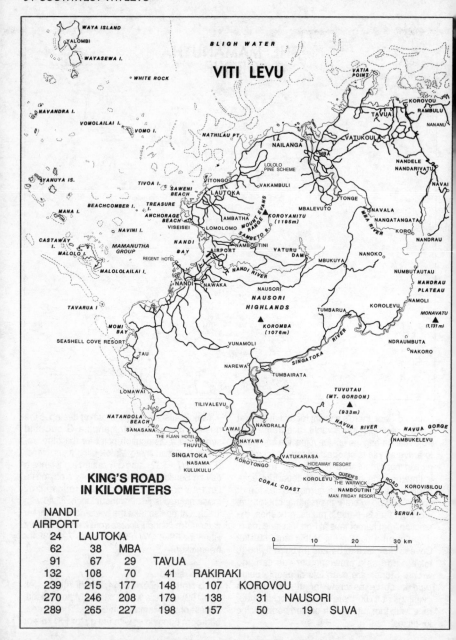

**KING'S ROAD
IN KILOMETERS**

NANDI AIRPORT								
24	LAUTOKA							
62	38	MBA						
91	67	29	TAVUA					
132	108	70	41	RAKIRAKI				
239	215	177	148	107	KOROVOU			
270	246	208	179	138	31	NAUSORI		
289	265	227	198	157	50	19	SUVA	

0   10   20   30 km

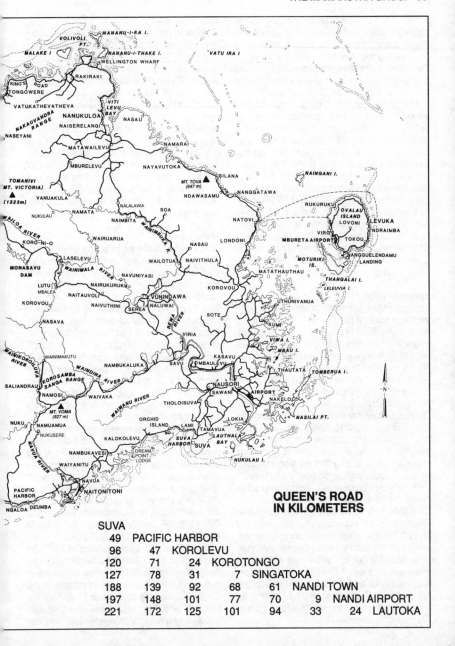

QUEEN'S ROAD IN KILOMETERS

SUVA							
49	PACIFIC HARBOR						
96	47	KOROLEVU					
120	71	24	KOROTONGO				
127	78	31	7	SINGATOKA			
188	139	92	68	61	NANDI TOWN		
197	148	101	77	70	9	NANDI AIRPORT	
221	172	125	101	94	33	24	LAUTOKA

d, the 10 two-bedroom family villas are F$295. Meals are extra, and while some breakfast groceries are available in the hotel boutique, it's best to bring your own food and make full use of the **cooking facilities** provided. The individual units are privately owned under a time-sharing scheme and each is decorated differently.

The compulsory F$30 pp club membership fee covers most nonmotorized water-sports activities; scuba diving with Aqua-Trek is extra. Club Naitasi staff will teach you how to sailboard, and this is the only resort offering parasailing on a regular basis. It also has a freshwater swimming pool. Get there on the twice-daily *Island Express* tourist boat from the Regent Hotel, Nandi, for F$28 OW, F$50 RT. The Turtle Airways seaplane from Nandi is F$70 OW, and there are also speedboats from Malololailai. No day-trippers are allowed at the club. Club Naitasi could be your choice if you're really into nautical activities or just want a quiet place to relax.

Tavarua Island

Tavarua Island, just south of Malololailai, operates as a **surfing** base camp (Dave Clark and Scott Funk, Box 1419, Nandi; tel. 723-513). There are both lefts and rights in Malolo Passage at Tavarua although the emphasis is usually on the lefts. When the swell is high enough you'll have some of the best surfing anywhere. On the off days you can get in some deep-sea fishing, sailboarding, snorkeling, or scuba diving. Only 15 surfers are allowed on the island at a time, and the US$100 s, US$115 d, US$175 t a day charge includes meals, accommodations, transfers from Nandi, and activities (three-day minimum stay). Nonsurfers are accommodated at half price, and couples get preference.

Bookings must be made through **Aquarius Tours** (18411 Crenshaw Blvd., #102, Torrance, CA 90504, U.S.A., tel. 805-683-6696). They're usually sold out, especially in June, July, and August. You can always try calling upon arrival, and they'll probably take you if vacancies have materialized. If not, or if you simply can't afford those prices, stay at **Seashell Cove Resort** south of Nandi and charter one of their boats out to Wilkes Passage or nearby Namotu Island. Registered guests are transferred out to Tavarua from Seashell Cove.

Castaway Island

Castaway Island Resort (Private Mail Bag, Nandi Airport; tel. 661-233), on Nggalito Island just west of Malolo and 15 km from Nandi, was erected in 1966 as Fiji's first outer-island resort. A small Fijian village shares the 80-hectare island. The 66 thatched *mbures* sleep four— F$232 and up (breakfast and dinner plan F$54 pp extra—no cooking facilities). Among the free water sports are water-skiing, sailboarding, canoeing, tennis, and snorkeling, but scuba diving and game fishing are extra. A daily catamaran departs from Nandi's Regent Hotel (F$28 OW, F$50 RT), and Turtle Airways has three seaplane flights a day from Nandi (F$70). Many Australian holidaymakers return to Castaway year after year.

Mana Island

Mana Island features beautiful white sandy beaches, crystal-clear waters, and a superb reef; topless and even nude sunbathing is said to be tolerated. **Mana Island Resort** (Box 610, Lautoka; tel. 661-455), northwest of Castaway and 32 km west of Lautoka, is popular with scuba divers. It's by far the largest of the resorts off Nandi, with 132 tin-roofed bungalows crowded together beneath the island's grassy, rounded hilltops. The rates (F$185 s or d, F$205 t) don't include meals at the three restaurants on Mana, and cooking facilities are not provided, so it's expensive (F$30 pp for breakfast and dinner only). Most of the guests are couples on all-inclusive package tours.

The price includes most nonmotorized water sports, though scuba diving and the five-day certification course are extra. There are two boat dives a day and night diving two or three times a week. Lots of other activities are offered, such as 45-minute semisubmersible rides (F$26 pp). The *Island Express* catamaran from the Regent Hotel, Nandi, calls twice a day (F$32 OW, F$56 RT), and Turtle Airways flies to Mana three times a day from Nandi (F$70).

Aqua-Trek offers scuba diving at Mana for F$50 (one tank) or F$250 for a six-dive package. Equipment rental is F$15 per dive. This is one of only two full PADI scuba diving centers in the South Pacific (the other is at Club Med on Moorea), and they run a great variety of dive courses, beginning with open-water certifica-

1. Waisomo Creek above Nasava, central Viti Levu (D. Stanley); 2. Maka Bay, Rotuma (Doug Hankin); 3. cane fields near Lautoka (D. Stanley); 4. cassava plantation, Mbukuya, Viti Levu (Don Pitcher); 5. female green iguana, Orchid Island, near Suva (Doug Hankin)

1. *mbure*, Viti Levu (Robert Kennington); **2.** house at Nasau, Koro I. (D. Stanley); **3.** pineapple fields, Viti Levu (D. Stanley); **4.** the chief's *mbure* at Nanggarawai on the Trans-Viti Levu Trek (D. Stanley); **5.** village on the Trans-Viti Levu Trek (D. Stanley)

tion for F$465. Divemaster Apisai Bati specializes in underwater shark feeding at a dive site called "Supermarket," just off Mana.

Matamanoa Island

Matamanoa Island Resort (Box 9729, Nandi Airport; tel. 660-511), to the northwest of Mana Island, has 26 a/c rooms for F$150 s or d, or F$260 for a *mbure* that sleeps four. Meals are extra (no cooking facilities). Matamanoa's rugged volcanic core gives it a certain character; and as if the tiny island's fine white beach and blue lagoon weren't enough, the resort also has a swimming pool and lighted tennis court. It's more expensive to reach because the launch transfers from Mana to Matamanoa (F$20 pp each way) are in addition to the catamaran from Nandi.

Tokoriki Island

Tokoriki Island Resort (Box 9729, Nandi Airport; tel. 661-999), 27 km due west of Lautoka, is the farthest offshore resort from Nandi. There are 19 *mbures* at F$260 for four adults and two children, and water sports such as water-skiing, sailboarding, and Hobie Cats are free. The resort faces west on a kilometer-long beach, and at the center of the island is a 94-meter-high hill offering good views of the Yasawa and Mamanutha groups. Tokoriki is under the same management as Matamanoa, and like Matamanoa, one must take the catamaran to Mana, then a launch to Tokoriki (F$30 pp each way). The regular launch to Matamanoa and Tokoriki leaves Mana at 1100 and 1600 daily.

Navini Island

Navini Island Resort (Box 9445, Nandi Airport; tel. 662-188), on a tiny coral islet between Malolo and Beachcomber islands, has 10 thatched *mbure* units with fan at F$170 s, F$190 d, F$213 t (meals extra—no cooking facilities). A 10% discount is available for stays over a week. At this smallest of Mamanutha resorts, everyone gets to know each other by dining at one long table. Boat transfers to Navini from Vunda Point near Lautoka are F$75 RT, the Turtle Airways seaplane from Nandi F$70 OW.

Beachcomber Island

Beachcomber Island (Box 364, Lautoka; tel. 661-500), or Tai Island as it used to be called, is 18 km west of Lautoka. This is Club Med at a fraction the price. The resort caters mostly to young Australians, and it's a good place to meet travelers of the opposite sex. You'll like the informal atmosphere and late-night parties: there's a sand-floor bar, dancing, and entertainment. The island is small. You can stroll around it in 10 minutes, but it has a white sandy beach and buildings nestled amongst coconut trees and tropical vegetation. A beautiful coral reef extends far out on all sides, though the scuba diving (F$48) here is nothing special. A full range of sporting activities are available at an additional charge (parasailing F$38, sailing F$28 an hour, water-skiing F$22, Jet Skis F$70 an hour).

Accommodations include all meals served buffet style. Most people opt for the big, open, coed dormitory where the 32 bunks cost F$57 each a night, but you can also get one of 27 thatched *mbures* with fan and private facilities for F$150 s, F$197 d. Prices include self-service meals. It lacks hot water, but in this heat, who needs it? Occasionally there's no cold water either, but this is rare. There's also the F$50 RT boat ride from Lautoka to consider, but that price includes lunch on departure day. You can make a day-trip to Beachcomber for the same price if you only want a few hours in the sun. There's a free shuttle bus from all Lautoka/Nandi hotels to the wharf; the connecting boat leaves daily at 1000 (1½ hours). Beachcomber is heavily booked, so reserve ahead at their Lautoka office or any travel agency.

Treasure Island Resort

Beachcomber's neighbor, **Treasure Island Resort,** (Box 364, Lautoka; tel. 661-500) caters to couples and families less interested in an intense singles' social scene. Instead of helping yourself at a buffet and eating at a long communal picnic table, regular meals are served in Treasure's restaurant (meal plan F$50 daily pp). Cooking facilities are not provided. The 68 units, each with three single beds (F$190 s, F$220 d), are contained in 34 functional duplex bungalows packed into the greenery behind the island's white sands. Some nautical activities—such as sailboarding, sailing, canoes, and spy board—that cost extra on Beachcomber, are free on Treasure. It's under the same management as Beachcomber, so guests take the same boat from Lautoka (which leaves daily at 1000) and are shuttled back to Treasure by speed-boat (F$46 RT). Unlike Beachcomber, however, Treasure doesn't get any day-trippers. There's no wharf here, so be prepared to wade ashore.

THE CORAL COAST

Shangri-La's Fijian Resort Hotel (Private Mail Bag, Nandi Airport; tel. 520-155) occupies all 40 hectares of Yanutha Island, connected to the main island by a causeway 10 km west of Singatoka and 61 km southeast of Nandi Airport. Built in the mid-1960s, this was Fiji's first large resort hotel. This 436-room complex of three-story Hawaiian-style buildings is still Fiji's largest hotel, catering to a trendy, high-rolling clientele. The a/c rooms begin at F$240 s or d, F$280 t, or F$660 for a deluxe beach *mbure*. Up to two children, 18 or under, stay free if sharing the parents' room. The Fijian offers a nine-hole golf course (par 31), five tennis courts, four restaurants and five bars, two swimming pools, and a white sandy beach. Weekly events include a *meke* on Tues. and Fri. and firewalking on Mon., Wed., and Fri. nights. Scuba diving is arranged by **Sea Sports Limited.** Avis Rent-A-Car has a desk in the Fijian.

A local attraction is the Fijian Princess, a restored narrow-gauge railway originally used to haul sugarcane, which runs 16-km day-trips from the Ka Levu Center (admission F$10), a mock-Fijian village opposite the Fijian Hotel, to Natandola Beach Mon.-Sat. at 0945. For information call the **Coral Coast Railway Co.** (Box 571, Singatoka; tel. 500-988). From the train station it's F$41 pp including a barbecue lunch, or F$55 pp including bus transfers from any Coral Coast hotel.

Singatoka

Singatoka town's setting is made picturesque by the long single-lane highway bridge crossing the Singatoka River here. You'll find the ubiquitous duty-free shops and a colorful local market (best on Sat.) with a large handicraft section. The town is the main center for the Coral Coast tourist district and the headquarters of Nandronga and Navosa Province.

Strangely, the traditional handmade **Fijian pottery** for which Singatoka is famous is not available here. Find it by asking in Nayawa

(where the clay originates), Yavulo, and Nasama villages near Singatoka. Better yet, take the two-hour **boat cruise** (F$16) up the river from Singatoka to Nakambuta and Lawai villages, where the pottery is displayed for sale.

Upriver from Singatoka is a wide valley known as Fiji's "salad bowl" for its rich market gardens by Fiji's second-largest river. Vegetables are grown on the west side of the valley, while the lands on the east bank are planted with sugarcane. Small trucks use the good dirt road up the west side of the river to take the produce to market, while a network of narrow-gauge railways collects the cane from the east side. You can drive right up the valley in a normal car.

The **Singatoka Hotel** (Box 35, Singatoka; tel. 500-000) is an older, commercial establishment not far from the center of town. The 18 rooms cost F$29 s, F$36 d, and there's a

LOUISE FOOTE

The original explorers of Oceania, the Polynesians, left distinctive lapita pottery, decorated in horizontal bands, scattered across the Pacific. Around 500 B.C. the art was lost and no more pottery was made in Polynesia. Melanesian pottery stems from a different tradition. This antique water pot was shaped and decorated by hand, as are those made in the Singatoka Valley today.

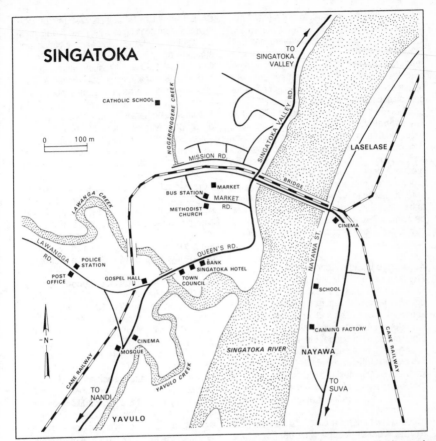

SINGATOKA

cramped six-person dormitory at F$9 pp, break-fast included (20% discount on dormitory accommodation upon presentation of a current YH card). A Chinese restaurant, open 24 hours a day, and a nightclub are on the premises. **Rattans Restaurant** (tel. 500-818) and **Reddy's Restaurant** (tel. 500-098), both on Market Rd., specialize in Indian dishes and sweets; nearby **Ching's Restaurant** (tel. 500-376) has Chinese food. Four banks have branches in Singatoka.

Kulukulu
Another favorite surfing beach is Kulukulu, five km south of Singatoka, where the Singatoka

River breaks through Viti Levu's fringing reef. Incredibly high **sand dunes** separate the cane fields from the shore. Winds sometimes uncover human bones from old burials, and potsherds lie scattered along the seashore—these fragments have been dated as far back as 2,000 years old. Giant sea turtles sometimes come ashore here to lay their eggs. Altogether a fascinating, evocative place, which unfortunately has received inadequate governmental protection. (Please show some sensitivity in the way you approach this unique environment.)

A group of American **surfers** have opened a base camp here called **Club Masa** (Box 710, Singatoka; no telephone). So far there's a dormitory cabin (F$9 pp), double cabin (F$20 pp), deluxe cabin (F$35), and camping area (F$6). Cooking facilities are available (bring food from Singatoka), or they'll prepare meals for you at reasonable rates. Have a beer in their nice, open lounge. There's plenty of firewood on the beach for evening bonfires. This is one of the only places for beach-break surfing on Viti Levu and boogie boards are for hire at F$5 a day. The **sailboarding** in this area is also fantastic, as you can either sail "flat water" across the river mouth or do "wave jumping" in the sea (all-sand bottom and big rollers with high wind). Be prepared, however, as these waters are treacherous for novices. About three buses a day run from Singatoka to Kulukulu village, but they tend to be unreliable. Taxi fare to Club Masa should be around F$4, and later you may only have to pay 50 cents for a seat in an empty taxi returning to Singatoka.

Korotongo Budget Accommodations

The south side of Viti Levu along the Queen's Rd. around Singatoka is known as the Coral Coast. The fringing reef here gives you the option of snorkeling at high tide or reefwalking at low tide. Most of the hotels are expensive, but there are several budget places to stay at Korotongo, eight km east of Singatoka.

Vakaviti Units and Cabins (Box 5, Singatoka; tel. 500-526), next to the Casablanca Beach Motel, has six motel units with cooking facilities at F$50 s, F$55 d. A four-person cabin is F$65. It's often full.

Just a few hundred meters east near the Reef Resort, **Waratah Lodge** (Box 86, Singatoka; tel. 500-278), has five very nice self-contained units—a good value at F$30 s, F$40 d. The swimming pool and charming management add to the allure.

Sandy Point Beach Cottages (Box 23, Singatoka; tel. 500-125), just east of the Reef Resort, has three fan-cooled double units with full cooking facilities at F$50 s, F$60 d or t, and one five-bed cottage at F$100. Set in spacious grounds right by the sea, Sandy Point has its own freshwater swimming pool. It's a good choice for families or small groups, but it's often full.

A kilometer farther east again is **Tumbakula Beach Cottages** (Box 2, Singatoka; tel. 500-097). Some of the 27 pleasant A-frame bungalows with fan, cooking facilities, and private bath are right on the beach, and each is capable of sleeping three or more (F$38). Their "Beach Club" consists of eight rooms, each with four beds at F$8 a bed. A communal kitchen is available, plus a swimming pool, games room, nightly videos, minimarket, and weekly *lovo* (F$8). The snorkeling here is good, there's surfing and diving nearby, and bus excursions are organized. Basically, Tumbakula is a quiet, do-your-own-thing kind of place for people who don't need lots of organized activities. Recommended.

One of the cheapest places to stay on the Coral Coast is **Korotongo Lodge** (Box 37, Singatoka; tel. 500-755). It has only five units, so you might call ahead (F$20 s or d, F$30 for a larger four-person family unit, or F$10 pp in the dorm). Cooking facilities and bicycle rentals are available and managers Ofa and Haroon Ali provide lots of special attention and information.

Korotongo Upmarket Accommodations

The Crow's Nest (Box 270, Singatoka; tel. 500-230) at Korotongo offers 18 split-level duplex bungalows with cooking facilities at F$82 s, F$110 d. The nautical touches in the excellent, moderately priced restaurant spill over into the rooms. Good views over the lagoon are obtained from the Crow's Nest's elevated perch.

The **Casablanca Beach Motel** (Box 164, Singatoka; tel. 500-766), next door to the Crow's Nest, is a pleasant two-story building on a hillside on the inland side of Queen's Road. Its eight a/c rooms with cooking facilities and arched balconies begin at F$70 s or d. A good pizzeria is on the premises.

The **Reef Resort** (Box 173, Singatoka; tel. 500-044), about a kilometer east of the Crow's Nest, is a three-story building facing right onto a white-sand beach. The 72 a/c rooms are F$130 for up to three persons, family suites F$150; most nonmotorized recreational activities are free. The hotel tennis courts, nine-hole, par-32 golf course, and horses are also available to outsiders at reasonable rates. Even if you're not staying there, check out the firewalking on Wed. and the Fijian dancing on Sat. night. Meals in the hotel restaurant are prepared to the taste of the mostly Australian clientele. Avis Rent-A-Car and Sea Sports Ltd. have desks in this hotel. Across the street from the resort is the **Kula Bird Park** (tel. 500-717), with a large collection of tropical birds (F$10 admission). It may be fun to visit this park, but the owners have displayed remarkable irresponsibility by importing highly undesirable species that could wreak ecological havoc if they escaped.

The **Tambua Sands Beach Resort** (Box 177, Singatoka; tel. 500-399), between Korotongo and Korolevu about 10 km east of the Reef Resort, has 23 beach bungalows at F$98 s or d, rooms in the back block at F$89 s or d (breakfast and dinner plan F$31 pp). Cooking facilities are not provided. There's live music most evenings and a *meke* on Fri. night. Thrifty Car Rental has a desk in this hotel.

Hideaway Resort

Most of the big Coral Coast hotels cater mostly to packaged tourists and the affluent. **Hideaway Resort** (Box 233, Singatoka; tel. 500-177), 20 km east of Singatoka near Korolevu, also makes itself available to young, budget travelers. Set on

Myriad snails crawl for the money at Hideaway's weekly mollusk marathon.

a palm-fringed beach before a verdant valley, the 42-room Hideaway offers everything the others offer, but also eight-bed, F$13-a-night dormitories (20% discount on the dormitory rate with a YH card). There's usually room for travelers who just happen to drop in, and if you're in a group, take one of the large *mbures* with fan suitable for up to six people (F$120), or smaller *mbures* for F$85 s or d.

Here's the catch: cooking your own food is not possible, the restaurant is expensive, and no grocery stores are to be found nearby. A F$40 pp meal plan is available, but only if you sign up for at least three nights. Even with the price of the meals, you'll still spend less at Hideaway than you would at Beachcomber Island. What Hideaway does offer is free live entertainment nightly, including a real *meke* on Tues. and Fri., Indian culture on Thurs., and an all-you-can-eat Fijian feast Sun. night. One of Fiji's best resort discos, Hernando's Hideaway, is on the premises, so this is a place to party! An afternoon excursion to a rainforest waterfall departs on Sat. at 1300. Surfing is possible in the pass here, and there's scuba diving with Sea Sports Limited. Avis Rent-A-Car is represented.

Korolevu Upmarket Accommodations

Korolevu is the heart of the Coral Coast hotel area. The family-oriented **Naviti Beach Resort** (Box 29, Korolevu; tel. 500-444), just west of Korolevu and 100 km from Nandi Airport, has 140 a/c rooms in its main two-story building beginning at F$175 s or d (meal plan F$47 pp). There's a *lovo* (F$18) on Friday night. Non-house guests may use the nine-hole golf course for F$7 (club rental F$1). Scuba diving is arranged by Sea Sports Ltd., but the hotel beach is rather poor.

The **Warwick Fiji** (Box 100, Korolevu; tel. 500-555), on the Queen's Rd. just east of Korolevu and 107 km from Nandi Airport, is the second-largest hotel on the Coral Coast (after the Fijian). Formerly the Hyatt Regency Hotel, it's under the same management as the Naviti and there's a shuttle bus between the two. The 250 a/c rooms in low-rise wings running east and west from the lobby begin at F$173 s or d, F$185 t, and rise to F$315 for a suite. There's live music in the Hibiscus Lounge nightly until 0100, disco dancing Sundays. This plush resort also offers a nine-hole golf course, a complete sports and fitness center, an excellent beach, an offshore artificial island, and scuba diving with Sea Sports Limited. Avis Rent-A-Car has a desk in the Warwick.

The **Man Friday Resort** (Box 20, Korolevu; tel. 500-185), right by the beach and six km off Queen's Rd. at Namboutini, is the most secluded place to stay on the Coral Coast. The 24 thatched *mbures* are F$75 s, F$80 d, F$85 t, with cooking facilities F$8 extra. The footprint-shaped, freshwater swimming pool alludes to Daniel Defoe's novel *Robinson Crusoe,* from which Man Friday takes its name.

Gaia Beach Resort (Box 109, Pacific Harbor; tel. 500-807), formerly known as Coral Village Resort, on the opposite side of Namanggu-manggua Village from Man Friday, has 12 modern bungalows at F$70 d in a one bedroom, F$90 d in a two bedroom, or F$14 pp in the dorm. There are no cooking facilities but many activities, including sailboarding, are free to bungalow guests. Gaia, a large property on a lovely beach, functions as a health resort dedicated to "permaculture," a system dedicated to earth-friendly agriculture and energy use. Special programs to help with weight loss and kicking the smoking habit are available.

Scuba Diving
Sea Sports Ltd. (Box 688, Singatoka; tel. 500-225) offers scuba diving from their dive shops at the Fijian and Warwick hotels. Their free red-and-blue minibus picks up clients at all other Coral Coast resorts just after 0700. They charge F$50 for one tank and F$85 for two tanks (both

on the same morning). Credit card payments are six percent more. Sea Sports runs PADI open-water certification courses and night dives are possible. Most dive sites are within 15 minutes of the resort jetties, so you won't waste much time commuting.

Getting Around
The easy way to get between the Coral Coast resorts and Nandi/Lautoka is on the a/c **Hyatt Express** shuttle bus, run by United Touring Company (UTC) (tel. 722-821). Every morning except Sun. at the bus departs the Warwick Hotel (0630), calling at Paradise Point (0635), Naviti Resort (0640), Reef Resort (0700), Fijian Hotel (0725), Nandi Hotel (0820), Regent Hotel (0830), Nandi Airport (0850), and Lautoka Wharf (0915). In the afternoon the return trip leaves Lautoka Wharf at 1715, reaching the Warwick at 2000. This bus connects with most day cruises to the Mamanutha Islands, and a full day at Mana Island, including bus, boat, and lunch, is F$74 (return from any Coral Coast hotel). Another UTC bus, the **Fiji Express**, departs the same hotels for Nandi Airport later in the morning. Fares from the Reef Resort run F$16 to the Regent Hotel or Nandi Airport, F$20 to Lautoka.

In the other direction the a/c **Queen's Coach** leaves the Fijian Hotel for Suva at 0910, the Warwick and Naviti Beach at 1030, and Pacific Harbor at 1115. The return trip departs Suva around 1700. Any of the above hotels will know about these services. Many less expensive, non-a/c buses pass on the highway, but make sure you're waiting somewhere they'll stop.

AROUND NAVUA

Deumba

The **Coral Coast Christian Camp** (Postal Agency, Pacific Harbor; tel. 450-178), 13 km west of Navua near Pacific Harbor, offers five-bed "Kozy Korner" cabins with a good communal kitchen and cold showers at F$10 s, F$18 d, F$24 t. The adjoining motel units go for F$18 s, F$30 d, F$38 t, complete with private bath, kitchen, fridge, and fan. Camping may be possible. A small grocery store is one km toward Pacific Harbor; for fruit and vegetables you must go to Navua. No alcoholic beverages or dancing are permitted on the premises; on Wed. and Sun. at 1930 you're invited to the Fellowship Meeting in the manager's flat. Recommended for an enjoyable weekend, but avoid arriving on Sunday. The Christian Camp and all the places listed below on the way to Suva are easily accessible on the fairly frequent Ngaloa bus from Suva market.

Pacific Harbor

Pacific Harbor is a misplaced Hawaiian condo development and instant-culture village, 152 km east of Nandi Airport and 44 km west of Suva. In July 1988 the Japanese corporation South Pacific Development purchased Pacific Harbor, and many of the 180 individual villas here are

a model of a fortified village at the Pacific Harbor Cultural Center

now owned by Australian or Hong Kong investors. The muggy Suva rain belt begins here.

There are three expensive hotels at Pacific Harbor, and **Sunflower Airlines** has direct flights from Nandi Airport (F$46). Pacific Harbor's beach here is unexciting, and the resort is best known for its 18-hole, par-72 championship **golf course** (tel. 450-048), designed by Robert Trent Jones Jr. and said to be the South Pacific's finest. It's Fiji's only fully sprinklered and irrigated golf course. Course records are 69 by Bobby Clampett of the U.S. (amateur) and 64 by Greg Norman of Australia (professional). Green fees are F$20 for hotel guests, F$50 for others, club rental F$15, an electric golf cart F$30. You'll find a restaurant and bar in the clubhouse.

Although golfing is the resort's main draw, **Beqa Divers** (tel. 361-088), a branch of Suva's Scubahire, is based at Pacific Harbor's marina and organizes diving on the nearby Mbengga Lagoon (F$115 with two tanks and lunch) daily at 0900.

The 84 a/c rooms at the **Pacific Harbor International Hotel** (Box 144, Pacific Harbor; tel. 450-022) are F$120 s, F$140 d, F$150 t. Equally plastic is the **Atholl Hotel** (Box 14, Pacific Harbor; tel. 450-100), right alongside the golf course itself, with 23 stuffy-plush rooms beginning at F$195 s, F$220 d. The advantage of the **Fiji Palms Beach Club Resort** (Box 6, Pacific Harbor; tel. 450-050) at Pacific Harbor is that the 14 two-bedroom apartments (F$135 s or d) have cooking facilities, which allows you to skip the many expensive restaurants in these hotels. Many of the units have been sold as part of a time-sharing scheme.

Pacific Harbor's **Cultural Center** (tel. 450-177) offers the chance to experience Fijian culture freeze-dried rather than fresh. This recreated Fijian village on a small "sacred island" is complete with natives attired in jungle garb and a 20-meter tall temple. Tourists see the island with a tour-guide "warrior" carrying a spear, from an hourly double-hulled *ndrua*. Crafts and village occupations such as canoe making, weaving, tapa, and pottery are demonstrated for the seated, canoe-bound tourists at various stops.

It's best to arrive with the tour buses in the early afternoon, as one-hour performances by the Dance Theater of Fiji (Mon., Wed., and Thurs.) or Fijian firewalking (Tues., Fri., and Sat.) begin at 1530. Admission is F$11 pp for the village tour (Mon.-Sat. 0930-1400), then another F$11 to see the dancing or firewalking, or F$20 for the village tour and a show. Packaged culture it may be, but it is informative. Entry to the Waikiki-style **Pacific Marketplace**, made up of mock-colonial boutiques and assorted historical displays, is free.

Navua

This untouristed river town is the center of a rice-growing delta area near the mouth of the Navua River and headquarters of Serua Province. **Heartbreak Hotel** (Box 87, Navua; tel. 460-310) occupies the building of the former Farmers Club by the river in the center of Navua, a hundred meters from the bus stand. The four rooms with shared bath and cooking facilities are good value at F$20 s, F$30 d. Manager Saimoni Ratu can arrange boat tours to both the highlands and Mbengga.

Village boats leave from the wharf beside Navua market for Mbengga Island (south of Viti Levu). Boats may leave any day, but more depart on Saturday. Also ask at Navua for village outboards that cruise 25 km up the Navua River to **Namuamua** on Thurs., Fri., and Sat. afternoons. The hour-long ride takes you between high canyon walls and over-boiling rapids with waterfalls on each side. Above Namuamua is the fabulous **Navua Gorge**, accessible only to intrepid river-runners in rubber rafts who fly in by helicopter. It's also possible to reach the river by road at Nambukelevu.

A great way to experience the picturesque lower Navua is with **Wilderness Tours** (Box 1398, Suva; tel. 386-498), which runs full-day canoe trips (F$49 pp) down the river. Their minibus collects participants at Suva hotels around 0800, then there's a scenic two-hour drive to the embarkation point, where the canoes will be waiting. A stop is made halfway down the river for swimming and a picnic lunch (included). The canoe trips are restricted to those aged 15-45, although physically fit older folk may join by signing a liability disclaimer. Everyone is welcome on Wilderness Tours' motorized boat trips (adults F$41, children F$25) up the river from Navua to Nukusere village, where lunch is taken and visitors get an introduction to Fijian culture. Bus pickups are at 0900 from Suva hotels, at 1000 from Pacific Harbor. These are probably the best day tours available in Fiji for the adventurous traveler.

Toward Suva

The **Ocean Pacific Club** (Box 3229, Lami; tel. 303-252), on a hillside between Navua and Suva, is an upmarket sportfishing camp with eight bungalows at F$170 s, F$190 d. Their nine-meter cruiser goes out for wahoo, mahimahi, giant trevally, yellowfin tuna, marlin, and sailfish each morning at 0830 (F$100 pp). Scuba diving is also offered here.

A much cheaper place to stay in the same area is **Dream Point Lodge** (Box 15406, Suva; tel. 304-834), near the South Pacific Bible College at Wainandoi, 20 km west of Suva. Follow the access road to the end, turn right and cross a causeway to the lodge. It's F$12 pp in double rooms or F$10 in the dorm.

DR. NIELSEN

The tortuous Navua River drains much of central Viti Levu.

Orchid Island Cultural Center (Box 1018, Suva; tel. 361-128), seven km northwest of Suva, offers a good synopsis of Fijian customs through demonstrations, dancing, and informative exhibits. Although the visit is invariably superficial and rushed, Orchid Island does afford a glimpse into traditions such as the kava ceremony, tapa and pottery making, etc., and the historical displays and miniature zoo are good. If a cruise ship is in port there may also be traditional dancing here. See and photograph Fiji's rare banded and crested iguanas up close. Replicas of a Fijian war canoe and thatched temple *(mbure kalou)* are on the grounds. Two-hour tours of the center are available every morning except Sun. around 1030, and the F\$20 pp cost includes transportation, admission, and entertainment (or F\$10 if you come by public bus and just show up at the gate). Bookings can be made through any travel agency in Suva. Though not as slick as Pacific Harbor's Cultural Center, Orchid Island has personal touches its counterpart lacks.

OFFSHORE ISLANDS

Vatulele Island

This small island, just south of Viti Levu, is famous for its tapa cloth. Vatulele reaches a height of only 34 meters on its north end; there are steep bluffs on the west coast, and gentle slopes on the east face a wide lagoon. Both passes into the lagoon are from its north end. Five different levels of erosion are visible on the cliffs as the uplifted limestone was undercut. There are rock paintings, but no one knows when they were executed.

Other unique features of Vatulele are the sacred **red prawns** found in a tidal pool in Korolamalama Cave near the island's rocky north coast. These scarlet prawns with remarkably long antennae are called *ura mbuta,* or cooked prawns, for their color. The red color probably comes from iron oxide in the limestone of their abode. It's strictly *tambu* to eat them or remove them from the pools. If one does, it will bring ill luck or even shipwreck. The story goes that long ago, a princess rejected a gift of cooked prawns from a suitor and threw them into the pools, where the boiled-red creatures were restored to life. Villagers can call the prawns by repeating a chant.

Village boats leave for the villages on the east side of Vatulele from the Naviti Beach Resort at Korolevu on Tues., Thurs., and Sat. mornings if the weather is good. Sunflower Airlines flies to Vatulele from Nandi four times a week (F\$48 OW). The island's small, private airstrip is near the villages, six km from Vatulele Island Resort (see below), to which tourists are transferred by bus.

In 1990 Vatulele got its own luxury resort, the **Vatulele Island Resort** (Box 9936, Nandi Airport; tel. 790-300) on Vatulele's west side. The 12 futuristic villas in a hybrid Fijian/New Mexico style sit about 50 meters apart on a magnificent white-sand beach facing a protected lagoon. As at Turtle Island in the Yasawas, the emphasis is on luxurious exclusivity. Villas cost F\$1000 d per day, including all meals—the most expensive lodging in Fiji. The minimum stay is five nights, and children under 12 are not accepted. Singles, triples, and children 12 and over are only admitted on a space-available basis. To preserve the natural environment motorized watersports are not offered, but there's lots to do, including sailing, snorkeling, sailboarding, paddling, tennis, and hiking, with guides and gear provided at no extra cost. Scuba diving is not available, however. This world-class resort is a creation of Australian TV producer Henry Crawford and local promoter Martin Livingston, a former manager of Turtle Island Resort in the Yasawas (after which this resort is closely modeled).

Mbengga Island

Mbengga is the home of the famous Fijian **firewalkers**; Rukua, Natheva, and Ndakuimbengga are firewalking villages. Nowadays, however, they perform only in the hotels on Viti Levu. At low tide you can walk the 27 km around the island: the road only goes from Waisomo to Ndakuni. Caves with ancient burials near Suliyanga can be reached on foot from Mbengga at low tide, but permission from the village chief is required to visit. Have your *sevu sevu* ready. Malumu Bay, between the two branches of the island, is thought to be a drowned crater. Climb Korolevu (439 meters), the highest peak, from Waisomo or Lalati.

Frigate Passage on the west side of the barrier reef is one of the best dive sites near Suva. A vigorous tide flows in and out of the passage, attracting large schools of fish; there are also large coral heads. **Sulfur Passage** on the east side of Mbengga is equally good.

The best beach is **Lawaki** to the west of Natheva. Present the village chief of Natheva with a nice bundle of *waka* if you want to camp. Kandavu Island is visible to the south of Mbengga.

The **Marlin Bay Resort** (Box 112, Deumba; tel. 304-042) opened in 1991 on a golden beach between Raviravi and Rukua villages on the west side of Mbengga. The 12 luxurious *mbures* (no cooking facilities) go for US$115 s, US$143 d, US$171 t. The meal plan is US$42 pp a day and boat transfers from Pacific Harbor are US$22 return. It's a favorite of scuba divers. Horseback riding is also available.

KANDAVU ISLAND

This big, 50-by-13-km island 100 km south of Suva is the fourth largest in Fiji. A mountainous, varied island with waterfalls plummeting from the rounded hilltops, Kandavu is outstanding for its vistas, beaches, and reefs. The three hilly sections of Kandavu are joined by two low isthmuses, with the sea biting so deeply into the island that on a map its shape resembles that of a wasp. Just northeast of the main island is the smaller Ono Island and the fabulous Astrolabe Reef, stretching halfway to Suva. The famous red-and-green Kandavu parrots may be seen and heard here.

In the 1870s steamers bound for New Zealand and Australia would call at the onetime whaling station at Ngaloa Harbor to pick up passengers and goods, and Kandavu was considered as a possible site for a new capital of Fiji. Instead Suva was chosen and Kandavu was left to lead its sleepy village life; only today is the outside world making a comeback with the arrival of roads, planes, and a handful of visitors.

Sights

The airstrip and wharf are each a 10-minute walk (in different directions) from the post office and hospital in the tiny government station of **Vunisea**, the largest of Kandavu's 60 Fijian villages. Vunisea is strategically located on a narrow, hilly isthmus where Ngaloa Harbor and Namalata Bay almost cut Kandavu in two.

The longest sandy beach on the island is at **Ndrue**, an hour's walk north from Vunisea. Another good beach is at **Muani** village, eight km south of Vunisea by road. Just two km south of the airstrip by road and a 10-minute hike inland is **Waikana Falls**. Cool spring water flows over a 10-meter-high rocky cliff between two deep pools, the perfect place for a refreshing swim on a hot day. A second falls six km east of Vunisea is even better.

The women of **Namuana** village, just west of the airstrip, can summon **giant turtles** up from the sea by singing traditional chants to the *vu* (ancestral spirits) Raunindalithe and Tinandi Thambonga. On a bluff 60 meters above the sea, the garlanded women begin their song, and in 15 minutes a large turtle will appear. This turtle, and sometimes its mates, will swim slowly up and down the shore just below the overhanging rocks. The calling of turtles is performed very rarely these days, but tour groups may be able to arrange it for a charge of F$400 (no photos allowed).

Hiking

Hike over the mountains from Namuana to **Tavuki** village, seat of the Tui Tavuki, paramount chief of Kandavu. A couple of hours beyond is the **Yawe** area, where large pine tracts are being established. In the villages of Nalotu, Yakita, and Nanggalotu at Yawe, traditional Fijian **pottery** is still made. Without a potter's wheel or kiln, the women shape the pots with a paddle and fire them in an open fire. Sap from the mangroves provides a glaze.

Carry on from Yawe to **Lomati** village, where

you'll begin the ascent of **Nambukelevu** (838 meters). There's no trail—you'll need a guide to help you hack a way. The abrupt cone of Nambukelevu (Mt. Washington) dominates the west end of Kandavu and renders hiking around the cape too arduous. Petrels nest in holes on the north side of the mountain.

There's **surfing** off Nambukelevuira village at the island's west point, but you'll need a boat. It's strongly suggested that you present a *sevu sevu* to the village chief before engaging in this activity. Unfortunately, the villagers have become rather hostile to stray tourists who turn up unannounced and pay no heed to local customs.

Cut south from Lomati to **Ndavinggele** village, where another trail leads east along the coast to **Mburelevu**, end of the road from the

airstrip. This whole loop can be done in three days without difficulty, but take food and be prepared to sleep rough. Mr. Sorovi on **Matanuku** off the south coast of Kandavu can arrange for you to stay on his island. To hire a boat from Muani to Matanuku is F$20

The Great Astrolabe Reef
The Great Astrolabe Reef stretches unbroken for 30 km along the east side of the small islands north of Kandavu. One km wide, the reef is unbelievably rich in coral and marinelife; because it's so far from shore, it still hasn't been fished out. The reef surrounds a lagoon containing 10 islands, the largest of which is Ono. The reef was named by French explorer Dumont d'Urville, who almost lost his ship, the *Astrolabe,* here in 1827.

There are frequent openings on the west side of the reef and the lagoon is never over 10 fathoms deep, which makes it a favorite of scuba divers and yachtspeople. The Astrolabe also features a vertical drop-off of 10 meters on the inside and 1,800 meters on the outside, with visibility of about 75 meters. The underwater caves and walls here must be seen to be believed.

The configuration of the Astrolabe Reef confirms Darwin's Theory of Atoll Formation. The famous formulator of the theory of evolution surmised that atolls form as high volcanic islands subside into lagoons. The original island's fringing reef grows into a barrier reef as the volcanic portion sinks. When the last volcanic material finally disappears below sea level, the coral ring of the reef/atoll remains to indicate how big the island once was. Of course, this takes place over millions of years, but deep down below any coral atoll is the old volcanic core. Darwin's theory is well illustrated here, where Ono and the small volcanic islands to the north remain inside the Astrolabe Reef. Return in 25 million years and all you'll find will be the reef itself.

Accommodations Near Vunisea
Reece's Place (Box 6, Vunisea, Kandavu; tel. 315-703), on tiny Ngaloa Island just off the northwest corner of Kandavu, was the first to accommodate visitors to Kandavu, though Joe Reece has now turned the operation over to his son Humphrey. It's a one-km walk from the airstrip to the dock at Vunisea station; the launch ride to Ngaloa costs F$6 pp each way. There are eight beds (F$12 pp) in four Fijian *mbures,* a F$9 dormitory, or pitch your tent for F$4 pp. Three mediocre meals cost F$24 pp, and unless you have a camp stove, cooking your own food is not possible. Don't show up late for a meal or there may not be anything left. The electricity is on 1800-2100 only.

The view of Ngaloa Harbor from Reece's Place is excellent, and there's a long, dark beach a 10-minute walk away, but the snorkeling in the murky water is only fair. For F$5-10 pp (minimum of four), Humphrey will arrange for someone to take you to the Ngaloa Barrier Reef, where the snorkeling is vastly superior. Scuba diving (F$50 one tank, F$75 two tanks) and

an early 19th century print of the southwest end of Kandavu Island

M.G.L. DOMENY DE RIENZI

even PADI certification courses (F$295) are offered by Humphrey's slightly chaotic company **Sun and Sea Dive**. The feedback we get from readers about this company is extremely contradictory: some claim the instructors are rather careless, while others say Kiwi divemasters Dennis and Kevin are super. We suggest you check with other travelers who've been to Reece's Place recently for current information.

A more upmarket operation is **Matana Resort** (Box 8, Vunisea, Kandavu; tel. 311-780), at Ndrue six km north of Vunisea. The four "budget rooms" with shared bath in the beachfront *mbure* are F$95 s, F$180 d; an attractive thatched *mbure* with private bath will run F$150 s, F$210 d on the hillside, F$180 s, F$240 d, F$255 t on the beach. Prices include all meals. Airport transfers by boat are F$6 pp. Matana caters mostly to a younger crowd that arrives on scuba tours booked from abroad to dive with **Dive Kandavu**. It's F$45 per boat dive to visit sites such as Yellow Wall, Crystal Crypt, Evil Trench, Blue Tang, Butterfly Bommie, Rainbow Tango, Tessa's Reef, Tavuki Trench, Featherstar Bazaar, Crazee Maze, Big Boy, Yellow Mellow, and several dozen other sites. The snorkeling off their white-sand beach is good and the fantastic Namalata Reef is straight out from the resort. Their open-water certification course is F$375. In Australia bookings for Matana Resort can be made through Bob Forster, G.P.O. Box 4900, Sydney, NSW 2001 (tel. 612-281-4155).

A kilometer or two beyond Matana is **Muaindule Paradise Point Resort** (tel. 383-617) at Ndrue village. The single dormitory-style *mbure* accommodates six people at F$40 pp, local meals included. Camping is F$15 pp with use of the cooking facilities. They're not always at the airstrip when the flights arrive, but information is available from Vo Niumatesere, who has a shop at Ndrue. Diving is available with Dive Kandavu Mon.-Sat. at 0930 and 1430.

Accommodations On North Kandavu
Albert's Place (Albert O'Connor, c/o P.O. Naletha, Kandavu; tel. 302-896), formerly Plantation Hideaway, at Langalevu at the east end of Kandavu, is similar to Reece's Place but more remote, more laid-back, and far less crowded. Each of the 10 *mbures* has a double and a single bed, coconut mats on the floor, and a

kerosene lamp for light. Accommodations are F$12 pp (share twin); camping is F$3.50 pp. The units share rustic flush toilets and cold showers with plenty of running water, and everything is kept fairly clean. Mosquito nets and coils are supplied.

Meals are another F$18 pp for all three, but Ruth O'Connor serves huge portions so breakfast and dinner (F$12) should suffice. Ruth's meals are exceptional, consisting of fish dishes with root vegetables, and she bakes her own bread daily. Campers used to be expected to bring all their own food with them, but this policy seems to have changed recently and there are now no cooking facilities for campers (ask about this if you ring up). Freddy's store nearby sells cabin crackers, eggs, rice, fresh fruit, and vegetables from his garden. There are several lovely waterfalls nearby where you can swim, and in the evening everybody sits around the kava bowl and swaps stories. As there are never more than 20 guests here at a time, it gets very chummy. The snorkeling right off Albert's beach is excellent and the Nukubalavu Dive Center (see below) picks up scuba divers and snorkelers here. Ocean kayaks are for rent at F$20 a half day, scuba gear F$15 a day, snorkeling gear F$5 a day.

You can get to Albert's on the weekly boat (F$30 OW) from Princes Wharf (ask for the *Princess Ashika, Sinikaloni, Adi Lau, Gurawa,* or *L. Tui*). The largest and most comfortable boat is the *Princess Ashika,* which leaves Suva Thurs. at midnight and stops at Kavala Bay every other week (weekly to Vunisea), a good hour west of Albert's on foot. Albert will pick you up at Vunisea Airport for F$50 each way for two persons, F$23 pp for three or more, for a two-hour boat ride (these prices are fixed, so don't bother bargaining). Be sure to let him know you're coming. It's best to allow plenty of time coming and going, so plan a stay at Albert's Place early on in your visit to Fiji so you don't have to be in a big rush to leave. People rave about this property, and it's highly recommended; just don't expect luxuries like electricity at those prices!

Orisi Qalomaiwasa's **Nukubalavu Adventure Resort** (Box 228, Suva; tel. 520-089), on a two-km stretch of white sandy beach on the north side of Kandavu between Albert's and

Kavala Bay, offers dorm beds at F$6 and shared *mbure* accommodations for F$12 pp. Camping is possible and local meals are prepared. The main attraction is the scuba diving with the resort's **Nukubalavu Dive Center**, also called Naiqoro Divers. This costs F$35 for a boat dive (F$65 for two tanks), F$20 for a shore dive, and F$5 for a snorkeling trip (minimum of four, no trips on Sundays). Naiqoro also runs five-day PADI open-water scuba certification courses (both here and at Albert's) for F$275—a great opportunity to learn how to dive! The gorgeous Great Astrolabe Reef (fantastic 75-meter visibility) is only a five-minute boat ride away and there's trekking up to waterfalls through dense rainforest. Orisi takes his launch to Vunisea fairly often (F$30 pp each way) or come on Whippy's boat (see below), which will drop you directly at the resort.

Accommodations On Ono

Kenia Resort (c/o P.O. Vambea, Ono, Kandavu; tel. 313-964 and ask for Lela), on the south side of Ono Island across the channel from Albert's, offers accommodation in traditional *mbures* for F$40 including local meals (camping F$3.50 pp). It's a small, family-style resort with a good beach and snorkeling, but no shopping possibilities exist here. The small local cargo boats *Tai Kambara* (tel. 312-668), *Tathake* (tel. 313-928), and *Gurawa* (tel. 321-426) arrive weekly from Suva (F$20).

Kini's Mbure Resort (John Flatt, c/o P.O. Nanggara, Ono, Kandavu; tel. 302-689), on the north side of Ono, offers accommodations in seven thatched *mbures* for F$55 pp (double occupancy) including Fiji-style meals. Lighting is by kerosene lamp, and the cold showers are in a separate building. The real attraction here is scuba diving with **Astrolabe Divers** (F$50, F$70 for a night dive), based right on the premises. Open-water scuba certification courses are offered at F$350; a one-tank resort course is F$75. Speedboat transfers from Vunisea airstrip (each way) are F$60 for one or two persons, F$30 pp for each additional person; in bad weather it can be a rough, wet trip.

Practicalities

There are no restaurants at Vunisea, but a coffee shop at the airstrip opens mornings, and two general stores sell canned goods. A lady at the market serves tea and scones Tues.-Saturday. Buy *waka* at the co-op store for formal presentations to village hosts. Occasional carriers ply the roads of Kandavu (about F$2 pp), but no buses. No banks are to be found on Kandavu either, so change enough money before coming.

Getting There

The easy way to arrive is on **Fiji Air** from Suva (F$47), four flights a week (air passes accepted). **Sunflower Airlines** flies Nandi-Kandavu four

Shoppers from outlying villages headed for Kandavu's market land on this beach near Vunisea. The hiking trails of Kandavu vie with untouched beaches such as this one in "downtown" Vunisea.

DAVID STANLEY

times a week (F$60 OW). The agent at Kandavu watches closely for overweight baggage and sometimes oversells seats on the plane, in which case the locals get priority. Be sure to reconfirm your return flight immediately upon arrival. Only Reece's Place meets all flights—pickups by the resorts on north Kandavu and Ono must be prearranged.

Boats arrive at Vunisea from Suva (F$30 OW) about twice a week, calling at villages along the north coast. The **Patterson Bros.** ferry *Princess Ashika* departs Suva's Narain's Wharf at Walu Bay every Thurs. night at midnight (F$30), returning to Suva on Friday morning. This ship gets crowded so arrive early. Also ask about **Whippy's** boat (tel. 340-015), which leaves Suva for Ono and northern Kandavu Tues. and Fri. at 0700 (F$37 pp).

SALVATORE CASA

SUVA

The pulsing heart of the South Pacific, Suva is the most cosmopolitan city in Oceania. The harbor is always jammed with ships bringing goods and passengers from far and wide. Busloads of commuters and enthusiastic visitors constantly stream into the busy market bus station nearby. In the business center are Indian women in saris, large sturdy chocolate-skinned Fijians, Australians and New Zealanders in shorts and knee socks, and wavy-haired Polynesians from Rotuma and Tonga.

Suva squats on a hilly peninsula between Lauthala Bay and Suva Harbor in the southeast corner of Viti Levu. The verdant northern and western mountains catch the southeastern trades, producing damp conditions year-round. Visitors sporting a sunburn from Fiji's western sunbelt resorts may appreciate Suva's warm tropical rains. In 1870 the Polynesia Company sent Australian settlers to camp along mosquito-infested Numbukalou Creek on land obtained from High Chief Cakobau. When efforts to grow sugarcane here failed, the company convinced the British to move their headquarters—since 1882 Suva has been the capital of Fiji.

Today this exciting multiracial city of 175,000—a fifth of Fiji's population—is also about the only place in Fiji where you'll see a building taller than a palm tree. High-rise office buildings and hotels overlook the compact downtown area. The British left behind imposing colonial buildings, wide avenues, and manicured parks as evidence of their rule. The Fiji School of Medicine, the University of the South Pacific, the Fiji Institute of Technology, the Pacific Theological College, and the headquarters of many regional organizations have been established here. In addition, the city offers some of the best nightlife between Kings Cross (Sydney) and North Beach (San Francisco), plus shopping, sightseeing, and many good-value places to stay and eat.

Keep in mind that on Sunday all shops are closed, restaurants keep reduced hours, and far fewer taxis or buses operate. It's smart to clear out of Suva for the weekend, though if you do find yourself there, the fantastic choral singing makes it worth dressing up and attending church. Most churches have services in English, but none compare with the Fijian service at 1000 at the Centenary Methodist Church on Stewart Street.

The lovely *Isa Lei*, a Fijian song of farewell, tells of a youth whose love sails off and leaves him alone in Suva, smitten with longing.

SIGHTS

South Suva

The most beautiful section of the city is the area around **Albert Park**. On 6 June 1928 aviator Charles Kingsford Smith landed his trimotor Fokker VII-3M in the middle of this park after arriving from Hawaii on the first-ever flight from California to Australia. (The first commercial flight to Fiji was a Pan Am flying boat, which landed in Suva Harbor in Oct. 1941.) To the north, the sinister, heavy lines of the **Government Buildings** (1939) reflect the tensions rampant in Europe at the time of construction. It was here that Col. Sitiveni Rabuka carried out his assault on parliament on 14 May 1987. During the following five years Fiji had no representative government, and the actual chamber where the elected members were arrested was demolished in 1988. Statues of Chief Cakobau and Ratu Sir Lala Sukuna stand outside. To the west is the elegant, Edwardian-style **Grand Pacific Hotel** (1914), dating from an earlier, more confident era; savor the interior for a taste of the old British *raj.*

South of Albert Park are the fine **Thurston Botanical Gardens**, opened in 1913, where tropical flowers such as cannas and plumbagos blossom. The original Fijian village of Suva once stood on this site. On the grounds of the gardens is the **Fiji Museum** (tel. 315-944), founded in 1904 and the oldest in the South Pacific. Small but full, this museum is renowned for its maritime displays: canoes, outriggers, the rudder from HMS *Bounty,* and *ndrua* steering oars that were manned by four Fijians. The collection of Fijian war clubs is outstanding. The history section is being greatly expanded as artifacts in overseas collections are returned to Fiji. The museum is open Mon.-Sat. 0830-1630, admission F$2.

South of the gardens is **Government House**, the residence of the president. The original building, erected after 1882, burned after being hit by lightning in 1921, and the present edifice, which dates from 1928, is a replica of the former British governor's residence in Colombo, Sri Lanka. The grounds cannot be visited. The sentry on ceremonial guard duty wears a belted red tunic and an immaculate white *sulu* (kilt). Military officers on duty here do not care to be photographed, though the sentry won't mind having his picture taken.

The seawall just opposite the sentry box is the perfect place to sit and enjoy the view across Suva Harbor to Mbengga Island (to the left) and the dark, green mountains of eastern Viti Levu punctuated by Joske's Thumb, a high volcanic plug (to the right). Take the Nasese bus around its loop through South Suva and back for a glimpse of the beautiful garden suburbs of the city. An impressive new **Parliament Building** has been constructed at Veiuto, near the southern tip of the peninsula.

University Of The South Pacific

Catch any bus eastbound along MacArthur or Gordon streets to reach this beautiful 72.8-hectare campus on a hilltop at Lauthala Bay. Founded in 1968, the USP is jointly owned by 12 Pacific countries for the purpose of building the skills needed back home. Although over 70% of the 1,800 full-time and 600 part-time students are from Fiji, the rest are on scholarships from every corner of the Pacific. The USP's School of Agriculture is in Western Samoa and Extension Services runs University Centers (with a total of 6,600 students) in all of the member countries except Tokelau. Another 1,600 people throughout the region are taking Continuing Education courses.

The site of the Lauthala Campus was a Royal New Zealand Air Force (RNZAF) seaplane base before the land was turned over to USP. As you enter from Lauthala Bay Rd. you'll pass the Botanical Garden (1988) and an information office on the right and the British-built Administration Building on the left. Then comes the university library (1988), erected with Australian aid, behind which is the School of Pure and Applied Sciences (1981), donated by Canada. The design of the Student Union Building (1975) next to the library was influenced by traditional Pacific building motifs of interlocking circles. Several buildings south of this is the **Institute of Pacific Studies** (Box 1168, Suva; tel. 314-306),

AROUND SUVA

1. cement factory
2. Raffles Tradewinds Hotel/Scubahire
3. Castle Restaurant
4. Fiji School of Medicine
5. Tamavua Reservoir
6. Queen Elizabeth Barracks
7. Suva Cemetery
8. Royal Suva Yacht Club
9. Suva Prison
10. Marine Department
11. Narain Wharf
12. Carlton Brewery
13. Marine Pacific Ltd.
14. General Post Office
15. New Haven Motel
16. hospital
17. mosque
18. Suva Apartments
19. South Seas Private Hotel
20. Fiji Museum
21. Thurston Botanical Gardens
22. Government House
23. Pacific Theological College
24. South Pacific Bureau of Economic Cooperation (SPEC)
25. University of the South Pacific
26. National Stadium
27. Beach Road Park
28. Raiwangga Market
29. Sangam Temple
30. Tanoa House
31. Fiji Institute of Technology

housed in the former RNZAF officers' mess. This Institute is a leading publisher of insightful books written by Pacific islanders, and these may be purchased at their bookstore without the markup charged by commercial stores in town.

Look for the pleasant canteen in the Student Union Building, or join the students for lunch or dinner in the dining hall just past the new library. The food's not too good, but it's interesting to observe the mixed batch of students and the ways they cope with the inconvenience of tiny chairs. There's a choice of Indian or island food.

Students from outside the Pacific islands pay about F$9500 a year tuition to study at USP. Room and board is available at F$3360 and books will run another F$400. There are academic minimum-entry requirements, and applications must be in by 31 Dec. for the following term. The two semesters are late Feb. to the end of June and late July until the end of November. Many courses in the social sciences have a high level of content pertaining to Pacific culture, and postgraduate studies in a limited number of areas are available. To obtain a calendar, application for admission, and other materials, send US$20 to: The Registrar, University of the South Pacific, Box 1168, Suva, Fiji Islands (tel. 313-900).

The USP is always in need of qualified staff, so if you're from a university milieu and looking for a chance to live in the South Seas, this could be it. The maximum contract is six years (and you need seven years residency to apply for Fijian citizenship). If your credentials are impeccable you should write to the registrar from home. On the spot it's better to talk to a department head about his/her needs before going to see the registrar. All USP staff, both local and expatriate, are barred from becoming involved in politics.

East on Lathala Bay Rd., past the National Stadium, is Beach Road Park, the closest beach to town. It's too muddy and dirty to swim, but the view across Lauthala Bay is worth the stop. The Vatuwangga bus passes nearby.

North Suva

Suva's wonderful, colorful **market**, the largest retail produce market in the Pacific, is a good place to linger. If you're a yachtie or backpacker, you'll be happy to know that the market overflows with fresh produce of every kind. It's worth some time looking around. Have some kava at the *yanggona* kiosk in the market for about F$1 a bowl (share the excess with those present). Unfortunately fumes, noise, and pollution from the adjacent bus station buffet through the market.

Continue north and turn right just before the bridge to reach the factory of **Island Industries Ltd.** Most of Fiji's copra is shipped to

Suva bowling club

DAVID STANLEY

Suva for processing. At this plant the copra is crushed to extract the coconut oil, which is then sent to the U.K. for further refining into vegetable oil. Crushed coconut meal for cattle feed is also produced at the factory and sold locally. Apply to the plant office for a free tour during business hours.

Farther Afield

About 600 meters beyond the brewery is the vintage **Suva Prison** (1913), a fascinating colonial structure with high walls and barbwire. Opposite is the **Royal Suva Yacht Club**, where you can buy a drink, meet some yachties, and maybe find a boat to crew on. Their T-shirts (F$10) are hot items. The picturesque **Suva Cemetery** is just to the north. The Fijian graves wrapped in colorful *sulus* and tapa cloth make good subjects for photographers.

Continuing west on Queen's Rd., you pass **Suvavou** village, home of the original Fijian inhabitants of the Suva area, and Lami Town before reaching the **Raffles Tradewinds Hotel** (tel. 362-450), seven km from the market. Many cruising yachts tie up here (see "Services" below), and the view of the Bay of Islands from the hotel is particularly good.

Hiking

For a bird's-eye view of Suva and the entire surrounding area, spend a morning climbing to the volcanic plug atop **Mt. Korombamba** (429 meters), the highest peak around. Take a Shore bus to the cement factory beyond the Tradewinds Hotel at Lami, then follow the dirt road past the factory up into the foothills. After about 45 minutes on the main track, you'll come to a fork just after a sharp descent. Keep left and cross a small stream. Soon after, the track divides again. Go up on the right and look for a trail straight up to the right where the tracks rejoin. It's a 10-minute scramble to the summit from here.

There's a far more challenging climb to the top of **Joske's Thumb**, a volcanic plug 15 km west of Suva. Take a bus to Naikorokoro Rd., then walk inland 30 minutes to where the road turns sharply right and crosses a bridge. Follow the track straight ahead and continue up the river till you reach a small village. Request permission of the villagers to proceed. From the village to the Thumb will take just under three hours, and a guide might be advisable. The last bit is extremely steep, and ropes may be necessary.

Another good trip is to **Wailoku Falls** below Tamavua, one of the nicest picnic spots near Suva. Take the Wailoku bus from lane two at the market bus station as far as its turnaround point. Continue down the road, cross a bridge, then follow a footpath on the left upstream till you reach the falls. There's a deep pool here, where you can swim among verdant surroundings.

Tholo-i-Suva Forest Park

This lovely park, at an altitude of 150-200 meters, offers 3.6 km of trails through the beautiful mahogany forest flanking the upper drainage area of Waisila Creek. Enter from the Forestry Station along the Falls Trail. A half-km nature trail begins near the Upper Pools, and aside from waterfalls and natural swimming pools there are thatched pavilions with tables at which to picnic. Unfortunately, there have been ripoffs, so keep an eye on your gear while you're swimming. Thefts from previous visitors have forced the rangers to prohibit camping in the park. Get there on the Sawani bus (50 cents), which leaves the Suva market every hour, but come on a dry day as it's even rainier than Suva and the creeks are prone to flooding. With lovely green forests in full view, this is one of the most breathtaking places in all of Fiji. Aside from the vegetation you may spot a few of Fiji's native butterflies, birds, reptiles, and frogs. The park is so unspoiled it's hard to imagine you're only 11 km from Suva.

THOLO - I - SUVA FOREST PARK

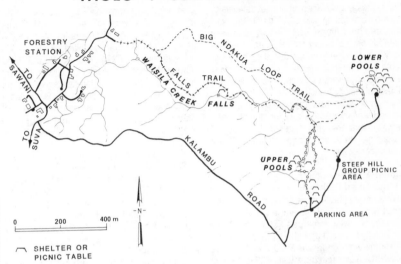

MINISTRY OF INFORMATION, GOVERNMENT OF FIJI

A good cross section of Fiji's tropical flora can be seen in Tholo-i-Suva Forest National Park near Suva.

ACCOMMODATIONS

Most of the decent places for budget travelers to stay are clustered on the south side of the downtown area near Albert Park. The commercially oriented hotels are near Marks St. and the market, while swingers gravitate to the establishments in the foothills up Waimanu Road. If you want to spend some time in Suva to take advantage of the city's good facilities and varied activities, look for something with cooking facilities and weekly rates. Many functional apartments are available on a short-term basis. When calculating costs, don't forget to add 10% tax to all prices below.

Budget Accommodations Around Albert Park

Suva's original backpacker's oasis is the **Coconut Inn** (Box 12539, Suva; tel. 312-904), 8 Kimberly St., which charges F$8.50 per bunk in the stuffy four-bed dormitories. The four double rooms with fridge are F$20 and there's a small flat upstairs for couples at F$32 d. A good breakfast is F$2 extra pp. The rooms are often full, but beds are usually available in the dorm. The Inn offers cooking facilities and luggage storage, and though it does get crowded, it's just the place to meet other young budget travelers and exchange experiences. Buy some kava powder and have an evening grog session in the lounge—one of the staff will do the honors as master of ceremonies. It's sometimes a little dirty and disorganized, though.

The **South Seas Private Hotel** (G.P.O. Box 157, Suva; tel. 312-296), 6 Williamson Rd. one block east of Albert Park, has 30 double rooms with fans and shared bath. Rates are F$11 s, F$14 d, or F$5 pp in the six-bed dorms. A room with private bath is F$22 d. This quiet hotel has a pleasant veranda and a large communal kitchen you may use to prepare your food (shortage of pots, pans, and plates). There's no hot water, and the kitchen and showers can get dirty. It's possible to leave excess luggage here while you visit other islands. However, because it's so popular, it's often full. When you first arrive, it's best to catch a taxi here from the market.

Loloma Lodge (Box 875, Suva; tel. 304-254), formerly known as Pacific Grand Apartments, an older two-story building at 19 Gorrie St., has 13 self-contained apartments for F$24 daily, with weekly rates available. One room in an apartment is F$14, and there's a F$6 pp dorm with access to cooking facilities. Visitors from other Pacific islands often stay here, as this is one of Suva's best buys. In 1991 Loloma was closed for renovations, and their new tariff may be much higher. Also check **Nukurua Apartments** (tel. 312-343) nearby at 25 Gorrie Street.

For a longer stay, consider the apartments at **Pender Court** (31 Pender St., Suva; tel. 313-973). The 13 studios with kitchenettes begin around F$29 s or d (10% reduction by the week), and there are also six one-bedroom apartments with kitchens for a bit more. The convenient location—just a few blocks east of Albert Park—makes this a very convenient place to settle in.

Eleven more self-contained units with cooking facilities are available at **Suva Apartments** (Box 12488, Suva; tel. 304-280), 17 Mbau St., a block or two east of Pender Court. They're F$25 s, F$30 d, F$39 t daily, with weekly rates available.

Budget Accommodations Downtown

Women are accommodated at the big, modern **Y.W.C.A.** (Box 534, Suva; tel. 304-829) on Sukuna Park at F$19 s, F$25 d—a good place to meet Fijian women. The main drawback is the loud late-night music from the disco across the street.

The **Metropole Hotel** (Box 404, Suva; tel. 304-124) on Usher St. opposite the market has 10 rooms with shared bath at F$21 s, F$27 d. Some hard drinking goes on in the public bar downstairs, but the hotel is well run, though often full.

The 26-room **Kings Suva Hotel** (Box 5141, Raiwangga; tel. 304-411) on Waimanu Rd. is similar at F$15 s, F$22 d, F$28 t, but the four noisy bars make it hardly a place for travelers. Check the rooms beforehand as quality varies. **Bhindi's Apartments** (Box 1089, Suva; tel.

315-520), nearby at 55 Toorak Rd., has a row of self-contained units at F$15 a night. The 12 units at **Amy Street Apartments** (98 Amy St.; tel. 315-113), several blocks east of Bhindi's, are F$17 s, F$22 d on the first floor, and F$22 s, F$28 d on the second and third floors. A larger family unit is F$55.

Budget Accommodations
Up Waimanu Road

The 42-room **Suva Oceanview Hotel** (270 Waimanu Rd.; tel. 312-129) charges F$10 s, F$14 d, or F$7 in the dorm. Though dirty, run-down, and frequented by prostitutes, it has a pleasant hillside location. Avoid the noisy rooms over the reception area.

The two-story **Outrigger Hotel** (Box 750, Suva; tel. 314-944), 349 Waimanu Rd., has 20 a/c rooms at F$45 s, F$55 d, and a four-person suite for F$60. Ask about their F$8 dormitory. The **Clifftop Motel** (94 Robertson Rd.; tel. 300-238) is F$25 s or d.

Farther up the hill at 587 Waimanu Rd. is the 14-room **New Haven Motel** (G.P.O. Box 992, Suva; tel. 315-220), which is cheap but rather dirty and seems to get a lot of couples for *very* short stays. The **Motel Crossroad Inn** (124 Robertson Rd.; tel. 313-820), F$12 s or d, and the **Motel Capital** (91 Robertson Rd.; tel. 313-246) also cater largely to people on the make. These three are not recommended for single women.

In contrast to these, **Tanoa House Private Hotel** (Box 704, Suva; tel. 381-575), 5 Princes Rd. in Samambula South, is a totally respectable guesthouse run by an ex-colonial from the Gilberts. The place has a garden with a view, and you meet genuine island characters. The 10 rooms with shared bath are F$15 s, F$25 d, F$30 t; breakfast is F$5 extra, and other meals are available. It's situated across from the Fiji Institute of Technology near the end of Waimanu Rd.; too far to walk from downtown, but get there easily on the Samambula bus.

Medium-priced Hotels

If yesteryear decadence at fading colonial prices has an appeal, don't miss the chance to stay at Suva's own 75-room **Grand Pacific Hotel** (Box 2524, Government Buildings, Suva; tel. 301-011); for decades this was the social center of the city. In 1914 the Union Steamship company built this charming white edifice to accommodate their transpacific passengers. The rooms were designed to appear as shipboard staterooms, with upstairs passageways surveying the harbor, like the promenade deck of a ship. In 1990 the Grand Pacific was purchased by the Republic of Nauru, and the hotel was closed for renovations in 1993. This may boost prices from the old F$70 s, F$80 d range, though it should still be worth splashing out on a night or two here.

The **Southern Cross Hotel** (G.P.O. Box 1076, Suva; tel. 314-233) is a high-rise concrete building at 63 Gordon Street. At F$75 s, F$85 d, F$90 t, the price of the 30 a/c rooms has increased sharply in recent years. Beware of smelly "budget" rooms on the main floor that are blasted by a band six nights a week. The hotel restaurant serves delicious Fijian and Korean dishes, and the lounge is a "safe," sedate night spot.

Elixir Motel Apartments (tel. 303-288), on the corner of Malcolm and Gordon streets, has two-bedroom apartments at F$50 daily or F$315 weekly without a/c, F$60 daily, F$375 weekly with a/c. Monthly rates are also available, so check it out for a long stay.

The less expensive **Endeavour Private Hotel** (Unit II, 8 Mitchell St.; tel. 303-092) charges F$30 s or d for a standard room, F$40 s or d for an a/c unit, or F$15 in the dorm. Breakfast is available for F$3.

The **Suva Peninsula Hotel** (Box 888, Suva; tel. 313-711), at the corner of Macgregor Rd. and Pender St., is a stylish four-floor building with a swimming pool. The 32 a/c rooms run F$45 s, F$55 d, while the eight suites with kitchenettes are F$70. The Peninsula's Japanese restaurant is expensive but good.

Two apartment-hotels behind the Central Police Station are worth a try if you want cooking facilities. The **Sunset Apartment Motel** (GPO Box 485, Suva; tel. 301-799), corner of Gordon and Murray streets, is a normal four-story suburban apartment block with 12 self-contained two-bedroom apartments beginning at F$36 s, F$48 d.

Nearby and under the same management is the congenial **Town House Apartment Hotel** (G.P.O. Box 485, Suva; tel. 300-055), 3 Forster

St., with 28 a/c units with cooking facilities beginning at F$44 s, F$52 d—good value. It's a five-story building with cars parked on the ground floor and a nice little bar on the roof.

Up in the Waimanu Rd. area the **Capricorn Apartment Hotel** (G.P.O. Box 1261, Suva; tel. 303-732), 7 St. Fort St., has 25 spacious a/c units with cooking facilities at F$65 s or d, F$75 t. It's very clean and comfortable—good value if you can find someone with whom to share. Three- and four-story apartment blocks are edged around the swimming pool with good views of the harbor from the individual balconies.

Tropic Towers Apartment Motel (Box 1347, Suva; tel. 304-470), 86 Robertson Rd., has 34 a/c apartments with cooking facilities in a four-story building at F$45 s, F$55 d, F$61 t. Ask about "budget" units without air-conditioning, which are about F$15 cheaper. Washing machines are available for guests. This and the Capricorn mentioned above are good choices for families.

Upmarket Hotels

Suva's largest and most expensive hotel is the **Suva Travelodge** (Box 1357, Suva; tel. 301-600) on the waterfront opposite the Government Buildings. The 132 a/c rooms begin at F$155 s, F$160 d. The swimming pool behind the two-story buildings compensates for the lack of a beach. Special events here include "island night" on Wed. with a *meke*, happy hour by the pool Fri. 1700-1930, and the Sun. poolside barbecue lunch. This is the only Suva hotel where reservations are recommended.

The nine-story **Suva Courtesy Inn** (G.P.O. Box 112, Suva; tel. 312-300), at the corner of Malcolm and Gordon streets, is the tallest hotel in Fiji. The 50 a/c rooms all face the harbor, but

at F$115 s or d they're overpriced. Suva's only Malaysian restaurant is at this hotel.

The turtle-shaped **Isa Lei Resort** (Private Bag, Lami; tel. 362-156), formerly the President Hotel, sits on a hill above Queen's Rd., between Suva and Lami. The 46 a/c units are F$120 s, F$180 d—not a very good deal considering the lack of a beach and isolation from central Suva. At last report the hotel was bankrupt.

The 110-room **Raffles Tradewinds Hotel** (Box 3377, Lami; tel. 362-450) at Lami just west of Suva reopened in Aug. 1992 after a US$ four-million renovation, complete with a convention center, shopping arcade, and floating seafood restaurant. Rates are F$110 s, F$125 d, F$145 t with private bath and a/c. Many cruising yachts anchor here and Suva's top dive shop is on the premises. Though bus service into Suva is good, the location is a little inconvenient for non-divers.

Camping

There's camping on **Nukulau**, a tiny reef island southeast of Suva. For many years Nukulau was the government quarantine station where most of the indentured laborers spent their first two weeks in Fiji. Now it's a public park. Get free three-day camping permits from the Department of Lands, Room 39, Government Buildings, during office hours. The island has toilets and drinking water, and the swimming is good. Problem is, the only access is the F$40 tourist boat (includes lunch) departing downtown Suva at 0930 when there are enough passengers. Contact **Coral See Cruises** (Box 852, Suva; tel. 321-570) for information. You're allowed to return to Suva a couple of days later at no extra charge. Mostly, Nukulau and nearby Makaluva Island attract **surfers**.

FOOD AND ENTERTAINMENT

Food

Suva has many excellent, inexpensive restaurants, with the emphasis on Chinese. Several places offer good weekday lunchtime Chinese smorgasbords, especially the **New Peking Restaurant** in the Pacific Arcade, (195 Victoria Parade; tel. 312-714) and the **Sichuan Pavilion Restaurant** (6 Thompson St.; tel. 314-865)—perhaps Suva's finest Asian restaurant. Chinese Consulate employees frequent this place for its spicy-hot Chinese dishes.

The **Shanghai Restaurant** (tel. 314-257), upstairs at 30 Cumming St. in the heart of the duty-free shopping area, serves inexpensive Chinese and European dishes. The staff and surroundings are pleasant, and the food good and ample. **Geraldyne's Restaurant** (160 Renwick Rd.; tel. 311-037) also serves Chinese food (closed Sunday). The best place to eat Chinese-style near the Raffles Tradewinds Hotel is the **Castle Restaurant** (tel. 361-223) in the Lami Shopping Center. Suva's most imposing Chinese restaurant is probably the **Ming Palace** (tel. 315-111) in the Old Town Hall next to the public library on Victoria Parade. **Phoenix Restaurant** (165 Victoria Parade; tel. 311-889) has more Chinese food and cheap beer.

Two other recommendable Chinese places are the **Lantern Restaurant** (10 Pratt St.; tel. 314-633), and **Fong's Restaurant** (8 Pratt St.; tel. 304-462). Nearby at the corner of Pratt and Joske streets are two of the best Indian restaurants in the entire South Pacific. The **Hare Krishna Restaurant** (closed Sun., tel. 314-154) specializes in luncheon vegetarian *thalis* (F$6), sweets, and ice cream (10 flavors), while the unpretentious **Curry Place** (tel. 313-885) next door offers nonvegetarian food. Study the menu carefully the first time you go into Hare Krishna; two distinct all-you-care-to-eat offers are available and the prices vary considerably. Ask about the special lunch on Sat., which allows you to sample six different dishes. A second **Hare Krishna Restaurant** (closed Sun.) is at 37 Cumming St.; both are highly recommended (no smoking or alcohol allowed).

Another excellent Indian place is the **Curry House** (255 Victoria Parade; tel. 313-000), with vegetarian curries for F$2 and meat curries from F$6. Beware of **Pizza Hut** (207 Victoria Parade; tel. 311-825), where they deliberately make you wait up to two hours for your order to get you to spend more money on alcohol.

For German or French cuisine Mon.-Sat., it's the **Swiss Tavern** (16 Kimberly St.; tel. 303-233), at Gordon (say hello to Hans). The Tudor England-style **Red Lion Restaurant** (215 Victoria Parade; tel. 312-968) is Suva's seafood and steak specialist (closed Sun.) and diners get free entry to Lucky Eddie's nightclub next door. **Tiko's Floating Restaurant** (tel. 313-625), a former Blue Lagoon cruise boat anchored off Stinson Parade behind the post office, also serves seafood (dinner only). These three are fairly expensive.

The **Y.W.C.A. cafeteria** (closed Sun., tel. 311-617) is the place to try native Fijian food, such as fish fried in coconut milk. You have to come early to get the best dishes. Another place where you may find Fijian food is the **Old Mill Cottage Cafe** (tel. 312-134), 49 Carnarvon St.—the street behind the Golden Dragon nightclub. At lunchtime they have curried freshwater mussels, curried chicken livers, fresh seaweed in coconut milk, taro leaves creamed in coconut milk, and fish cooked in coconut milk. Also stop by for afternoon tea.

If you just want a snack, check out **Donald's Kitchen** in the arcade at 45 Cumming Street. This is an excellent place to take a break. One block over on Marks St. are cheaper Chinese restaurants, such as **Kim's Cafe**, 128 Marks St., where you can get a toasted egg sandwich and coffee for a dollar. Snack bars around town often sell large bottles of cold milk—cheap and refreshing.

The very cheapest and most colorful places to eat in Suva are down near the market. At lunchtime Fijian women run a food market beside Princes Wharf, about F$1 a plate for real Fijian food. At night a dozen Indian food trucks park beside the market just opposite Burns Philp and dispense great curries.

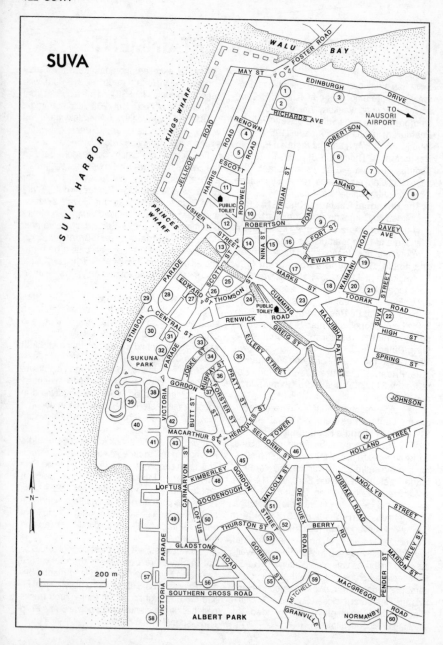

SUVA

SUVA

1. Bali Hai Cabaret	21. Bhindi's Apartments	40. Suva Olympic Pool
2. Phoenix Theater	22. Immigration Office	41. Suva City Library
3. Island Industries Ltd.	23. Chequers Nightspot	42. Fiji Air/Lucky Eddie's
4. Health Office	24. Morris Hedstrom	43. Government Handicraft
5. buses for Lautoka	Supermarket	Center
6. Tropic Towers	25. Harbor Center	44. Anglican Cathedral
Apartment Motel	26. Fiji Visitors Bureau	45. Southern Cross Hotel
7. Motel Crossroad Inn	27. General Post Office	46. The Playhouse
8. Suva Oceanview Hotel	28. Curio and Handicraft Center	47. Hindu Temple
9. Capricorn Apartment Hotel	29. Coral See Cruise Landing	48. Coconut Inn
10. Morris Hedstrom Store	30. Y.W.C.A.	49. Golden Dragon
11. bus station	31. Air Pacific Office	50. U.S. Embassy
12. market	32. Regal Theater	51. Suva Courtesy Inn
13. Metropole Hotel	33. Hare Krishna Restaurant	52. Forestry Dept.
14. Burns Philp Supermarket	34. police station	53. Gordon St. Medical Center
15. Patterson Bros.	35. Catholic Cathedral	54. Loloma Lodge
16. Centenary Methodist	36. Town House Apartment	55. Fiji Arts Council
Church	Hotel	56. Government Buildings
17. Century Theater	37. Sunset Apartment Motel	57. Suva Travelodge
18. Kings Suva Hotel	38. Fiji International	58. Grand Pacific Hotel
19. Alankar Theater	Telecommunications Office	59. Tuvalu High Commission
20. Lilac Theater	39. Suva Civic Auditorium	60. Suva Peninsula Hotel

Entertainment

Movie houses are plentiful downtown, charging F$1 for a hard seat, F$1.60 for a soft seat. The selection of films is fairly good, and they change every three days, so it's a paradise for movie lovers. The best time to be in Suva is around the end of Aug. or early Sept., when the **Hibiscus Festival** fills Albert Park with stalls, games, and carnival revelers.

The numerous nightclubs all have cover charges of around F$4 and require neat dress; nothing much happens until after 2200 and women shouldn't enter alone. The most interracial and relaxed of the clubs is **Chequers Nightspot** (127 Waimanu Rd.; tel. 313-563), which has live music Tues.-Sat. after 2100. Hang on to your wallet here. Gays will feel comfortable at **Lucky Eddie's** (217 Victoria Parade; tel. 312-884) daily except Sun. after 1900; it's not really a gay bar, as the Fijian women there try to prove. The Lucky Eddie's cover charge is also valid for the more sedate **Rockefeller's Night Club** in the same building. The **Golden Dragon,** open Fri. and Sat. 0730-0100 (379 Victoria Parade; tel. 311-018), is

similar. **Traps** (305 Victoria Parade; tel. 312-922), offers free admission (reasonable dress), jazz twice a week, and pitchers of beer anytime; they're open till 0200 weekends.

For a real earthy atmosphere try the **Bali Hai** (tel. 315-868) on Rodwell Rd., the roughest club in Suva. Friday and Sat. nights the place is packed with Fijians (no Indians) and tourists are rare, so beware. If you're looking for action, you'll be able to pick a partner within minutes. Watch out for aggressive males. The dance hall on the top floor is the swingingest, with body-to-body jive—the Bali Hai will rock you.

Unescorted female travelers and those in search of a more subdued drinking place should try the bar at Tiko's Floating Restaurant or the lounge at the Southern Cross Hotel. The piano bar at the Travelodge is more upmarket.

For information on the exciting day-trips from Suva offered by **Wilderness Tours** (tel. 386-498), turn to the "Around Navua" and "Around Nausori" sections in this book. Wilderness also runs excellent two-hour city sightseeing tours three times a day (adults F$20, children F$10).

OTHER PRACTICALITIES

Sports And Recreation

Scubahire (G.P.O. Box 777, Suva; tel. 361-088) at the Raffles Tradewinds Hotel arranges full-day diving trips to the Mbengga Lagoon for F$115, including two tanks, weight belt, backpack, and lunch. Other equipment can be rented. Scubahire is also happy to take snorkelers out on all their full-day dive trips for F$55 pp, gear and lunch included. The 65 km of barrier reef around the Mbengga Lagoon features multicolored soft corals and fabulous sea fans at Side Streets and an exciting wall and big fish at Cutter Passage. Scubahire's four-day PADI certification course (F$450) involves six boat dives, an excellent way to learn while getting in some great diving. An introductory dive is F$125. You'll need to show a medical certificate proving you're fit for diving. Several readers have written in praising this company, Fiji's oldest (established 1970) and most experienced dive shop.

Dive Centre Ltd. (Box 3066, Lami; tel. 300-599), 4 Matua St., Walu Bay, rents and sells scuba gear at daily and weekly rates and fills tanks.

The Suva **Olympic Swimming Pool** (224 Victoria Parade; tel. 313-433) charges 50 cents admission; open Mon.-Fri. 1000-1800, Sat. 0800-1800 (April to Sept.), or Mon.-Fri. 0900-1900, Sat. 0600-1900 (Oct. to March). Lockers are available.

At the 18-hole, par-72 **Fiji Golf Club** (15 Rifle Range Rd., Vatuwangga; tel. 382-872), the course record is 65. Green fees are F$6 for nine holes, F$12 for 18 or 36 holes, plus F$10 for club and trolley hire. Visitors are welcome, though Tues. and Sat. afternoons are reserved for club competitions (General Rabuka and Ratu Mara are regulars). Near Nausori Airport is another well-designed 18-hole golf course (tel. 4772-911) with green fees of only F$3.

Yacht races to Suva from Auckland and Sydney occur in April or May on alternate years, timed from the cruisers' return just after the hurricane season. There's a powerboat race from Suva to Levuka on the long weekend around 10 October.

The Fijians are a very muscular, keenly athletic people who send champion teams far and wide in the Pacific. You can see rugby (April to Sept.) and soccer (March to Oct.) on Sat. afternoons at 1500 at the **National Stadium** near the University of the South Pacific. Rugby and soccer are also played at Albert Park Sat., and you could also see a cricket game here (mid-Oct. to Easter).

Shopping

Items of the best workmanship are sold in the **Government Handicraft Center** behind Ratu Sukuna House, MacArthur and Carnarvon streets. Familiarize yourself here with what is authentic in a relaxed, fixed-price atmosphere before plunging into the hard-sell establishments. Another good place to start is the **Fiji Museum** shop. The large **Curio and Handicraft Market** on the waterfront behind the post office is intended mostly for cruise-ship passengers; bargain hard here.

Some of the most offbeat places to buy things in Suva are the **pawn shops**, most of which are in the vicinity of the Suva Hotel. Ask for the behind-the-counter selection.

Cumming St. (site of the main Suva produce market until the 1940s) is Suva's **duty-free** shopping area. The wide selection of goods in the large number of shops makes this about the best place in Fiji to shop for electrical and other imported goods. Expect to receive a 10-40% discount by bargaining. **Premier Electronic Co.** (54 Cumming St.; tel. 312-232) may offer the best prices, but *shop around* before you buy. Dealers with a sticker from the Fiji Duty Free Merchants Association in their windows tend to be more reliable.

Be wary when purchasing gold jewelry, as it might be fake. Never buy anything on the day when a cruise ship is in port—prices shoot up. And watch out for hustlers who will take you around to the shops and get you a "good price" after tempting you with the possibility of profits to be made by selling the items in New Zealand. The only profits will be your loss and their gain.

For clothing see the very fashionable hand-printed shirts and dresses at **Tiki Togs** (tel. 304-381) across from the post office, or at their sec-

FIJI VISITORS BUREAU

Suva's business district adjoins Suva Harbor.

ond location next to the Pizza Hut: you could come out looking like a real South Seas character at a very reasonable price.

The **Philatelic Bureau** (Box 100, Suva; tel. 312-928) at the main post office sells the stamps of Tuvalu, Western Samoa, Kiribati, Pitcairn, Solomon Islands, and Vanuatu, as well as those of Fiji. **Lotu Pasifika Productions** (Box 208, Suva; tel. 301-314), 7 Thurston St. near the Government Buildings, sells books on island social issues and Nuclear-Free Pacific posters.

In Suva beware of the seemingly friendly sword and mask sellers (usually toting canvas bags) who will approach you on the street or near the Fiji Museum, ask your name, then quickly carve it on a sword and demand F$15 for a set that you could buy at a Nandi curio shop for F$5. The masks and swords themselves have nothing to do with Fiji.

Services

Thomas Cook Travel (21 Thomson St; tel. 301-603), next to the post office, will change foreign currency Sat. 0830-1200 at the usual rate (1% commission). The **Fiji International Telecommunications** office (158 Victoria Parade; tel. 312-933) is open 24 hours a day for trunk calls and telegrams. The basic charge for three minutes is F$4.80 to Australia or New Zealand, US$8.10 to North America and Europe. There's a row of public telephones outside the post office, most out of service.

The **Immigration Office** for extensions of stay, etc. is at the corner of Toorak Rd. and Suva Street (open Mon.-Fri. 0830-1200/1400-1530; tel. 312-622). Bring along your departure ticket, traveler's checks, and credit cards. Cruising yachties wishing to tour the Lau Group must first obtain permission from the prime minister. Fijian Affairs gives approval to cruise the other

Fijian islands. Right after the 1987 military coups they weren't giving permission to anyone (out of fear of gunrunning), but things may have quieted down by now.

The following countries have diplomatic missions in Suva: Australia (tel. 312-844), Britain (tel. 311-033), Canada (tel. 300-589), China (tel. 311-836), the Federated States of Micronesia (tel. 314-528), Finland (tel. 313-188), France (tel. 312-233), Germany (tel. 315-000), Israel (tel. 303-420), Japan (tel. 302-122), Korea (tel. 300-977), Malaysia (tel. 312-166), Marshall Islands (tel. 302-479), Nauru (tel. 313-566), New Zealand (tel. 311-422), Papua New Guinea (tel. 304-244), Sweden (tel. 313-188), Tuvalu (tel. 301-355), and the U.S.A. (tel. 314-466). Almost everyone needs a visa to visit Australia, and these are available at the Australian Embassy, 8th Floor, Dominion House, near the Fiji Visitors Bureau.

Mooring charges for **yachts** at the Raffles Tradewinds Hotel (Box 3377, Lami; tel. 362-450) are F$15 a week per boat to tie up alongside (includes water, electricity, dinghy pontoon, telephone message service, use of hotel pool, etc.). There's a notice board by the pool for people seeking passage or crew for yachts. At the Royal Suva Yacht Club (tel. 312-921), it costs F$15 a week for such amenities as mooring privileges, warm showers, laundry facilities, cheap drinks, Sun. barbecues, and the full use of facilities by the whole crew. People have reported thefts off boats anchored here, so watch out.

Hunts Travel (Box 686, Suva; tel. 315-288), in the Dominion Building arcade behind the Fiji Visitors Bureau, is the place to pick up air tickets. They often know more about Air Pacific flights than the Air Pacific employees themselves!

Also compare **Travelworld Services** (tel. 315-870) in the Honson Arcade on Thompson St.; it sometimes gives five percent discounts on plane tickets to other Pacific countries.

The **Fiji Society** (Box 1205, Suva) can help researchers on Fiji and the other Pacific islands. Contact them locally through the Fiji Museum. The **Fiji Arts Council** (34 Gorrie St.; tel. 311-754) can be of assistance to visiting musicians and artists.

The **Fijian Indian Cultural Center** (tel. 300-050), upstairs at the corner of Raojibhai Patel St. and Waimanu Rd., offers classes in Indian

music, dancing, art, etc. It's well worth dropping in to find out if any public performances are scheduled during your visit.

Health

You can see a doctor at the Outpatients Deptment of the **Colonial War Memorial Hospital** (tel. 313-444) for F$5 (tourists) or 50 cents (locals). It can be extremely crowded, so take along a book to read while you're waiting for them to call your number. You'll receive better attention at the **Gordon St. Medical Center** (tel. 313-355), Gordon and Thurston streets (consultations F$10). Women note: there's a female doctor here. The **J.P. Bayly Clinic** (190 Rodwell Rd.; tel. 315-888), opposite the Phoenix Theater, is a church-operated low-income clinic.

The **Health Office** (open Tues. and Fri. 0830-0930; tel. 314-988), on Rodwell Rd. past the market, gives tetanus, polio, cholera, typhoid, and yellow-fever vaccinations.

Information

The **Fiji Visitors Bureau** (tel. 302-433) is in the old customs house in front of the post office on Thompson St., open Mon.-Fri. 0830-1630, Sat. 0830-1200. You may use their toilet. The **Ministry of Information** (211-305), Ground Floor, New Wing, Government Buildings, hands out a few official booklets on the country. Across the parking lot in the same complex is the Maps and Plans Room (tel. 211-395) of the **Lands and Surveys Division**, which sells excellent maps of Fiji (open Mon.-Thurs. 0900-1300/1400-1530, Fri. 0900-1300/1400-1500). Carpenters Shipping (tel. 312-244), 3rd Floor, Neptune House, Tofua St., Walu Bay, sells navigational charts (F$15 each).

The **Suva Public Library** is worth a look (open Mon., Tues., Thurs., Fri. 0930-1800, Wed. 1200-1800, Sat. 0900-1300). Visitors can use the library upon payment of a refundable deposit. This library opened in 1909 thanks to a grant from American philanthropist Andrew Carnegie.

The **Desai Bookshop** (tel. 304-654), on Pier St. opposite the post office, has the best selection of books on Fiji (ask for *The Fantasy Eaters,* by Fiji's leading novelist Subramani). There's a good secondhand book exchange upstairs in the building at 45 Marks Street. The **Seamen's**

Mission (open Mon.-Fri. 1200-1400), near the main wharf, trades paperback books, one for one. Lotu Pasifika Productions (7 Thurston St.; tel. 301-314) publishes a number of excellent books on regional social problems and carries Nuclear-Free Pacific posters.

Airline Offices

Reconfirm your onward flight at your airline's Suva office:

Air Calédonie International, 64 Renwick Rd., tel. 302-133.

Air Marshall Islands, 30 Thompson St., tel. 303-888.

Air Nauru, Ratu Sakuna House, 249 Victoria Parade, tel. 312-377.

Air New Zealand, Queensland Insurance Centre, Victoria Parade, tel. 313-100.

Air Pacific, CML Building, Victoria Parade, tel. 384-955.

Fiji Air, 129 Victoria Parade, tel. 314-666, represents Air Vanuatu and Solomon Airlines.

Qantas Airways, CML Building, Victoria Parade, tel. 313-888.

TRANSPORT

Although nearly all international flights to Fiji arrive at Nandi, Suva is still the most important transportation center in the country. Interisland shipping crowds the waterfront, and if you can't find a ship going your way at precisely the time you want to travel, Fiji Air flies to all the major Fiji islands, while Air Pacific services Tonga, Samoa, and Vanuatu—both from Nausori Airport. Make the rounds of the shipping offices listed below, then head down to the wharf to check the information. Compare the price of a cabin and deck passage and ask if meals are included. Start checking early, as many domestic services within Fiji are only once a week and trips to other countries are far less frequent.

A solid block of buses await your patronage at the market bus station near the harbor, with continuous local service to Lami and Raiwangga, among others, and frequent long-distance departures to Nandi and Lautoka. (See "Getting Around By Bus" in the Introduction.) Most of the points of interest around Suva are accessible on foot. If you wander too far, jump on any bus headed in the right direction and you'll end up back in the market. Taxis are also easy to find and relatively cheap (F$1 in the city center, F$1.50 to the suburbs).

Ships To Other Countries

The Wed. issue of the *Fiji Times* carries a special section on international shipping, though most of the services listed don't accept passengers. Most shipping is headed for Tonga and Samoa—there's not much going westward and actually getting on any of the ships mentioned below requires considerable persistence. You can also try to sign on as crew on a yacht. Try both yacht anchorages in Suva: put up a notice, ask around, etc. Yacht Help (141 Foster Rd., Walu Bay; tel. 311-982) has a "crew wanted" notice board, and they keep their ears to the ground.

Burns Philp Shipping (tel. 315-556), above Burns Philp Supermarket on Rodwell Rd., is an agent for the monthly Banks Line service to Lautoka, Nouméa, Honiara, Kieta, Port Moresby, and on to Europe. They cannot sell you a passenger ticket; they can only tell you when the ship is due in and where it's headed. It's up to you to make arrangements personally with the captain.

Time Shipping Agency Ltd. (Box 15093, Suva; tel. 303-618), corner of Stewart and Marks streets, offers limited passenger service to Auckland and Apia every three weeks on the MV *Cotswold Prince.*

The Tuvalu Embassy (Box 14449, Suva; tel. 300-697), 8 Mitchell St., runs the *Nivaga II* to Funafuti about six times a year, but the dates are variable. Fares run F$53 deck, F$144 second class, F$182 first class OW, meals included. It's less if you take your own food or patronize the snack bar aboard. After reaching Funafuti the ship cruises the Tuvalu Group.

Marine Pacific Ltd. (25 Eliza St., Walu Bay; tel. 312-488), upstairs near the dry dock, handles Warner Pacific Line ships to Tonga and Samoa. Passengers are sometimes accepted, but you must bring your own food.

The Inter-Ports Shipping Corporation (tel.

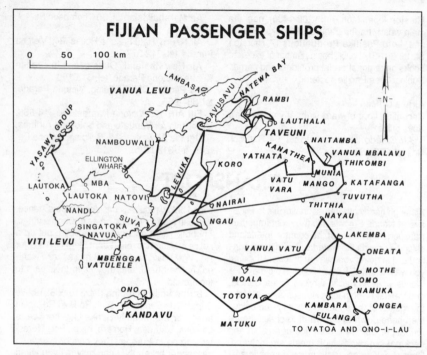

FIJIAN PASSENGER SHIPS

0   50   100 km

LAMBASA
VANUA LEVU
SAVUSAVU
NATEWA BAY
RAMBI
LAUTHALA
TAVEUNI
NAITAMBA
NAMBOUWALU
KANATHEA
VANUA MBALAVU
ELLINGTON WHARF
YATHATA
KORO
THIKOMBI
MUNIA
YASAWA GROUP
LEVUKA
VATU VARA
MANGO
KATAFANGA
LAUTOKA
MBA
NATOVI
ONAIRAI
TUVUTHA
NANDI
LAUTOKA
THITHIA
SINGATOKA
SUVA
NGAU
NAYAU
VITI LEVU
NAVUA
LAKEMBA
VANUA VATU
ONEATA
MBENGGA
VATULELE
MOTHE
MOALA
KOMO
ONO
NAMUKA
TOTOYA
KAMBARA
ONGEA
KANDAVU
FULANGA
MATUKU
TO VATOA AND ONO-I-LAU

-N-

313-344), Tofua St., Walu Bay, has regular passenger services to Apia (monthly, F$200) and Rotuma.

Carpenters Shipping (tel. 312-244), 3rd Floor, Neptune House, Tofua St., Walu Bay, is an agent for the *Moana III* and *Moana IV*, which sail about every two months from Suva to Futuna and Wallis, then on to Nouméa. They can't sell the ticket but will tell you when the ship is expected in, and you can book with the captain. This is a beautiful trip, and not at all crowded between Fiji and Wallis. Book a cabin, however, if you're going right through to Nouméa.

Sofrana Unilines (tel. 304-528) ships sometimes accept work-a-passage crew for New Zealand, Australia, or any other port when they need hands. You must arrange this with the captain.

Ships To Other Islands
Patterson Bros. (Private Mail Bag, Suva; tel. 315-644), Suite 1, 1st Floor, Epworth Arcade off Nina St., takes reservations for the Suva-Natovi-Nambouwalu-Lambasa bus/ferry/bus combination that departs Suva's General Post Office Mon.-Sat. at 0400 and Lambasa at 0530. The fare is F$26 Suva to Nambouwalu, F$30 right through to Lambasa, an excellent 10-hour trip. Their *Princess Ashika* or *Ovalau II* links Suva to Ngau, Koro, Savusavu (F$27), and Taveuni (F$30) weekly, departing Narain's Wharf at Walu Bay at midnight Mondays. Thursday at midnight this ship departs Suva for Kandavu (F$30, six hours). Patterson Bros. also has offices in Lambasa, Lautoka, Levuka, and Savusavu.

Consort Shipping Line (G.P.O. Box 152, Suva; tel. 302-877), in the Dominion House arcade on Thompson St., operates the ferry *Spirit of Free Enterprise* from Suva to Savusavu twice a week (F$27 OW), departing Suva on Wed. and Sat. at 0500. Some trips call at Koro and Taveuni (F$31). This 450-passenger car ferry formerly shuttled between the north and

the reef off Ovalau (Don Pitcher)

1. Beachcomber Island (Islands in the Sun); **2.** the tourist boat *Tui Tai* (islands in the Sun); **3.** camping at Natandola Beach, Viti Levu (D. Stanley); **4.** dormitory at Beachcomber Island (D. Stanley); **5.** *mbure* on Beachcomber Island (Islands in the Sun)

south islands of New Zealand. Consort has the advantage over Patterson in that its ships leave right from Suva rather than Natovi, a 1½-hour bus ride north. On the down side, its services aren't as reliable as those of Patterson, so be there early.

Walu Shipping (tel. 312-668) at Millers Wharf has regular shipping services to Lau and Rotuma on the MV *Katika,* F$53 deck, F$63 cabin to any island in Lau. Food is included in the price and on the outward journey it will probably be okay, but on the return don't expect much more than rice and tea.

Also check at the Narain Wharf in Walu Bay for private ships to different islands. Also at Walu Bay, the **Marine Dept.** handles government barges to all the Fiji islands, and passenger fares are generally lower than on private ships, but no meals are included. Departures are listed on a blackboard at their office. The government barge to Rotuma leaves approximately once a month. Ask about boats to Western Samoa and Tokelau here.

Ask on the smaller vessels tied up at **Princes Wharf** for passage to Nairai, Ngau, Kandavu, etc. Don't believe the first person who tells you no boat is going where you want to go—*ask around.* If you're planning a long voyage by interisland ship, a big bundle of kava roots to captain and crew as a token of appreciation for their hospitality works wonders.

To Ovalau Island

Fiji Air flies from Nausori to Levuka (F$27) two or three times a day, but the most popular trip is the bus/launch/bus combination via Natovi or Mbau Landing. Three different companies operate these four- to five-hour, F$17 trips. Reservations are recommended on weekends and public holidays.

The Patterson Bros. service (book at their office mentioned above) leaves from behind the post office in Suva Mon.-Sat. at 1230. This express bus goes from Suva to Natovi, where it drives onto a ferry to Mburesala on Ovalau, then continues on to Levuka, where it arrives around 1730. For the return journey, you leave the Patterson Bros. office in Levuka Mon.-

Fiji's emerald green banded iguana is the most striking reptile of the Pacific.

THE FIJI TIMES

Sat. at 0400, arriving in Suva at 0800. Tickets must be purchased in advance at the office—no exceptions.

Bula Ferry Services (G.P.O. Box 15072, Suva) runs a similar service to Levuka (F$17), departing the Suva Bus Station twice daily Mon.-Sat. at 0800 and 1330. Their boat, the MV *Ana Tupou,* sails direct from Natovi to Levuka in two hours. The return service leaves Levuka at 0730

and 1300. Tickets are available from Jina Brothers Hairdressing Salon, Shop 1, Metropole Bldg., Scotts Street, Suva (tel. 312-794), or the Talanoa Bookshop at the bus station.

A third choice is the *Emosi Express,* departing Suva Post Office at 1100 for Mbau Landing, where one boards a launch to Leleuvia Island and Levuka (2½ hours). To book this, call the Old Capital Inn in Levuka at 440-057.

AROUND NAUSORI

NAUSORI

In 1881 the Rewa River town of Nausori, 19 km northeast of Suva, was chosen as the site of Fiji's first large sugar mill, which operated until 1959. In those early days it was believed incorrectly that sugarcane grew better on the wetter eastern side of the island. Today cane is grown only on the drier, sunnier western sides of Viti Levu and Vanua Levu. The old sugar mill is now a rice mill and storage depot, as the Rewa Valley has become a major rice-producing area. Today Nausori is Fiji's fifth-largest city (population 14,018 in 1986) and the headquarters of Central Division. The nine-span bridge across the river here was built in 1937.

Nausori is better known for its large international airport three km southeast, built as a fighter strip to defend Fiji's capital during WW II. It's a good place to stay if your flight leaves very early the next morning. The business area is compact, so it's easy to attend to odds and ends like getting a haircut, last-minute shopping at the small stores and the few duty-free shops, and taking in a movie at one of the three cinemas. Nausori has three banks.

Accommodations And Food
The **Hotel Nausori** (Box 67, Nausori; tel. 478-833), also known as "Kings Nausori Hotel," 99 King's Rd., beside the rice mill, has seven grubby rooms with private bath and hot water at F$21 s, F$26 d. One redeeming feature is that as a hotel guest you can buy beer on Sunday. Nausori has several basic restaurants, plus the **Whistling Duck** pub.

From Nausori
Buses to the airport (35 cents) and Suva (80 cents) are fairly frequent, but the last bus to Suva is at 2130. You can also catch buses here to Lautoka and Natovi (for Levuka).

Take a bus to **Nakelo Landing** to explore the **Rewa River Delta**. Many outboards leave from here to take villagers to their riverside homes. Passenger fares are less than a dollar for short trips. Larger boats leave sporadically from Nakelo for Levuka, Ngau, and Koro, but finding one would be pure chance. Some also depart from nearby **Wainimbokasi Landing**.

Wilderness Tours (Box 1389, Suva; tel. 386-498) runs half-day boat tours of the Rewa Delta, with stops at Nailili Catholic Mission to visit St. Joseph's Church (1901), and Nambua village where Fijian pottery is still made. The tour leaves twice daily at 0930 and 1400, and the F$29 pp price includes minibus transfers from Suva hotels (only operates if at least four people sign up). This is a refreshing change of pace.

OFFSHORE ISLANDS

Mbau Island
Mbau, a tiny, eight-hectare island just east of Viti Levu, has a special place in Fiji's history: this was the seat of High Chief Cakobau, who used European cannons and muskets to subdue most of western Fiji in the 1850s. At its pinnacle Mbau had a population of 3,000, hundreds of war canoes to guard its waters, and over 20 temples on the island's central plain. After the Battle of Verata on Viti Levu in 1839, Cakobau and his father, Tanoa, presented 260 bodies of men, women, and children to their closest friends and allied

chiefs for gastronomical purposes. Fifteen years after this slaughter, Cakobau converted to Christianity and prohibited cannibalism on Mbau. In 1867 he became a sovereign, crowned by European traders and planters desiring a stable government in Fiji to protect their interests.

Tanoa, the cannibal king of Mbau. Tanoa was about 65 years of age in 1840 when the United States Exploring Expedition, under Lt. Charles Wilkes, toured Fiji. His rise to power threw the island into several years of strife, as Tanoa had to do away with virtually every minor chief who challenged his right to rule. With long colorful pennants playing from the mast and thousands of Cypraea ovula shells decorating the hull, his 30-meter outrigger canoe was the fastest in the region. One of Tanoa's favorite sports was overtaking and ramming smaller canoes at sea. The survivors were then fair game for whoever could catch and keep them. At feasts where most nobles were expected to provide a pig, Tanoa always furnished a human body. Wilkes included this sketch of Tanoa in volume three of the Expedition's monumental Narrative, published in 1845.

Sights Of Mbau

The great stone slabs that form docks and seawalls around much of the island, once accommodated Mbau's fleet of war canoes. The graves of the Cakobau family and many of the old chiefs lie on the hilltop behind the school. The large, sturdy stone church located near the provincial offices was the first Christian church in Fiji. Inside its nearly one-meter-thick walls, just in front of the altar, is the old sacrificial stone once used for human sacrifices; today it's the baptismal font. Now painted white, this font was once known as King Cakobau's "skull crusher." It's said a thousand brains were splattered against it. Across from the church are huge ancient trees and the thatched Council House on the site of the one-time temple of the war god Cagawalu. The family of the late Sir George Cakobau, governor-general of Fiji 1973-82, has a large traditional-style home on the island. You can see everything on the island in an hour or so.

Getting There

Take the Mbau bus from Nausori to Mbau Landing. There are punts to cross over to the island: F$1 at high tide from the old landing, F$2 at any time from the new landing.

Note that Mbau is not considered a tourist attraction, and from time to time visitors are prevented from going to the island. It's important to get someone to invite you across, which they'll do willingly if you show a genuine interest in Fijian history. Like all Fijians, the inhabitants of Mbau are very friendly people. Bring a big bundle of *waka* for the *turanga-ni-koro,* and ask permission very politely to be shown around. There could be some confusion about who's to receive the *sevu sevu,* however, as everyone on Mbau's a chief! The more respectable your dress and demeanor, the better your chances of success. If you're told to contact the Ministry of Fijian Affairs in Suva, just depart gracefully, as that's only their way of saying no. After all, it's up to them.

Viwa Island

Before Cakobau adopted Christianity in 1854, Methodist missionaries working for this effect resided in Viwa Island, just across the water from Mbau. Here the first Fijian New Testament was printed in 1847; the Reverend John

Hunt, who did the translation, lies buried in the graveyard beside the church that bears his name.

Viwa is a good alternative if you aren't invited to visit Mbau itself. To reach the island, hire a punt at Mbau Landing for about F$5. If you're lucky, some locals will be going and you'll be able to get a ride for less. A single Fijian village stands on the island.

Tomberua Island

Tomberua Island Resort (Michael Dennis, Box 567, Suva; tel. 479-177), on a tiny reef island off the east tip of Viti Levu, caters to upmarket honeymooners, families, and professionals. Built in 1968, this was one of Fiji's first outer-island resorts. The 14 thatched *mbures* are designed in the purest Fijian style, yet it's all very luxurious and the small size means peace and quiet. The tariff is F$270 s, F$297 d, F$337 t, plus F$72 pp for three gourmet meals, F$59 pp for two meals, and baby-sitters are F$12 a day. Tomberua is out of eastern Viti Levu's wet belt, so it doesn't get a lot of rain like nearby Suva; weather permitting, all meals are served outdoors.

Don't expect tennis courts or a golf course at Tomberua, though, believe it or not, there's tropical golfing on the reef at low tide! Deep-sea fishing is F$40 an hour and free activities include snorkeling, water-skiing, sailing, sailboarding, and boat trips. There's no resident divemaster, but scuba diving can be arranged through Suva dive shops with a pickup here at F$90 for one person, F$55 pp for two or more (one tank). The launch transfer from Nakelo landing to Tomberua is F$19 pp each way; a Turtle Airways seaplane from Nandi will be F$286 pp OW (three-person minimum).

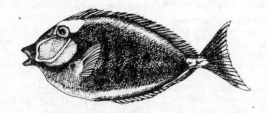

The surgeonfish gets its name from the knifelike spines just in front of its tail. Extreme care must be taken in handling the fish to avoid severe cuts.

DIANA LASICH-HARPER

SALVATORE CASA

CENTRAL VITI LEVU
THE CROSS-ISLAND HIGHWAY

Vunindawa

If you have a few days to spare, consider exploring the river country northwest of Nausori. The main center of Naitasiri Province is Vunindawa on the Wainimala River, a big village with four stores, a hospital, post office, police station, two schools, and a provincial office. Four buses a day depart Suva for Vunindawa but there's no bus connection to Korovou.

Go for a swim in the river or borrow a horse to ride around the countryside. Stroll two km down the road to Waindawara, where there's a free hourly punt near the point where the Wainimbuka and Wainimala rivers unite to form the mighty Rewa River. Take a whole day to hike up to Nairukuruku and Navuniyasi, then back.

Regular bus service operates along the Cross-Island Highway, with routes from both Suva and Tavua at either end, connecting at Monasavu in the middle. Buses depart Suva for Monasavu at 0800 and 1300 daily. If you want to make a connection at Monasavu for Nandarivatu or Tavua, you'll have to catch the 0800 bus. The 0800 bus to Monasavu passes Naluwai, across the river from Vunindawa, at about 1000, and Mbalea, trailhead of the Trans-Viti Levu Trek, about noon. A bus leaves Tavua for Monasavu at about 1500 daily (be at the stop by 1430), passing through Nandarivatu. We've heard that bus service via Monasavu is now greatly reduced, so check.

River-running

An exciting bamboo raft *(mbilimbili)* trip runs through the Waingga Gorge between Naitauvoli and Naivuthini, two villages on the Cross-Island Highway west of Vunindawa. The Monasavu bus passes nearby. Two men with long poles guide each raft through the frothing rapids as the seated visitor views towering boulders enveloped in jungle. The charge for the two-hour ride is F$25 pp, but reservations must be made in advance, as an individual *mbilimbili* will have to be constructed for you. (There's no way to get a used *mbilimbili* back up to Naitauvoli.)

Write Turangi-ni-koro, Naitauvoli Village, Wainimala, Naitasiri, P.A. Naikasanga, Fiji Islands, at least two weeks ahead, giving the exact date of your arrival in the village and the number in your party. The Fiji Visitors Bureau in Suva may be able to help you arrange this trip. No trips are made on Sunday. If you plan to spend the night at Naitauvoli, specify whether you require imported European-style food or will be satisfied with local village produce. If you stay overnight a *sevu sevu* and monetary contribution to your hosts are expected in addition to the F$25 pp for the raft trip.

Monasavu Hydroelectric Project

The largest development project ever undertaken in Fiji, this massive F$234 million scheme at Monasavu on the Nandrau Plateau (near the center of Viti Levu) took 1,500 men and six years to complete by 1985. This earthen dam, 82 meters high, was built on the Nanuka River to supply water to the four 20-megawatt generating turbines at the Wailoa Power Station on the Wailoa River, 625 meters below. The dam forms a lake 17 km long, and the water drops through a 5.4-km tunnel at a 45-degree angle, one of the steepest engineered dips in the world. Overhead transmission lines carry power from Wailoa to Suva and Lautoka, and Monasavu is capable of filling Viti Levu's needs well into the 1990s, representing huge savings on imported diesel oil.

Mount Victoria

The two great rivers of Fiji, the Rewa and the Singatoka, originate on the slopes of Mt. Victoria (Tomanivi), the country's highest mountain (1,323 meters). The climb begins near the bridge at Navai, 10 km from Nandarivatu. Turn right up the hillside a few hundred meters down the jeep track, then climb up through native bush on the main path all the way to the top. Beware of misleading signboards. There are three small streams to cross; no water after the third. Bright red epiphytic orchids *(Dendrobium mohlianum)* are sometimes in full bloom. There's a flat area up there where you could camp—if you're willing to take your chances with Mbuli, the devil king of the mountain. On your way down, stop for a swim at the largest stream. Allow about six hours for the roundtrip. Local guides are available. Mount Victoria is on the divide between the wet and dry sides of Viti Levu, and from the summit you should be able to distinguish the contrasting vegetation in these zones.

THE TRANS-VITI LEVU TREK

Experienced hikers can try the rugged two-day trek from the Cross-Island Highway to Wainimakutu, up and down jungle river valleys through the rainforest. It will take a strong, fast hiker about three hours from Mbalea on the highway to Nasava, then another four hours over the ridge to Wainimakutu. The Trans-Viti Levu Trek passes through several large Fijian villages and gives you a good cross section of village life.

On this traditional route, you'll meet people going down the track on horseback or on foot. Since you must cross the rivers innumerable times, the trek is probably impossible for visitors during the rainy season (Dec. to April), although the locals still manage to do it. If it's been raining, sections of the trail become a quagmire, stirred up by horses' hoofs. Hiking boots aren't much use here; you'd be better off with shorts and an old pair of running shoes in which to wade across the rivers. There are many refreshing places to swim along the way. Some of the villages have small trade stores, but you're better off carrying your own food. Pack some *yanggona* as well. You can always give it away if someone invites you in.

But remember, you are not the first to undertake this walk; the villagers have played host to trekkers many times. Some previous hikers have not shown much consideration to local residents along the track. Unless you have been specifically invited, do not presume automatic hospitality. If a villager provides food or a service, be prepared to offer adequate payment. This applies equally to the Singatoka River Trek. Camping is a good alternative, so take your tent if you have one. Hopefully, the locals will soon recognize the popularity of these treks and set up simple rest houses along the way for trekkers to use.

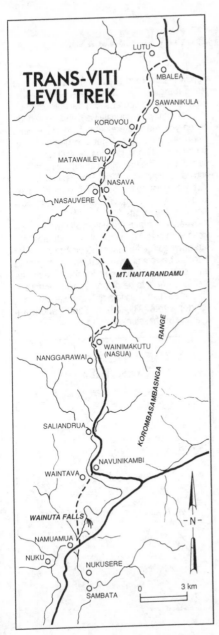

The Route

Take the Monasavu bus to **Mbalea**, which is just before Lutu. From Mbalea walk down to the Wainimala River, which must be crossed three times before you reach the bank opposite Sawanikula. These crossings can be dangerous and well-nigh impossible in the rainy season, in which case it's better to stop and wait for some local people who might help you across. From Sawanikula it's not far to **Korovou**, a fairly large village with a primary school, clinic, and two stores. Between Korovou and **Nasava** you cross the Wainimala River 14 times, but it's easier because you're farther upstream. Try to reach Nasava on the first day. If you sleep at Korovou you'll need an early start and a brisk pace to get to the first village south of the divide before nightfall on the second day.

From Nasava, follow the course of the Waisomo Creek up through a small gorge and past a waterfall. You zigzag back and forth across the creek all the way up, almost to the divide. After a steep incline you cross to the south-coast watershed. You could camp in a clearing among the bamboo groves on top, but there's no water. Before **Wainimakutu** (Nasau) the scenery gets better as you enter a wide valley with Mt. Naitarandamu (1,152 meters) behind you and the jagged outline of the unscaled Korombasambasanga Range to your left. Wainimakutu is a large village with two stores and bus service to Suva twice daily, at 0600 and 1300.

Namosi

The bus from Wainimakutu to Suva goes via **Namosi**, spectacularly situated below massive Mt. Voma (927 meters), with sheer stone cliffs on all sides. You can climb Mt. Voma in a day from Namosi for a sweeping view of much of Viti Levu. It's steep but not too difficult. Allow at least four hours up and down. Mr. Anani Lorosio at Namosi village is available as a guide (F$10). Visit the old Catholic Church at Namosi.

There are low-grade copper deposits, estimated at one-half million tonnes, at the foot of the Korombasambasanga Range, which Rupert Brooke called the "Gateway to Hell," 14 km north of Namosi by road. No mining has begun due to depressed world prices and high production costs, though feasibility studies continue. A 1979 study indicated that an investment of F$ one billion would be required.

THE SINGATOKA RIVER TREK

One of the most rewarding trips you can make on Viti Levu is the three-day hike south across the center of the island from Nandarivatu to Korolevu on the Singatoka River. There are many superb campsites along the trail.

Nandarivatu

Nandarivatu, on the Cross-Island Highway, is an important forestry station; its 900-meter altitude means a cool climate and a fantastic panorama of the north coast from the ridge. An excellent viewpoint is just above the district officer's residence. This is the source of the Singatoka River.

While you're at Nandarivatu, make a sidetrip to Mt. Lomalangi (Mt. Heaven), which has a fire tower on top that provides a good platform for viewing Mt. Victoria. Actually the tower seems about to collapse, but you might still risk climbing up onto its shaky roof. It's an hour's hike to the tower past the Forestry Training Center; the governor-general's swimming hole is also on the way. Pine forests cover the land.

Practicalities

Nandarivatu is a good place to catch your breath before setting out on the trek. The **Forestry Rest House** at Nandarivatu charges F$5, but you must reserve in advance at the Ministry of Forestry in Suva (tel. 301-611) or Lautoka (tel. 812-077). The rest house originally served as a summer retreat for expats from the nearby Vatukoula gold mine. When booking, explain that you don't mind sharing the facilities with other travelers, otherwise they might reserve the whole building (nine beds) just for you, or turn you away for the same reason. (An unverified late report indicates that this rest house has burned down.) Also ask about camping permits for this area. Some canned foods are available at the canteen opposite the rest house, but bring most of the food you'll need for the hike from Suva or Lautoka. Cabin crackers are handy.

Get there on the Monasavu bus that leaves Suva at 0800 (change of buses at Monasavu) and Tavua at 1500. Arrive at the stop at least 30 minutes ahead, as these buses do fill up.

The Route

Follow the dirt road south from Nandarivatu to **Nangatangata**. Fill your canteen here; the trail ahead of you is rigorous and no water is to be found. From Nangatangata walk about one hour. When you reach the electric high-power line, where the road turns right and begins to descend toward Koro, look for the well-worn footpath ahead. The trail winds along the ridge, and you can see as far as Mba. The primeval forests that once covered this part of Fiji were destroyed long ago by the slash-and-burn agricultural techniques of the Fijians.

When you reach the pine trees the path divides, with Nanoko to the right and **Numbutautau** down to the left. If you decide to make for Nanoko, beware of a very roundabout loop road on the left. The Reverend Thomas Baker, the last missionary to be clubbed and devoured in Fiji (in 1867), met his fate at Numbutautau. Jack London wrote "The Whale Tooth" about the death of the missionary.

THE SINGATOKA RIVER TREK

Numbutautau gets more than its share of hikers looking for a place to stay. A simple guesthouse would make things easier for all concerned and would provide a little income for the villagers. Suggest it to them. Nangatangata, Namoli, and Korolevu have also been visited far too often for it to be pure Fijian hospitality anymore: a monetary *sevu sevu*, spiced with a bundle of *waka*, is in order. Camping is an excellent alternative, but please don't spoil things by littering or causing fires.

The Numbutautau-Korolevu section involves 22 crossings of the Singatoka River—easy enough in the dry season (cut a bamboo staff for balance), but almost impossible in the wet season (Dec. to April). During the rainy season it's best to turn right and head to Nanoko, where you may be able to find a carrier to Mbukuya or all the way to Nandi. Bus service is available between Mbukuya and Mba. Still, it's a fantastic trip down the river to **Korolevu** if you can make it. Hiking boots will be useless in the river, so wear a pair of old running shoes. From Korolevu you can take a carrier to Tumbarua, which has four buses a day to Singatoka (F$2).

The Korolevu villagers can call large eels up from a nearby pool with a certain chant. A few hours' walk from Korolevu are the **pottery villages**, Ndraumbuta and Nakoro, where traditional, long Fijian pots are still made. The pots are not sold, but you can trade mats or salt for one.

NORTHERN VITI LEVU

Korovou To Natovi And Beyond

Korovou is an engaging small town 31 km north of Nausori on the east side of Viti Levu at the junction of King's Rd. and the road to **Natovi**, terminus of the Ovalau and Vanua Levu ferries. Its crossroads position in the heart of Tailevu Province makes it an important stop for buses plying the northern route around the island. (**Note:** since "korovou" means "new village," there are many places called that in Fiji—don't mix them up.) The large dairy farms in this area were set up just after WW I. The very enjoyable **Tailevu Hotel** (tel. 43-28) in Korovou has 10 rooms beginning at F$14 s, F$20 d. The hotel's public bar can get wild.

Nanggatawa, eight km north of Natovi, has a camping area near a good beach (but no surf). Ask about this place at the Coconut Inn in Suva, which owns the property. For a sweeping view of the entire Tailevu area, climb **Mt. Tova** (647 meters) in a day from Silana village, eight km northwest of Nanggatawa.

At Wailotua #1, 20 km west of Korovou, is a large **cave** (admission F$2) right beside the village, easily accessible from the road. One stalactite in the cave is shaped like a six-headed snake. From Wailotua, King's Rd. follows the Wainimbuka River north almost all the way to Viti Levu Bay.

Ra Province

The old Catholic Church of St. Francis Xavier at **Naiserelangi**, on a hilltop above Navunimbitu Catholic School on King's Rd. about 25 km southeast of Rakiraki, was beautifully decorated with frescoes by Jean Charlot in 1962-63. Typically Fijian motifs such as the *tambua, tanoa,* and *yanggona* blend in the powerful composition behind the altar. Father Pierre Chanel, who was martyred on Futuna Island in 1841, appears on the left holding the weapon that killed him, a war club. Christ and the Madonna are portrayed in black. The church is worth stopping to see, and you'll find an onward bus, provided it's not too late in the day. Ask the driver.

Three banks are at **Rakiraki**, a small town that grew up beside the Penang Sugar Mill,

erected in 1880. The mill is connected by an 11-km cane railway to Ellington Wharf, where the sugar is loaded aboard ships. The two-story **Rakiraki Hotel** (Box 31, Rakiraki; tel. 694-101) has 36 a/c rooms with fridge and private bath at F$80 s, F$90 d. In 1991 this hotel was thoroughly renovated, though the old colonial atmosphere was retained. The hotel's outdoor bowling green draws lawn bowling enthusiasts from Australia and New Zealand.

Navatu Rock a few kilometers west of Rakiraki was the jumping-off point for the disembodied spirits of the ancient Fijians. A fortified village once stood on its summit. The **Nakauvandra Range** towering south of Rakiraki is the traditional home of the Fijian serpent-god Degei, who is said to dwell in a cave on the summit of Mt. Uluda (866 meters). This "cave" is little more than a cleft in the rock. To climb the mountain, hire a guide at Tongowere village between Rakiraki and Tavua.

Nananu-i-ra Island

This small island five km off the northernmost tip of Viti Levu is a good place to spend some time amid perfect tranquillity and beauty without the commercialization of the resorts off Nandi. Here too the climate is dry and sunny. In the early 19th century the original Fijian inhabitants were wiped out by tribal warfare and disease, and an heir sold the island to Europeans whose descendants now operate small resorts and a 219-hectare plantation on the island. Great beaches, reefs, snorkeling, walks, sunsets, and moonrises over the water—Nananu-i-ra has it all; only the roads are absent.

Boat transfers from Ellington Wharf to Nananu-i-ra are around F$14 pp return (F$28 minimum, 20 minutes). Kontiki picks up at Volivoli tidal flat, but check when you call to make your booking. **Empire Taxi** (tel. 694-275) in Rakiraki provides transport to the landings at around F$6 for the car. The resorts are in touch with Empire several times a day and will send their boat over to pick you up, but you may have to wade out. Several budget hotels in Nandi (including Sunny Holiday Motel, the Nandi Town

Motel, and Kontiki Nandi) arrange minibus rides direct from Nandi to Ellington Wharf at F$21 pp, though it's cheaper to take an express bus to Rakiraki (F$4), then a taxi to the landing. When it's time to leave you can hike three km out to the main highway and flag down a Sunbeam bus to Suva (F$5) or Lautoka. Only local buses will stop at this junction; for the express you must go to Rakiraki. Ask about the direct ferry connection from Ellington Wharf to Nambouwalu, a great shortcut to Vanua Levu. It departs Ellington Wharf around 0700 on Tues., Thurs., and Sat., and there's a connecting bus to Lambasa.

The number of beds on the island is limited, and with Nananu-i-ra's growing popularity, it's strongly recommended that you call the resorts ahead to arrange to be picked up at Ellington, as they simply don't bother coming over when they're fully booked. If you want an individual room or *mbure* make 100% sure one is available immediately, otherwise you could end up spending quite a few nights in the dormitory waiting for one to become free. All the budget places have

NANANU - I - RA

cooking facilities, but it's necessary to take your own supplies as the island has no store or village. If you run out, groceries can be ordered from Rakiraki for a F$2 service charge, but it's best to bring everything with you when you come. The Nandi minibus stops at the market in Mba to give everyone a chance to stock up. Bring enough cash, as only the Mokusingas Island Resort accepts credit cards.

Somehow the island's South Sea flavor is captured best at **Kontiki Island Lodge** (Box 87, Rakiraki; tel. 694-290), offering shared accommodations in three seven-bed bungalows at F$10 pp, or F$25 d in one of the four *mbures* (usually full) with fridge and full cooking facilities. The generator runs until 2200. Enjoy the beach, snorkel, and rest—four nights is the average stay, though some people stay four weeks. Highly recommended. George and Oni at Kontiki have poor relations with Mr. Sanford Kent, manager of the adjacent Harper Plantation, and Kontiki guests are actively discouraged from trespassing on Harper property, where cattle graze beneath coconuts. The entire coastline is public, however, but only as far as two meters above the high-tide line. Avoid becoming stranded by high tide and forced to cut across private property.

At the other end of Nananu-i-ra and accessible only by boat are several slightly more expensive places to stay. **Betham's Bungalows** (Box 5, Rakiraki; tel. 694-132) has four units at F$40 s, F$48 d. Next door is MacDonald's **Nananu Beach Cottages** (Box 140, Rakiraki; tel. 694-633) with five cottages at F$40 s or d or F$45 deluxe. **Charley's Place** (Charley Anthony, Box 407, Rakiraki; tel. 694-676) is F$50 d in a deluxe *mbure* or F$13 in an eight-bed dorm. Charley's very friendly, though the kitchen and beds are in the same room. All these offer cooking facilities but there's no camping.

In Aug. 1991 **Mokusingas Island Resort** (Box 268, Rakiraki; tel. 694-449) opened on a white-sand beach in the center of Nananu-i-ra. The 20 comfortable duplex bungalows with fridge are F$145 for up to three persons, but cooking facilities are not provided and meals at the restaurant/bar are extra. Launch transfers are F$16 pp return. The resort's dive shop offers scuba diving at F$40 from a boat or F$25 from shore. A five-day PADI certification course costs

F$300. To create a diving attraction, the 43-meter *Papuan Explorer* was deliberately sunk in 25 meters of water just off the 189-meter Mokusingas jetty, which curves out into the sheltered lagoon. Happy hour on the jetty is a tradition here.

An American couple, Edward and Betty Morris, have lived at nearby Sunset Point since 1970. Ed is a former president of the International Brotherhood of Magicians and he always enjoys sharing magic with visitors.

Tavua

West of Rakiraki, King's Rd. gets much better, and at Tavua, an important junction on the northern coast, buses on the Cross-Island and northern coast highways meet. Catching a bus from Tavua to Rakiraki or Lautoka is usually no problem, but buses to Nandarivatu are less frequent (one leaves at 1500). **Eagle Lodge** in Tavua has good curries and videos. There are two banks in town but the Tavua Hotel (Box 81, Tavua; tel. 680-522) was recently reported closed, so ask.

Vatukoula

Gold was first discovered at Vatukoula, eight km south of Tavua, in 1932 by Bill Borthwick, an old prospector from Australia. Borthwick and his partner P. Costello of Suva sold their rights to an Australian company in 1934, and in 1935 the **Emperor Gold Mine** opened. The Western Mining Corporation of Australia sold its interest in the mine in 1991 but retains a management contract that runs until 1994. When it was suggested in 1987 that the Coalition government intended to nationalize the mine or at least introduce strict safety regulations, company officials allegedly provided support for the Taukei extremists to set up roadblocks and create public disorders.

The ore is mined both underground and in an open pit, and the mine presently extracts 135,000 ounces of gold annually from 600,000 tonnes of ore. A tonne of silver is also produced each year and waste rock is crushed into gravel and sold. Proven recoverable ore reserves at Vatukoula are sufficient for another decade of mining, and in 1985 additional deposits were discovered at nearby Nasomo where extraction began in 1988. At Vatukoula the ore comes up from the underground area through the Smith Shaft. There's also a crushing section, ball mill, and flotation area where gold and silver are separated from the ore.

Vatukoula is a genuine company town, with education and social services under the jurisdiction of the Emperor. Company housing consists of WW II-style Quonset huts. The 1,200 miners employed here (most of them indigenous Fijians) live in primitive, racially segregated ghettos. They are paided low wages, and benefits like overtime and public holiday pay are unknown. Workers with large families often end up going in the hole figuratively as well as physically—by running up high bills with the company for supermarket vouchers. Compensation to the families of five miners killed in accidents between 1987 and 1990 was paid only after feature articles about the situation ran in the *Fiji Times*. In contrast, tradesmen and supervisors, most of them Rotumans and part-Europeans, enjoy much better living conditions, and senior staff and management live in colonial-style comfort. Sensitive to profitability, the Emperor has tenaciously resisted the unionization of its work force, leading to bitter strikes in 1977 and 1991. It's not possible to visit the mine.

Mba

The large Indian town of Mba (population 10,255 in 1986) on the Mba River is seldom visited by tourists. As the attractive mosque in the center of town indicates, nearly half of Fiji's Muslims live in Mba Province. Small fishing boats depart from behind the Shell service station opposite the mosque, and it's fairly easy to arrange to go along on all-night trips. A wide belt of mangroves covers much of the river's delta. Mba is better known for the large Rarawai Sugar Mill, opened by the Colonial Sugar Refining Co. in 1886.

The **Mba Hotel** (Box 29, Mba; tel. 674-000), 110 Bank St., is the only organized accommodation. The 13 a/c rooms are F$33 s, F$42 d—very pleasant with a swimming pool, a bar, and a restaurant.

Four banks have branches in Mba.

If you'd like to stay in a village try **Navala** on the road to Mbukuya; ask for Semi and say the guy from the Peace Corps sent you (don't arrive on a Sunday).

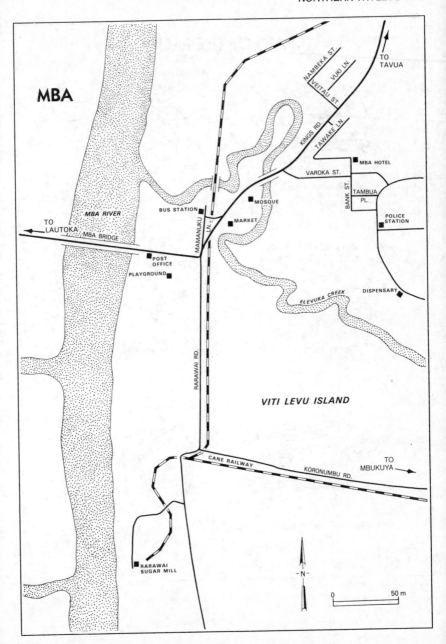

MBA

MBA RIVER

TO LAUTOKA

MBA BRIDGE

POST OFFICE

PLAYGROUND

BUS STATION

MAMANUKU LN.

MARKET

MOSQUE

ELEVUKA CREEK

RARAWAI RD.

VITI LEVU ISLAND

NAMBEKA ST.

VUKI LN.

VEITAU ST.

TO TAVUA

KINGS RD.

TAWAKE LN.

VAROKA ST.

BANK ST.

MBA HOTEL

TAMBUA PL.

POLICE STATION

DISPENSARY

CANE RAILWAY

KORONUMBU RD.

TO MBUKUYA

RARAWAI SUGAR MILL

-N-

0   50 m

CRABS OF THE PACIFIC

Carpilius maculatus

kalahimu

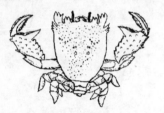

Ranina ranina

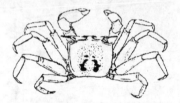

racing crab (Octypode ceratophthalma)

swimming crab (Portunus pelagicus)

kalavi

LOUISE FOOTE / 6

SALVATORE CASA

LAUTOKA AND VICINITY

LAUTOKA

Fiji's second-largest city (population 50,000), Lautoka is the main center of the sugar and timber industries, a major port, and Western Division headquarters. It's an amiable place with a row of towering royal palms along its main street. Though Lautoka grew up around the Fijian village of Namoli, it's a predominantly Indian town today. Shuttle boats to the Beachcomber and Treasure Island resorts in the Mamanutha Group depart from Lautoka, and this is the gateway to the Yasawa Islands. Lautoka offers a rambunctious nightlife (though not as good as Suva's), but it's also a religious city, with all the main religions of India (except the Jains and Buddhists) well represented. The mosque is also very prominent, located in the center of town. Unless you're into tourist-oriented activities, Lautoka is a good alternative to staying in Nandi.

SIGHTS OF LAUTOKA AND VICINITY

Sugar Mill
Before the 1987 military coups the Lautoka Sugar Mill (founded in 1903, on the southwest side of town) offered free tours during the crushing season (June to Nov.). Then the mill was reclassified as a potential target for sabotage, and all tours were stopped. Call the Fiji Sugar Corporation at 660-800 to find out if things are back to normal. You can see quite a bit of this mill, one of the largest in the Southern Hemisphere, from outside, even if you're not allowed in. Ask before taking photos.

Sikh Temple
Both males and females must cover their heads (handkerchiefs are all right) when they visit the

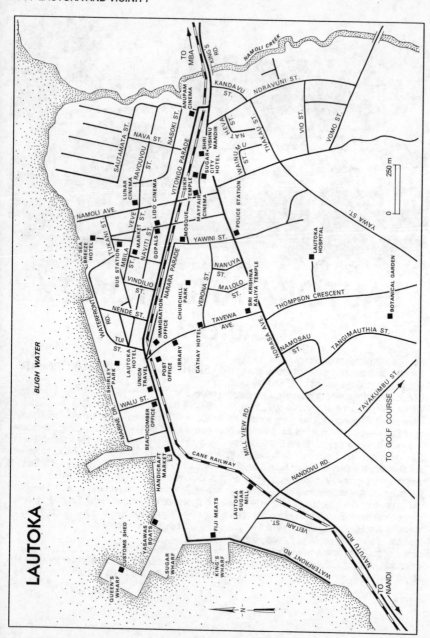

LAUTOKA

Sikh Temple. Sikhism began in the Punjab region of northwest India in the 16th century as a reformed branch of Hinduism much influenced by Islam: for example, Sikhs reject the caste system and idolatry. The teachings of the 10 gurus are contained in the *Granth,* a holy book prominently displayed in the temple. The Sikhs are easily recognized by their beards and turbans. There is a *dharamshala* (hostel) in the temple where sensitive visitors may spend the night, but cigarettes, liquor, and meat are forbidden. It has a communal kitchen, and lunch is served weekdays after the noon service. Make a contribution to the temple when you leave. In Oct. 1989 the old Sikh Temple was burned down by a gang of fundamentalist Christians, but the temple has since been rebuilt.

LOUISE FOOTE

Hare Krishna Temple

The Sri Krishna Kaliya Temple on Tavewa Ave. (open daily until 2030) is the most prominent Krishna temple in the South Pacific. The images inside on the right are Radha and Krishna, while the central figure is Krishna dancing on the snake Kaliya to show his mastery over the reptile. The story goes that Krishna chastised Kaliya and exiled him to the island of Ramanik Deep, which Fiji Indians believe to be Fiji. (Curiously, the native Fijian people have also long believed in a serpent-god, named Degei, who lived in a cave in the Nakauvandra Range.) The two figures on the left are incarnations of Krishna and Balarama. At the front of the temple is a representation of His Divine Grace A.C. Bhaktivedanta Swami Prabhupada, founder of the International Society for Krishna Consciousness (ISKCON).

The big event of the week at the temple is the Sun. evening *puja* (prayer) from 1630-2030, followed by a vegetarian feast. Visitors are encouraged to join in the singing and dancing. Take off your shoes and sit on the white marble floor, men on one side, women on the other.

The female devotees are especially stunning in their beautiful *saris.* Bells ring, drums are beaten, conch shells are blown, and stories from the Vedas, Srimad Bhagavatam, and Ramayana are acted out as everyone chants, *"Hare Krsna, Hare Krsna, Krsna Krsna, Hare Hare, Hare Rama, Hare Rama, Rama, Rama, Hare, Hare."* It's a real celebration of joy and a most moving experience. At one point children will circulate with small trays covered with burning candles, on which it is customary to place a modest donation; you may also drop a dollar or two in the yellow box in the center of the temple. You'll be readily invited to join the feast later, and no more money will be asked of you.

If you are interested in learning more about Vedic philosophy, several spiritual teachers who reside in the temple ashram would be delighted to talk to you about the *Bhagavad-gita,* and who can supply literature for a nominal fee. It's also possible to stay at the temple. On Sun. 15 Oct. 1989, members of a Methodist youth group carried out a firebomb attack on this temple and

DAVID STANLEY

The Sunday afternoon festival and feast at Lautoka's Hare Krishna Temple, fifth largest in the South Pacific, is worth attending.

three other Indian places of worship in Lautoka, causing hundreds of thousands of dollars in damage.

North Of Lautoka

Timber is becoming important as Fiji attempts to diversify its economy away from sugar. One of the largest reforestation projects yet undertaken in the South Pacific is the **Lololo Pine Scheme**, eight km off King's Rd. between Lautoka and Mba. The logs are sawn into timber if straight or ground into chip if twisted, then exported from Lautoka. You could swim at a shady picnic area along a dammed creek at the forestry station, but even if you don't stop, it's worthwhile to take the roundtrip bus ride from Lautoka to see this beautiful area and learn how it's being used.

East Of Lautoka

Ambatha village, east of Lautoka, is the perfect base for hiking into the **Mt. Evans Mountains** behind Lautoka. Guides are available. Take a *sevu sevu* of *yanggona* roots and pay F$2 pp a day hiking tax to the *turanga-ni-koro*. Four waterfalls are near the village, and **Table Mountain**, with sweeping views of the coast and Yasawas, is only an hour away. More ambitious hikes to higher peaks are possible. The landscape of wide green valleys set against steep slopes is superb.

You can get there by taking the Tavakumba bus as far as Ambatha junction, then hiking another 10 km to the village. A better idea is to hire a carrier direct to Ambatha from Lautoka

market for about F$10. Fiji-style accommodations are provided in the village for F$10 pp, including basic meals. It's all part of a local income-generating project, so you'll be well received. Avoid arriving in Ambatha on Sun., the traditional day of worship and rest.

South Of Lautoka

A popular legend invented in 1893 holds that **Viseisei** village between Lautoka and Nandi (frequent buses) is the oldest settlement in Fiji. It's told how the first Fijians, led by chiefs Lutunasobasoba and Degei, came from the west, landing their great canoe, the *Kaunitoni,* at Vunda Point, where the oil tanks are now. A Centennial Memorial (1835-1935) in front of the church commemorates the arrival of the first Methodist missionaries in Fiji. Opposite the memorial is a traditional Fijian *mbure*—the residence of the present king of Vunda. Near the back of the church is another monument topped by a giant war club.

All this is only a few minutes' walk from the bus stop, but you're expected to have someone accompany you (Fijian villages are private property). Ask permission of anyone you meet at the bus stop and he or she will send a child with you. You could give the child a pack of chewing gum as you part. Nearby is a **Memorial Cultural Center,** where souvenirs are sold to cruise ship passengers. There's a fine view of Nandi Bay from the Center. The late Dr. Timoci Bavadra, former prime minister of Fiji deposed by the Rabuka coup in 1987, hailed from Viseisei.

the guns of Lomolomo on a hilltop between Lautoka and Nandi

DAVID STANLEY

A couple of kilometers from the village on the airport side of Viseisei, just above Lomolomo Public School, are two **British six-inch guns** set up here during WW II to defend the northern side of Nandi Bay. It's a fairly easy climb from the main highway, and you'll get an excellent view from the top.

Scuba Diving

The closest scuba locale to Lautoka is **Tivoa Island** (20 km roundtrip), which has clean, clear water (except when it rains), abundant fish, and beautiful coral. Farther out is **Vomolailai Island** (50 km RT), a sheer wall covered with Gorgonian soft coral, visibility 30 meters plus. The **Mana Main Reef** off Mana Island (65 km RT) is famous for its drop-offs. It has turtles, fish of all descriptions, plus the occasional crayfish. Visibility on this reef is never less than 25 meters. At **Yalombi**, on Waya Island (100 km RT) in the Yasawas, see cabbage coral, whip coral, and giant fan corals in the warm, clear waters teeming with fish.

   Dive Expeditions Ltd. (Box 502, Lautoka; tel. 664-422) has a dive shop at the corner of Nende and Naviti streets in Lautoka where you can arrange scuba trips and rent snorkeling gear. Tank air fills at offshore islands can also be arranged. Six-day trips to Waya Island in the Yasawas are also offered for scuba divers and snorkelers. Divers should call for free pickup at Nandi/Lautoka hotels.

PRACTICALITIES

Accommodations

The 16-room **Sugar City Hotel** (Box 736, Lautoka; tel. 6619-201) on Nathula St. charges F$7 pp in the dorm (four beds) or F$15 s, F$22.50 d for a private room with bath. It's rather noisy at night.

   More appealing is the clean, quiet **Sea Breeze Hotel** (Box 152, Lautoka; tel. 660-717), 5 Bekana Lane on the waterfront near the bus station, from F$24 s, F$29 d, F$35 t for one of the 26 rooms with private bath (rooms with a/c F$5 more). The food served here is good, and it even has a swimming pool.

   Also recommended are the 40 rooms at the **Cathay Hotel** (Box 239, Lautoka; tel. 660-566),

Tavewa Ave., which features a small swimming pool. The charge is F$25 s, F$30 d with a/c and private bath, F$18 s, F$22 d with fan. Several dormitories of varying size, cleanliness, and facilities are available at F$6 pp.

   To be close to the action, stay at the 36-room **Lautoka Hotel** (Box 51, Lautoka; tel. 660-388), 2 Naviti St., which has several good bars and nightclubs on the premises. It also has a pool. Room prices vary from F$12.50 s, F$17.50 d for a fan-cooled room with shared bath, to F$30 s or d for a/c and private bath, and F$55 s or d for a/c, private bath, fridge, and water bed.

   Lautoka's most expensive hotel is the **Waterfront Hotel** (Box 4653, Lautoka; tel. 664-777), a two-story building erected in 1987 on Marine Drive. The 41 water-bed-equipped a/c rooms are F$80 s, F$90 d and there's a swimming pool. Those with a late flight out of Nandi can get a room for half price if they arrange to vacate by 2300. Members of groups departing Lautoka on Yasawa Islands tours often stay here.

At The Beach

Several beach hotels are located between Lautoka and Nandi airport, two km off the main road. The first two are alike in offering dormitory accommodations with good cooking facilities, fridge, swimming pool, and nearby stores. **Saweni Beach Apartments** (Box 239, Lautoka; tel. 661-777) offers a row of 12 self-contained apartments with fan at F$35 s or d, plus a F$10 dorm. Campers are welcome at F$4 pp. Saweni is quieter and has a better beach than the Anchorage mentioned below. Fishermen on the beach sell fresh fish every morning. Cruising yachts often anchor off Saweni Beach—much better than anchoring at Lautoka. A bus runs right to the hotel from Lautoka four times a day. There's been talk of a megadevelopment at Saweni with hundreds of condos, a marina, and Holiday Inn, Meridien, and Westin hotels, but so far nothing has happened. The beach only comes alive on weekends, when local picnickers arrive.

   The **Anchorage Beach Resort** (Box 9472, Nandi Airport; tel. 662-099), between Viseisei and Vunda Point a few km south of the Saweni Beach, has 10 rooms at F$75 s, F$90 d, and a F$15 pp dorm with cooking facilities. A swimming pool, washing machine, and panoramic views are among the other attractions. Stay at the Anchorage if you like meeting people, at Saweni if you want to regenerate.

Mediterranean Villas (Box 5240, Lautoka; tel. 664-011), on Vunda Hill overlooking Viseisei village, has six attractive villas beginning at US$90 s, F$120 d. Cooking facilities are not provided, but a licensed Italian seafood restaurant is on the premises.

Paradise Island

Paradise Island Resort (Helene Kelly, Private Mail Bag, Lautoka; tel. 665-222), on Mbekana Island just a few km north of Lautoka, opened in 1991. They offer 12 thatched fan-cooled *mbures* with private bath and fridge (but no cooking facilities) at F$120 s, F$135 d, F$150 t, breakfast included. Accommodation in Paradise's 12-bed dormitory is F$15 pp to sleep or F$45 pp including all meals. Add F$15 pp for return boat transfers from Lautoka, and ask about special five-night dormitory packages that include transfers and all meals. Activities here include horseback riding and water sports, and guests can be dropped off on uninhabited islands. The proximity to Lautoka makes Paradise Island Resort a good choice for those who want to combine beach life with organized shopping and sightseeing. A day-trip to the island from Lautoka is F$25 including lunch.

For information on Beachcomber Island and Treasure Island resorts, both accessible from Lautoka, see "The Mamanutha Group" above.

Food

The **Ming Wah Cafe** (tel. 661-719) on Yasawa St. across from the bus station is a good choice if you roll into Lautoka hungry. Their menu is surprisingly extensive and reasonable. **Narsey's Restaurant** (tel. 660-357) nearby has the best Indian food—very spicy.

Rennee's Restaurant (62 Naviti St.; tel. 662-473) has the standard curry- and chop suey-type dishes, but tasty big portions and reasonable prices. The **Hot Snax Shop**, 56 Naviti St., is also good for Indian dishes.

Enjoy ample servings of good Cantonese food at the a/c **Sea Coast Restaurant** (tel. 660-675) on Naviti St.; F$3-7 menu. Also try the **Empress of China** (tel. 661-969), 143 Vitongo

Parade. For dessert, try the ice cream at **Gopals** (tel. 662-990) on Naviti St. near the market.

Entertainment

Four movie houses feature several showings daily. The disco scene in Lautoka centers on the **Hunter's Inn** (open Fri. and Sat. 2100-0100 only; F$4 cover) near the Lautoka Hotel. Next door is **Cinderella's**, with a rougher atmosphere. Roughest is **Galaxy Disco** in the center of town. Nothing happens at Galaxy before 2200. The **Captain Cook Lounge** at the Lautoka Hotel is a safe place for an early evening drink (they close at 2100).

Catch an exciting rugby or soccer game at the stadium in Churchill Park. Admission is reasonable—check locally for the times of league games.

Day cruises to Beachcomber Island (F$50 pp including lunch) depart Lautoka daily at 1000—a great way to spend a day.

Shopping And Services

Lautoka has a big, colorful market, open daily except Sun., but it's busiest on Saturday. The duty-free shopping in Lautoka is poor compared to Suva, but the sellers aren't as pushy as those in Nandi.

Lautoka Hospital (Mon.-Fri. 0800-1600, Sat. 0800-1100; tel. 660-399) has an outpatient service and dental clinic. A consultation with Dr. Y. Raju, whose office is across the street from Desai Bookstore, is more convenient. Vaccinations for international travelers are available at the Health Office (Tues. and Fri. 0800-1200).

The **Forestry Dept.** (tel. 661-085) in the Department of Agriculture Bldg. takes reservations for the Nandarivatu Forestry Rest House (see "The Singatoka River Trek" above).

The **Western Regional Library** (tel. 660-091) nearby has a good collection of topographical maps you could use to plan your trip.

Transport

Buses, carriers, taxis—everything leaves from the bus stand beside the market. **Pacific Transport** (tel. 660-499) has express buses to Suva via Queen's Rd. daily at 0630, 0700, 1210, and 1730 daily (five hours). Four other "stage" buses also operate daily (six hours) along this route. **Sunbeam Transport** (tel.

662-822) has three expresses a day to Suva (six hours) via Tavua, plus two local buses on the same route (nine hours).

Anyone headed toward Vanua Levu should check with **Patterson Bros.** (71 Vitongo Parade; tel. 661-173), which runs a bus/ferry/bus service between Lautoka, Rakiraki, Nambouwalu, Lam-basa, departing Lautoka around 0400.

Time Shipping Agency Ltd. (Box 4027, Lautoka; tel. 660-365), 1st Floor, Sunnybrook Building, Wharf Rd., books passage to Auckland and Apia on the container ship MV *Cotswold Prince,* with sailings every three weeks. Book well ahead, as capacity is limited.

CORALS OF THE PACIFIC

acropora

staghorn fire coral *(Millepora alcicornis)*

table coral

mushroom coral
(Fungia fungites)

elkhorn fire coral
(Millepora platyphylla)

honeycomb coral *(Favia matthaii)*

brain coral *(Meandrina)*

DIANA LASICH-HARPER / 7

SALVATORE CASA

THE YASAWA ISLANDS

The Yasawas are a chain of 16 main volcanic islands and dozens of smaller ones stretching 80 km in a north-northeastern direction roughly 35 km off the west coast of Viti Levu; they offer beautiful, isolated beaches, cliffs, bays, and reefs. In the lee of Viti Levu, the Yasawas are dry and sunny. The waters are crystal clear and almost totally shark-free. The group was romanticized in two movies titled *The Blue Lagoon:* a 1949 original starring Jean Simmons and the 1980 remake with Brooke Shields. It was from the north end of the Yasawas that two canoeloads of cannibals appeared in 1789 and gave Capt. William Bligh and his 18 companions a chase less than a week after the famous mutiny.

Two centuries later, increasing numbers of cruise ships ply the chain. Though an abundance of luxury resorts dot the islands off Nandi, you won't find many regular, inexpensive places to stay. The usual thing for backpackers is to visit Tavewa (see below) by village boat from Lautoka. Visiting any of the other islands usually involves some local contact, a *sevu sevu* of *yanggona* (which doesn't grow in the Yasawas) for the chief, and observing the etiquette outlined under "Staying In Villages" in the Intro-

duction. You'll also have to take most of your own food.

Waya Island
The 579-meter peak on Waya is the highest in the Yasawas. A sheer mass of rock rises above **Yalombi** village, which also has a beautiful beach. At low tide you can wade from here across to neighboring Wayasewa Island: there's good snorkeling here. A remarkable 354-meter-high volcanic thumb overlooks the south coast of Wayasewa. Also from Yalombi it's a 30-minute hike across the ridge to Natawa village on the east side of Waya. A deserted beach is located another 20 minutes north of Natawa.

For a place to stay at Yalombi, ask for Miss Andi or her brother Monasa, who rent 15 two-person thatched *mbures* at F$18 pp, plus F$25 pp for local meals (bring your own drinks). The huts are usually used by scuba divers sent over by **Dive Expeditions Ltd.** (Box 502, Lautoka; tel. 664-422), so you might inquire at their Lautoka office at the corner of Nende and Naviti streets. They may even be able to provide boat transportation to Waya at F$50 pp return. This local resort makes a good base for observing

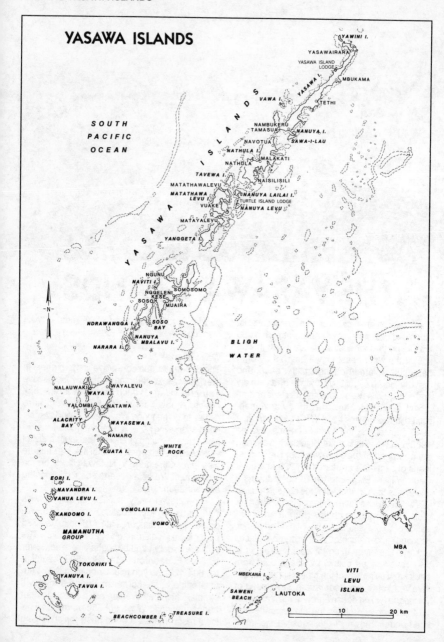

YASAWA ISLANDS

YAWINI I.

YASAWAIRARA

YASAWA ISLAND LODGE

MBUKAMA

SOUTH PACIFIC OCEAN

VAWA I.

TETHI

NAMBUKERU
TAMASUA
NANUYA I.
NAVOTUA
SAWA-I-LAU
NATHULA I.
MALAKATI
NATHULA
TAVEWA I.
NAISILISILI
MATATHAWALEVU
NANUYA LAILAI I.
MATATHAWA
LEVU I.
TURTLE ISLAND LODGE
VUAKE
NANUYA LEVU I.
MATAYALEVU
YANGGETA I.

NGUNU
NAVITI I.
SOMOSOMO
NGGELENI
KESE
SOSO
MUAIRA
NDRAWANGGA I.
SOSO
BAY
NANUYA
MBALAVU I.
NARARA I.

BLIGH WATER

NALAUWAKI
WAYALEVU
WAYA I.
YALOMBI
NATAWA
ALACRITY
BAY
WAYASEWA I.
NAMARO
KUATA I.
WHITE
ROCK

EORI I.
NAVANDRA I.
VANUA LEVU I.
KANDOMO I.
VOMOLAILAI I.
MAMANUTHA
GROUP
VOMO

MBA

TOKORIKI I.
YANUYA I.
TAVUA I.

VITI
LEVU
ISLAND

MBEKANA I.

SAWENI
BEACH
LAUTOKA

BEACHCOMBER I.
TREASURE I.

0   10   20 km

traditional Fijian life and enjoying nature while retaining one's privacy.

Tavewa Island

Tavewa is a strikingly beautiful small island about two km long with a population of around 50 souls. It has no store, telephones, or electricity, but tall grass covers the hilly interior, the bathing is excellent at a picture-postcard beach on the southeastern side, and there's a good fringing reef. This is freehold land, so there's no chief on Tavewa.

In the past we've recommended that travelers visiting Tavewa stay with Auntie Lucy Doughty and Auntie Amelia, who put up guests for around F$10 pp. Unfortunately, numerous contradictory complaints about these two places came in from readers who felt they'd been "used." Evidently the food they supplied didn't come back to them in their meals and there was tampering with the agreed-upon prices. Auntie Lucy even set up a

Captain William Bligh. *In 1789, after being cast adrift by the mutineers on his HMS* Bounty, *Capt. Bligh and 18 others in a seven-meter longboat were chased by two Fijian war canoes through what is now called Bligh Water. His men pulled the oars desperately, heading for open sea, and managed to escape the cannibals. They later arrived in Timor, finishing the most celebrated open-boat journey of all time. Captain Bligh did some incredible charting of Fijian waters along the way.*

small store to resell the supplies and kava tendered by guests! What's really going on is hard to judge, and there's a tremendous jealousy and rivalry among the families on Tavewa. One group often berates the other to visitors—don't let yourself be taken in by it! Ask other travelers who have visited Tavewa recently and write us a letter about how it went for you.

Tavewa's still an idyllic island to visit if you don't mind a non-Fijian atmosphere and a lack of privacy. The snorkeling in the surrounding waters is great—tourists on the Blue Lagoon cruises pay hundreds of dollars for this! If you stay at Auntie Lucy's it's probably best to camp (F$5 pp), but consider hanging on to all of your own food and only paying at the end of your visit. Check out the accommodations Lucy offers in the house and ask if you can cook.

David and Kara Doughty's Place between Auntie Lucy's and the small church has several *mbures* for travelers at F$20 s or d, F$36 for four. Camping is F$5 pp, and since they started cutting the grass the mosquito problem has declined. The water supply is often exhausted, and the only way to shower is with a bucket of well water. There's no light in the toilet, so bring a flashlight and toilet paper if you need it. The Doughtys offer meals at F$8 for all three, but it's safer to bring your own food with you, especially green vegetables. They'll offer to cook your stuff for you for a F$1 fee, but it's traditional in Fiji to cook and eat communally, so you may not get back much of what you put in! Better cook it yourself and keep track of your own supplies. The Doughtys will invite you to join in family activities, and the results of David's fishing trips often appear at dinner. He'll take you to a scenic cave, and in the evening you can sit around drinking kava with David, playing backgammon, or (if you're a woman) helping Kara weave a mat.

Recently the redoubtable Doughty clan has added to its empire. This time it's **Otto & Fanny Doughty's Place** (Box 1349, Lautoka), with bungalows at F$30 s, F$45 d, F$52 t, or F$20 in the dorm.

You could also stay with **Uncle Robert de Bruce** who has huts with glass windows and mosquito nets at F$8 pp, plus F$1 for cooking (bring all your own food). For current information call 660-566 and ask for Don (Robert's son).

Contact is often made at the Cathay Hotel in Lautoka on Thursdays, and Don also represents Otto & Fanny. A German reader who stayed at Robert's liked Meca's meals of fresh fish seasoned with garlic and ginger and enjoyed Robert's evening tales of ten-headed snakes and buried treasure. Uncle Robert takes guests to the Sawa-i-Lau cave and to another island for folkloric "entertainment" (F$20 pp).

Also check out **Murray's Place** (Amelia, Jack, and Moses), which a Canadian couple who wrote in strongly recommended. Murray charges F$8 pp in simple *mbures*.

Exercise caution with persons you meet in Lautoka who say they can arrange your trip for you. Never pay any money up front for the food, boat, kava, etc., as your contact will probably pocket half the money and give you very basic supplies (if you see him again at all). You'll later be charged extra for the boat. It's okay to agree to go, but don't promise to stay with anyone in particular. Once on Tavewa you can size up the situation.

To get to Tavewa ask for the weekly Nathula boats, such as the *Calm Sea, Babale, Tai Vo, Ratu Levu, Andi Sulva, Vatuvula,* or *Nukunindreke* which leave the old King's, or "Fisherman's," Wharf at Lautoka on Tues. and Sat. at 0600, returning to Lautoka on Wed. or Thursday. Take all your own food, matches, candles, one kilo of kava, mosquito coils, and a *sulu* to cover up. If you'd like to take something to your hosts, they'll appreciate flour, sugar, powdered milk, and oil. Reader Miguel DaSilva sent us this:

Getting to Tavewa involves a 6-to-10-hour trip on small three-to-five-meter boats with weak, noisy engines. The boats are usually overloaded with passengers and cargo, and there's no radio or life vests. Usually the captain will tell you to sit/squat in one position and you will not be allowed to move/stretch very often because it might rock the boat too much. When the winds are strong the swells are high, and the trip is not for those who get seasick easily. Also, don't expect to go to the toilet—there is none, and for women this is a problem. The biggest of the weekly boats is the Bundi, but it is usually the most over-loaded. The captain tries to charge F$20-25 for the trip, but stick to F$15. The boats leave at 0500, and it is wise to arrange transport to the wharf the night before.

Turtle Island

If you've been looking for the South Pacific's ultimate resort, it may be **Turtle Island Lodge** (Richard Evanson, Box 9317, Nandi Airport; tel. 663-889) on 200-hectare Nanuya Levu in the middle of the Yasawa Group. Only 14 fan-cooled, two-room *mbures* grace Turtle, and eccentric American owner-resident Richard Evanson, who bought the island in 1972 for US$300,000, swears there'll never be more. The 28 guests (English-speaking mixed couples only, please) pay US$690 per couple per night, but that includes all meals, drinks, and activities (scuba diving not available). You'll find the fridge in your cottage well stocked with beer, wine, soft drinks, and champagne, refilled daily, and no extra bill to pay when you leave. Sports such as sailing, snorkeling, canoeing, sailboarding, glass-bottom boating, deep-sea fishing, catamaraning, horseback riding, guided hiking, and moonlight cruising are all included in the tariff. They'll even do your laundry at no charge.

If you want to spend the day on an uninhabited island, just ask and they'll drop you off. Later someone will be back with lunch and a cooler of wine or champagne. Otherwise use any of the dozen secluded beaches on the main island, including one a few steps from your door. Meals are served at your cottage or taken at the community table; every evening Richard hosts a small dinner party. He's turned down many offers to develop the island with hundreds more units or to sell out for a multimillion-dollar price. That's not Richard's style and he's quite specific about who he *doesn't* want to come: "Trendies, jetsetters, obnoxious imbibers and plastic people won't get much out of my place. Also, opinionated, loud, critical grouches and anti-socials should give us a miss."

Of course, all this luxury and romance has a price. Aside from the per diem, it's another US$520 per couple for roundtrip seaplane transportation to the island from Nandi. There's also a seven-night minimum stay, but as nearly half the guests are repeaters that doesn't seem to be

KARL PARTRIDGE

village house, Nathula, Yasawa Island

an impediment. (Turtle Island is off-limits to anyone other than hotel guests.) Turtle's success may be measured by its many imitators, including the Vatulele Island Resort, the Wakaya Club, Lauthala Island, Kaimbu Island, Yasawa Island Lodge, and others. Turtle Island has also set the standard for environmentally-conscious resort development. Aside from planting thousands of trees and providing a safe haven for birds, Evanson has preserved the island's mangroves, cleverly erecting a boardwalk to turn what others may have considered an eyesore into a major attraction. Nanuya Lailai Island, adjacent to Turtle, is being developed by Blue Lagoon Cruises as a beach facility for passengers on their Yasawa cruises.

Yasawa Island

In March 1991 **Yasawa Island Lodge** (Box 10128, Nandi Airport; tel. 663-364) opened on a creamy white beach on the upper west side of Yasawa Island, the groups largest and northernmost. For many years the Fiji government had a policy that the Yasawas were "closed" to land-based tourism development, and construction of this $8.5-million Australian-owned resort was only approved after the 1987 coups. Most of the resort's employees come from Mbukama village, which owns the land.

At present Yasawa Island Lodge has only eight thatched *mbures,* but plans exist to build another 10 and a golf course. The five one-room units are F$470 s, F$650 d, F$950 t, while the three two-bedroom *mbures* are F$785 d, F$1150 t, F$1200 for four. All meals are included, but unlike most other resorts in this category alcoholic drinks are *not.* Scuba diving and game fishing also cost extra. The resort's 21-meter ketch, *Ariadne,* does sunset cruises.

Guests arrive on a chartered Sunflower Airlines flight (F$100 pp each way) that lands on the resort's private airstrip. Here they're met by a thatched six-wheel-drive truck called the "*mbure* bus" that carries them to the resort, while they sit on hard wooden benches in back. Children are admitted to the lodge only at Christmas and in July.

Others

One of the captains of the Tavewa boats, Mr. Aborisa Bogisa, will gladly take you to his home village on **Nathula,** where you can stay for F$10 pp a night including local meals (do bring ample supplies, however). You'll be introduced to the village chief who will expect from each person a *sevu sevu* of F$20 and 500 grams of kava. After that you'll be free to move around. This is much more of a Fijian experience than Tavewa; you'll be able to go out fishing with the men and even visit the Sawa-i-Lau caves. Ask around the harbor for Aborisa late Thurs. afternoon or early Fri. morning to allow yourself enough time to obtain a Yasawas permit from the district officer (see below). In 1991 a Nautilus Lagoon Resort was proposed for the southeast side of Nathula Island.

The Tui Yasawa, highest chief of the group, resides at Yasawairara village at the north end of **Yasawa Island**. On the island of **Sawa-i-Lau** is a large limestone cave illuminated by a crevice at the top. Within the cave is a clear, deep pool where you can swim, and an underwater opening leads back into a smaller, darker cave (bring a light). A Fijian legend tells how a young chief once hid his love in this cave when her family wished to marry her to another. Each day he brought her food until both could escape to safety on another island. All the cruise ships stop at this cave. If you get there on your own and wish to visit, pay F$2 pp to the chief of Nambukeru village just west of the cave.

Naviti (33 square km) is the largest of the Yasawas. Its king, one of the group's highest chiefs, resides at Soso. The church there houses fine woodcarvings. Every Wed. at noon the people of Soso gather to sell shells to the button factory. On the hillside above Soso are two caves containing the bones of ancestors. Yawe-sa, the secondary boarding school on Naviti, is a village in itself. Navitino has no wharf, so you must wade ashore from the boat.

The most remote of the Yasawas is **Viwa**, squatting alone 25 km northwest of Waya. Traditional Fijian pottery is made in the village on **Yanuya Island** in the Mamanutha Group. Of the 13 northern Mamanutha islands, only it and nearby Tavua have Fijian villages.

Permissions

Before going to the Yasawas you're expected to get a free permit from the district officer (tel. 660-710) in the Department of Agriculture and Fisheries building beside the public library (open Mon.-Fri. 0800-1300/1400-1600). He will only issue the permit if you have an invitation from the village you intend to visit, though it's sometimes enough simply to explain who your host will be. You don't need a permit or letter to go to Tavewa, which is freehold land.

Getting There

Village boats from the Yasawas arrive both at Lautoka's old King's Wharf and the old jetty near Fiji Meats on Wed. or Thurs. and depart on Fri. or Sat. morning. This means you must spend either five or 12 days in the Yasawas. The fare is around F$30 pp OW. There are always Yasawans around Lautoka market on Fridays.

SALVATORE CASA

THE LOMAIVITI GROUP

The Lomaiviti, or Central Fiji, Group lies in the Koro Sea near the heart of the archipelago, east of Viti Levu and south of Vanua Levu. Of its nine main volcanic islands, Ngau, Koro, and Ovalau are among the largest in Fiji. Lomaiviti's climate is moderate, neither as wet and humid as Suva nor as dry and hot as Nandi. The population is mostly Fijian, engaged in subsistence agriculture and copra making.

OVALAU ISLAND

The old capital island, Ovalau, is by far the best known and most visited of the group. Naingani has a tourist resort all its own, but Koro and Ngau are seldom visited, due to a lack of facilities for visitors. Ferries ply the Koro Sea to Ovalau, while onward ferries run to Savusavu a couple of times a week. Fiji Air flies several times a day to Ovalau, but only a couple of times a week to Koro and Ngau.

Ovalau, a large volcanic island just east of Viti Levu, is the main island of Lomaiviti Group. Almost encircled by high peaks, the Lovoni Valley in the center of Ovalau is actually the island's volcanic crater and about the only flat land. The crater's rim is pierced by the Mbureta River, which escapes through a gap to the southeast. The highest peak is 626-meter Nandelaiovalau (meaning, "the top of Ovalau") behind Levuka.

LEVUKA

The town of Levuka on Ovalau's east side was Fiji's capital until the shift to Suva in 1881. Founded as a whaling settlement in 1830, Levuka became the center for European traders in Fiji. A British consul was appointed in 1857. The cotton boom of the 1860s brought new settlers, and Levuka quickly grew into a boisterous town with over 50 hotels and taverns along Beach Street. Escaped convicts and debtors fleeing creditors in Australia swelled the throng, until it was said that a ship could find the reef

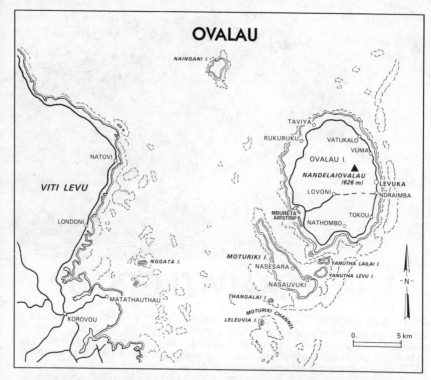

OVALAU

passage into Levuka by following the empty gin bottles floating out on the tide. The honest traders felt the need for a stable government, so in 1871 Levuka became capital of Cakobau's Kingdom of Fiji. The disorders continued, with certain elements forming a rebel faction defiant of any form of Fijian authority.

On 10 Oct. 1874, a semblance of decorum came as Fiji was annexed by Great Britain. A municipal council was formed in 1877. Ovalau's central location seemed ideal for trade, and sailing boats could easily reach the port from Lau or Vanua Levu. Yet the lush green hills that rise behind the town were its downfall, as colonial planners saw that there was no room for the expansion of their capital. In Aug. 1882 Governor Sir Arthur Gordon moved his staff to Suva. After a hurricane in 1886, Levuka's devastated buildings were not replaced.

Levuka remained the collection center for the copra trade right up until 1957. When that industry also moved to Suva, the town seemed doomed. With the establishment of a fishing industry in 1964 things picked up, and today it's a minor educational center, the headquarters of Eastern Division, and a low-profile tourist center. The false-fronted buildings and covered sidewalks along Beach St. give this somnolent town of 2,871 inhabitants (1986) a 19th-century, Wild West flavor. It's a perfect base for excursions into the mountains, along the winding coast, or out to the barrier reef one km offshore. Levuka is one of the more peaceful, pleasant, and picturesque places in Fiji.

SIGHTS

Near Queen's Wharf is the old Morris Hedstrom Ltd. store (erected in 1878 by Percy Morris and

Maynard Hedstrom), great-granddaddy of today's Pacific-wide Morris Hedstrom chain. In 1980 the building was restored and converted into a **museum and library** (closed Sun.) where cannibal forks vie with war clubs and clay pots for your attention. Ask at the museum about guided walking tours of historic Levuka and hikes to Lovoni (F$4 pp).

Stroll along Levuka's sleepy waterfront. The **Church of the Sacred Heart**, with its square stone clock tower, was erected by French Marist Fathers who arrived in 1858. When you reach the former movie house, turn left onto Hennings St. and head inland on the left side of Tongonga Creek to the **Levuka Public School** (1879), birthplace of Fiji's present public educational system. Other Levuka firsts include the first newspaper (1869), the first Masonic Lodge (1875), and the first bank (1876) in Fiji. Farther up Bath Rd. the creek has been dammed to create a pond. Continue straight up and you'll eventually reach the source of the town's water supply.

As you come back down the hill, on your left across the small bridge is the **Ovalau Club**. Despite the "Members Only" sign, you're welcome to go in. On the wall by the bar is a framed letter from Count Felix von Luckner, the WW I German sea wolf. Von Luckner left the letter and some money at the unoccupied residence of a trader on Katafanga Island in the Lau Group,

from which he took some provisions. In the letter, Count von Luckner identifies himself as Max Pemberton, an English writer on a sporting cruise through the Pacific. The old Town Hall (1898) and Masonic Lodge adjoin the Club. A few blocks north of the club, past the Royal Hotel, are the 199 steps up **Mission Hill** to an old Methodist school and a fine view.

On a low hill farther north along the waterfront is a **war memorial** to British residents of Levuka who died in WW I. Before Fiji was ceded to Britain the Cakobau government headquarters was installed on this hill. The Anglican Church (1904) beyond has stained-glass windows from that period.

North Of Levuka

Follow the coastal road north from Levuka to the second yellow bridge, where you'll see the old **Methodist church** (1869) on the left. In the small cemetery behind the church is the grave of the first U.S. consul to Fiji, John Brown Williams. For the story of Williams' activities see "European and Tongan Pentration" under "History" in the Introduction. Across the bridge and beneath a large *ndilo* tree is the tomb of an old king of Levuka. The large house in front of the tree is the residence of the present Tui Levuka.

Directly above is **Gun Rock**, used as a target in 1849 to show Cakobau the efficacy of a ship's cannon so he might be more considerate to res-

view of Levuka, as
seen from Gun Rock

ident Europeans. The early Fijians had a fort atop the rock to defend themselves against the Lovoni hill tribes. Ask permission of the Tui Levuka (the "Roko") or a member of his household to climb Gun Rock for a splendid view of Levuka. If a small boy leads you up and down, it wouldn't be out of place to give him something for his trouble. From the summit, let your eyes follow the horizon from right to left with the islands of Ngau, Mbatiki, Nairai, Wakaya, Koro, Makongai, and Vanua Levu, respectively, in view.

Continue north on the road, round a bend, pass the ruin of a large concrete building, and you'll reach a cluster of government housing on the site of a cricket field where the Duke of York (later King George V) played in 1878. There's a beautiful deep pool and waterfall behind **Waitovu** village, about two km north of Levuka. You may swim here but please don't skinny-dip; this is offensive to the local people and has led to serious incidents in the past. Since they're good enough to let you use this idyllic spot, which they own, it's common courtesy to respect their wishes.

South Of Levuka

The **Pacific Fishing Company** tuna cannery is south of the main wharf. A Japanese cold-storage facility opened here in 1964, the cannery in 1976. In 1986 the Japanese company involved in the joint venture pulled out, turning the facility over to the government. In 1989 a F$2 million state-of-the-art can-making factory opened alongside the cannery after investments by Kingfisher Holdings of Thailand. The facility is supplied with albacore tuna by Taiwanese longline fishing boats, and skipjack and yellowfin by pole-and-line ships of the government-owned Ika Corporation. Environmentally destructive fishing methods, such as gillnetting and purse seining, are not used by Pacific Fishing's suppliers. The canned fish, caught in the pollution-free South Pacific and processed using spring water from the source of Totongo Creek, has a good reputation. Most of the F$50 million worth of canned tuna produced each year is marketed in Britain by Sainsbury and John West and in Canada by B.C. Packers. A thousand residents of Ovalau have jobs related to tuna canning.

The **Cession Monument** is a little farther along; the Deed of Cession, which made Fiji a British colony, was signed here by Chief Cakobau in 1874. A traditional *mbure* used for Provincial Council meetings is on the other side of the road.

When you reach Ndraimba village (two km), take the road to the right before the four condominiums and follow a path for 4½ hours through enchanting forests and across clear streams to **Lovoni** village. The trail is no longer used by the locals and requires attentiveness to follow, so consider hiring a guide through the Visitors Bureau unless you're a very experienced hiker.

The Provincial Council meeting place at Levuka is built like a traditional Fijian chief's mbure.

THE FIJI TIMES

1. Yasawa boats at Lautoka, Viti Levu (D. Stanley); 2. Prince's Wharf, Suva (D. Stanley);

1. Queen's Wharf, Levuka, Ovalau (D. Stanley);
2. unloading gear, Mbalea, central Viti Levu (D. Stanley)

Swim and picnic, then catch the 1500 bus from Lovoni back to Levuka. It's also possible to hike to Lovoni from Rukuruku. In 1855 the fierce Lovoni tribesmen, the Ovalau, burned Levuka and continued to threaten it right up until 1871 when they were finally captured during a truce and sold to European planters as laborers. In 1875 the British government allowed the survivors to return to their valley, where their descendants live today.

If you forgo this hike and continue on the main road, you'll come to an old cemetery a little south of Ndraimba. A few kilometers farther is the **Devil's Thumb**, a dramatic volcanic plug towering above **Tokou** village, one of the scenic highlights of Fiji. Catholic missionaries set up a printing press at Tokou in 1889 to produce gospel lessons in Fijian. In the center of the village is a sculpture of a lion made by one of the early priests. It's five km back to Levuka.

Just off the south end of Ovalau is tiny **Yanutha Lailai Island,** where on 14 May 1879 the first 463 indentured Indian laborers to arrive in Fiji landed from the ship *Leonidas.* They spent two months in quarantine on Yanutha Lailai to avoid the introduction of cholera or smallpox into Fiji. Later Nukulau Island off Suva became Fiji's main quarantine station.

PRACTICALITIES

Accommodations
Levuka hasn't yet been blemished by an up-market hotel; instead you have a choice of five inexpensive places to stay. The first hotel you come to after disembarking is the **Old Capital Inn** (Box 50, Levuka; tel. 440-057) on Convent Rd., a favorite of budget travelers who want to be with their counterparts where the action is. The Inn has six double rooms at F$10 s, F$17 d, and 28 dormitory beds at F$7 pp, breakfast included (if you want to skip breakfast you'll save a dollar). There's no hot water. Don't leave food in your luggage; it attracts pests. An inn annex with additional rooms opened in 1989 on Beach St., but food is served only in the main building.

Recommended for its pleasant family atmosphere is **Mavida Lodge** (Box 91, Levuka; tel. 440-051), on the waterfront near the Levuka Club. This spacious colonial house has been functioning as a guesthouse since 1869; it's Fiji's oldest. The 13 rooms are F$16 s, F$20 d, F$7 dormitory, and a full English breakfast is included. Fijian dishes and vegetarian meals are served here. Owner Irene Thomas bears an uncanny facial and vocal resemblance to the late Pearl Bailey, and Irene can play a mean piano and sing, too, a legacy of her years as a hotel entertainer in Papua New Guinea.

For the full Somerset Maugham flavor, stay at the 14-room **Royal Hotel** (Box 47, Levuka; tel. 440-024). Built in 1852 and renovated in the 1890s, this is Fiji's oldest regular hotel. Ceiling fans revolve above the potted plants and rat-

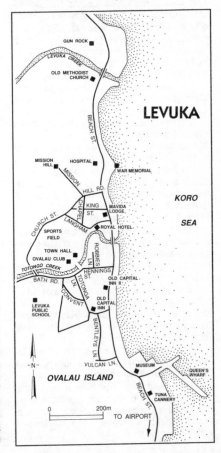

tan sofas in the lounge. The colonial atmosphere and impeccable service make it about the best value in Fiji (F$16 s, F$23 d, F$25 t). The 15 fan-cooled rooms with private bath are pleasant, and much-needed mosquito nets are provided. There's also a F$6 dorm and cottages for F$50. Meals are served, but you have to order dinner before 1400. Their bar and beer garden are worth a visit, though the snooker and videos are strictly for guests.

Beach Resorts

The **Ovalau Holiday Resort** (Stephen and Rosemary Diston, Box 113, Levuka; tel. 440-329), also known as the "Levuka Holiday Resort," is at Vuma on a rocky beach five km north of Levuka (taxi F$3). *Mbures* are F$20 s, F$25 d, F$35 t, or F$7 pp in the dorm. Camping is F$4 pp, with use of the dorm facilities. Cooking facilities and hot showers are provided, and the Mbula Beach Bar is in a converted 150-year-old whaler's cottage. Their restaurant does some good home cooking and the snorkeling is good here. They'll rent you their car for F$25.

The perfect escape from it all is quiet, lovely **Rukuruku Resort** (Box 112, Levuka; tel. 303-377) on the northwestern side of Ovalau, 20 km from Levuka. A large campground (F$5 pp) comes complete with toilets, showers, barbecue, and a kitchen. Dormitory-style accommodations (F$12 pp including breakfast) are also available, or rent a private four-person *mbure* for F$60 a day. The restaurant/bar is somewhat overpriced, but basic groceries may be purchased in the adjacent Fijian village. The black-sand beach is only so-so, but the snorkeling out on the reef is good, and there's a natural freshwater swimming pool in the river adjacent to the resort. A vanilla plantation and beautiful verdant mountains cradle Rukuruku on the island side. A small boat is available to charter for day-trips (F$40-60 for the boat) to Naingani Island, the reef, or for fishing.

Get to Rukuruku on a carrier or bus from Levuka (F$1.40 pp); no service on Sun. or late in the afternoon. When you're ready to return to Suva, the resort launch will shuttle you out to the Natovi ferry (F$5 for the boat), making a return to Levuka unnecessary. Just don't expect a flashy tourist hotel like the ones near Nandi—Rukuruku is Fiji-style.

Offshore Island Resorts

Several tiny islands on opposite sides of Moturiki bear beautiful beaches and small budget resorts popular among backpackers who like being "pampered" for a low price. **Lost Island Resort** is on Yanutha Lailai, just off the southern end of Ovalau. The eight double rooms cost F$7 pp, and three meals a day are another F$12 (F$5 for the *lovo* special). Camping is F$4 pp. Reef tours from Lost Island are F$3 pp, and day-trips are offered from Levuka at F$18 pp, lunch included. Transfers from Levuka are F$10 each way. Details are available at Mavida Lodge (tel. 440-051) in Levuka.

Emosi Yee Show at the Old Capital Inn (tel. 440-057) runs **Leleuvia Island**, a lovely isolated reef island with nothing but coconut trees and sandy beaches. Accommodations and three basic meals (rationed, not buffet) run F$17 each in the dorm, F$20 pp in a thatched hut, or F$15 pp to camp. Water is in short supply on Leleuvia, and bathing is with a bucket. The small shop sells candy and drinks. Leleuvia is popular among travelers who like to drink and party a lot (live music in the evening), so don't come expecting a rest. The owners drop off as many people as they can, and it can get *very* crowded. Snorkeling trips (F$3 pp), scuba diving (F$40), and other activities are arranged, and on Sun. they'll even take you to church! For F$4 pp they'll drop you on one-tree "Honeymoon Island." A day-trip from Levuka to Leleuvia with lunch is about F$15 pp, or F$7 OW. The "Emosi Express" departs Levuka for Leleuvia at 0800 (F$10); otherwise, catch the bus at Suva post office at 1100 and come via Mbau Landing (F$14), both daily except Sunday. Book through the Old Capital Inn in person or by phone.

A similar resort on neighboring **Thangalai Island** is owned by the Methodist Church of Fiji and much more peaceful (no alcohol allowed). The 12 *mbures* are F$11 pp (triple occupancy), otherwise pay F$7 pp in the dormitory without meals, or camp for F$6 pp. Three meals are F$10. Information should be available at Paak Kum Loong Chinese Restaurant next to the Catholic church in Levuka (boat from here daily at 1000, F$10 pp), otherwise you'll just have to show up and be prepared to camp if they don't have a room. It's primitive, but the island and people are great. Dress up for Sun. service in the village church.

Small outboards to **Moturiki Island** depart Nangguelendamu Landing most afternoons (50 cents). You can charter one to take you over anytime for about F$10. The best beaches are on the east side of Moturiki. Camping is officially discouraged, but possible.

Food And Entertainment
About the only place to get dinner on Sun. evening is the restaurant at the **Old Capital Inn**, which has a F$8 all-you-can-eat buffet that night. Otherwise try the curry house on the waterfront. **Paak Kum Loong Chinese Restaurant** (tel. 440-382) on Beach St. is reasonable, and you can eat with chopsticks if you want. Try the prawns. The little carryout behind the library/museum serves fish and curry dinners and tasty homemade desserts, plus it's open on Sundays. The **Levuka Cafe** (closed Sun. and Mon.) next to the museum serves a three-course dinner for F$6.

Although the sign says "Members Only," visitors are welcome at the **Ovalau Club** (cheap beer). Stop in for a drink at the **Royal Hotel** (1882) to absorb some of the atmosphere of old Levuka. To have dinner here you must place your order before 1700.

Money
The **Westpac Bank** (tel. 440-346) has a branch on Beach St., Lekuka, the only bank on Ovalau.

Transport
Fiji Air (tel. 440-139) has three flights a day from Nausori to Mbureta airport on Ovalau (F$27), with one continuing to Koro (F$24). Standby fares (35% reduction) are available on these flights but they don't like giving them to tourists. Fiji Air has a minibus from their Levuka office to the airstrip for F$3 pp.

Inquire at the **Patterson Bros.** office (tel. 440-126) on the waterfront beside the market in front of the Royal Hotel about the direct ferry from Levuka to Nambouwalu, Vanua Levu, via Natovi. The connecting bus departs Levuka at about 0400 Mon.-Saturday. Also ask about the Suva-Savusavu ferry (F$21), which calls at Levuka on Fri. or Sat. northbound and Tues. southbound. Village boats leave sporadically for Mbatiki, Nairai, and Koro.

The bus/ferry/bus service between Levuka and Suva was discussed above under "Transport" in the "Suva" section. Three competing services are available, each taking around five hours right through and costing around F$17. The Patterson Bros. combination involves an express bus from Levuka to Mburesala at 0400, a 45-minute ferry ride from Mburesala to Natovi, then the same bus on to Suva. Bula Ferry Services (Mr. Koroi Ramusu) is different in that the MV *Ana Tupou* sails direct from Levuka Wharf at 0730 and 1300 daily except Sunday, a two-hour boat ride that connects at Natovi with a bus to Suva. The third choice is the "Emosi Express" from Levuka at 0800 to Mbau Landing via Leleuvia Island, then a minibus to Suva. Inquire at the Old Capital Inn. Advance bookings are recommended on holidays.

Due to steep hills on the northwestern side of Ovalau, there isn't a bus around the island. Northbound they go as far as historic St. John's College, while those headed south don't reach farther than Viro. Carriers run as far as Rukuruku village (F$1) along a beautiful, hilly road. Go in the morning.

Tours
The Royal Hotel runs a day tour to Lovoni for F$12, including a tour of the fort and lunch. Ask at the Old Capital Inn and elsewhere about land tours around Ovalau with lunch at Rukuruku for F$12. The reef tours (F$5 pp, plus F$2 for gear) are great for swimming and snorkeling, and you'll be shown sharks if you ask. Five people are required for either of these tours. Sometimes boat charters to Naingani or Makongai are possible if enough people are interested. If you'd like to climb the peak that towers behind Levuka, a guide can be arranged for a nominal amount. Ask about all this at the **Ovalau Visitors Bureau** on the main street, which can also arrange a guide for the hike to Lovoni and other trips.

OTHER ISLANDS
OF THE LOMAIVITI GROUP

Naingani

Naingani, 11 km off Viti Levu, is a lush tropical island near Ovalau on the west end of the Lomaiviti Group, with pristine beaches and only one Fijian village in the southwestern corner. It's just the right size for exploring on foot, and fortunately there's a reasonable place to stay.

Mystery Island Resort (Box 12539, Suva; tel. 440-364), also known as Naingani Island Resort or Islanders Village, offers 22 comfortable fan-cooled units at F$120 for a one-bedroom apartment (four persons), F$200 for a two-bedroom villa (six persons), and F$285 for a three-bedroom villa (eight persons). These units have cooking facilities and fridges, so bring food. Rooms without cooking facilities are F$80 s, F$120 d, including all meals in the dining room. Children under 13 get a 50% discount, so this is a good place for families; lower off-season rates apply from mid-Sept. to May (excepting Christ-mas)—ask. It also has a six-bed dormitory (F$10). Sporting activities such as sailboarding and deep-sea fishing are extra. In Suva, for information on Mystery ask at Suites 7 and 8, Procera House, Waimanu Rd., which often has all-inclusive four-night packaged trips to Naingani. The minibus/launch connection from Suva daily at 1000 is F$50 RT, and the same launch also connects Naingani to Levuka. This is a great place to come for a rest and, unlike some other resorts, you won't feel at all cramped here. Mystery Island Resort recently changed ownership again, and some of the above may have changed, so check carefully.

Makongai

Makongai shares a figure-eight-shaped barrier reef with neighboring Wakaya. The anchorage is in Dalithe Bay on the northwestern side of the island. From 1911 to 1969 this was a leper colony

Mangroves (Rhizophora) flourish along Fijian shorelines. The many spidery stilt roots, which anchor and support the tree, allow it to breathe more easily in the oxygen-poor environment.

As saltwater floods the mud flats, the mangroves serve to reclaim new land and create a specialized habitat. Where mangroves have been cleared, coastal fisheries decline.

THE FIJI TIMES

staffed by Catholic nuns, which also received patients from various other Pacific island groups. Many of the old hospital buildings still stand. Today Makongai is owned by the Deptment of Agriculture, which runs an experimental sheep farm here, with some 2,000 animals. A new breed obtained by crossing British and Caribbean sheep bears little wool and is intended as a source of mutton.

Wakaya

Chief Cakobau sold Wakaya to Europeans in 1840, and it has since had many owners. In 1862 David Whippy set up Fiji's first sugar mill on Wakaya. At one time the Pacific Harbor Corporation had grandiose plans to develop Wakaya for condotourists, but these have proved impractical. Red deer imported from New Caledonia run wild across Wakaya. On the west coast a high cliff is known as Chieftain's Leap, named for a young chief who threw himself over the edge to avoid capture by his foes.

The German raider, Count Felix von Luckner, was captured on Wakaya during WW I. His ship, the *Seeadler,* had foundered on a reef at Maupihaa in the Society Islands on 2 Aug. 1917. The 105 survivors (prisoners included) camped on Maupihaa while von Luckner and five men set out in an open boat on 23 Aug. to capture a schooner and continue the war. On 21 Sept. 1917 they found a suitable ship at Wakaya. Their plan was to go aboard as passengers and capture it, but a British officer and four Indian soldiers happened upon the scene. Not wishing to go against the rules of chivalry and fight in civilian clothes, the count gave himself up and was interned at Auckland as a prisoner of war. He later wrote a book, *The Sea Devil,* about his experiences.

In 1985 Canadian industrialist David Harrison Gilmour bought the island for US$6 million, and five years later he opened **The Wakaya Club** (Box 15424, Suva; tel. 440-128), with eight spacious cottages at US$742 s, US$962 d, all-inclusive (four-night minimum stay). There's a nine-hole golf course open to guests and an airstrip for charter flights from Nandi. Mr. Gilmour's 150 employees, who live in a barracks alongside the Club, are forbidden to drink alcohol while on the island. The rest of Wakaya has been subdivided into 150 parcels that are

being sold to foreigners as homesites at a quarter million dollars a hectare.

Mbatiki

Mbatiki has a large interior lagoon of brackish water surrounded by mud flats. Four Fijian villages are on Mbatiki, but due to hazardous reefs there's no safe anchorage for ships. Fine baskets are made here.

Nairai

Seven Fijian villages are found on this 336-meter-high island between Koro and Ngau. The inhabitants are known for their woven handicrafts. Hazardous reefs stretch out in three directions, and in 1808 the brigantine *Eliza* was wrecked here. Among the survivors was Charles Savage, who served as a mercenary for the chiefs of Mbau for five years until falling into the clutches of Vanua Levu cannibals.

Koro

Koro is an eight-by-16-km island shaped like a shark's tooth. A ridge traverses the island from northeast to southwest, reaching 561 meters near the center. High jungle-clad hillsides drop sharply to the coast. The best beach is along the southern coast between Mundu and the lighthouse at Muanivanua Point. Among the 14 large Fijian villages, the government center with post office, hospital, and schools is at **Nasau**.

The road to **Vatulele** village on the northern coast climbs from Nasau to the high plateau at the center of the island. The coconut trees and mangos of the coast are replaced by great tree ferns and thick rainforest. Mr. Amena Tave, chief of Vatulele village, can arrange accommodations for visitors or give you a place to camp.

At **Nathamaki** village, in the northeastern corner of Koro, turtle calling is still practiced. The caller stands on Tuinaikasi, a high cliff about a kilometer west of the village, and repeats the prescribed words to bring the animals to the surface. The ritual does work, although the turtles are becoming scarce and only one or two may appear. If anyone present points a finger or camera at a turtle, they quickly submerge. Actually, it's not possible to photograph the turtles, as magic is involved (the photos wouldn't show any turtles). You're so high above the

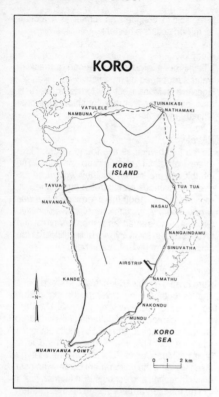

KORO

water you'd need the most powerful telephoto lens just to pick them out, anyway. (One reader wrote in to report that no turtles have appeared since 1987, due to the killing of a shark by a local villager.)

The track south between Nathamaki and Tua Tua runs along a golden palm-fringed beach. A cooperative store at **Nangaindamu** sells *yanggona* and supplies. Koro kava is Fiji's best. A 30-minute hike up a steep trail from the co-op brings you to a waterfall and idyllic swimming hole. Keep left if you're on your own (a guide would be preferable).

Koro has an unusual inclined **airstrip** on the east side of the island near Namathu village. You land uphill, take off downhill. Fiji Air can bring you here from Suva (F$47) or Levuka (F$24), and several carriers meet the flights.

The weekly Patterson Bros. and Consort

Shipping line ships from Suva anchor off Nangaindamu (no wharf). All the large ships plying between Suva and Savusavu/Taveuni call here. The *Spirit of Free Enterprise* calls northbound on Wed. and Sat. afternoons, southbound Mon. and Thurs. nights. The Patterson Bros. ferry *Princess Ashika* leaves Suva for Koro at midnight Mon., departs Koro for Savusavu at noon Tues., then leaves Savusavu again for Koro Thurs. at 0100, departing Koro for Suva at 0530. This vessel can also be used to travel between Koro and Ngau.

Koro and Ngau don't have hotels, so you'll have to stay with the locals or ask permission to camp. On both islands your best bet is to wait till you meet someone here, then ask them to write you a letter of introduction to their relatives back home on the island. It's always best to know someone before you arrive. Make it clear you're willing to pay your own way, then don't neglect to do so.

Ngau

Ngau is the fifth-largest island in Fiji, with 16 villages and 13 settlements. There's a barrier reef on the west coast, only a fringing reef on the east. Near the P.W.D. depot at **Waikama** is a hot-spring swimming pool. From Waikama, hike

NGAU

along the beach and over the hills to **Somoso-mo** village. If you lose the way, look for the creek at the head of the bay and work your way up it until you encounter the trail. Somosomo has a bathing pool with emerald green water.

A road runs from Somosomo to **Sawaieke** village, where the Takalaingau, high chief of Ngau, resides. The remnants of one of the only surviving pagan temples *(mbure kalou)* in Fiji is beside the road at the junction in Sawaieke. The high stone mound is still impressive.

It's possible to climb **Mt. Ndelaitho** (760 meters), highest on the island, from Sawaieke in three or four hours. The first hour is the hardest. From the summit there is a sweeping view. MacGillivray's Fiji petrel, a rare seabird of the albatross family, lays its eggs underground on Ngau's jungle-clad peaks. Only two specimens have ever been taken: one by the survey ship *Herald* in 1855, and a second by Dick Watling of Nandi in 1984.

The co-op and government station (hospital, post office, etc.) are at **Nggarani** at the north end of Ngau. Two ships a week arrive here from Suva on an irregular schedule, but there is no wharf so they anchor offshore. The wharf at **Waikama** is used only for government boats.

The east coast offers a number of waterfalls, the best known behind **Lekanai** and up Waimboteingau Creek, both an hour's walk off the main road. The "weather stone" is on the beach, a five-minute walk south of **Yandua** village. Bad weather is certain if you step on it or throw a stone at it.

To arrange accommodations try asking at the Fiji Air office in Suva. Tom Koroi, driver of the carrier serving the airstrip, may be able to arrange accommodations in Waikama village at F$10 pp including meals. Tom connects with another carrier down the east coast to Lamiti. The airstrip is on Katundrau Beach at the south end of Ngau. Flights to/from Suva are F$40 one-way.

The Patterson Bros. ferry *Princess Ashika* departs Suva for Ngau at midnight Mon., leaving Ngau for Savusavu Tues. at 0700. Southbound the same ship departs Savusavu for Ngau Thurs. at 0100, leaving Ngau for Suva Thurs. at 1030. The same vessel also calls at Koro and Taveuni.

LOUISE FOOTE

The leatherback (Dermodhelys coriacea), one of four species of sea turtles found in Fiji, is the only turtle that cannot retract its head or limbs. Its shell is a leathery skin rather than a horny plate. The seven lengthwise ridges on its back and five on its underside make it easily recognizable. Leatherbacks can grow up to 2½ meters long and weigh up to a ton. In the Fiji Islands all leatherbacks and their eggs are fully protected year-round under the Fisheries Act.

SALVATORE CASA

VANUA LEVU

Though only half as big as Viti Levu, Vanua Levu ("Great Land") has much to offer. The transport is good, scenery varied, people warm and hospitable, and far fewer tourists visit than reach heavily promoted Nandi/Singatoka/Suva. Fijian villages are numerous all the way around the island—here you'll be able to experience real Fijian life, so it's worth the effort to visit Fiji's second-largest island (5,556 square km).

The drier northwestern side of Vanua Levu features sugarcane fields, while on the damper southeastern side copra plantations predominate, with a little cocoa around Natewa Bay. Toward the southeast it's more the bucolic beauty of coconut groves dipping down toward the sea. Majestic bays cut into the island's south side, and one of the world's longest barrier reefs flanks the northern coast. Some superb locations here, both above and below the waterline, are just waiting to be discovered.

Fiji Indians live in the large market town of Lambasa and the surrounding cane-growing area; most of the rest of Vanua Levu is Fijian. Together Vanua Levu, Taveuni, and adjacent is-

lands form Fiji's Northern Division, which is subdivided into three provinces: the western end of Vanua Levu is Mbua Province; most of the northern side of Vanua Levu is Mathuata Province; and the southeastern side of Vanua Levu and Taveuni are Thakaundrove Province.

Nambouwalu
The ferry from Viti Levu ties up to the wharf at this friendly little government station near the southern tip of Vanua Levu. From here it's 137 km by bus to Lambasa, 141 km to Savusavu. Nambouwalu has no restaurants or hotels, but **Mr. Sukha Prasad**, a jolly ol' boy, runs a very basic *dharamshala* (guesthouse) with cooking facilities near the wharf. He doesn't charge, but make a contribution upon departure.

Another possibility is the lovely **Government Rest House** on the hillside. They have two rooms where you can cook at F$5 pp. Make reservations with the District Officer Mbua in Nambouwalu (tel. 84-010, ext. 60). If the Rest House is booked, ask the D.O.'s clerk if you may camp on the grounds.

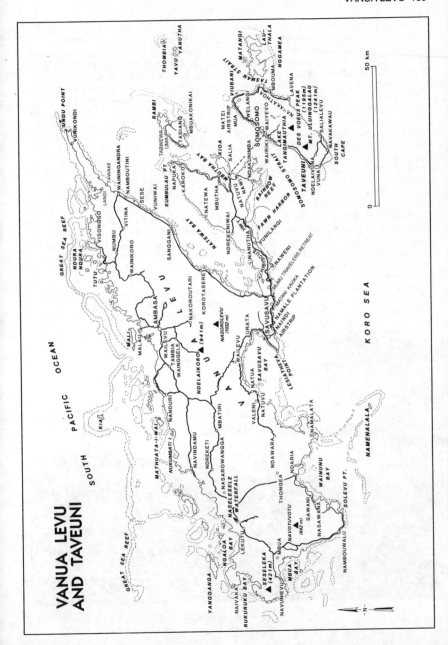

VANUA LEVU
AND TAVEUNI

50 km

The large Patterson Bros. car ferry sails from Natovi on Viti Levu to Nambouwalu, daily except Sun. around 0700, F$22 for the four-hour trip. From Nambouwalu the same boat departs for Natovi daily except Sun. at 1100. Natovi has ferry connections to/from Ovalau Island. Patterson Bros. runs an express bus from Nambouwalu to Lambasa (four hours—F$7) for ferry passengers. This bus is quicker than the four regular buses to Lambasa (five hours), which make numerous detours and stops. Several times a week at 1100 there's also a direct ferry from Nambouwalu to Ellington Wharf near Rakiraki, where you can connect for Nananu-i-ra Island or Lautoka.

The Road To Lambasa

This twisting, tiring bus ride takes you past Fijian villages, rice paddies, and cane fields. The early sandalwood traders put in at **Mbua Bay**, and the dry open countryside west of Mbua stretches out to Seseleka (421 meters). Nukungasi Beach on **Ngaloa Bay** is three km off the main highway, just south of Lekutu postal agency (keep right).

About 13 km west of Lekutu, near Ngaloa Bay on the northern side of the narrow neck of land that joins the Naivaka Peninsula to the main island, is **Dillon's Rock**. In Sept. 1813 a party of Europeans took refuge here after being ambushed during a raid on a nearby village. After witnessing Swedish mercenary Charles Savage being killed and eaten by enraged Fijian warriors when he descended to negotiate a truce, Peter Dillon of the *Hunter* and two others managed to escape to their boat by holding muskets to the head of an important chief and walking between the assembled cannibals. (In 1826 Dillon earned his place in Pacific history by discovering relics from the La Pérouse expedition on Vanikoro Island in the Solomons, finally solving the mystery of the disappearance in 1788 of that famous French contemporary of Capt. Cook.)

About five km north of Lekutu Secondary School, one km off the main road (bus drivers know the place), is Fiji's most accessible yet least-known waterfall, the **Naselesele Falls**. This is a perfect place to picnic between buses, with a nice grassy area where you could camp. The falls are most impressive during the rainy

M.G.L. DOMENY DE RIEZNI

the death of Charles Savage

season, but the greater flow means muddy water, so swimming is best in the dry season. Below the falls is a large basalt pool; nobody lives in the immediate vicinity. You'll probably have the place to yourself. Much of this part of the island has been reforested with pine.

Farther east the road passes a major rice-growing area and runs along the Ndreketi River, Vanua Levu's largest. A rice mill at Ndreketi and citrus project at Mbatiri are features of this area. In the Seanggangga settlement area between Mbatiri and Lambasa, about 60 square km of native land was cleared and planted with sugarcane during the 1980s.

LAMBASA

Lambasa is a busy Indian market town, which services Vanua Levu's major cane-growing area. It's Fiji's third-largest city with 16,736 (1986) inhabitants, four banks, and the Northern Division headquarters. Built on a delta where three rivers enter the sea, maritime transport is limited to small boats able to navigate the shallow Lambasa River. Large ships must anchor off Malau, 11 km away. Lambasa's lack of an adequate port has hindered development.

Other than providing a good base from which to explore the surrounding countryside and a place to spend the night, Lambasa has little to interest the average tourist. That's its main attraction: since few visitors come, there's adventure in the air, good food, and fun places to drink (for males). It's not beautiful but it is real, and the bus ride that brings you here is great.

SIGHTS

A library is in the **Civic Center** near the Lambasa bus station. The **Lambasa Sugar Mill**, opened in 1894 a kilometer east of town, is in operation from May to December. Walk a little farther along the road for a view of **Three Sisters Hill** to the right.

Anyone with an interest in archaeology should take the short ride on the Nakoroutari bus to **Wasavula** on the southern outskirts of Lambasa. Parallel stone platforms bearing one large monolith and several smaller ones are found among the coconut trees to the east of the road. This site (Fiji's first "national monument") is not well-known, so just take the bus to Wasavula, get off, and ask.

Other easy side trips with frequent bus service include the Fiji Forests plant at **Malau**, where Lambasa's sugar production is loaded, and the

Wainggele hot springs (no bathing) beyond the airport. If you're a surfer, ask about hiring a boat out to the **Great Sea Reef** north of Kia Island, 40 km northwest of Lambasa.

Near Lambasa
You can get a view of much of Vanua Levu from atop **Ndelaikoro** (941 meters), 25 km south of Lambasa. There's no public transport, but you might swing a ride by asking the telecommunications engineer in the building behind the Lambasa Post Office if any of his staff is going to the summit to service the equipment. Only a four-wheel-drive vehicle can make it to the top.

PRACTICALITIES

Accommodations
The single-story **Grand Eastern Hotel** (Box 641, Lambasa; tel. 811-022) on Gibson St. has 26 clean rooms with shared bath in the main building at F$18 s, F$24 d, F$2 extra with fan, F$6 extra for a/c. Prices in the new wing are much higher at F$48 s, F$54 d with a/c. The meals in the dining room are good.

The **Lambasa Club** (tel. 811-304) on Nanuku St. has two dark and dingy rooms for men only at F$5 pp. Also try the **Farmers Club** on the main street, though it's often permanently occupied.

The **Riverview Private Hotel** (Box 129, Lambasa; tel. 811-367), on Namara St. beyond the police station, charges F$17 s, F$22 d for a room with shared bath in a new concrete building.

The **Lambasa Guest House** (Box 259, Lambasa; tel. 812-155) has 10 rooms with shared bath and cooking facilities at F$6 pp. Ask about this place at Prakash Sharma Photo Shop on Nasekula Road.

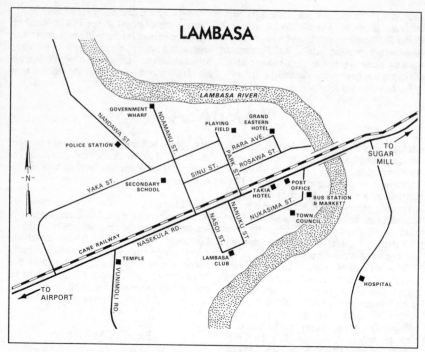

LAMBASA

Food And Entertainment

The **Takia Hotel** (Box 7, Lambasa; tel. 811-655), at 10 Nasekula Rd. above the shopping area right in the middle of town, has 32 rooms at F$45 s, F$55 d, with fan, F$55 s, F$70 d with a/c. If you have a business card, try asking for the "commercial rate."

In 1992 the upmarket **Nukumbati Island Resort** (Box 1928, Lambasa; tel. 813-901), formerly known as Coral Island Resort, opened on remote Nukumbati Island, 40 km west of Lambasa. The four spacious bungalows are A$440 d, including meals (emphasis on seafood) and activities, with a seven-night minimum stay. Children are not allowed, and alcoholic drinks are extra. It's A$500 a day to hire their game-fishing boat; land safaris are A$300. Access is by speedboat from Lambasa or by chartered seaplane direct from Nandi (A$600).

Food And Entertainment

Of the nine restaurants along Nasekula Rd. the best for the money is the **Wun Wuh Cafe** (tel.

811-653), across from the bus station. Also very popular are **Chands Restaurant** (tel. 813-215), **Jennys Wine & Dine** (tel. 813-244), and the Bamboo Hut in the Takia Hotel. The friendly **China Friendship Restaurant** (tel. 813-932), diagonally opposite the Takia Hotel, serves ample meals at reasonable prices. For Indian food try the **Isa Lei Restaurant** (tel. 811-490) on Sangam Avenue.

Naidu's Nite Club and Restaurant (tel. 811-220), Rara Ave. near the Grand Eastern Hotel, serves a reasonable curry lunch made more appealing by the cold beer; it has music and dancing Fri. and Sat. around 2200.

Lambasa has three movie houses.

Transport

Fiji Air (tel. 811-188) has service three or four times a day from Lambasa to Suva (F$61). **Sunflower Airlines** (tel. 811-454) flies direct to Nandi (F$82) twice daily and to Taveuni (F$38) five times a week. A local bus shuttles between the airport and town.

Patterson Bros. (tel. 812-444) has an office in the arcade beside the Takia Hotel where you can book your bus/ferry/bus ticket through to Suva (F$30) via Nambouwalu and Natovi. This bus leaves Lambasa at 0530 daily except Sun. and passengers arrive in Suva at 1700. There's also a direct bus/boat/bus connection from Lambasa to Ellington Wharf and Lautoka.

Rental cars are available from **Budget Rent-A-Car** (tel. 811-199) on Dongo Road. **Northern Rentals** (tel. 811-361) has one car to rent. Few roads on Vanua Levu are paved, and obtaining gasoline outside the two main towns is difficult.

Four regular buses leave daily for Nambouwalu (F$7) and another four leave for Savusavu (three hours—F$5). The ride from Nambouwalu to Lambasa is dusty and tiring, so if time is short catch a morning flight from Suva to Lambasa and an afternoon bus on to Savusavu, the best part of the trip. Otherwise stay in Savusavu and make Lambasa a day-trip. The 0700 Lambasa-Savusavu bus connects with the bus/ferry service to Taveuni, making it possible to go straight through from Lambasa to Taveuni in a day. It's a very beautiful ride over the Waisali saddle between the Korotini and Valili mountains, and along the palm-studded coast.

SAVUSAVU

Savusavu is a picturesque small town opposite Nawi Island on Savusavu Bay. This is one of the most scenic spots in Fiji—the view across to the mountains of southwestern Vanua Levu and down the coast toward Nambouwalu is superlatively lovely. In the 1860s Europeans arrived to establish coconut plantations. They mixed with the Fijians, and although business went bust in the 1930s, their descendants and Fijian villagers still supply Savusavu's small mill with copra, giving this side of Vanua Levu a pleasant agricultural air.

Savusavu is Vanua Levu's main port, and cruising yachts often rock at anchor offshore. The surrounding mountains and reefs make Savusavu a well-protected hurricane refuge. Savusavu is also the administrative center of Thakaundrove Province and has three banks. In the past few years tourism has really taken off around Savusavu, with new resorts springing up all the time, though it's far from being spoiled.

The one main street through Nakama (the precise name of Savusavu town) consists of a motley collection of Indian and Chinese shops, parked taxis, loitering locals, and the odd tourist. Visit the small **hot springs** boiling out among fractured coral behind Morris Hedstrom. Residents use the springs to cook native vegetables (bathing is not possible). Follow the road six km southwest from Savusavu to Lesiatheva Point. From here **Nukumbalavu Beach** stretches along the southern coast as far east as the airstrip.

PRACTICALITIES

Accommodations In Savusavu Town
We've arranged this accommodation section beginning at Savusavu bus station and working west through town to Lesiatheva Point, then east along the coast.

The **Copra Shed Marina** (Box 3, Savusavu; tel. 850-651) near the bus station rents one-bedroom apartments at F$60, two bedrooms at F$80. Cook your own meals or dine at the Captain's Cafe. The **Savusavu Yacht Club** is based here, and visiting yachts can moor alongside for F$40 a week (offshore hurricane moorings are F$150 a month). The Fiji Air office, a dive shop, and a bakery are also here.

Hidden Paradise Guest House (Box 41, Savusavu; tel 850-106), behind Hari Chand Store just beyond Morris Hedstrom, has six rooms at F$11 s, F$17 d, including breakfast. Cooking facilities are provided and it's clean and friendly—don't be put off by the exterior.

thatched tourist accommodations

BRIAN RUTHERFORD

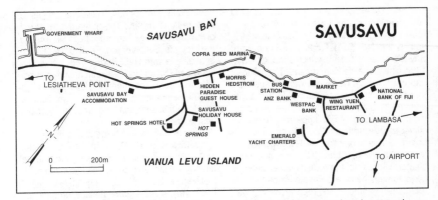

The **Hot Springs Hotel** (Box 208, Savusavu; tel. 850-195), on the hillside overlooking Nakama, is named for the nearby thermal springs and steam vents. The 48 rooms begin at F$55 s, F$65 d, F$70 t without a/c, F$70 s, F$80 d, F$85 t with a/c. (Sometimes special reduced rates are in effect—ask. Dormitory beds may also be available.) There's no beach nearby, but you'll get a fantastic view from the pool terrace. A slightly run-down fromer Travelodge, this four-story hotel has had numerous changes of ownership and name during the past few years, which needn't detract from its utility as a convenient, medium-priced choice. Friday and Sat. nights there's live music in the hotel bar.

David Manohar Lal's six-room **Savusavu Budget Holiday House** (Box 65, Savusavu; tel. 850-216), just up from the Hot Springs Hotel, has bed and Fijian breakfast for F$12 s, F$18 d, F$24 t (shared bath), or F$10 dorm, including a well-equipped kitchen. David's a strict Seventh-Day Adventist so no alcoholic beverages are allowed on the premises, though he may loan you his bicycle. Actually, he's a delightful character.

Savusavu Bay Accommodation (Lal Chand and Suresh Chand, Box 290, Savusavu; tel. 850-100), above Patterson Bros. on the main street, has four a/c rooms at F$25 s or d and seven standard rooms at F$10 s, F$15 d. Cooking facilities are provided, and a restaurant downstairs serves huge Chinese meals for F$3.50. On the roof is a terrace where travelers can wash and dry their clothes, or just sit and relax. Many of the rooms are taken on a long-term basis, and the atmosphere is not as nice as in the places above.

The Anglican Diocese of Polynesia operates the **Daku Estate Resort** (Box 18, Savusavu; tel 850-046) just west of the ferry landing. The six thatched *mbures* with fan and fridge go for F$100 s, F$165 d, F$198 t, or F$253 for four. These prices include all meals, served in a large *mbure* next to the swimming pool. Two houses with fully equipped kitchens rent for F$75 s or d, F$100 t, without meals. Income from the resort is used to send gifted children from remote areas to boarding school, so you'll be contributing to a worthy cause.

Right next to Daku is **Jim's Place** (Box 18, Savusavu; tel. 850-563), run by Daku's former manager, ex-Aussie Jim Matheson. The two new units with cooking facilities are each suitable for a couple with one or two small children at F$245 a week for extended stays only. Daku and Jim's share a beach with good snorkeling possibilities.

Accommodations Around Savusavu

Lesiatheva Point Beach Apartments (Rhonda and Glenn Mulligan, Box 57, Savusavu; tel. 850-250), near Lesiatheva Point five km west of Savusavu town, has two plain, functional apartments, each with one double room and two bunk beds. Cooking facilities are provided, as is free transportation to the shops in town weekdays. Rates are F$49 s, F$60 d, F$70 t, camping F$10 per tent. The weekly rate for an entire apartment is F$294 s, F$360 d, F$420 t (no refunds). Lesiatheva would make a good base from which to explore the surrounding area while settling in for a restful, inexpensive week.

Just 400 meters away and right on the point itself is the **Na Koro Resort** (Private Bag, Savusavu; tel. 850-188), which opened in mid-1987. The name Na Koro means "The Village," and that's what it recreates, with 20 authentic thatched Fijian *mbures* (F$225 s, F$250 d with fan) and a restaurant built like a towering pagan temple (meal plan is F$63 pp—no cooking facilities). Free activities include sailing, sailboarding, and snorkeling, and **H2O Sportz** offers scuba diving, scuba instruction, and yacht charters with diving. Snorkeling off their beach is good, though the hotel's Private Property signs aren't inviting, and at last report Na Koro was facing bankruptcy.

The **Vatukaluvi Holiday House** (Box 3, Savusavu; tel. 850-143), on the southern side of the peninsula, west of Savusavu airport, accommodates six people at F$45 s or d. Cooking facilities are provided, and the nearby snorkeling is good.

The most upmarket place around Savusavu is **Namale Plantation** (Box 244, Savusavu; tel. 850-435), a working copra plantation founded in 1874, nine km east of Savusavu. The superb food and homey atmosphere amid exotic landscapes and refreshing white beaches make this one of Fiji's most exclusive resorts. The 10 thatched *mbures* start at F$250 s, F$290 d—meal plan F$65 pp extra (no cooking facilities). The mosquito nets over the beds, ceiling fans, and louvered windows give the units a rustic charm. Rental cars are available at Namale and airport transfers are free. Namale caters only to in-house guests—there's no provision for sightseers who'd like to stop in for lunch.

Matani Kavika (Private Mail Bag, Savusavu; tel. 850-262), formerly known as Kontiki Resorts, on the Hibiscus Highway 15 km east of Savusavu, has 17 small thatched bungalows from F$90 s, F$150 d, F$165 t, including airport transfers. The three-person deluxe dormitory here is F$25 pp. Significant reductions are possible if you book direct. Their restaurant offers a good selection of Fijian and Indian dishes with main courses averaging F$15. No groceries are sold in the resort shop, only souvenirs and sun cream. Set in a well-kept coconut grove, Matani Kavika has many interesting caves,

pools, trails, falls, ponds, lakes, and jungles to explore in its vicinity. The name means "land of the wild plum tree," and such trees still exist on the grounds. Scuba diving (F$80 for two tanks) is available with H2O Sportz and a dive site known as Dream House is right at Matani Kavika's front door. The snorkeling is fine as well. It also has a swimming pool, nine-hole golf course, tennis courts, a marina, and many other activities, but no beach.

A more affordable choice would be **Mumu Travelers Retreat** (Box 240, Savusavu; tel. 850-416), also east of Savusavu about three km beyond Matani Kavika. The site is the spiritual home of Radini Mumu, a legendary queen of Fiji. In 1970 owner Gordon Edris, a former world traveler, did what many of us dream of doing: he retired to the South Seas and slowly created a small resort, which now accommodates 11 persons. Rooms are F$25 s or d, F$35 t, the five-person "dream house" goes for F$50 d, and there's also a F$12 dorm (often full). Camping is possible (F$4 pp), and Mumu's kitchen serves tasty Fijian and European dishes at budget prices. It's right beside the ocean, the snorkeling and scenery are good, the staff friendly, and there's even scuba diving. Paths wind endlessly through the property to cliff-top lookouts with chairs, through natural rock arches, and right along the water's edge. A natural swimming hole is surrounded by a concrete terrace. A taxi here from Savusavu should be around F$10, a bus around F$1. Gordon promises you'll get the most for your dollar at Mumu, but unless you've got a tent, call ahead to make sure there's a room for you.

Offshore Island

Moody's Namenalala Island Resort (Private Bag, Savusavu; tel. 813-764), on a tiny high island in the Koro Sea southwest of Savusavu, is one of Fiji's top hideaways. Tom and Joan Moody ran a similar operation in Panama's San Blas Islands for 15 years until June 1981, when they were attacked by Cuna Indians who shot Tom in the leg and tried to burn their resort. The media reported at the time that the Indians had been scandalized by hotel guests who smoked marijuana and cavorted naked on the beach, but Joan Moody claims it was part of a move to evict all foreigners from San Blas to cover up drug-running activities. In 1984, after a long search for a replacement, the couple leased Namenalala from the Fiji government, which needed a caretaker to protect the uninhabited island from poachers.

The cost to stay here is F$176 s or d, plus F$70 pp extra for the meal plan, and you have to consider the cost of getting there by chartered yacht from Savusavu (F$220) or seaplane from Nandi (F$700). The Moodys have tried to keep everything as natural as possible. There's no electricity and the five lovely thatched *mbures* are well tucked away in the lush vegetation to ensure maximum privacy.

This 45-hectare island within 24 km of barrier reef is perfect for birdwatching, fishing, and snorkeling. Scuba diving with Phil McComber is F$42 per tank. Giant clams proliferate in the surrounding waters, and sea turtles pull themselves up onto the island's golden sands to lay their eggs from Nov. to January. Great numbers of red-footed boobies nest here. If you want a holiday that combines unspoiled nature with interesting characters and a certain elegance, you won't go wrong here. Moody's closes from 15 March to 15 May every year.

Food And Entertainment

The **Captain's Table** at the Copra Shed Marina was mentioned above. If you don't drop into this yachtie hangout for the pizza and beer, it's still worth stopping to peruse their notice board, bearing photos of all the yachts that have called at Savasavu recently.

Have a meal at the **Ping Ho Cafe** (tel. 850-300), opposite the market, or try the more modern **Wing Yuen Restaurant**, next to the National Bank farther east. At **Mereta's**, behind the market, Vuki prepares good local food; her husband Abram is an excellent diver. The cook at the **Sea Breeze Restaurant** below Savusavu Bay Accommodation can prepare a special Sat. evening dinner if you let him know the day before. The **A1 Restaurant** in front of Hidden Paradise Guest House has curries from F$3.

Drinkers can repair to the **Planters Club** (tel. 850-233) toward the wharf—they're never out of Fiji Bitter. The weekend dances at the club are local events. The video cinema in Savusavu shows poor-quality films, has broken seats, and is right next to a pool parlor with five bad tables.

Activities

H2O Sportz (tel. 850-188) at the Na Koro Resort offers dive trips (F$70 with two tanks) and PADI scuba certification courses. Mark Hinton of **Pacific Island Divers** (tel. 850-435) takes divers out from his camp on Barioi Island in Natewa Bay. Mark charges F$45 per dive or F$265 for PADI certification.

Emerald Yacht Charters (Box 15, Savusavu; tel. 850-440) has three skippered yachts, the *Romer, Rainbow,* and *Kita,* available for day charters at F$49 pp including lunch, snorkeling gear, and tax. An afternoon charter is F$27 pp. This makes for an excellent day out. Longer overnight cruises to Taveuni and the Lomaiviti Group can be arranged beginning around F$390 a day for two, F$425 daily for three, F$465 daily for four, meals included but 10% tax extra. Their office is up the road from the Westpac Bank (ask). Due to hazardous reefs in this area, bareboat charters are not available.

Transport

Fiji Air (tel. 850-538) flies into Savusavu twice daily from Nausori (F$56) and daily from Taveuni, while **Sunflower Airlines** (tel. 850-141) has flights to Savusavu twice daily from Nandi (F$82) and daily from Taveuni (F$38). The airstrip is beside the main highway, three km east of town, and you *will* pay for excess baggage here. Local buses to Savusavu (30¢) pass about once an hour, or take a taxi for F$3.

Consort Shipping Line Ltd. (tel. 850-279) runs the large car ferry *Spirit of Free Enterprise* from Suva to Savusavu, calling at Koro en route, a 12-hour trip (F$27 deck, F$50 cabin). The ferry leaves Suva northbound Wed. and Fri. at 0500, leaves Savusavu southbound Mon. and Thurs. around 1700. The Wed. trip continues on to Taveuni. The **Patterson Bros.** (tel. 850-161) car ferries *Ovalau II* or *Princess Ashika* depart Suva for Savusavu (F$27) Mon. at midnight via Ngau and Koro. The return journey departs Savusavu Thurs. at 0100. All of the above schedules change frequently, so check.

Numerous taxis congregate at Savusavu market. About six buses a day run to Lesiatheva Point (40 cents), a favorite snorkeling spot. If you catch the 1000 bus there you can return to Savusavu at 1230, 1430, 1600, or 1730 (these times could change). Four buses a day go from

Savusavu to Lambasa (F$5). The 1030 bus from Savusavu to Napuka connects at Mbutha Bay with the daily ferry *Grace* to Taveuni (F$5), departing Natuvu around 1300. It's a beautiful trip but can be rough if the wind is up. The five-hour bus/boat connection goes straight through from Savusavu to Taveuni, so use a toilet before leaving and bring along a snack (westbound the connection is poor, involving a wait of several hours at Mbutha Bay). **Avis Rent-A-Car** (tel. 850-184) has an office in Savusavu.

ALONG THE HIBISCUS HIGHWAY

This lovely coastal highway runs 77 km east from Savusavu to Natuvu, then up the eastern side of Vanua Levu to the old Catholic mission station of **Napuka** at the end of the peninsula. Old frame mansions remaining from the heyday of the 19th-century planters can be spotted among the palms. **Mbutha Bay** is a recognized "hurricane hole," where ships can find shelter during storms. Coupmaster Sitiveni Rabuka hails from **Ndrekeniwai** village on Natewa Bay.

Large red prawns inhabit a saltwater crevice in the center of a tiny limestone island off **Naweni** village between Savusavu and Natuvu. The villagers believe the prawns are the spirit Urumbuta and call them up by singing:

Keitou onggo na marama ni vuna
keitou mai sara Urumbuta
I tumba i tumba e
I tumba i tumba e

The island is accessible on foot at low tide, but a *sevu sevu* must first be presented to the chief of Naweni for permission to visit (no photos). Local guides must also be compensated. Ask to be shown the weather stone on the beach and, perhaps, a second pool of prawns on the other side of the village.

There are petroglyphs *(vatuvola)* on large stones in a creek near **Ndakunimba** village, 10 km south of Natuvu (no bus service). Look for a second group of rock carvings a couple of hundred meters farther up the slope. The figures resemble some undeciphered ancient script.

OFFSHORE ISLANDS

Kioa

The Taveuni ferry passes between Vanua Levu and Kioa, home of some 300 Polynesians from Vaitupu Island, Tuvalu (the former Ellice Islands). In 1853 Capt. Owen of the ship *Packet* obtained Kioa from the Tui Cakau, and it has since operated as a coconut plantation. In 1946 it was purchased by the Ellice Islanders, who were facing overpopulation on their home island.

The people live at **Salia** on the southeastern side of Kioa. The women make baskets for sale to tourists, while the men go out fishing alone in small outrigger canoes. If you visit, try the coconut toddy *(kalevi)* or the more potent fermented toddy *(kamangi)*. Kioa and nearby Rambi are the only islands in Fiji where the government allows toddy to be cut.

Rambi

In 1855 a Tongan army conquered Fijian rebels on Rambi at the request of the Tui Cakau on Taveuni. On their departure a few years later, this chief sold the island to Europeans to cover outstanding debts. In 1941 the British government purchased Rambi Island from the Australian firm Lever Brothers for 25,000 pounds to serve as a new home for the Micronesian Banabans of Ocean Island (Banaba) in Kiribati, whose home island was being ravaged by phosphate mining. The war began before they could be resettled, and it was not until Dec. 1945 that the move was made. Today the Banabans are citizens of Fiji and live among Lever's former coconut plantations at the northwest corner of the island. The Rambi Island Council administers the island.

The island reaches a height of 472 meters and is well wooded. The former Lever headquarters is at Tabwewa, while the airstrip is near Tabiang. Rambi's other two villages are Uma and Mbuakonikai. At Nuku between Uma and Tabwewa is a post office and small guesthouse. For permission to visit wire the chairman of the Rambi Island Council, explaining your interest in the island.

Fiji Air flies direct to Rambi from Nausori (F$76). A chartered speedboat from Karoko on Vanua Levu to Tabiang on Rambi costs F$15-20 each way.

The Banabans

The Banaban people on Rambi are from Banaba, a tiny, six-square-km raised atoll 450 km southwest of Tarawa in the Gilbert Islands. Like Nauru, Banaba was once rich in phosphates, but from 1900 through 1979 the deposits were exploited by British, Australian, and New Zealand interests in what is perhaps the best example of a corporate/colonial rip-off in the history of the Pacific islands.

After the Sydney-based Pacific Islands Company discovered phosphates on Nauru and Banaba in 1899 a company official, Albert Ellis, was sent to Banaba in May 1900 to obtain control of the resource. In due course "King" Temate and the other chiefs signed an agreement granting Ellis's firm exclusive rights to exploit the phosphate deposits on Banaba for 999 years in exchange for £50 a year. Of course, the guileless Micronesian islanders had no idea what it was all about.

As Ellis rushed to have mining equipment and moorings put in place, a British naval vessel arrived on 28 Sept. 1901 to raise the British flag, joining Banaba to the Gilbert and Ellice Islands Protectorate. The British Government reduced the term of the lease to a more realistic 99 years and the Pacific Phosphate Company was formed in 1902.

Things ran smoothly until 1909 when the islanders refused to lease the company any additional land after 15% of Banaba had been stripped of both phosphates and food trees. The British government arranged a somewhat better deal in 1913, but in 1916 changed the protectorate to a colony so the Banabans could not withhold their land again. After WW I the company was renamed the British Phosphate Commission (BPC), and in 1928 the resident commissioner, Sir Arthur Grimble, signed an order expropriating the rest of the land against the

Banabans' wishes. The islanders continued to receive their tiny royalty right up until WW II.

On 10 Dec. 1941, with a Japanese invasion deemed imminent, the order was given to blow up the mining infrastructure on Banaba, and on 28 Feb. 1942 a French destroyer evacuated company employees from the island. In August some 500 Japanese troops and 50 laborers landed on Banaba and began erecting fortifications. The six Europeans they captured eventually perished as a result of Japanese mistreatment, and all but 150 of the 2,413 local mine laborers and their families present were eventually deported to Tarawa, Nauru, and Kosrae. As a warning the Japanese beheaded three of the locals and used another three to test an electrified anti-invasion fence.

Meanwhile the BPC decided to take advantage of this situation to rid itself of the island's original inhabitants for once and for all, thus avoiding any future hindrance to mining operations. In March 1942 the commission purchased Rambi Island off Vanua Levu in Fiji for £25,000 as an alternative homeland for the Banabans. In late Sept. 1945 the British returned to Banaba with Albert Ellis the first to step ashore. Only surrendering Japanese troops were found on Banaba, and the local villages had been destroyed.

Two months later an emaciated and wild-eyed Gilbertese man named Kabunare emerged from three months in hiding and told his story to a military court:

We were assembled together and told that the war was over and the Japanese would soon be leaving. Our rifles were taken away. We were put in groups, our names taken, then marched to the edge of the cliffs where our hands were tied and we were blindfolded and told to squat. Then we were shot.

Kabunare either lost his balance or fainted, and fell over the cliff before he was hit. In the sea he came to the surface and kicked his way to some rocks where he severed the string that tied his hands. He crawled into a cave and watched the Japanese pile up the bodies of his companions and toss them into the sea. He stayed in the cave two nights and, after he thought it was safe, made his way inland, where he survived on coconuts until he was sure the Japanese had left. Kabunare said he thought the Japanese had executed the others to destroy any evidence of their cruelties and atrocities on Banaba.

As peace returned the British implemented their plan to resettle all 2,000 surviving Banabans on Rambi, which seemed a better place for them than their mined-out homeland. The first group arrived on Rambi on 14 Dec. 1945, and in time they adapted to their mountainous new home and traded much of their original Micronesian culture for that of the Fijians. There they and their descendants live today.

During the 1960s the Banabans saw the much better deal Nauru was getting from the BPC, mainly through the efforts of Hammer DeRoburt and the "Geelong Boys," who were trapped in Australia during the war and thus received an excellent education and understanding of the white man's ways. Thanks to this the Nauruan leadership was able to hold its own against colonial bullying, while the Banabans were simply forgotten on Rambi.

In 1966 Mr. Tebuke Rotan, a Banaban Methodist minister, journeyed to London on behalf of his people to demand reparations from the British for laying waste to their island, a case that would drag on for nearly 20 bitter years. After some 50 visits to the Foreign and Commonwealth offices, he was offered (and rejected) £80,000 compensation. In 1971 the Banabans sued for damages in the British High Court. After a lengthy litigation, the British government in 1977 offered the Banabans an *ex gratia* payment of A$10 million, in exchange for a pledge that there would be no further legal action.

In 1975 the Banabans asked that their island be separated from the rest of Kiribati and joined to Fiji, their present country of citizenship. Gilbertese politicians, anxious to protect their fisheries zone and wary of the dismemberment of the country, lobbied against this, and the British rejected the proposal. The free entry of Banabans to Banaba was guaranteed in the Kiribati constitution, however. In 1979 Kiribati obtained independence from Britain and mining on Banaba ended the same year. Finally, in 1981 the Banabans accepted the A$10 million compensation money, plus interest, from the

British, though they refused to withdraw their claim to Banaba. The present Kiribati government rejects all further claims from the Banabans, asserting that it's something between them and the British. The British are trying to forget the whole thing. (For more information on Rambi and the Banabans see *On Fiji Islands*, by Ronald Wright.)

DIANA LASICH-HARPER

Golden cowry pendant. *The golden cowry (*Cypraea aurantium*), which the Fijians call* mbuli kula, *is one of the rarest of all seashells. On important ceremonial occasions, high chiefs would wear the shell around the neck as a symbol of the highest authority. This example in the Fijian Museum was collected in the mid-19th century by one of the first Methodist missionaries.*

SALVATORE CASA

TAVEUNI

Long, green, coconut-covered Taveuni is Fiji's third-largest island (470 square km). Only eight km across the Somosomo Strait from Vanua Levu's southeast tip, Taveuni is known as the Garden Island of Fiji for the abundance of its flora. Its surrounding reefs and those off nearby Vanua Levu make up one of the world's top dive sites. The strong currents in the strait nurture the corals but can make diving a tricky business for the unprepared. These waters are also famous for deep-sea fishing. Because Taveuni is free of the mongoose, many wild chickens, *kula* parrots, and orange doves abound, making this a special place for birders.

The island's 16-km-long, 1,000-meter-high volcanic spine causes the prevailing trade winds to dump colossal amounts of rainfall on the island's southeastern side and considerable quantities on the northwestern side. At 1,241 meters, **Uluinggalau** in southern Taveuni is the second-highest peak in Fiji. **Des Voeux Peak** (1,195 meters) in central Taveuni is the highest point in the country accessible by road. The European discoverer of Fiji, Abel Tasman, sighted this ridge on the night of 5 Feb. 1643. The almost inaccessible southeastern coast features plummeting waterfalls, soaring cliffs, and crashing surf. The people live on the island's gently sloping northwestern side.

The deep, rich volcanic soil nurtures indigenous floral species such as *Medinilla spectabilis*, which hang in clusters like red sleigh bells, and the rare *tangimauthia (Medinilla waterousei)*, a climbing plant with red-and-white flower clusters 30 cm long. *Tangimauthia* grows only around Taveuni's 900-meter-high crater lake and on Vanua Levu. It cannot be transplanted and flowers only in mid-December. The story goes that a young woman was fleeing from her father, who wanted to force her to marry a crotchety old man. As she lay crying beside the lake, her tears turned to flowers. Her father took pity on her when he heard this and allowed her to marry her young lover.

In the past four or five years Taveuni has become very popular as a destination for scuba divers or those in search of a much more natural vacation area than the overcrowded Nandi/Coral Coast strips. Even the producers of the film *Return to the Blue Lagoon* chose Taveuni for their 1990 remake. Despite all this attention Taveuni is still about the most beautiful, scenic, and friendly island in Fiji.

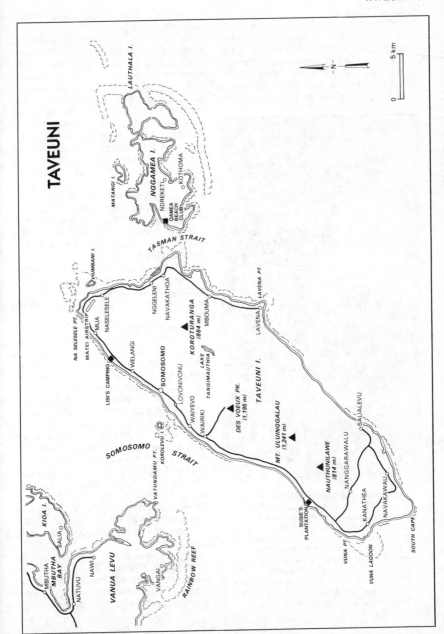

TAVEUNI

Southern Taveuni

The post office, hospital, and government offices are on a hilltop at **Waiyevo** above the Garden Island Resort. Ask directions to the **Waitavala Natural Waterslide** in a stream just off the main road a little north of the Garden Island Resort. It's especially fast after heavy rains, yet the local kids go down standing up!

THE FIJI TIMES

The ruins of the century-old Bilyard Sugar Mill as Salialevu, Taveuni, lie incongruously in the midst of today's coconut plantation. In the early days, planters believed sugar grew best in a wet, tropical environment such as that at southeastern Taveuni. Sugar fields in the Rewa Valley near Suva fed another mill at Nasusori, which now processes rice. Today all of Fiji's sugar is grown on the sunny, dry, northwestern sides of Viti Levu and Vanua Levu, with bustling sugar mills at Lambasa, Rakiraka, Mba, and Lautoka.

Tiny Korolevu Island off Waiyevo is rumored to be haunted.

The 180th degree of longitude passes through a point just south of Waiyevo marked by a signboard. One early Taveuni trader overcame the objections of missionaries to his doing business on Sunday by claiming the international date line ran through his property and if it was Sunday at the front door it was already Monday around back. Similarly, European planters got their native laborers to work seven days a week by having Sunday at one end of the plantation, Monday at the other. An 1879 ordinance ended this by placing all of Fiji west of the date line, so you're no longer able to stand here with one foot in the past and the other in the present.

Beyond the date line about eight km south of Waiyevo are the **Taveuni Estates**, an ill-fated condo development standing out like a pimple on the face of Taveuni. The golf course, tennis courts, and bowling green are well maintained but the 40 condominiums stand vacant, and behind are seemingly endless stretches of empty paved roads, sewers, and flashy signs—another dismal monument to bad planning and greed.

At **Vuna** the lava flows have formed pools beside the ocean, which fill up with fresh water at low tide and are used for washing and bathing. There's good snorkeling on the reef and spectacular **blowholes** at nearby Namboundrau Bay, especially on a southern swell.

Buses run to **Navakawau** village at the southeastern end of the island, from where you can hike through the coconut plantations for an hour and a half along a dirt track northeast to **Salialevu**, site of the Bilyard Sugar Mill (1874-96), one of Fiji's first. In the 1860s European planters tried growing cotton on Taveuni, turning to sugar when the cotton market collapsed. Later, copra was found to be more profitable. Some of Fiji's only Australian magpies (large black-and-white birds) inhabit this plantation. A tall chimney, boilers, and other equipment remain below the school at Salialevu.

From Salialevu, another road climbs over the island to **Ndelaivuna**, a tiring two hours. The bus comes up this road from the northwestern coast as far as Ndelaivuna, so you could also start from there and do the above in reverse.

Northern Taveuni

Somosomo is the chiefly village of Thakaundrove and seat of the Tui Cakau: Ratu Sir Penaia Ganilau, the president of Fiji, hails from here. The large hall in the village was erected for a 1986 meeting of the Great Council of Chiefs. Missionary William Cross, one of the creators of today's system of written Fijian, is buried in this village.

The three waterfalls at **Mbouma** on the northwestern side of the island are set high above sea level. Before heading in, stop at the Information Center just south of the village to pay the F$5 pp admission fee and pick up a map. The track to the falls leads along the right bank of the second stream south of Mbouma. The falls plunge 20 meters into a deep pool, where you could swim, and from here a trail leads up to a second falls, also with a pool. Unscrupulous business interests wanted to log this virgin rainforest, but fortunately sanity prevailed and a **national park** is now being developed in this area, complete with additional trails and camping facilities. (If the admission fee rankles consider the easy royalties the local people have forfeited to preserve this area.) The Mbouma villagers are very friendly, and it's possible to stay with them.

Some of the Mbouma buses go on another six km to **Lavena**, with another waterfall and one of Fiji's most spectacular beaches (be careful with the currents if you snorkel). The film *Return to the Blue Lagoon* was filmed here. The enterprising Lavena locals now offer daily "Return to the Blue Lagoon Cruises," that include a boat trip down the Ravilevo Coast to Savuleveavonu Falls (which cascade down into the ocean), a hike to Wainibau Falls, and lunch, all for F$25 pp. Ask your hotel or call Kaba's Motel (tel. 880-233) at Somosomo for information.

A good plan is to catch the 0900 to Mbouma and see the waterfalls, walk to Lavena from Mbouma (nearly two hours), then catch the bus from Lavena back to Waiyevo at 1430 (though you can only do this on certain days). Otherwise, camp or stay with the locals at Mbouma and allow yourself more time to see this beautiful area.

To The Interior

The trail up to lovely **Lake Tangimauthia**, high in the mountainous interior, begins behind the Mormon church at Somosomo. The first half is the hardest. You'll need a full day to do a roundtrip, and a guide (F$20-30) will be necessary, as there are many trails to choose from. You must wade for a half hour through knee-deep mud in the crater to reach the lake's edge. Much of the lake's surface is covered with vegetation, and the water is only five meters deep.

The adventuresome might try hiking to Lake Tangimauthia from Lavena on the southeast coast, or southwest from Lavena to Salialevu, lesser-known but feasible routes. Intrepid kayakers sometimes paddle the 20 km down the back side of Taveuni, past countless cliffs and waterfalls.

An easier climb is up the jeep track from the Marist school one km south of Waiyevo to the telecommunications station on **Des Voeux Peak**. This is an all-day trip with a view of Lake Tangimauthia as a reward (clouds permitting). The less ambitious will settle for the short hike up to the cross above the Marist mission.

PRACTICALITIES

Budget Accommodations

The **Airport Motel** (c/o Postal Agency, Matei, Taveuni; tel. 880-406), also known as Niranjan's Budget Accommodation, is just a few minutes' walk from the airport. The four rooms, each with two beds, fridge, and cooking facilities, go for F$35 d, F$45 t. Campers are welcome.

Bibi's Hideaway (Box 80, Waiyevo, Taveuni; tel. 880-443), about 500 meters south of the airport, offers three units with cooking facilities. One room in the two-room cottage is F$30 s or d, while the larger family unit is F$70 d, F$80 t. The film crew from *Return to the Blue Lagoon* stayed here, and with the extra income the owner built a deluxe *mbure*, which is F$50 s or d. The nearest store is a 15-minute walk away. Bibi's is located on lush, spacious grounds a few minutes' walk from the beach. It's a good choice for scuba groups, and James, Victor, and Agnes Bibi will make you feel right at home.

The original budget hotel on Taveuni was **Kaba's Motel & Guest House** (Box 4, Taveuni; tel. 880-233) at Somosomo, which charges F$12 s, F$20 d, F$28 t for a bed in one of three double rooms with shared facilities in the guest-house. The cooking facilities are very good, and you may camp behind the guesthouse and use the facilities for half price. A new motel section is also available at F$25 s, F$32 d, F$40 t for one of the five large units with kitchenette, fridge, fan, phone, and private bath—good value. Check in at Kaba's Supermarket across the street. The supermarket also has a huge selection of videos you can rent to play on the guesthouse VCR.

A friendly Indian family runs **Kool's Accommodation** (Box 10, Waiyevo, Taveuni; tel. 880-395), just south of Kaba's at Somosomo. The six clean rooms are F$8 s, F$12 d, and cooking facilities are provided. Manageress Chitra Singh will arrange a four-wheel-drive jeep able to carry five persons to the top of Des Voeux Peak for F$40 for the vehicle, plus another F$25 if you want them to wait around a couple of hours to bring you back.

Mr. Seru Ladua of Lovonivonu village puts up visitors in his home for F$10 pp including all meals.

Susie's Plantation (Navatha Estate, Taveuni; tel. 880-125), just north of Vuna Point at the south end of Taveuni, offers peace and quiet amid picturesque rustic surroundings, at the right price. Rates begin at F$25 d for a room with shared bath in the plantation house or F$35 d for a simple seaside *mbure*. Their dorm is F$10 pp, camping F$8 per tent. You can cook your own food (an Indian shop is a five-minute walk away), or pay F$20 pp extra for a good breakfast and dinner in their restaurant, which is housed in the oldest missionary building on the island (nonguests welcome). This professionally run resort right on the ocean has its own resident diving instructor, who leads daily trips to the Great White Wall and Rainbow Reef (F$40 one tank, F$70 two tanks). A PADI scuba-certification course costs F$380, including seven ocean dives and five-nights accommodation (double occupancy)—a great opportunity to learn how to dive. Even if you're not a diver, the snorkeling's superb right off their beach. Recommended.

Camping Grounds

Just over a kilometer south of the airstrip is **Beverly Campground** (tel. 880-381), run by Bill Madden. It's F$4 pp (your tent), F$5 pp (Bill's

tent), or F$10 pp in a *mbure*. Cooking facilities (one-time charge of F$2 for gas) are available in a nearby *mbure*, but bring food. Bill can supply fresh fruit and vegetables, and he even serves a good dinner for F$6. It's a clean, quiet place right on a great beach with excellent snorkeling. Horseback riding can be arranged.

Another good place right on a white-sand beach is **Lisi's Campground** (Vathala Estate, P.A. Matei; tel. 880-136), two km southeast of Beverly. It's F$4 pp to camp or F$10 s, F$15 d, F$20 t in a small *mbure*. If you don't have a tent, they may be able to rent you one. Cooking facilities are available in a *mbure* (fresh fruit provided every morning), and hosts Mary and Lote Tuisago serve excellent Fijian meals at reasonable prices. The snorkeling is good, outrigger canoes rent for (F$3), horseback riding is possible, and you're welcome to help with the "work," collecting fruit or making copra, if you want. It's primitive but adequate and you'll get to meet local people. Everyone joins the afternoon volleyball game, and in the evening there's kava drinking, often along with music. One traveler wrote in to say, "It's hard to describe the atmosphere of love and harmony at this place."

Upmarket Accommodations

The **Garden Island Resort** (Box 1, Waiyevo, Taveuni; tel. 880-286), by the sea at Waiyevo three km south of Somosomo, has 30 a/c rooms in an attractive two-story building at F$48 s, F$65 d, F$75 t, or F$16 in the dorm. Prices seem to fluctuate a lot here, so call and check. The buffet breakfast and dinner plan is F$25 pp. Formerly known as the Castaway, this used to be Taveuni's premier hotel; several changes of ownership later, however, Garden Island has been eclipsed by the offshore resorts. Although it has no beach, Garden Island offers a restaurant, bar, evening entertainment, swimming pool, excursions, snorkeling trips to Korolevu Island (F$10), and water sports. It's a nice place to hang out.

Maravu Plantation Resort (c/o Matei Postal Agency, Taveuni; tel. 880-555) is a village-style resort in a real 20-hectare copra-making plantation a kilometer south of the airport opposite Dive Taveuni. It has 10 comfortable *mbures* with ceiling fans at F$150 s, F$180 d, F$207 t. The meal plan at the resort restaurant is F$64 pp extra. There's also a bar and swimming pool on the landscaped grounds. Nonguests must make reservations to eat here (the food is good, but count on F$32 for dinner). Airport transfers are F$5.

The **Matei Lagoon Resort** (c/o Matei Postal Agency, Taveuni; tel. 880-422), also known as Matei Lodge, overlooks a beach opposite the airport. The three pleasant wooden bungalows set in spacious grounds are F$110 s or d, F$137 t. Reductions may be possible if you book direct. The facilities are clean and new, each unit with a kitchen and fridge, and a two-bedroom house is available for small groups or families. A grass tennis court is on the property, and an eight-meter fishing launch is available for hire.

Food And Entertainment

Clusters of small shops sell groceries at Somosomo and Wairiki, a couple of kilometers north and south of Waiyevo respectively. The restaurant at the **Garden Island Resort** is reasonable, and a Chinese takeaway is next door. In Somosomo the **Central Restaurant** has curries and simple Chinese dishes from F$2. **Audrey's** is an upmarket coffee shop run by an American woman at Matei. Afternoon tea while enjoying the great view from her terrace will run F$5, and she has various homemade goodies to go. There still isn't any tourist-oriented nightlife beyond the hotel bars, though the **Taveuni Country Club** (tel. 880-133) at Waiyevo is a local drinking place. This island is mostly a place for active people who like to be out and about by day and early to bed at night, and it's also fine for those in need of rest.

Scuba Diving

Taveuni and surrounding waters have become known as one of Fiji's top diving areas. The fabulous 31-km Rainbow Reef off the south coast of eastern Vanua Levu abounds in turtles, fish, overhangs, crevices, and soft corals, all in 5-10 meters of water. Favorite dive sites here include White Sandy Gulley, Jack's Place, Cabbage Patch, Pot Luck, Blue Ribbon Eel Reef, the Ledge, Jerry's Jelly, Coral Garden, and especially the Great White Wall.

Strong currents in the Somosomo Strait call for experienced dive leaders, and **Dive Taveuni** (Ric and Do Cammick, P.A., Matei, Taveuni; tel. 880-441) pioneered diving in this area way back in 1976. They charge F$94 for two tanks including lunch (hire gear not available). Ten divers are accommodated in six very pleasant *mbures* at "Ric's Place" (US$114 pp including three meals and transfers) on Dive Taveuni's premises just southwest of Matei airstrip across from Maravu Plantation Resort. The property is on a cliff overlooking the ocean, with great views from the open terrace dining area. No alcohol is sold, so bring your own. They're closed in February and March. Do Cammick recently sent us this:

As you can see, the resort and dive boat are not for the budget-minded diver. The food is prepared by an international chef and the resort accommodations beautifully appointed. We find a lot of people arrive here expecting cheap accommodation and rough conditions and are shocked when they actually see the resort. So in our latest literature we are trying to change the image we have.

Now that Dive Taveuni has developed from humble beginnings into one of the top medium-priced scuba operations in Fiji the budget-minded diver should check out **Rainbow Divers** (tel. 880-125), based at Susie's Plantation, which offers five-day packages providing accommodation and NAUI scuba certification for F$380, or F$80 for a full day of diving on the Rainbow Reef (plus F$15 extra for gear). The **Garden Island Resort Dive Center** (tel. 880-286) also has competitive prices with one-tank dives at F$55, two tanks F$90, and PADI scuba certification F$400. Offshore dive resorts such as Matangi Island and Qamea Beach Club receive mostly upmarket divers who book from outside Fiji, and accommodations there are much more expensive than those on Taveuni.

Money

Although the Westpac Banking Corporation has an agency at Waiyevo (tel. 880-035), it's probably wise to change enough money to cover your stay before arriving on Taveuni.

Getting There

Matei airstrip at the northern tip of Taveuni is serviced twice daily by **Fiji Air** (tel. 880-062) from Nausori (F$73) and **Sunflower Airlines** (tel. 880-461) from Nandi (F$98) and Savusavu (F$38). Sunflower also arrives from Lambasa (F$38) five times a week. Flights to/from Taveuni are often heavily booked, though it's still worth trying to go standby (F$47 to/from Nausori). You get superb views of Taveuni from the plane; sit on the right side going up, the left side coming back. A taxi from the airport to Somosomo will be F$10.

Patterson Bros. has the ferries *Princess Ashika* and *Ovalau II* from Suva to Taveuni (29 hours, F$31) every Mon. at midnight, departing Taveuni for the return trip Wed. at 1100. **Consort Shipping** operates the weekly *Spirit of Free Enterprise* service from Suva to Taveuni (call Ian Simpson at 880-261) via Koro and Savusavu (24 hours, F$31). This ferry departs Suva northbound Wed. at 0500 and leaves Taveuni southbound Thurs. at 1300. These times could change.

The ferry *Grace* to Natuvu at Mbutha Bay on Vanua Levu leaves Waiyevo daily except Sun. at 0800 (F$5, two hours), but you must wait a couple of hours for the connecting bus to Savusavu (F$3) on the other side. Combined tickets for a boat/minibus service Taveuni-Lambasa three times a week are F$15, but you also have to wait a few hours at Natuvu for the connection, so it ends up taking a full day, though the lovely scenery makes it worthwhile. It's much better to travel overland on a Suva/Ovalau-Nambouwalu-Lambasa-Savusavu-Taveuni routing, then fly directly back to Suva from Taveuni, as eastbound the bus/boat connection at Mbutha Bay is immediate.

the spider conch (Lambis chiragra)

DIANA LASICH HARPER

Getting Around

Bus service is infrequent. Buses leave Waiyevo northbound to Mbouma (F$1.60) at 0900 and 1230, southbound to Navakawau (F$2) at 0830 and 1300. The service is reliable on Mon., Fri., and Sat., unreliable Tues., Wed., and Thurs., and uncertain on Sunday. Check the schedule carefully as soon as you arrive.

Kaba's Motel (tel. 880-233) in Somosomo rents cars at F$45 a day. Taxis are available on Taveuni but are somewhat more expensive than elsewhere and may have to be called.

OFFSHORE ISLANDS

Nggamea Island

Nggamea (Qamea) Island, just three km east off Taveuni, is the 12th-largest island in Fiji. It's 10 km long with lots of lovely bays, lush green hills and secluded white-sand beaches. Land crabs *(lairo)* are gathered in abundance during their migration to the sea here in late Nov. or early December. The birdlife is also rich, due to the absence of the mongoose. Outboards from villages on Nggamea land near Navakathoa village on the northeastern side of Taveuni. Best time to try for a ride over (F$3 pp) is Thurs. or Fri. afternoons. Vatusongosongo village on Nggamea is inhabited by descendants of blackbirded Solomon islanders.

Fiji's top yuppie hideaway, the **Qamea Beach Club Resort** (Postal Agency, Matei, Taveuni; tel. 880-220), opened on the west side of Nggamea in 1984. The 11 tastefully designed thatched *mbures* with fans and fridges go for F$270 s, F$315 d, F$345 t (no children under 12 allowed), and the meal plan is another F$70 pp a day (no cooking facilities). Meals are served in a central dining room and lounge designed like a *mburekalau* (temple). The boat transfer from Taveuni airport is F$50 pp return. Activities such as sailboarding, snorkeling, sailing, outrigger canoeing, hiking, and night fishing are included in the basic price, but scuba diving is F$55 a tank extra. Some of the best dive sites in the world are close at hand. To prevent Qamea from degenerating into a scuba camp, half the resort's beds are reserved for nondivers who are satisfied with the superb snorkeling right off the beach, or who come mainly to relax.

Matangi Island

Matangi is a tiny volcanic island just north of Nggamea, its sunken crater forming a lovely palm-fringed bay. The island is privately owned by the Douglas family, who has been producing copra on Matangi for five generations. Recently they've diversified into the hotel business.

Matangi Island Resort (Box 83, Waiyevo, Taveuni; tel. 880-260) makes no bones about being intended almost exclusively as a base for scuba divers. Guests are accommodated in 10 neat thatched *mbures* (F$151 s, F$197 d), well spaced among the coconut palms below Matangi's high jungly interior. The compulsory meal package is another F$60 pp (no cooking facilities), and boat transfers from Taveuni are F$45 pp return. Diving here costs US$67 for two tanks and a F$35 pp per day "Aqua Club" membership fee includes sailboarding, Hobie Cat sailing, 10 minutes of water-skiing, snorkeling gear, scuba initiation, and boat tours to neighboring islands. The live-aboard dive boat *Matangi Princess* is based here (from US$200 pp a day).

Lauthala Island

Lauthala Island, which shares a barrier reef with Nggamea, was depopulated and sold to Europeans in the mid-19th century by the chief of Taveuni, after the inhabitants sided with Tongan chief Enele Ma'afu in a local war. Today it's owned by the estate of the late multimillionaire businessman and New York publisher Malcolm Forbes, who was buried on the island. In 1972 Forbes bought 12-square-km Lauthala from the Australian company Morris Hedstrom for US$1 million. He then spent another US$5 million on an airstrip, wharf, and roads. The thatched *mbures* of the 350 residents of the one Fijian village on Lauthala were replaced by red-roofed cement-block houses with running water. Forbes's private residence at the top of a hill overlooks the village, the inhabitants of which make copra. General Manager Tim Reid (Box 9952, Nandi Airport; tel. 880-077) is the only chief on Lauthala, and misbehavers are promptly booted off the island.

Prior to his death, Mr. "Capitalist Tool" Forbes deigned to share his island with eight tourists who stay in four a/c cottages, each with living room, bar, and kitchen. A private cook prepares guests' meals in their cottages; dinner is served in the plantation house. The price is US$2600 pp plus tax for seven nights (the minimum stay), all meals, "a reasonable supply" of liquor, sports, scuba diving, deep-sea fishing, and the 300-km trip from Nandi in Forbes's private plane included.

SALVATORE CASA

THE LAU GROUP

Lau is by far the most remote part of Fiji, its 57 islands scattered over a vast area of ocean between Viti Levu and Tonga. Roughly half of them are inhabited. Though all are relatively small, they vary from volcanic islands to uplifted atolls to some combination of the two. Vanua Mbalavu (52 square km) and Lakemba (54 square km) are the largest and most important islands of the group. Tongan influence has always been strong in Lau, and due to Polynesian mixing the people have a somewhat lighter skin color than other Fijians. Historically the chiefs of Lau have always had a political influence on Fiji far out of proportion to their economic or geographical importance.

Once accessible only after a long sea voyage on infrequent copra-collecting ships, four islands in Lau (Lakemba, Vanua Mbalavu, Moala, and Thithia) now have regular air service from Nausori. Organized accommodations are available on Lakemba and Vanua Mbalavu; the latter is more rewarding. Similarly, Moala is a large mountainous island with much to offer, while there is little for the average visitor on Thithia.

Both government and private ships circulate through Lau, usually calling at five or six islands on a single trip. To experience what life in the group is really about, try to go at least one way by ship (see "Transport" in the "Suva" section for details). If you're planning to stay on any of the islands, take along rice, flour, sugar, kava, corned beef, soap, and bonbons to give as *sevu sevu*. As none of these islands is prepared for tourism, the reception you may receive varies. Sometimes you'll be welcomed as a guest, other times they'll only want to know when you're leaving. Lau has no banks.

NORTHERN LAU

VANUA MBALAVU

The name means the "long land." The southern portion of this unusual, seahorse-shaped island is mostly volcanic, while the north is uplifted coral. An unspoiled environment of palm-fringed beaches backed by long grassy hillsides and sheer limestone cliffs, this is a wonderful area to explore. There are varied vistas and scenic views on all sides. To the east is a barrier reef enclosing a lagoon 37 by 16 km. The Bay of Islands at the northwestern end of Vanua Mbalavu is a recognized hurricane shelter. The villages of Vanua Mbalavu are impeccably clean, the grass cut and manicured. Large mats are made on the island and strips of pandanus can be seen drying before many of the houses.

In 1840 Commodore Wilkes of the U.S. Exploring Expedition named Vanua Mbalavu and its adjacent islands enclosed by the same barrier reef the Exploring Isles. In the days of sail, Lomaloma, the largest settlement, was an important Pacific port. The early trading company Hennings Brothers had its headquarters here. The great Tongan warlord Enele Ma'afu conquered northern Lau from the chiefs of Vanua Levu in 1855 and made Lomaloma the base for his bid to dominate Fiji. A small monument, flanked by two cannons, on the waterfront near the wharf, recalls the event. Fiji's first public botanical garden was laid out here over a century ago, but nothing remains of it. History has passed Lomaloma by. Today it's only a big sleepy village with a hospital and a couple of general stores. Some 400 Tongans live in Sawana, the south portion of Lomaloma village, and many of the houses have the round ends characteristic of Lau.

Sights

Copra is the main export and there's a small coconut oil mill at **Lomaloma**. A road runs inland from Lomaloma up and across the island to **Ndakuilomaloma**. An excellent view extends from the small communications station on a grassy hilltop midway.

Follow the road south from Lomaloma three km to **Narothivo** village, then continue two km beyond to the narrow passage separating Vanua Mbalavu and Malata islands. At low tide you can easily wade across to **Namalata** village. Alternatively, work your way around to the western side of Vanua Mbalavu, where there are isolated tropical beaches. There's good snorkeling in this passage.

There are **hot springs** and **burial caves** among the high limestone outcrops between Narothivo and Namalata, but you'll need a guide to find them. This can be easily arranged at Nakama, the tiny collection of houses closest to the cliffs, upon payment of a F$2 pp fee. Small bats inhabit some of the caves.

Rent a boat (F$15) to take you over to the **Raviravi Lagoon** on Susui Island, the favorite picnic spot near Lomaloma for the locals. The beach and snorkeling are good, and there's even a cave if you're interested. **Munia Island** is a privately owned coconut plantation where paying guests are accommodated in two *mbures*.

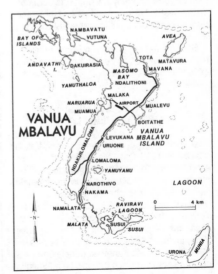

Events

A most unusual event occurs annually at Masomo Bay, west of **Mavana** village, usually around Christmastime. For a couple of days the Mavana villagers, clad only in skirts of *ndrauninggai* leaves, enter the waters and stir up the muddy bottom by swimming around clutching logs. No one understands exactly why, and magic is thought to be involved, but this activity stuns the *yawi* fish that inhabit the bay, rendering them easy prey for the waiting spearmen. Peni, the *mbete* (priest) of Mavana, controls the ritual. No photos are allowed.

Accommodations

Mr. Poasa Delailomaloma and his brother Laveti operate a charming traditional-style resthouse in the middle of Lomaloma village. For F$15 pp you'll get a bed and all meals. If you'd like to camp, ask Alfred Miller, the Fiji Air agent, if he knows of a place. Bread is baked locally.

Getting There

Fiji Air flies in weekly from Nausori (F$89 OW) and Thithia. The flights are heavily booked, so reserve your return journey before leaving Suva. The bus from the airstrip to Lomaloma is 50 cents. After checking in at the airstrip for departure you'll probably have time to scramble up the nearby hill for a good view of the island. Boat service from Suva is only every couple of weeks.

Several carriers a day run from Lomaloma north to Mualevu (40 cents), and some carry on to Mavana (70 cents).

OTHER ISLANDS
OF NORTHERN LAU

After setting himself up at Lomaloma on Vanua Mbalavu in 1855, Chief Ma'afu encouraged the establishment of European copra and cotton plantations, and several islands are freehold land to this day. **Kanathea**, to the west of Vanua Mbalavu, was sold to a European by the Tui Thakau in 1863 and is now owned by the Australian firm Carpenters. In 1991 Carpenters was trying to sell the island to overseas buyers for F$6 million, though Kanathea people now resident on Taveuni claimed it should be returned to

them. **Mango Island**, a copra estate formerly owned by English planter Jim Barron, was purchased by the Tokyu Corporation of Japan in 1985 for F$6 million.

In 1983 **Naitamba Island** was purchased from TV star Raymond Burr by the California spiritual group Johannine Daist Communion (750 Adrian Way, San Rafael, CA 94903, U.S.A.) for US$2.1 million. Johannine Daist holds four-to-eight-week meditation retreats on Naitamba for long-time members of the communion. The communion's founder and teacher, Baba Da Free John, the former Franklin Albert Jones, who attained enlightenment in Hollywood in 1970, resides on the island.

Yathata Island offers a single Fijian village and a gorgeous white beach. **Kaimbu Island**, right next to Yathata and sharing the same lagoon, has been owned by fiberglass millionaire Jay Johnson (Box 7, Suva; tel. 880-333) since 1969. His four luxurious guest *mbures* go for US$995 per couple per day, including gourmet meals, drinks, sport fishing, scuba diving, and just about anything else you desire (minimum stay six nights). A chartered Fiji Air flight from Nausori to Kaimbu's central airstrip is also included in the price. Bookings are handled by Kaimbu Island Associates, Box 10392, Newport Beach, CA 92658 U.S.A.; tel. 714-552-0332).

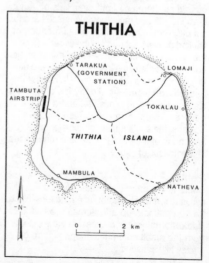

THITHIA

1. Sri Krishna Kaliya Temple, Lautoka, Viti Levu (D. Stanley);
2. Government House, Suva (D. Stanley); **3.** Renwick Road, Suva (John Penisten);
4. Grand Pacific Hotel, Suva (D. Stanley); **5.** Sikh Temple, Lautoka, Viti Levu (D. Stanley)

1. boy at Tholo-i-Suva Forest Park near Suva (David Bowden); **2.** carver at Mbukuya, Viti Levu (Don Pitcher); **3.** washing clothes, Lovoni, Ovalau (Karl Partridge); **4.** planting kava, Ovalau (Karl Partridge); **5.** Lawaki Beach, Mbengga (D. Stanley)

Vatu Vara to the south, with its soaring interior plateau, golden beaches, and azure lagoon, is privately owned and unoccupied much of the time. The circular, 314-meter-high central limestone terrace makes the island look like a hat when viewed from the sea, giving it its other name, Hat Island. Buried treasure is reputed to be somewhere on Vatu Vara.

Katafanga to the southeast of Vanua Mbalavu was at one time owned by Harold Gatty, the famous Australian aviator who founded Fiji Airways (later Air Pacific) in 1951.

Weekly Fiji Air flights from Nausori call at **Thithia** (F$86), between Northern and Southern Lau. Several Fijian villages are found on Thithia, and land is leased to European companies for copra planting. Fiji's only black-and-white Australian magpies have been introduced to Thithia and Taveuni.

Wailangi Lala, northernmost of the Lau Group, is a coral atoll bearing a lighthouse that beckons to ships entering Nanuku Passage, the northwestern gateway to Fiji.

CENTRAL AND SOUTHERN LAU

LAKEMBA

Lakemba is a rounded volcanic island reaching 215 meters. The fertile red soils of the rolling interior hills have been planted with pine, but the low coastal plain, with eight villages and all the people, is covered with coconuts. To the east is a wide lagoon enclosed by a barrier reef. In the olden days, the population lived on Delai Kendekende, an interior hilltop well suited for defense.

The original capital of Lakemba was Nasanggalau on the northern coast. The present inhabitants of Nasanggalau retain strong Tongan influence. When the Nayau clan conquered the island their paramount chief, the Tui Nayau, became ruler of all of Central and Southern Lau from his seat at Tumbou. During the 1970s and 1980s Ratu Sir Kamisese Mara, the Tui Nayau, served as prime minister of Fiji.

Sights

A 29-km road runs all the way around Lakemba. From the Catholic church you get a good view of **Tumbou**, an attractive village and one of the largest in Fiji, with a hospital, wharf, and several stores. Tumbou was originally situated at Korovusa just inland, where the foundations of former houses can still be seen. Farther inland on the same road is the forestry station and a nursery.

The Tongan chief Enele Ma'afu (died 1881) is buried on a stepped platform behind the Provincial Office near Tumbou's wharf. In 1869 Ma'afu

united the group into the Lau Confederation and took the title Tui Lau. Two years later he accepted the supremacy of Cakobau's Kingdom of Fiji, and in 1874 he signed the cession to Britain. Alongside Ma'afu is the grave of Ratu Sir Lala Sukuna (1888-1958), an important figure in the development of indigenous Fijian self-government. The first Methodist missionaries to arrive in Fiji landed on the beach just opposite the burial place on 12 Oct. 1835. Here they invented the present system of written Fijian.

Coconut Factory

Four km west of Tumbou is the coir (husk fiber) and coconut oil factory of the **Lakemba Cooperative Association** at Wainiyambia. First, truckloads of coconuts are brought in and dehusked by hand. Then the meat is removed and sent to the copra driers. Finally, the coconut oil is pressed from the copra and exported in drums. Nothing, however, is wasted. The dry pulp remaining after the extraction is bagged and sold locally as feed for pigs. The husks are flattened and soaked, then fed through machinery that separates the fiber. This is then made into twine, rope, brushes, and doormats, or bundled to be used as mattress fiber. Behind the factory is Wainiyambia Beach, one of the most scenic on Lakemba.

Nasanggalau And Vicinity

The best limestone caves on the island are near the coast on the northwestern side of Lakemba, 2½ km southwest of Nasanggalau. **Oso Nambukete** is the largest; the entrance is behind a

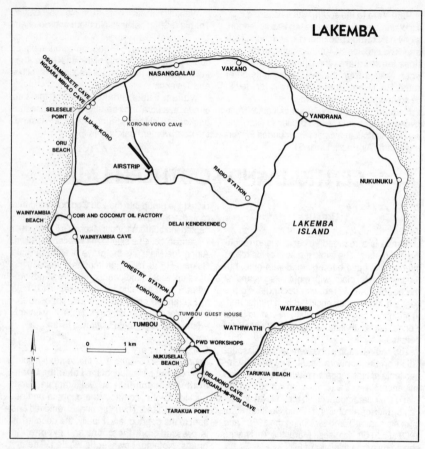

raised limestone terrace. You walk through two chambers before reaching a small, circular opening about one meter in diameter, leading into a third chamber. The story goes that women attempting to hide during pregnancy are unable to pass through this opening, thus giving the cave its name, the "Tight Fit to the Pregnant" Cave.

Nearby is a smaller cave, **Nggara Mbulo** ("Hidden Cave"), which one must crawl into. Warriors used it as a refuge and hiding place in former times. The old village of Nasanggalau was located on top of the high cliffs behind the caves at Ulu-ni-koro. The whole area is owned by the Nautonggumu clan of Nasanggalau, and

they will arrange for a guide to show you around for about F$5. Take a flashlight and some newspapers to spread over the openings to protect your clothing.

Each Oct. or Nov. the Nasanggalau people perform a shark-calling ritual. A month before the ritual, a priest *(mbete)* plants a post with a piece of tapa tied to it in the reef. He then keeps watch to ensure that no one comes near the area, while performing a daily kava ceremony. When the appointed day arrives, the caller wades out up to his neck and repeats a chant. Not long after, a large school of sharks led by a white shark arrives and circles the caller. He leads them to shallow water, where all but the white shark are formally killed and eaten.

East Of Tumbou

Two less impressive caves can be found at Tarakua, southeast of Tumbou. **Nggara-ni-pusi** has a small entrance, but opens up once you're inside. **Delaiono Cave** is just below a huge banyan tree; this one is easier to enter and smaller inside.

The best beach near Tumbou is **Nukuselal**, accessible by walking east along the coastal road as far as the P.W.D. workshops. Turn right onto the track that runs along the west side of the compound to Nukuselal Beach.

Into The Interior

Many forestry roads have been built throughout the interior of Lakemba. Walk across the island from Tumbou to Yandrana in a couple of hours, enjoying excellent views along the way. A radio station operates on solar energy near the center of the island. **Aiwa Island**, which can be seen to the southeast, is owned by the Tui Nayau and is inhabited only by flocks of wild goats.

Accommodations

The **Tumbou Guest House** (Provincial Office, Tumbou, Lakemba) has four rooms at F$8 pp bed/breakfast, F$4 extra for lunch or dinner. Be sure to call ahead for reservations (tel. 42-090,

ext. 35). The locals at Tumbou concoct a potent homebrew *(umburu)* from cassava.

Getting There

Fiji Air flies to Lakemba (F$89) twice weekly from Suva and weekly from Moala. The bus from the airstrip to Tumbou is 50 cents. Buses around the island run four times weekdays, three times a day on weekends.

OTHER ISLANDS

Central Lau

Aside from Lakemba, other islands of Central Lau include Nayau, Vanua Vatu, Aiwa, and Oneata. **Oneata** is famous for its mosquitos and tapa cloth. In 1830 two Tahitian teachers from the London Missionary Society arrived on Oneata and were adopted by a local chief who had previously visited Tonga and Tahiti. The men spent the rest of their lives on the island, and there's a monument to them at Ndakuloa village.

In a pool on **Vanua Vatu** are red prawns similar to those of Vatulele and Vanua Levu. Here too the locals can summon the prawns with a certain chant.

Southern Lau

Mothe is known for its tapa cloth, which is also made on Namuka, Vatoa, and Ono-i-Lau. **Komo**

The Tumbou Guest House (Lakemba) is typical of the simple yet comfortable accommodations available on the outer islands.

DAVID STANLEY

is known for its beautiful girls and the dances (*meke*) that are performed whenever a ship arrives. Mothe, Komo, and Olorua are unique in that they are volcanic islands without uplifted limestone terraces.

The **Yangasa Cluster** is owned by the people of Mothe, who visit it occasionally to make copra. Fiji's best *tanoa* are carved from *vesi* wood at **Kambara**, the largest island in southern Lau. The surfing is also said to be good at Kambara, if you can get there.

Fulanga is known for its woodcarving; large outrigger canoes are still built on Fulanga, as well as **Ongea**. Over 100 tiny islands in the Fulanga lagoon have been undercut into incredible mushroom shapes. The water around them is tinged with striking colors by the dissolved limestone, and there are numerous magnificent beaches. Yachts can enter this lagoon through a narrow pass.

Ono-i-Lau, far to the south, is closer to Tonga than to the main islands of Fiji. It consists of three small volcanic islands, remnants of a single crater, in an oval lagoon. A few tiny coral islets sit on the barrier reef. The people of Ono-i-Lau make the best *mangi mangi* (sennit rope) and *tambu kaisi* mats in the country. Only high chiefs may sit on these mats. Ono-i-Lau formerly had air service from Nausori, but this has been suspended.

The Moala Group

Structurally, geographically, and historically, the high volcanic islands of Moala, Totoya, and Matuku have more to do with Viti Levu than with the rest of Lau. In the mid-19th century they were conquered by the Tongan warlord Enele Ma'afu, and today they're still administered as part of the Lau Group. All three islands have varied scenery, with dark green rainforests above grassy slopes, good anchorage, many villages, and abundant food. Their unexplored nature, yet relative proximity to Suva by boat, make them an ideal escape for adventurers. No tourist facilities of any kind exist in the Moala Group.

Triangular **Moala** is an intriguing 68-square-km island, the ninth largest in Fiji. Two small crater lakes on the summit of Delai Moala (467 meters) are covered with matted sedges, capable of supporting a person's weight. Though the main island is volcanic, an extensive reef system flanks the shores. Ships call at the small government station of Naroi, also the site of an airstrip that receives weekly Fiji Air flights from Nausori (F$66) and Lakemba.

Totoya is a horseshoe-shaped high island enclosing a deep bay on the south. The bay, actually the island's sunken crater, can only be entered through a narrow channel known as the Gullet, and the southeastern trades send high waves across the reefs at the mouth of the bay, making this a dangerous place. Better anchorage is found off the southwestern arm of the island. Five Fijian villages are found on Totoya, while neighboring **Matuku** has seven. The anchorage in a submerged crater on the west side of Matuku is one of the best in Fiji.

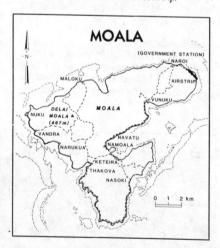

SALVATORE CASA

ROTUMA

This isolated six-by-14-km volcanic island, 500 km north of Viti Levu, is surrounded on all sides by more than 322 km of open sea. There's a saying in Fiji that if you can find Rotuma on a map, it's a fairly good map. In the beginning Raho, the Samoan folk hero, dumped two basketfuls of earth here to create the twin islands, joined by the Motusa Isthmus, and installed Sauiftonga as king. Tongans from Niuafo'ou conquered Rotuma in the 17th century and ruled from Noa'tau until they were overthrown.

The first recorded European visit was by Capt. Edwards of the HMS *Pandora* in 1791, while searching for the *Bounty* mutineers. Christianity was introduced in 1842 by Tongan Wesleyan missionaries, followed in 1847 by Marist Roman Catholics. Their followers fought pitched battles in the religious wars of 1871 and 1878, with the Wesleyans emerging victorious. Escaped convicts and beachcombers also flooded in but mostly succeeded in killing each other off. Tiring of strife, the chiefs asked Britain to annex the island in 1881, and it has been part of Fiji ever since. European planters ran the copra trade from their settlement at Motusa until local cooperatives took over.

Rotuma is run like a colony of Fiji, with the administration in the hands of a district officer responsible to the district commissioner at Levuka. Decisions of the appointed Rotuma island council are subject to veto by the national government. The island wasn't directly represented in the old house of representatives, being lumped into the Lau Group constituencies, although it did have an appointed senator. In early 1988 Rotuma attempted to secede from Fiji, citing human rights violations by the military-backed republican regime. The Fijian district officer on the island promptly demonstrated his disgust by blasting the flag of the new Republic of Rotuma with a shotgun. Soon after, a "peace-keeping force" of 13 Rotuman soldiers arrived, and the protesters were taken to Suva and charged with sedition.

Some 2,800 Rotumans presently inhabit the island, and another 4,600 of their number live in Suva. The light-skinned Polynesian Rotumans are easily distinguished from Fijians. The climate is damp. Rotuma kava is noted for its strength, and the women weave fine white mats. Fiji's best oranges are grown here.

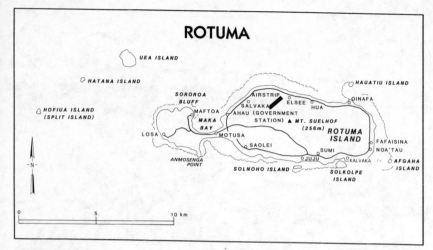

ROTUMA

Sights Of Rotuma

Shipping arrives at a wharf on the reef edge, connected to Oinafa Point by a 200-meter coral causeway that acts as a breakwater. **Oinafa** also has a lovely white beach. The airstrip is to the west, between Oinafa and Ahau, the government station. At **Noa'tau** southeast of Oinafa is a co-op store; nearby, at **Sililo,** a hill with large stone slabs and old cannons scattered about marks the burial place of the kings of yore. Fine stained-glass windows are in the Catholic church at **Sumi** on the southern coast. Inland near the center of the island is Mt. Suelhof (256 meters), Rotuma's highest peak. Climb it for the view.

Maftoa across the Motusa Isthmus has a cave with a freshwater pool. In the graveyard at Maftoa are huge stones brought here long ago. It's said four men could go into a trance and carry the stones with their fingers. **Sororoa Bluff** (218 meters) above Maftoa should be climbed for the view. Deserted **Vovoe Beach** on the western side of Sororoa is one of the finest in the Pacific. A kilometer southwest of Sororoa is **Solmea Hill** (165 meters), with an inactive crater on its northern slope. On the coast at the northwestern corner of Rotuma is a natural **stone bridge** over the water.

Hatana, a tiny islet off the western end of Rotuma, is said to be the final resting place of Raho, the demigod who created Rotuma. A pair of volcanic rocks before a stone altar surrounded by a coral ring are said to be the King and Queen stones. Today Hatana is a refuge for seabirds. *Hofiua*, or Split Island, looks like it was cut in two with a knife. A circular boulder bridges the gap.

Getting There

Fiji Air flies to Rotuma from Nausori weekly (F$184). The monthly government boats carry mixed cargo out, copra back. Unless you really want to spend a month on Rotuma, book your return flight before leaving Suva.

As yet there are no organized accommodations on Rotuma. Many Rotumans live in Suva, however, and if you have a Rotuman friend he/she may be willing to send word to his/her family to expect you. Ask your friend what you could take along as a gift. Tourism is discouraged, so flying to Rotuma without knowing anyone isn't a good idea; if you go by ship you'll probably have made some local friends by the time you get there. Although the National Bank of Fiji has a branch on Rotuma, you should change enough money before leaving Suva.

BOOKLIST

GUIDEBOOKS

Bruce, Erroll. *Deep Sea Sailing*. London: Stanley Paul, 1953. The classic text on ocean cruising. Study it beforehand if you're thinking of working as crew on a yacht.

Douglas, Norman, and Ngaire Douglas. *Fiji Handbook: Business and Travel Guide*. Sydney: Pacific Publications. Though the emphasis is on administrative structures, official statistics, and economic data, this encyclopedic overview does provide useful background reading.

Gravelle, Kim. *Fiji Explorer's Handbook*. Suva: Pacific Graphics. A thorough guide to the roads of Viti Levu and Ovalau with excellent highway maps. You'll find it at local bookstores around Fiji.

Hatt, John. *The Tropical Traveler*. Pan Books, 1985. Over a thousand tips covering every aspect of tropical travel.

Hinz, Earl R. *Landfalls of Paradise: The Guide to Pacific Islands*. Western Marine Enterprises, 3611 Motor Ave., Ste. 102, Los Angeles, CA 90034-5749, U.S.A. The only genuine cruising guide to all 32 island groups of Oceania. Western Marine also handles *A Yachtsman's Fiji*.

Schutz, Albert J. *Suva: A History and Guide*. Sydney: Pacific Publications, 1978. This slim volume is all you'll need to *really* get to know the city.

Stanley, David. *South Pacific Handbook*. Chico, CA: Moon Publications. Covers the whole South Pacific in the same manner as the book you're reading. There's also a *Micronesia Handbook* and a *Tahiti-Polynesia Handbook* by the same author.

Street, Donald. *The Ocean Sailing Yacht*. New York: Norton, 1973. A complete handbook on the operation of a cruising yacht.

DESCRIPTION AND TRAVEL

Siers, James. *Fiji Celebration*. New York: St. Martin's Press, 1985. Primarily a color-photo, coffee-table book, Siers also provides a good summary of the history of Fiji.

Stewart, Robert A.C., ed. *Pacific Profiles*. Suva: Extension Services, University of the South Pacific, 1982. A hundred heartwarming tales of island life. Probably no other book will bring you closer to the Pacific peoples than this.

Wibberley, Leonard. *Fiji: Islands of The Dawn*. New York: Ives Washburn, Inc., 1964. A masterful mixture of history and travel

Wright, Ronald. *On Fiji Islands*. New York: Penguin Books, 1986. Wright relates his travels to Fijian history and tradition in a most pleasing and informative way.

GEOGRAPHY

Derrick, R.A. *The Fiji Islands: Geographical Handbook*. Suva: Government Printing Office, 1965. Along with 140 maps and diagrams, this handbook contains a complete list of all of the islands of Fiji.

Freeman, Otis W., ed. *Geography of the Pacific*. New York: John Wiley, 1951. Although dated, this book does provide a wealth of background information on the islands.

NATURAL SCIENCE

DeLuca, Charles J., and Diana MacIntyre DeLuca. *Pacific Marine Life: A Survey of Pacific Ocean Invertebrates*. Rutland, VT: Charles E. Tuttle Co., 1976. An informative 82-page pamphlet.

Hargreaves, Bob, and Dorothy Hargreaves. *Tropical Blossoms of the Pacific*. Ross-Hargreaves, Box 11897, Lahaina, HI 96761 U.S.A.. A handy 64-page booklet with color photos to assist in identification; a matching volume is *Tropical Trees of the Pacific*.

Martini, Frederic. *Exploring Tropical Isles and Seas*. Englewood Cliffs, NJ: Prentice-Hall, 1984. A fine introduction to the natural environment of the islands.

Mayr, Ernst. *Birds of the Southwest Pacific*. Rutland, VT: Charles E. Tuttle Co., 1978. Though poor on illustrations, this paperback reprint of the 1945 edition is an essential reference list for birders.

Merrill, Elmer D. *Plant Life of the Pacific World*. Rutland, VT: Charles E. Tuttle Co., 1981. First published in 1945, this handy volume is a useful first reference.

Mitchell, Andrew W. *A Fragile Paradise: Man and Nature in the Pacific*. London: Fontana, 1990. Published in the U.S. by the University of Texas Press under the title *The Fragile South Pacific: An Ecological Odyssey*. Andrew Mitchell, an Earthwatch Europe deputy director, utters a heartfelt plea on behalf of all endangered Pacific wildlife is this brilliant new book.

Pratt, Douglas. *A Field Guide to the Birds of Hawaii and the Tropical Pacific*. Princeton, NJ: Princeton University Press, 1986. The best in a poorly covered field.

Tinker, Spencer Wilkie. *Fishes of Hawaii: A Handbook of the Marine Fishes of Hawaii and the Central Pacific Ocean*. Hawaiian Service, Inc., Box 2835, Honolulu, HI 96803, U.S.A.; $30. A comprehensive, indexed reference work.

Zug, George R. *The Lizards of Fiji*. Honolulu: Bishop Museum Press, 1991. A comprehensive survey of the 23 species of Fijian lizards.

HISTORY

Bain, Atu, and Tupeni Baba, eds. *Bavadra:*
Prime Minister, Statesman, Man of the People. Nandi: Sunrise Press, 1990. A selection of Dr. Bavadra's speeches and writings, 1985-1989.

Brewster, A.B. *The Hill Tribes of Fiji*. London: Seely, Service & Co., 1922. Reprinted in 1967 by the Johnson Reprint Corp., New York. A record of 40 years' intimate connection with the tribes of the mountainous interior of Fiji with a description of their way of life.

Davis Wallis, Mary. *Five Years Among the Cannibals*. Parnassus Books, 1967. First published in 1851, this book is the account of a New England missionary in Fiji.

Dean, Eddie, and Stan Ritova. *Rabuka: No Other Way*. Sydney: Doubleday, 1988. An "as told to" biography of coup master Rabuka, in which he outlines his motives for overthrowing the elected government of Fiji.

Derrick, R.A. *A History of Fiji*. Suva: Government Press, 1950. This classic work by a former director of the Fiji Museum deals with the period up to 1874 only.

Gravelle, Kim. *Fiji's Times: A History of Fiji*. Suva: Fiji Times and Herald, 1979. An anthology of stories from the *Fiji Times*.

Howard, Michael C. *Fiji: Race and Politics in an Island State*. Vancouver: University of British Columbia Press, 1991. Perhaps the best scholarly study of the background and root causes of the Fiji coups.

Lal, Brij V. *Broken Waves: A History of the Fiji Islands in the 20th Century*. Honolulu: University of Hawaii Press, 1991. Lal is a penetrating writer who uses language accessible to the layman.

Lal, Brij V. *Fiji: Coups in Paradise: Race, Politics, and Military Intervention*. London: Zed Books, 1990.

Lal, Brij V. *Power and Prejudice: The Making of the Fiji Crisis*. Wellington: New Zealand Institute of International Affairs, 1988.

Lawson, Stephanie. *The Failure of Democratic Politics in Fiji.* Oxford: Clarendon Press, 1991. Lawson claims that democracy failed in Fiji because the Fijian chiefs were unwilling to accept any change that threatened their traditional privileges.

Robertson, Robert T., and Akosita Tamanisau. *Fiji—Shattered Coups.* Australia: Pluto Press, 1988. The first detailed analysis to emerge from Fiji of events which shook the South Pacific. Robertson, a history lecturer at the University of the South Pacific until expelled by Rabuka, and his wife Tamanisau, a reporter with the *Fiji Sun* until Rabuka closed the paper down, wrote the book secretly in Fiji and smuggled out the manuscript chapter by chapter. A military raid on their Suva home failed to uncover the book in preparation.

Robie, David. *Blood on their Banner: Nationalist Struggles in the South Pacific.* London: Zed Books, 1989. Robie's three chapters on Fiji provide excellent background on the Rabuka coups. In the U.S. it's available from Zed Books, 171 First Ave., Atlantic Heights, NJ 07716; in Britain from Zed Books, 57 Caledonian Rd., London N1 9BU; in Australia from Pluto Press, Box 199, Leichhardt, NSW 2040.

Scarr, Deryck. *Fiji: A Short History.* Hawaii: Institute for Polynesian Studies, 1984. An academic look at Fijian history from first settlement to 1982.

Sutherland, William. *Beyond the Politics of Race: An Alternative History of Fiji to 1992.* Canberra: Research School of Pacific Studies, 1992. William Sutherland was Dr. Bavadra's personal secretary.

Walker, Ranginui, and William Sutherland, eds. *The Pacific: Peace, Security & the Nuclear Issue.* London and Atlantic Heights, NJ: Zed Books, 1988. Published as part of the Studies on Peace and Regional Security program of the United Nations University, Tokyo. Provides a useful history of the antinuclear movement in Fiji and background on the coups.

SOCIAL SCIENCE

Bayliss-Smith, Tim, Richard Bedford, Harold Brookfield, and Marc Latham. *Islands, Islanders and the World.* Cambridge, England: University Press, 1988. The colonial and postcolonial experience of Eastern Fiji. Written shortly before the Rabuka coups, the authors freely admit in their introduction that "the reader will seek in vain for any real premonition of this disaster for Fijian democracy, social harmony and economic progress." Like almost all outside observers, they failed to recognize the "complex and changing play of contradictions, in which allegiance and rebellion, ethnic confrontation and cordial interdependence, traditionalism and modernity, clan and class, east and west with the nation, all had their parts." This admission adds a second focus of interest to their work.

Bigay, John, Mason Green, Dr. Freda Rajotte, and others. *Beqa: Island of Firewalkers.* Suva: Institute of Pacific Studies, 1981. Focuses on the interaction between the people and their environment, plus the transition from traditional to modern life.

Lifuka, Neli, edited and introduced by Klaus-Friedrich Koch. *Logs in the Current of the Sea: Neli Lifuka's Story of Kioa and the Vaitupu Colonists.* Canberra: Australian National University, 1978. The troubled story of the purchase in 1946 and subsequent settlement of Kioa Island off Vanua Levu by Polynesians from Tuvalu, as told by one of the participants.

Norton, Robert. *Race and Politics in Fiji.* St. Lucia, Queensland: University of Queensland Press, 1990. A revised edition of the 1977 classic. Norton emphasizes the flexibility of Fijian culture, which was able to absorb the impact of two military coups without any loss of life.

Oliver, Douglas L. *Native Cultures of the Pacific Islands.* Honolulu: University of Hawaii Press, 1988. Intended primarily for college-level courses on precontact anthropology, history, economy, and politics of the entire region; an abridged version of Oliver's *Oceania,* listed below.

Oliver, Douglas L. *Oceania: The Native Cultures of Australia and the Pacific Islands*. Honolulu: University of Hawaii Press, 1989. A massive, two-volume, 1,275-page anthropological survey.

Prasad, Shiu. *Indian Indentured Workers in Fiji*. Suva: South Pacific Social Studies Association, 1974. Describes the life of laborers in the Lambasa area.

Ravavu, Asesela. *The Fijian Way of Life*. Suva: Institute of Pacific Studies, 1983. Contributes to an understanding of the organization of Fijian society and its effects on attitudes and behavior.

Roth, G. Kingsley. *Fijian Way of Life*. 2nd ed. Melbourne: Oxford University Press, 1973. A standard reference on Fijian culture.

Sahlins, Marshall D. *Moala: Culture and Nature on a Fijian Island*. Ann Arbor: University of Michigan Press, 1962. The results of a thorough study carried out in 1954 and 1955.

LANGUAGE AND LITERATURE

Kikau, Eci. *The Wisdom of Fiji*. Suva: Institute of Pacific Studies, 1981. This extensive collection of Fijian proverbs opens a window to understanding Fijian society, culture, and philosophy.

Schutz, Albert J. *Say It In Fijian*. Sydney: Pacific Publications, 1979. An entertaining introduction to the language. Another text by Schutz, *The Fijian Language*, is published by the University of Hawaii Press.

Subramani. *South Pacific Literature*. Suva: Institute of Pacific Studies, 1985. The most comprehensive survey of Pacific Island writers to date.

REFERENCE BOOKS

Douglas, Ngaire, and Norman Douglas, eds. *Pacific Islands Yearbook*. Australia: Angus & Robertson Publishers. Despite the name, a new edition of this authoritative sourcebook has come out about every three years since 1932. Copies may be ordered through *Pacific Islands Monthly*, G.P.O. Box 1167, Suva, Fiji Islands.

Far East and Australasia. London: Europa Publications. An annual survey and directory of Asia and the Pacific. Provides abundant and factual political, social, and economic data; an excellent reference source.

Fry, Gerald W., and Rufjno Mauricio. *Pacific Basin and Oceania*. Oxford: Clio Press, 1987. A selective, indexed Pacific bibliography that actually describes the contents of the books, instead of merely listing them.

Jackson, Miles M., ed. *Pacific Island Studies: A Survey of the Literature*. Westport: Greenwood Press, 1986. In addition to comprehensive listings, there are extensive essays that put the most important works in perspective.

Snow, Philip A., ed. *A Bibliography of Fiji, Tonga, and Rotuma*. Coral Gables, FL: University of Miami Press, 1969.

BOOKSELLERS AND PUBLISHERS

Many of the titles listed above are out of print and not available in regular bookstores. Major research libraries should have a few; otherwise write to the specialized antiquarian booksellers or regional publishers listed below for their printed lists of recycled or hard-to-find books on the Pacific.

Australia, the Pacific and South East Asia. Serendipity Books, Box 340, Nedlands, WA 6009, Australia. The largest stocks of antiquarian, secondhand and out-of-print books on the Pacific in Western Australia.

Boating Books. International Marine Publishing Co., Box 220, Camden, ME 04843, U.S.A. All the books you'll ever need to teach yourself how to sail.

Books & Series in Print. Bishop Museum Press, Box 19000-A, Honolulu, HI 96817-0916, U.S.A. An indexed list of publications on the Pacific available from Hawaii's Bishop Museum.

Books from the Pacific Islands. Institute of Pacific Studies, University of the South Pacific, Box 1168, Suva, Fiji Islands. Many books on Fiji are included in this extensive catalog. Their specialty is books about the islands written by the Pacific islanders themselves.

Books, Maps & Prints of Pacific Islands. Colin Hinchcliffe, 12 Queens Staith Mews, York, YO1 1HH, England. An excellent source of antiquarian books, maps, and engravings.

Books on Africa, Archaeology & Anthropology, Asia, & Oceania. Michael Graves-Johnston, Bookseller, Box 532, London SW9 0DR, England.

Catalogue of Pacific Region Books. Pacific Book House, 17 Park Ave., Broadbeach Waters, Gold Coast, QLD 4218, Australia. A Queensland source of out-of-print books on the Pacific, including many on Fiji.

Defense Mapping Agency Catalog of Maps, Charts, and Related Products: Part 2—Hydrographic Products, Volume VIII, Oceania. Defense Mapping Agency Combat Support Center, ATTN: DDCP, Washington, DC 20315-0010, U.S.A. For a copy of this complete index and order form for nautical charts of the South Pacific, send US$2.50.

Hawaii and Pacific Islands. The Book Bin, 2305 N.W. Monroe St., Corvallis, OR 97330, U.S.A. (tel. 503-752-0045). An indexed mail-order catalog of hundreds of rare books on the Pacific. If there's a particular book about the Pacific you can't find anywhere, this is the place to try.

Hawaii and the Pacific. University of Hawaii Press, 2840 Kolowalu St., Honolulu, HI 96822, U.S.A. Lists many new and current titles on Fiji.

Pacificana. Messrs Berkelouw, "Bendooley," Hume Highway, Berrima, NSW 2577, Australia (tel. 048-77-1370). A detailed listing of thousands of rare Pacific titles. Payment of an annual subscription of A$25 entitles one to 25 catalogs a year.

Pacificana. Books of Yesteryear, Box 19, Mosman, NSW 2088, Australia. Another good source of old, fine, and rare books on the Pacific.

Polynesian Bookshop Catalogues. Box 68-446, Newton, Auckland 1, New Zealand. Mostly new books on the South Pacific, but a good starting point for New Zealanders.

The "Nesias" & Down Under: Some Recent Books. The Cellar Book Shop, 18090 Wyoming, Detroit, MI 48221, U.S.A. A wide range of new books on the Pacific.

The Peoples of the Pacific. AMS Press, Inc., 56 East 13th St., New York, NY 10003, U.S.A. Reprint editions of the classics of Polynesian and Melanesian anthropology.

PERIODICALS

Bulletin of Concerned Asian Scholars. 3239 9th St., Boulder, CO 80302-2112, U.S.A. The Volume 19, Number Four, 1987, issue contains several excellent articles on Fiji.

Ccmmodores' Bulletin. Seven Seas Cruising Assn., 521 South Andrews Ave., Ste. 10, Fort Lauderdale, FL 33301, U.S.A. (US$29 a year worldwide by surface mail). This monthly bulletin is chock-full of useful information for anyone wishing to tour the South Pacific by sailing boat. All Pacific yachties and friends should be Seven Seas associate members!

ENVIRONWatch. South Pacific Action Committee for Human Ecology and Environment, Box 1168, Suva, Fiji Islands (US$10 a year). This quarterly newsletter from SPACHEE provides excellent background on environmental concerns in Fiji and throughout the region.

Fiji Voice. Box 78, Balmain, Sydney, NSW 2041, Australia (US$40 a year to North America). Published by the Fiji Independent News Service, this monthly newsletter is perhaps the best way of keeping up with political developments in Fiji.

German Pacific Society Bulletin. Feichmayrstr. 25, 8000 München 50, Germany. At DM70 a year, Society membership is a good way for German speakers to keep in touch.

Globe Newsletter. The Globetrotters Club, BCM/Roving, London WC1N 3XX, England. This informative travel newsletter, published six times a year, provides lots of practical information on how to tour the world "on the cheap." Club membership (US$18 plus a US$5 joining fee) includes a subscription to *Globe*, a globetrotter's handbook, a list of other members, etc. This is "the" club for world travelers.

Islands Business. Box 12718, Suva, Fiji Islands (annual airmailed subscription US$38 to North America, US$50 to Europe, A$32 to Australia, NZ$40 to New Zealand). A monthly newsmagazine with the emphasis on political, economic, and business trends in Fiji.

Journal of Pacific History. Division of Pacific and Asian History, RSPacS, Australian National University, GPO Box 4, Canberra, ACT 2601, Australia (annual subscription US$35). Since 1966 this publication has provided reliable scholarly information on the Pacific. The Volume XXI, 3-4, 1986 issue includes several scholarly articles on recent events in the South Pacific. Outstanding.

Journal of the Polynesian Society. Department of Anthropology, University of Auckland, Private Bag, Auckland, New Zealand. Established in 1892, this quarterly journal contains a wealth of specialized material on Pacific culture.

Mana. South Pacific Creative Arts Society, Box 5083, Raiwaqa, Suva, Fiji Islands. This South Pacific literary journal with poems, short stories, and articles by island writers, should come out twice a year, but in practice it's irregular.

NFIP Bulletin. Jan Symington, 52 Salisbury Road, Crookes, Sheffield S10 1WB, England (£10 a year). This bulletin of Women Working for a Nuclear-Free and Independent Pacific appears six times a year.

Pacific Islands Communication Journal. Institute of Pacific Studies, Box 1168, Suva, Fiji Islands. This irregular publication of the Pacific Islands News Association carries interesting articles on press freedom in the South Pacific.

Pacific Islands Monthly. G.P.O. Box 1167, Suva, Fiji Islands (annual subscription A$30 to Australia, US$45 to North America, and A$63 to Europe). Founded in Sydney by R.W. Robson in 1930, *PIM* is the granddaddy of regional magazines. In June, 1989, the magazine's editorial office moved from Sydney to Suva.

Pacific Issues. Social Responsibility and Justice, Uniting Church in Australia, 130 Little Collins St., Melbourne, Victoria 3000, Australia (A$20 a year in Australia). Photocopies of significant articles from other publications on regional social and political problems.

Pacific Magazine. Box 25488, Honolulu, HI 96825, U.S.A. (every other month; US$15 annual subscription). This business-oriented magazine, published in Hawaii since 1976, will keep you up-to-date on what's happening around the Pacific. An excellent means of keeping in touch with the region.

Pacific News Bulletin. Pacific Concerns Resource Center, Box 489, Petersham, NSW 2049, Australia (A$12 a year in Australia, A$25 a year elsewhere). A 16-page monthly newsletter for use worldwide by members of the Nuclear-Free and Independent Pacific Movement.

Pacific Report. Box 25, Monaro Cres. P.O., ACT, 2603, Australia. Helen Fraser's fortnightly newsletter providing up-to-the-moment coverage of political and business affairs in the South and Central Pacific region. Airmail subscriptions are A$110 in Australia, A$120 elsewhere for six months.

Pacific Viewpoint. Information and Publications Section, Victoria University of Wellington, Private Bag, Wellington, New Zealand. Twice a year; annual subscription US$28 worldwide. A scholarly journal with in-depth articles on regional social issues.

The Contemporary Pacific. University of Hawaii Press, 2840 Kolowalu St., Honolulu, HI 96822, U.S.A. (published twice a year, annual subscription US$25). Publishes a good mix of articles of interest to both scholars and general readers; the country-by-country "Political Review" in each number is a concise summary of events during the preceding year. Those interested in current topics in Pacific island affairs should check recent volumes for background information. Recommended.

The South Sea Digest. G.P.O. Box 4245, Sydney, NSW 2001, Australia (fortnightly, A$150 a year in Australia, US$175 a year overseas). Editor John Carter has many years of experience in the region.

Third World Resources. 464 19th St., Oakland, CA 94612-9761, U.S.A. (two-year subscription US$35 to the U.S. and Canada, US$50 overseas). A quarterly review of books, articles, and organizations involved with development issues in the third world.

Tok Blong SPPF. South Pacific Peoples Foundation of Canada, 415-620 View St., Victoria, BC V8W 1J6, Canada ($25 a year). This quarterly of news and views focuses on regional environmental, development, human rights, and disarmament issues. Recommended.

Wellington Pacific Report. Box 9314, Wellington, New Zealand (10 issues NZ$14 in N.Z., US$14 elsewhere). An incisive newsletter with startling revelations of covert U.S. activities in the Pacific.

AN IMPORTANT MESSAGE

Authors, editors, and publishers wishing to see their publications listed here should send review copies to:

David Stanley,
c/o Moon Publications Inc.,
P.O. Box 3040,
Chico, CA 95927-3040 U.S.A.

GLOSSARY

Andi—the female equivalent of Ratu

ANZUS Treaty—a mutual-defense pact signed in 1951 between Australia, New Zealand, and the U.S.

archipelago—a group of islands

atoll—a low-lying, ring-shaped coral reef enclosing a lagoon

bare-boat charter—chartering a yacht without crew or provisions

barrier reef—a coral reef separated from the adjacent shore by a lagoon

bêche-de-mer—sea cucumber, trepang; an edible sea slug

blackbirder—a European recruiter of slave labor in the South Seas during the 19th century

breadfruit—a large, round fruit with starchy flesh, grown on a tree (*Artocarpus altilis*)

caldera—a wide crater formed through the collapse or explosion of a volcano

cassava—manioc; the starchy edible root of the tapioca plant

ciguatera—a form of fish poisoning caused by microscopic algae

coir—coconut-husk sennit used to make rope, etc.

confirmation—A confirmed reservation exists when a supplier acknowledges, either orally or in writing, that a booking has been accepted.

copra—dried coconut meat used in the manufacture of coconut oil, cosmetics, soap, and margarine

coral—a hard, calcareous substance of various shapes, comprised of the skeletons of tiny marine animals called polyps

coral bank—a coral formation over 150 meters long

coral head—a coral formation a few meters across

coral patch—a coral formation up to 150 meters long

custom owner—traditional tribal or customary owner based on usage

cyclone—Also known as a hurricane (in the Caribbean) or typhoon (in the north Pacific). A tropical storm that rotates around a center of low atmospheric pressure; it becomes a cyclone when its winds reach 64 knots. In the Northern Hemisphere cyclones spin counterclockwise, while south of the equator they move clockwise. The winds of cyclonic storms are deflected toward a low-pressure area at the center, although the "eye" of the cyclone may be calm.

direct flight—a through flight with one or more stops but no change of aircraft, as opposed to a nonstop flight

dugong—a large plant-eating marine mammal; called a manatee in the Caribbean

EEZ—Exclusive Economic Zone; a 200-nautical-mile offshore belt of an island nation or seacoast state that controls the mineral exploitation and fishing rights

endemic—native to a particular area and existing only there

FAD—fish aggregation device

filaria—parasitic worms transmitted by biting insects to the blood or tissues of mammals. The obstruction of the lymphatic glands by the worms can cause an enlargement of the legs or other parts, a disease known as elephantiasis.

FIT—foreign independent travel; a custom-designed, prepaid tour composed of many individualized arrangements

fringing reef—a reef along the shore of an island

guano—manure of seabirds, used as a fertilizer

ivi—the Polynesian chestnut tree (*Inocarpus edulis*)

jug—a cross between a ceramic kettle and a pitcher, used to heat water for tea or coffee in Australian-style hotels

kai—freshwater mussel

kaisi—a commoner

kava—a Polynesian word for the drink known in the Fijian language as *yanggona*. This traditional beverage is made by squeezing a mixture of the grated root of the pepper shrub *(Piper methysticum)* and cold water through a strainer of hibiscus bark fiber.

kokonda—chopped raw fish and sea urchins with onions and lemon

koro—village

kumala—sweet potato

kumi—stenciled tapa cloth

lagoon—an expanse of water bounded by a reef

lali—hollow log drum

lapita **pottery**—pottery made by the ancient Polynesians from 1600 to 500 B.C.

leeward—downwind; the shore (or side) sheltered from the wind, as opposed to windward

LMS—London Missionary Society, a Protestant group which spread Christianity from Tahiti (1797) across the Pacific

lolo—coconut cream

lovo—an underground, earthen oven (called an *umu* in the Polynesian languages); after A.D. 500 the Polynesians had lost the art of making pottery, so they were compelled to bake their food rather than boil it.

mana—authority, prestige, virtue, "face," psychic power, a positive force

mangiti—feast

mangrove—a tropical shrub with branches that send down roots forming dense thickets along tidal shores

manioc—cassava, tapioca, a starchy root crop

masa kesa—freehand painted tapa

masi—*see* tapa

mata ni vanua—an orator who speaks for a high chief

matanggali—basic Fijian landowning group

matrilineal—a system of tracing descent through the mother's familial line

mbalawa—pandanus, screw pine

mbalolo—a reef worm *(Eunice viridis)*

mbete—a traditional priest

mbilimbili—a bamboo raft

mbilo—a kava cup

Mbose vaka-Turanga—Great Council of Chiefs

Mbose vaka-Yasana—Provincial Council

mbula **shirt**—a colorful Fijian aloha shirt

mbuli—Fijian administrative officer in charge of a *tikina;* subordinate of the Roko Tui

Melanesia—the high island groups of the western Pacific (Fiji, New Caledonia, Vanuatu, Solomon Islands, Papua New Guinea)

mbure—a village house

meke—traditional song and dance

Micronesia—chains of high and low islands mostly north of the equator (Carolines, Gilberts, Marianas, Marshalls)

mynah—an Indian starlinglike bird *(Gracula)*

ndalo—*see* taro

Ndengei—the greatest of the pre-Christian Fijian gods

ndrua—an ancient Fijian double canoe

overbooking—the practice of confirming more seats, cabins, or rooms than are actually available to insure against no-shows

Pacific rim—the continental land masses and large countries around the fringe of the Pacific

PADI—Professional Association of Dive Instructors

palusami—a Samoan specialty of young taro leaves wrapped around coconut cream and baked

pandanus—screw pine with slender stem and prop roots. The sword-shaped leaves are used for plaiting mats and hats.

parasailing—a sport in which participants are carried aloft by a parachute pulled behind a speedboat

pass—a channel through a barrier reef, usually with an outward flow of water

passage—an inside passage between an island and a barrier reef

patrilineal—a system of tracing descent through the father's familial line

pelagic—relating to the open sea, away from land

Polynesia—divided into Western Polynesia (Tonga and Samoa) and Eastern Polynesia (Tahiti-Polynesia, Cook Islands, Hawaii, Easter Island, and New Zealand)

punt—a flat-bottomed boat

rain shadow—the dry side of a mountain sheltered from the windward side

rara—a grassy village square

Ratu—a title for male Fijian chiefs, prefixed to their names

reef—a coral ridge near the ocean surface

Roko Tui—senior Fijian administrative officer

roti—a flat Indian bread

salusalu—garland, lei

scuba—self-contained underwater breathing apparatus

self-contained—a hotel room with private facilities (a toilet and shower not shared with other guests); as opposed to a "self-catering" unit with cooking facilities

sennit—braided coconut-fiber rope

sevu sevu—a presentation of *yanggona*

shareboat charter—a yacht tour for individuals or couples who join a small group on a fixed itinerary

shifting cultivation—a wasteful method of farming involving the rotation of fields instead of crops

shoal—a shallow sandbar or mud bank

shoulder season—a travel period between high/peak and low/off-peak

SPARTECA—South Pacific Regional Trade and Economic Cooperation Agreement; an agreement that allows certain manufactured goods from Pacific countries duty-free entry to Australia and New Zealand

subduction—the action of one tectonic plate wedging under another

subsidence—geological sinking or settling

sulu—a sarong-like wraparound skirt, kilt, or loincloth

takia—a small sailing canoe

tambu—taboo, forbidden, sacred, set apart, a negative force

tambua—a whale's tooth, a ceremonial object

tanoa—a special, wide wooden bowl in which *yanggona* (kava) is mixed; used in ceremonies in Fiji, Tonga, and Samoa

tapa—a cloth made from the pounded bark of the paper mulberry tree *(Broussonetia papyrifera)*. It's soaked and beaten with a mallet to flatten and intertwine the fibers, then painted with geometric designs; called *masi* in Fijian.

taro—a starchy elephant-eared tuber *(Colocasia esculenta)*, a staple food of the Pacific islanders; called *ndalo* in Fijian

tavioka—tapioca, cassava, manioc, arrowroot

teitei—a garden

tikina—a group of Fijian villages administered by a *mbuli*

TNC—transnational corporation (also referred to as a "multinational" corporation)

toddy—The spathe of a coconut tree is bent to a horizontal position and tightly bound before it begins to flower. The end of the spathe is then split and the sap drips down a twig or leaf into a bottle. Fresh or fermented, toddy *(tuba)* makes an excellent drink.

trade wind—a steady wind blowing toward the equator from either northeast or southeast

trench—the section at the bottom of the ocean where one tectonic plate wedges under another

tridacna clam—eaten everywhere in the Pacific, its size varies between 10 cm and one meter

tropical storm—a cyclonic storm with winds of 35-64 knots

tsunami—a fast-moving wave caused by an undersea earthquake

tui—king

turanga—chief

turanga-ni-koro—village mayor

umara—see *kumala*

umu—see *lovo*

vakaviti—in the Fijian way

vigia—a mark on a nautical chart indicating a dangerous rock or shoal

volcanic bomb—lumps of lava blown out of a volcano, which take a bomblike shape as they cool in the air

windward—the point or side from which the wind blows, as opposed to leeward

yam—the starchy, tuberous root of a climbing plant

yanggona—see *kava*

zories—rubber shower sandals, thongs, flip-flops

CAPSULE FIJIAN VOCABULARY

Although most people in Fiji speak English fluently, mother tongues include Fijian, Hindi, and other Pacific languages. Knowledge of a few words of Fijian, especially slang words, will make your stay more exciting and enriching. Fijian has no pure *b, c,* or *d* sounds as they are known in English. When the first missionaries arrived, they invented a system of spelling, with one letter for each Fijian sound. To avoid confusion, all Fijian words and place names in this book are rendered phonetically, but the reader should be aware that, locally, "mb" is written *b,* "nd" is *d,* "ng" is *g,* "ngg" is *q,* and "th" is *c.*

Au lako mai Kenada.—I come from Canada.
Au sa lako ki vei?—Where are you going?
au la o—Vanua Levu version of *mbarewa*
au lili—affirmative response to *au la o* (also *la o mai*)
Au ni lako mai vei?—Where do you come from?

dua tale—once more
dua oo—said by males when they meet a chief or enter a Fijian *mbure*

e rewa—a positive response to *mbarewa*

io—yes

kambawangga—prostitute
kana—eat
kiavalangi—foreigner
Kothei na yathamu?—What's your name?

lailai—small
lako mai eke—come here
levu—big, much

loloma yani—please pass along my regards

maleka—delicious
mbarewa—a provocative greeting for the opposite sex
mbula—a Fijian greeting
mothe—goodbye
Ndaru lako!—Let's go!
nggara—cave
Nice mbola.—You're looking good.
Ni sa mbula.—Hello, how are you? (can also say *sa mbula* or *mbula vinaka;* the answer is *an sa mbula vinaka*)
ni sa mothe—good night
ni sa yandra—good morning

phufter—a gay male (a disrespectful term)

rewa sese—an affirmative response to *mbarewa*

sa vinaka—it's okay
senga—no, none

talatala—reverend
tambu rewa—a negative response to *mbarewa*
tilou—excuse me

vaka lailai—a little
vinaka—thank you
vinaka vaka levu—thank you very much
vu—an ancestral spirit

wai—water

yalo vinaka—please
yanggona—kava, grog

CAPSULE HINDI VOCABULARY

accha—good
bhaahut julum—very beautiful (slang)
dhanyabaad—thank you
hum jauo—I go (slang)
jalebi—an Indian sweet
kaise hai?—how are you?
khana—food
kitna?—how much?

namaste—hello, goodbye
pani—water
rait—okay
ram ram—same as *namaste*
roti—a flat Indian bread
seedhe jauo—go straight
thik hai—I'm fine

ALTERNATIVE PLACE NAMES

Ba—*see* Mba
Bau—*see* Mbau
Beqa—*see* Mbengga
Buca—*see* Mbutha
Bukuya—*see* Mbukuya
Cicia—*see* Thithia
Colo-i-Suva—*see* Tholo-i-Suva
Deuba—*see* Deumba
Galoa—*see* Ngaloa
Gau—*see* Ngau
Kadavu—*see* Kandavu
Korotogo—*see* Korotongo
Labasa—*see* Lambasa

Lakeba—*see* Lakemba
Laucala—*see* Lauthala
Mamanuca—*see* Mamanutha
Nabouwalu—*see* Nambouwalu
Nadarivatu—*see* Nandarivatu
Nadi—*see* Nandi
Natadola—*see* Natandola
Qamea—*see* Nggamea
Rabi—*see* Rambi
Sigatoka—*see* Singatoka
Toberua—*see* Tomberua
Vanua Balavu—*see* Vanua Mbalavu

INDEX

Page numbers in **boldface** indicate primary reference; *Italicized* page numbers indicate material in charts, callouts, captions, illustrations, or maps.

ABOUT THE AUTHOR

A quarter century ago, David Stanley's right thumb carried him out of Toronto, Canada, on a journey that has so far wound through 149 countries, including a three-year trip from Tokyo to Kabul. His travel guidebooks to the South Pacific, Micronesia, Alaska, and Eastern Europe opened those areas to budget travelers for the first time.

During the late 1960s, Stanley got involved in Mexican culture by spending a year in several small towns near Guanajuato. Later he studied at the universities of Barcelona and Florence, before settling down to get an honors degree (with distinction) in Spanish literature from the University of Guelph, Canada.

In 1978 Stanley linked up with future publisher Bill Dalton, and together they wrote the first edition of *South Pacific Handbook* (now in its fifth edition). Since then Stanley has gone on to write additional definitive guides for Moon Publications, including *Micronesia Handbook, Tahiti-Polynesia Handbook,* and early editions of *Alaska-Yukon Handbook*. His books informed a generation of budget travelers.

From his base in Amsterdam, Stanley makes frequent research trips to the areas covered in his guides, jammed between journeys to the 104 countries and territories worldwide he still hasn't visited. To maintain his independence, Stanley does not accept subsi-

dized travel arrangements or "freebies" from any source. A card-carrying member of the National Writers Union, in travel writing David Stanley has found a perfect outlet for his restless wanderlust.

Travel books by David Stanley:

ALASKA-YUKON HANDBOOK

EASTERN EUROPE ON A SHOESTRING

FIJI ISLANDS HANDBOOK

MICRONESIA HANDBOOK

SOUTH PACIFIC HANDBOOK

TAHITI-POLYNESIA HANDBOOK

MOON HANDBOOKS—THE IDEAL TRAVELING COMPANIONS

Open a Moon Handbook and you're opening your eyes and heart to the world. Thoughtful, sensitive, and provocative, Moon Handbooks encourage an intimate understanding of a region, from its culture and history to essential practicalities. Fun to read and packed with valuable information on accommodations, dining, recreation, plus indispensable travel tips, detailed maps, charts, illustrations, photos, glossaries, and indexes, Moon Handbooks are ideal traveling companions: informative, entertaining, and highly practical.

To locate the bookstore nearest you that carries Moon Travel Handbooks or to order directly from Moon Publications, call: (800) 345-5473, Monday-Friday, 9 a.m.-5 p.m. PST.

THE PACIFIC/ASIA SERIES

BALI HANDBOOK by Bill Dalton
Detailed travel information on the most famous island in the world. 428 pages. **$12.95**

BANGKOK HANDBOOK by Michael Buckley
Your tour guide through this exotic and dynamic city reveals the affordable and accessible possibilities. Thai phrasebook. 214 pages. **$10.95**

BLUEPRINT FOR PARADISE: How to Live on a Tropic Island by Ross Norgrove
This one-of-a-kind guide has everything you need to know about moving to and living comfortably on a tropical island. 212 pages. **$14.95**

FIJI ISLANDS HANDBOOK by David Stanley
The first and still the best source of information on travel around this 322-island archipelago. Fijian glossary. 213 pages. **$11.95**

INDONESIA HANDBOOK by Bill Dalton
This one-volume encyclopedia explores island by island the many facets of this sprawling, kaleidoscopic island nation. Extensive Indonesian vocabulary. 1,000 pages. **$19.95**

MICRONESIA HANDBOOK: Guide to the Caroline, Gilbert, Mariana, and Marshall Islands
by David Stanley
Micronesia Handbook guides you on a real Pacific adventure all your own. 345 pages. **$11.95**

NEW ZEALAND HANDBOOK by Jane King
Introduces you to the people, places, history, and culture of this extraordinary land. 571 pages. **$18.95**

OUTBACK AUSTRALIA HANDBOOK by Marael Johnson
Australia is an endlessly fascinating, vast land, and *Outback Australia Handbook* explores the cities and towns, sheep stations, and wilderness areas of the Northern Territory, Western Australia, and South Australia. Full of travel tips and cultural information for adventuring, relaxing, or just getting away from it all. 355 pages. **$15.95**

PHILIPPINES HANDBOOK   by Peter Harper and Evelyn Peplow
Crammed with detailed information, *Philippines Handbook* equips the escapist, hedonist, or business traveler with thorough coverage of the Philippines's colorful history, landscapes, and culture. 587 pages.   **$12.95**

SOUTHEAST ASIA HANDBOOK   by Carl Parkes
Helps the enlightened traveler discover the real Southeast Asia. 873 pages.   **$16.95**

SOUTH KOREA HANDBOOK   by Robert Nilsen
Whether you're visiting on business or searching for adventure, *South Korea Handbook* is an invaluable companion. Korean glossary with useful notes on speaking and reading the language. 548 pages.   **$14.95**

SOUTH PACIFIC HANDBOOK   by David Stanley
The original comprehensive guide to the 16 territories in the South Pacific. 740 pages.   **$19.95**

TAHITI-POLYNESIA HANDBOOK   by David Stanley
All five French-Polynesian archipelagoes are covered in this comprehensive guide by Oceania's best-known travel writer. 235 pages.   **$11.95**

THAILAND HANDBOOK   by Carl Parkes
Presents the richest source of information on travel in Thailand. 568 pages.   **$16.95**

THE HAWAIIAN SERIES

BIG ISLAND OF HAWAII HANDBOOK   by J.D. Bisignani
An entertaining yet informative text packed with insider tips on accommodations, dining, sports and outdoor activities, natural attractions, and must-see sights. 347 pages.   **$11.95**

HAWAII HANDBOOK   by J.D. Bisignani
Winner of the 1989 Hawaii Visitors Bureau's Best Guide Award and the Grand Award for Excellence in Travel Journalism, this guide takes you beyond the glitz and high-priced hype and leads you to a genuine Hawaiian experience. Covers all 8 Hawaiian Islands. 879 pages.   **$15.95**

KAUAI HANDBOOK   by J.D. Bisignani
Kauai Handbook is the perfect antidote to the workaday world. Hawaiian and pidgin glossaries. 236 pages.   **$9.95**

MAUI HANDBOOK   by J.D. Bisignani
"No fool-'round" advice on accommodations, eateries, and recreation, plus a comprehensive introduction to island ways, geography, and history. Hawaiian and pidgin glossaries. 350 pages. **$11.95**

OAHU HANDBOOK   by J.D. Bisignani
A handy guide to Honolulu, renowned surfing beaches, and Oahu's countless other diversions. Hawaiian and pidgin glossaries. 354 pages.   **$11.95**

THE AMERICAS SERIES

ALASKA-YUKON HANDBOOK by Deke Castleman and Don Pitcher
Get the inside story, with plenty of well-seasoned advice to help you cover more miles on less money. 384 pages. **$13.95**

ARIZONA TRAVELER'S HANDBOOK by Bill Weir
This meticulously researched guide contains everything necessary to make Arizona accessible and enjoyable. 505 pages. **$14.95**

BAJA HANDBOOK by Joe Cummings
A comprehensive guide with all the travel information and background on the land, history, and culture of this untamed thousand-mile-long peninsula. 356 pages. **$13.95**

BELIZE HANDBOOK by Chicki Mallan
Complete with detailed maps, practical information, and an overview of the area's flamboyant history, culture, and geographical features, *Belize Handbook* is the only comprehensive guide of its kind to this spectacular region. 212 pages. **$13.95**

BRITISH COLUMBIA HANDBOOK by Jane King
With an emphasis on outdoor adventures, this guide covers mainland British Columbia, Vancouver Island, the Queen Charlotte Islands, and the Canadian Rockies. 381 pages. **$13.95**

CANCUN HANDBOOK by Chicki Mallan
Covers the city's luxury scene as well as more modest attractions, plus many side trips to unspoiled beaches and Mayan ruins. Spanish glossary. 257 pages. **$12.95**

CATALINA ISLAND HANDBOOK: A Guide to California's Channel Islands
by Chicki Mallan
A complete guide to these remarkable islands, from the windy solitude of the Channel Islands National Marine Sanctuary to bustling Avalon. 245 pages. **$10.95**

COLORADO HANDBOOK by Stephen Metzger
Essential details to the all-season possibilities in Colorado fill this guide. Practical travel tips combine with recreation—skiing, nightlife, and wilderness exploration—plus entertaining essays. 422 pages. **$15.95**

IDAHO HANDBOOK by Bill Loftus
A year-round guide to everything in this outdoor wonderland, from whitewater adventures to rural hideaways. 275 pages. **$12.95**

JAMAICA HANDBOOK by Karl Luntta
From the sun and surf of Montego Bay and Ocho Rios to the cool slopes of the Blue Mountains, author Karl Luntta offers island-seekers a perceptive, personal view of Jamaica. 213 pages. **$12.95**

MONTANA HANDBOOK by W.C. McRae and Judy Jewell
The wild West is yours with this extensive guide to the Treasure State, complete with travel practicalities, history, and lively essays on Montana life. 393 pages. **$13.95**

NEVADA HANDBOOK by Deke Castleman
Nevada Handbook puts the Silver State into perspective and makes it manageable and affordable. 400 pages. **$14.95**

NEW MEXICO HANDBOOK by Stephen Metzger
A close-up and complete look at every aspect of this wondrous state. 375 pages. **$13.95**

NORTHERN CALIFORNIA HANDBOOK by Kim Weir
An outstanding companion for imaginative travel in the territory north of the Tehachapis. 759 pages. **$16.95**

OREGON HANDBOOK by Stuart Warren and Ted Long Ishikawa
Brimming with travel practicalities and insider views on Oregon's history, culture, arts, and activities. 422 pages. **$12.95**

TEXAS HANDBOOK by Joe Cummings
Seasoned travel writer Joe Cummings brings an insider's perspective to his home state. 483 pages. **$13.95**

UTAH HANDBOOK by Bill Weir
Weir gives you all the carefully researched facts and background to make your visit a success. 445 pages. **$14.95**

WASHINGTON HANDBOOK by Dianne J. Boulerice Lyons and Archie Satterfield
Covers sights, shopping, services, transportation, and outdoor recreation, with complete listings for restaurants and accommodations. 433 pages. **$13.95**

WYOMING HANDBOOK by Don Pitcher
All you need to know to open the doors to this wide and wild state. 427 pages. **$14.95**

YUCATAN HANDBOOK by Chicki Mallan
All the information you'll need to guide you into every corner of this exotic land. Mayan and Spanish glossaries. 391 pages. **$14.95**

THE INTERNATIONAL SERIES

EGYPT HANDBOOK by Kathy Hansen
An invaluable resource for intelligent travel in Egypt. Arabic glossary. 510 pages. **$18.95**

MOSCOW-ST. PETERSBURG HANDBOOK by Masha Nordbye
Provides the visitor with an extensive introduction to the history, culture, and people of these two great cities, as well as practical information on where to stay, eat, and shop. 205 pages. **$13.95**

NEPAL HANDBOOK by Kerry Moran
Whether you're planning a week in Kathmandu or months out on the trail, *Nepal Handbook* will take you into the heart of this Himalayan jewel. 378 pages. **$12.95**